Start your day with a hearty breakfast of *ham and egg pancakes*. . . .

For lunch, whip up a light and refreshing *California chicken avocado salad*. . . .

And for dinner regale yourself and your family with *Chicken cordon bleu*. . . .

Simple-to-follow directions and inexpensive, easy-to-find ingredients will give you *carte blanche* in the creation of a new and surprisingly original menu for your home.

Spend less time cooking, more time relaxing, morning, noon and night, with

THE CHICKEN AND THE EGG COOKBOOK

HOME SAVINGS & LOAN ASSOCIATION

THE
CHICKEN
AND THE
EGG COOKBOOK

Maria Luisa Scott
and
Jack Denton Scott

BANTAM BOOKS
Toronto • New York • London • Sydney

THE CHICKEN AND THE EGG COOKBOOK
A Bantam Book / December 1981

ISBN 0-553-20050-X

Published simultaneously in the United States and Canada

Bantam Books are published by Bantam Books, Inc. Its
trademark, consisting of the words "Bantam Books" and
the portrayal of a rooster, is Registered in U.S. Patent
and Trademark Office and in other countries. Marca Reg-
istrada. Bantam Books, Inc., 666 Fifth Avenue, New York,
New York 10103.

PRINTED IN THE UNITED STATES OF AMERICA

0 9 8 7 6 5 4 3 2 1

This is for our editor, Linda Price, who not only had the idea for this book, but whose creative ability, enthusiasm and encouragement were always there when needed.

MLS
JDS

Table of Contents

THE
CHICKEN
AND THE
EGG COOKBOOK

Part One

CHICKEN, THE VERSATILE INFLATION FIGHTER

Foreword

We are not going to attempt to solve that old conundrum, "Which came first, the chicken or the egg?"

Alphabetically the chicken comes first, so we will begin with the remarkable animal that has made America become the most chicken-conscious nation in the world.

Inflation has forced us all to face the harsh realities of putting meat on the table. Pork prices spiral, beef continues its spectacular rise, lamb is in orbit, veal is out of sight and even that old standby, hamburger, is heading for $2 a pound. Inflation: the housewife's lament, that no one seems to be listening to, or trying to do anything about except the chicken producers who are keeping prices down and gaining new converts daily.

We confess to a small smugness about this current rediscovery of chicken, as we were converted to its delicious and unlimited possibilities years ago by a master French chef friend when we watched him create a superb hash, using only potatoes, seasonings—and crisp chicken skin.

Of such culinary legerdemain, Jean Anthelme Brillat-Savarin, famed chronicler of French Cuisine, wrote, "Poultry is for the cook what canvas is for a painter."

Poultry for most of us is chicken, which comes conveniently and economically to market in about 30 ways—whole, halved, quartered, in parts, breasts boned, partially cooked or precooked. Increasingly, we are buying all varieties of chicken, but the whole fresh bird remains popular because it is so easily prepared—baked, barbecued, braised, broiled, fricasseed, fried, grilled, poached, roasted, sauteed, steamed and stewed.

Classic creations roll off the tongue in all languages: arroz con pollo, cacciatore, chasseur, cock-a-leekie, cordon bleu, coq au vin, galantine, kiev, marengo, tandoori, teriyaki, weiner backhendle, and the American favorites, Southern fried and potpie.

5

Special dishes and variations from soup to livers in various offerings, salad, hash, kabobs, scallops to pâté are almost endless.

According to the National Broiler Council, the spokesman for the U.S. industry, per capita consumption for 1979 reached a new high of 48 pounds, more than 16 chickens, or a total of 10.6 billion pounds.

The beef, pork and veal eaters may be turning to chicken because of price, but the National Broiler Council believes that many also have discovered that old secret of the chefs, that chicken combines well with everything from anchovies to zucchini, yet retains its own personality.

Paradoxically, despite inflation, we are a nation of shoppers who suspect a bargain, many of us believing if something is inexpensive it is inferior. For such skeptics, the facts about the American chicken should sweep away prejudices.

But only in the U.S. is chicken a bargain. In Rome, for example, it costs about $1.50 a pound, in Tokyo, $2.

For those who put chicken on the shopping list as a "make-do" budget meal, consider that the delicate flesh of the chicken is low in calories and high in protein. Nutrition experts recommend it over red meats for a healthier diet. Half a chicken breast supplies 61.1 percent of protein needed daily and two drumsticks 55.7 percent. Containing vitamin A, niacin and calcium, chicken also has all of those essential amino acids, the building blocks necessary for growth and general good health.

Weight watchers take notice: Half of a chicken breast contains only 160 calories, one drumstick 88. A hamburger has 303; an 8-ounce club steak, fat-trimmed, 553; a pork chop 227.

There's more: Being short-fibered, chicken is among the most easily digested of all meats, making it the perfect food for the young and old, the ill and the convalescent. Low in sodium, it is recommended for those on this restricted diet. With less fat than other meats, it is the dieter's delight; the small amount of fat chicken contains is mostly unsaturated (which cannot be claimed for beef or pork), a boon to those on low-cholesterol diets. Another fact for the weight-conscious: No additional fat is needed to broil, bake or roast a chicken. The fat in the skin is sufficient for self-basting.

How many who downgrade chicken are aware that often it is the first choice of three-star chefs and goumets? Asked to name a favorite food, noted French chef Antoine Gilly, who *has cooked for kings, not only replied that it was roast chicken, but also stated that he rated chefs and restaurants by how well they prepared it.*

A gourmet who treasured a unique chicken dish was the Emperor Napoleon, who started a lasting chicken controversy between France and Italy. Napoleon defeated the Austrian army at Marengo, in the Italian Piedmont. Exultant, he commanded his orderly to have the Catering Corps prepare a victory dinner. Low on supplies, the Corps found a peasant woman who offered to cook a dish she served on festa days, chicken in a wine and tomato sauce, dramatically encircled by shrimps, fried bread, mushrooms and fried eggs.

"Napoleon," according to Francesco Ghedini in Northern Italian Cooking, *"liked 'chicken marengo' so much that he incorporated it into the French cuisine, depriving the peasant woman of any credit."*

In times past, chicken was considered a special dish in the U. S. "Chicken on Sunday," and a politician's ploy, "a chicken in every pot" were familiar phrases.

Today, all of us can have chicken in our pots. Remarkably, it is the only meat that is as good a buy today as it was before the decline of the dollar, costing little more than it did in the late 1940's and early 1950's.

Due to the efforts of the broiler-chicken industry, which poultry expert and consultant H. D. Weber believes may be the only counter-inflationary industry in the U. S., chicken is steadfastly holding the line. Instead of keeping the price-pace of all other foods in 1978, which would have hiked chicken to $1.64 a pound, incredibly efficient broiler production (which Dr. Max Brunk, Professor of Marketing at Cornell University, called "the world's most advanced system of food production") kept the price at an average of 64 cents.

America's versatile inflation-fighter started off far from that technological wonder it is today, beginning life as a sinewy wild fowl of the Asian jungles. Early studies by naturalist Charles Darwin concluded that domestic chickens came from the Indian Red Jungle Fowl. Later, some believed that other wild fowl were also the progenitors, the Jungle Grey, the Ceylon and the Java. Jungle fowls are closely related to pheasants; in fact, they are considered by some ornithologists to actually be a species of pheasant with a fleshy comb, thus placed in the genus Gallus, *which means comb. So today we may be enjoying pheasant, not chicken. It's open to discussion.*

No one knows who tamed the first jungle fowl, but the bird, domesticated in India in 3000 B.C., was held in high respect and even worshipped. The National Geographic *details Indian Parsees writing of the cock in their sacred book, "Who is he who sets the world in motion, a mighty speared and lordly god? It is Parodaro the cock who lifts up his voice against the mighty dawn."*

The cock was sacred in the Persian Zoroaster religion. One of their poets, Chanakya, declared in 300 B.C. that four social lessons could be learned from the cock: "To fight, to arise early, to eat with your family, and to protect your spouse when she gets into trouble."

To most of the ancients, "The cock was a bird of magic, a symbol of three remarkable powers, the sun, resurrection, and sexuality."

The Chicken Book *by Page Smith and Charles Daniel records that the Greeks and Romans believed that the cock had power even greater than the lion's. Men who rubbed their bodies with garlic and broth created from a cock could not be harmed by lions and panthers.*

The Egyptians may have been the first people who appreciated the chicken as food. The Greeks, records The Chicken Book, *claimed that Egyptians so effectively utilized chickens for food that four thousand years ago they used clay incubators warmed by constant fires to hatch as many as 10,000 chicks at one time.*

The Chinese also domesticated the chicken early, about 1400 B.C., and, like the Egyptians, raised them for food.

The Romans gave the chicken its name, Gallus Domesticus, *and may have been responsible for our popular Leghorn.*

We were latecomers. Our first chickens probably arrived in the 16th century when Spanish explorers brought them to the Southwest. But our supply grew fast. In 1841, when the Department of the Interior took the first poultry census, it was discovered that there were 98,984,232 chickens in the U.S.

We are a long way from that first poultry exhibition in Boston in 1849 when no American chicken took the forefront, as ten thousand fanciers thronged to view 1,023 birds. The hit of the show was an enormous chicken from China, a shaggy-shanked Cochin, followed by the Indian Brahman, the British Dorking, the German Hamburg, the Asian Malay and the Sumatra.

Silver-tongued Daniel Webster appeared at the exhibition

to praise chickens, and suddenly America became chicken-conscious and serious breeding began. But it got off to a hap-hazard start; for years it mainly was a hit-or-miss "backyard" operation.

Today, five U.S. companies produce 90 percent of the breeding chickens for the world. One of the leaders is Arbor Acres, Inc., in Glastonbury, Connecticut, which we visited to discover why the U.S. continues to lead the world in the pro-duction of the chicken of tomorrow, today.

There 50 poultry scientists, geneticists, technicians and as-sistants work with computers and data processing in the research and development of improved strains of poultry, also training people from all over the world in all aspects of ad-vanced poultry production.

Not only are individual chickens constantly placed under the scientific microscope for the study of good feathering, skin color, life span, conformation, uniformity, growth rate, yield, feed conversion, but entire generations are monitored for these qualities.

The South, however, has long dominated the "broiler belt" with growing farms dotting the countryside from the Del-marva Peninsula (where Delaware, Maryland and Virginia form a tri-state finger of land between the Chesapeake Bay and the Atlantic Ocean) into the Carolinas, Georgia, Ala-bama, Arkansas and Texas. A tongue-in-cheek theory for the South's leadership attributes it to Prohibition.

Large amounts of corn were raised by Southern farmers, ostensibly to feed chickens. But much of the grain actually went to produce moonshine in stills hidden in the mountains. When Prohibition was repealed and thus the demand for corn liquor greatly reduced, the farmers decided that perhaps corn did have other uses after all. And, reluctantly, they began feeding it to their chickens, which soon gained a reputation for plumpness, golden color and good flavor.

Whether this is humor or history, it remains a fact that the U.S. produces the greatest number and the best chickens in the world, so good that practically every other nation comes to us for advice and for breeding stock.

Nutritionist Jean Mayer may have best summed up the rea-son for the spectacular success of our chickens. "At this point American scientists know more about the nutrition of the chicken than they do human beings," he says. "We are just beginning to write computer programs for human diets, while computerized programs for chickens have been available for at least ten years."

Also, without the remarkable American chicken, we wouldn't have our other valuable inflation-fighter: The egg, which we laud in Part III.

NOTE

Before we get into recipes for either the chicken or the egg, we would like to point out that inasmuch as both chicken and eggs are always a bargain, in some recipes we decided that we could splurge a little and use expensive items like brandy, butter, wine, heavy cream and olive oil. However, if you have to keep all costs down, substitutes are fine. Expensive wines aren't necessary; jug wines are very good. So is half-and-half instead of heavy cream, margarine instead of butter, vegetable oils rather than olive oil. We find that we like the cooking results and the flavor of the combination of butter and olive oil, but try your own combinations.

Also, if time is a factor and homemade chicken broth isn't available (and it is always the best), then canned chicken broth or chicken bouillon cubes work well. The best bouillon we've discovered, which is closest to the desired homemade flavor, is Knorr-Swiss Chicken Bouillon; each cube makes two cups of tasty chicken broth.

Although this entire book is written with economy and ease of preparation in mind, to assist the reader-cook, we have selected special recipes and marked them with simple symbols.

When you note a recipe marked with a single asterisk*, it means that this is an especially inexpensive recipe to prepare.

If the recipe is marked with a double asterisk**, this means that it is fast and easy to prepare.

Finally, here are some helpful hints on buying, storing and cooking chicken from the experts at the National Broiler Council.

TYPES OF CHICKENS:
Broiler-fryer, weighing 2 to 3½ pounds, an all-purpose bird, comprising 90 percent of all chickens sold.
Roaster, older, larger than broilers, weighing 3½ to 6 pounds.
Capon, largest bird, weighing 4 to 7 pounds, 16 weeks old,

male that has been surgically desexed to increase size and tenderness.

Heavy hen, a plump, meaty, mature laying hen of the broiler industry, about 1½ years old, weighing 4½ to 6 pounds. Usually used for stewing and to make broth and soup.

Cornish Game Hens, 4 to 6 weeks old, weighing 1 to 1½ pounds, sold whole for individual serving.

When buying fresh chicken look for plumpness and a clean skin free of bruises and discoloration. Skin color is not a measure of nutritional value, flavor, tenderness or fat content. All chicken meat should be bright in color; beware of grayish or pasty-looking meat. Chicken parts should be well-shaped and meaty.

It is much more economical to buy a whole bird, and save money by cutting it up yourself. The larger chicken is the best buy; it offers a higher proportion of meat to bone. Instead of buying boned chicken choose whole or half chicken breasts, and save at least 50 percent in cost by boning them yourself.

Multiple-bagged chickens or parts, should be rinsed, patted dry with paper towels, separated into portions and repacked in clean bags.

When packaged chicken, opened the day of purchase, has a strong odor, do not be concerned. This is due to oxidation, and is considered normal. However, if a few minutes after opening, the odor still lingers, the product should be returned to the store.

Whole, cooked chicken stores well in a refrigerator for three days, uncooked, for two days. Store on the bottom shelf, the coldest section.

Save energy and plan ahead by roasting two chickens instead of one. Slice some to serve immediately and save some for sandwiches at another meal. It is also handy for a cold summer meal. Or the remainder can be diced for casseroles, salads or crepes.

Use small appliances designed for a specific job; they require less energy than the range. Cook a whole bird in a slow cooker, fry chicken in an electric skillet or small deep-fryer. Or, if you have a microwave oven, cook a whole chicken or chicken casserole with a 75 percent saving in energy.

When cooking chicken in the oven, save energy by keeping the door closed for the entire cooking time. When cooking on the stove top use pans the same size as the surface units, and speed cooking time by using lids that fit tightly.

Chapter One
Chicken Appetizers

There is a new wave of entertaining sweeping the country: the Appetizer Party. It is superseding the Cocktail Party. Such an abundant, tasty variety of appetizers and snacks are served with drinks that the guests leave not only delighted, but also satiated, and with no desire to have dinner.

To produce an interesting and appetite-satisfying array of finger foods and other cocktail offerings is no easy task for the host or hostess. But this chapter will make it easier, for the chicken is the complete answer, offering a remarkable variety of appetizers, ranging from Oriental wings and drumsticks, through pâtés, dips, rolls, "bites," canapés, loaves and molds to unique "sates" on skewers.

QUICK CHICKEN-ALMOND MOUSSE TO FILL CHEESE PUFFS

Fills about 40 puffs: Excellent for filling "Cocktail Cheddar Cheese Shells" (page 363).

2 large whole chicken
  breasts, poached, skinned
  and boned
⅔ cup of mayonnaise
1 teaspoon of salt
½ teaspoon of pepper
24 almonds, blanched,
  skinned and minced
1¼ cup of heavy cream,
  whipped

The food processor is best for this, but a blender will suffice. Cut up chicken, then puree it in the processor. Blend in the mayonnaise, season with salt and pepper, mix in the almonds and fold in the whipped cream.

CHICKEN BALLS INDIENNE

Makes about 50 balls, depending on size:

1 (8-ounce) package of cream cheese at room temperature, well creamed
2 cups of finely chopped cooked chicken
1 cup of chopped walnuts
¼ cup of mayonnaise

1 tablespoon of prepared mustard
½ tablespoon of dried dill weed
2½ teaspoons of curry powder
1 cup of grated coconut

In a large bowl, combine all the ingredients, except the coconut, blending well. Roll into small, bite-sized balls (if they don't hold together, add additional mayonnaise). Dredge in coconut. Chill.

DEVILED CHICKEN BALLS

Makes about 40 balls, depending on size:

2½ cups of minced cooked chicken
3 tablespoons of minced fresh chives
2 tablespoons of minced broadleaf parsley
2 tablespoons of minced celery
2 tablespoons of minced onion

4 tablespoons of fine fresh bread crumbs
2 teaspoons of salt
2½ tablespoons of Dijon mustard
3 tablespoons of mayonnaise
Bread crumbs for dredging
2 small eggs, beaten with 2 tablespoons of heavy cream
Oil for deep frying

In a large bowl, combine chicken, chives, parsley, celery, onion, bread crumbs, salt, mustard and mayonnaise. Blend well. Shape into small bite-sized balls (if mixture doesn't hold together, add more mayonnaise).

Dredge the balls in the bread crumbs, dip in the egg mixture, then dredge in bread crumbs again. Refrigerate for 2 hours. Just before serving, deep fry until golden and crisp. Drain on paper towels and serve immediately on a heated dish.

CHICKEN, BLUE CHEESE AND CREAM CHEESE SPREAD

Makes about 2 cups:

3 ounces of blue (or Roquefort or Gorgonzola) cheese

2 (3-ounce) packages of cream cheese

¼ cup of sour cream

2 tablespoons of mayonnaise

Good pinch of cayenne

1 cup of finely chopped cooked chicken

Fresh dill, minced

In a blender container, thoroughly blend the cheeses, sour cream, mayonnaise and cayenne. Transfer to a bowl and blend in the chicken. Serve on small toast squares (or crackers), garnished with a pinch of dill.

JDS'S BOUDINS BLANCS

Serves 10: These delicate little French chicken sausages not only make an elegant appetizer, but are also excellent as a luncheon dish atop light, creamy mashed potatoes.

2½ pounds (after boning and skinning) of raw, skinned and boned chicken breasts

¾ pound unsalted fatback of pork with streaks of lean (often labeled "Pork for cooking beans")

3 tablespoons of butter

3 medium-sized onions, minced

⅓ teaspoon of dried thyme

1 bay leaf

1½ teaspoons of salt

½ teaspoon of white pepper

¼ teaspoon of nutmeg

2 tablespoons of minced broadleaf parsley

3 egg whites, unbeaten

3 tablespoons of heavy cream

Sausage casings

Put chicken and fatback through the fine blade of a grinder (or use a food processor). In a saucepan, over medium heat, melt butter and sauté onion with thyme and bay leaf for 4 minutes. Discard bay leaf. In a bowl, blend onion (with the cooking butter), salt, pepper, nutmeg, parsley and the ground meats.

Put the mixture through the grinder again. (Not, however, if a food processor has been used.) In a bowl, blend it well with the egg whites and cream (an electric blender or food processor will help).

Make a small patty of the sausage meat and cook it in butter in a frypan and taste for seasoning.

Fill the sausage casings (don't stuff them too full or the sausages might burst in cooking). Twist into 4-inch links (or any size desired) and tie each link with thread.

In a saucepan, bring water to the boil. Add the sausages to be cooked. Immediately take the saucepan from the heat and let the sausages stand for 10 minutes. Drain well, then sauté in butter, browning evenly.

PICKLED DRUMSTICKS

24 drumsticks:

24 broiler drumsticks
1 tablespoon of salt

heated to a simmer, well
stirred and cooled

3 cups of cider vinegar
2 tablespoons of sugar
1 tablespoon of pickling spice

In a pot, place the drumsticks, cover with water and add salt. Simmer for about 25 minutes, or until fork tender. Drain, reserving 2 cups of the cooking liquid. Blend that liquid with the vinegar-sugar-pickling spice mixture. Place cooked drumsticks in a large bowl, and pour over the vinegar mixture. Cover and refrigerate for 48 hours. Drain and serve cold.

CHICK STICKS WITH DIPS

24 drumsticks:

1½ cups of flour
2 teaspoons of salt
1 tablespoon of Hungarian paprika

½ teaspoon of dried thyme
½ teaspoon of pepper

24 broiler drumsticks
Cooking oil for frying

Blend all ingredients except chicken and oil.
Spread seasoned flour on a piece of waxed paper and dredge the drumsticks well. Fry in ½ inch of hot oil in a deep fry-pan until evenly colored golden brown and fork tender. Pass the "chick sticks" with the following dips.

TOMATO DIP

well blended
1 cup of chili sauce
3 tablespoons of horscrad-ish

⅓ cup of minced ripe olives
2 teaspoons of Worcestershire sauce

PICKLE DIP

well blended
½ cup of mayonnaise
½ cup of pickle relish

4 tablespoons of prepared mustard
3 tablespoons of minced onion

HONG KONG CHICKEN GINGER BALLS

Serves 8:

1½ pounds of ground uncooked chicken, (both light and dark meat)
1 egg, beaten
½ cup of minced water chestnuts

1½ tablespoons of soy sauce
1 teaspoon of salt
1½ tablespoons of grated fresh ginger root
½ cup of bread crumbs
Peanut oil for frying

In a bowl, thoroughly blend all ingredients except the peanut oil. Form into small, bite-sized balls. In a frypan, wok or deep fryer, heat the oil, deep enough to completely immerse the chicken balls. Brown evenly. Drain on paper towels and serve warm on toothpicks with a sauce of your choice.

JAPANESE MOTSU

Serves 8: The Japanese have a tasty method of serving chicken gizzards (that we mainly waste) as appealing appetizers. The gizzard can simply be cut in two, but the Japanese trim them to resemble little meatballs.

2 pounds of chicken giz-
 zards, trimmed
2 cups of soy sauce
3 cups of water

6 cloves of garlic, crushed
2 tablespoons of minced
 fresh ginger root

Place all ingredients in a pot, bring to a boil, then cover. Lower the heat to a simmer and cook for 1 hour, or until the gizzards are tender. Serve either hot or cold on toothpicks, with a dip of soy sauce or *wasabi*, Japanese horseradish.

CHOPPED CHICKEN LIVER

Serves 8:

4 tablespoons of chicken fat
 (or butter)
1½ pounds of chicken livers
3 medium-sized onions

2 small cloves of garlic,
 minced
4 hard-cooked egg yolks
Salt and pepper to taste

In a saucepan, over medium heat, melt chicken fat and evenly brown the livers (do not overcook, they should be slightly pink inside). Remove livers. Sauté onion and garlic in the same saucepan for 4 minutes. In a blender or a food processor (the processor is excellent for this task), combine the livers, onions, garlic (and the cooking fat) and egg yolks. Puree. Season with salt and pepper. (If mixture seems a little dry, add more melted chicken fat or soft butter.) Serve on toast or crackers.

CHICKEN LIVER DIP

Makes about 2 cups:

2 tablespoons of butter
½ pound of chicken livers, washed, trimmed, dried and cut into small pieces
1 clove of garlic, minced
Salt and pepper
2 tablespoons of dark rum

1 (8-ounce) package of cream cheese, at room temperature
¼ cup of yogurt
¼ cup of mayonnaise
Pinch of thyme
Chopped parsley

In a frypan, over medium heat, melt the butter. Add the livers and garlic and cook until the livers are just cooked through. Sprinkle with salt and pepper. Cool, then transfer to a blender container or food processor. Add the rum, cream cheese, yogurt, mayonnaise and thyme and blend until smooth. Taste for seasoning. Transfer to a bowl and chill thoroughly. Sprinkle with parsley. Serve with chips, crackers, small squares of toast or use as a vegetable dip.

HAWAIIAN LOMI LOMI LIVERS

Serves 6 to 8:

1 pound of chicken livers, cut into bite-sized pieces
4 tablespoons of hoisin sauce

(available in gourmet shops)
Batter (see below)
Cooking oil for deep frying (peanut oil is best)

In a bowl, mix the livers with the hoisin sauce, tossing gently to coat the livers well. Marinate for 4 hours. Drain. Spoon the livers into the batter and deep-fry in hot, but not smoking, oil in a pot, wok or deep fryer. Cook each batch for 1 minute, or until crisply brown outside and pink inside. Cook one first as a sample, testing both the oil and the livers. Over-cooking can make them tasteless, with the batter having the predominate personality.

BATTER

1½ cups of flour
3 tablespoons of cornstarch
2 teaspoons of salt

2 teaspoons of baking powder
1 cup of water

Place all ingredients in a bowl and blend thoroughly.

CHICKEN LIVER MOUSSE

Makes about 2 cups:

6 tablespoons of butter (2 softened)
2 scallions, minced, using most of the green tails
1 pound of chicken livers, washed, trimmed, dried, dusted with flour and quartered

1 small clove of garlic, minced
1 teaspoon of salt
¼ teaspoon of pepper
Pinch of mace
Pinch of ground sage
¼ cup of brandy

In a frypan, over medium heat, melt 4 tablespoons of the butter (do not use the "soft" butter). Add the scallions and cook for 2 minutes, or until soft. Add the livers and cook until livers are evenly browned on the outside and still slightly pink on the inside. Add the garlic, salt, pepper, mace, sage and brandy. Raise the heat and quickly cook off half of the brandy. Puree the mixture in a blender or processor, or push it through a sieve (this will make the smoothest mixture). Stir in the remaining 2 tablespoons of soft butter. Taste for seasoning. Pack into a crock and chill. Serve with cornichons and toast.

CHICKEN LIVER AND MUSHROOM CRESCENTS

Makes about 48:

THE PASTRY

2 cups of all-purpose flour
1½ teaspoons of salt
⅓ cup *each* of butter and
Crisco

⅓ cup of water
1 egg, beaten with 1
teaspoon of water
(egg wash)

In a bowl, combine and thoroughly blend with a pastry mixer (or use a processor) the flour, salt, butter and Crisco. Add the water and mix well with a fork. Roll into a ball, wrap in waxed paper and refrigerate until ready to use.

THE FILLING

4 tablespoons of butter
2 scallions, finely chopped,
using half of the green
tails
4 medium-sized mushrooms,
coarsely chopped

½ pound of chicken livers,
washed, trimmed, dried,
coarsely chopped and
lightly dredged with flour
3 tablespoons of Madeira
Salt and pepper to taste

In a frypan, over medium heat, melt 2 tablespoons of the butter. Add the scallions and mushrooms and cook for 2 minutes, or until they are a little less crisp. With a slotted spoon transfer to a bowl. Melt the remaining 2 tablespoons of butter in the frypan. Add the livers and cook for 2 minutes, or until they start to brown but are still slightly pink inside. Pour on the Madeira, add the salt and pepper and quickly cook off most of the wine. Add the livers to the onion-mushroom mixture and blend.

Divide the chilled pastry in half. Roll out one-half at a time on a floured board to a ⅛-inch thickness. With a 3-inch cutter, cut rounds of each round. Spoon some of the liver mixture on one half of the dough. Fold the other half over and seal the edges. Prick the tops with a fork. Place on an ungreased baking sheet. Brush the tops with the egg wash. Bake in a preheated 400°F. oven for 10 to 12 minutes, or just until the top is golden (do not overcook). Serve hot.

LIVER-STUFFED FRESH MUSHROOMS

Serves 4:

3 tablespoons of butter
1 tablespoon of olive oil
2 tablespoons of chopped
  shallots
8 large mushrooms, stems
  removed and chopped

½ pound of chicken livers,
  coarsely chopped
Salt and pepper to taste
2 tablespoons of Madeira
2 tablespoons of heavy
  cream
½ cup of bread crumbs

In a frypan, heat 2 tablespoons of the butter and the oil over medium heat and sauté the shallots and mushroom stems for 3 minutes. Stir in the livers, season with salt and pepper and cook for 2 minutes, or until they are brown on the outside but slightly pink inside. Add 1 tablespoon of the Madeira, the cream and bread crumbs, blending thoroughly.

Sprinkle salt on the inside of the mushroom caps. Fill with the stuffing. Sprinkle with the remaining 1 tablespoon of Madeira and dot with the remaining 1 tablespoon of butter. Place on a greased baking sheet and bake in a preheated 350°F. oven for 15 minutes. Serve hot.

TUSCAN CHICKEN LIVER PÂTÉ ON TOAST

Serves 6 to 8:

6 tablespoons of butter
1 medium-sized onion, finely
  chopped
3 tablespoons of Marsala
¼ cup of chicken broth
1 pound of chicken livers,
  washed, trimmed, dried
  and put through a meat
  grinder or use a processor

Salt and pepper to taste
⅛ teaspoon of leaf sage,
  powdered
2 tablespoons of minced
  broadleaf parsley
Small slices of French or
  Italian bread, sautéed in
  butter until golden and
  crisp on both sides

In a frypan, over medium heat, melt the butter. Add the onion and cook until soft. Add the Marsala and broth and cook for 3 minutes, or until reduced by half. Stir in the livers, salt, pepper and sage. Cook, stirring, until the pink of the livers has just about disappeared (do not overcook). Stir in the parsley. Taste for seasoning. Pack into a small serving bowl and chill. Spread on the crisp warm bread.

CHICKEN LIVER RAMAKI

Makes about 35:

1 (5-ounce) can of water chestnuts, drained and quartered

1 pound of chicken livers, trimmed, and halved

blended in a bowl
  1 cup of soy sauce

⅓ cup of light brown sugar

⅛ teaspoon of ginger

16 to 20 extra thin, lean slices of bacon, cut into halves

Marinate the water chestnuts and livers in the soy sauce mixture for 3 hours. Drain well. Wrap a half slice of bacon around a half liver and a quarter water chestnut. Secure with toothpicks. Broil for 4 minutes on each side, or until bacon is crisp.

CHICKEN PUFFS

Makes about 2½ cups:

1½ cups of cooked chopped chicken

1 cup of grated sharp Cheddar cheese

1½ tablespoons of brandy

1½ tablespoons of mayonnaise

1 tablespoon of grated onion

Salt and pepper to taste

2 tablespoons of chopped parsley

Toast squares

Using a blender or food processor, combine the chicken, cheese, brandy, mayonnaise and onion and blend until almost a puree (be careful that the mixture doesn't get too thin and soupy). Taste and season with salt and pepper. Mix in the parsley. Spread generous amounts on the toast squares and place under a broiler until golden brown and puffed. Serve hot.

SESAME SNACKS

Serves 6:

2 small onions, minced, sautéed in butter for 5 minutes (or until soft) and drained
1 teaspoon of dry mustard
½ cup of mayonnaise

2 cups of cooked chicken (thigh meat is excellent), cut into ¾-inch cubes

blended
    ¾ cup of bread crumbs
    ½ cup of sesame seeds

In a bowl, blend onion, mustard and mayonnaise. Dip chicken cubes in the mayonnaise mixture, then dredge in the bread crumbs-and-sesame seed mixture. Space on a cookie sheet so cubes do not touch. Bake in a preheated 400°F. oven for 10 minutes or until golden. Serve with a dip, either soy, a mixture of apricot jam and horseradish, or any other favorite. These snacks are excellent, however, as cocktail-chasers without any dip.

CHICKEN-SHRIMP BALLS

Serves 4:

1 whole chicken breast, skinned, boned and coarsely diced
½ pound of shrimp, shelled and deveined
3 scallions, coarsely chopped
4 water chestnuts, quartered
½ teaspoon of monosodium glutamate

1 egg white, lightly beaten
1 tablespoon of cornstarch, blended with 2 tablespoons of water
2 slices of ginger, minced
Bread crumbs for dredging
Vegetable oil for deep frying

Put the chicken, shrimp, scallions and water chestnuts through the fine blade of a meat grinder or use a food processor. In a bowl combine them with the remaining ingredients (except the bread crumbs and vegetable oil) and mix well. Shape the mixture into balls, ¾ inch in diameter. Roll in the bread crumbs to lightly coat. Heat the oil to medium-hot and deep fry the balls a few at a time (do not crowd), turning until balls are golden brown. Drain on paper towels. Serve with a commercial Plum Sauce or with the following Marmalade and Horseradish Sauce:

MARMALADE AND HORSERADISH SAUCE

¾ cup of orange marmalade
2 tablespoons of lemon juice
1 tablespoon of fresh grated horseradish (or use prepared)

¼ teaspoon of powdered ginger
½ teaspoon of salt

Place all ingredients into a blender and blend for several seconds until well mixed.

SKEWERED CHICKEN

This one leans upon your imagination. You can vary this recipe any way you like, with many combinations. We offer you a spark with this favorite of ours.

Cooked leftover chicken, cut into bite-sized cubes (breast is best, but any cooked chicken that can be cubed will do)

Seasoned salt
Honeydew melon, cubed
Pistachio nuts, crushed

Amount depends upon the number of guests you will serve. Very lightly sprinkle the chicken cubes with seasoned salt. Roll the cubes of melon in the pistachios. Thread them alternately onto skewers and serve cold.

SKEWERED BREAST OF CHICKEN AND PINEAPPLE

Serves 4:

¼ cup of peanut oil
½ cup of soy sauce
1 (8-ounce) can of sliced pineapple, juice reserved
2 tablespoons of brown sugar

3 cloves of garlic, coarsely chopped
Pinch of cinnamon
1 large whole chicken breast, skinned and boned

In a bowl, combine the oil, soy sauce, reserved pineapple juice, brown sugar, garlic and cinnamon to make a marinade. Cut the chicken and pineapple slices into small bite-sized cubes. Marinate in the soy sauce mixture for 1½ to 2 hours. Divide the pieces of chicken and pineapple into 8 portions. Put each portion on thin wooden skewers and broil for 3 or 4 minutes on each side until the chicken is golden. Brush with the marinade when you turn to broil the other side (do not overcook the chicken or it will toughen).

SPANISH SNACKS

Serves 8: This is an excellent summer dish.

2 whole chicken breasts, halved
4 onions, chopped
3 cloves of garlic, halved and crushed

3 slices of fresh ginger root
2½ teaspoons of salt
2 cups of dry sherry

Place chicken breasts in a pot, cover with water, then add onion, garlic and ginger. Bring to a boil, reduce to a simmer, cover and cook for 15 minutes, or until just tender. Remove from the heat and let set, covered, for 20 minutes. Drain. Sprinkle the breasts liberally with salt. Place in a large mason jar with screw-top lid. Cover the chicken with the sherry, screw on the top and refrigerate for 3 days. Just before serving, drain and remove skin and bones from the breasts. Cut into bite-sized cubes and serve cold with cocktails.

CHICKEN SURPRISES

Poached or roasted breast of chicken, cold
Stuffed green olives and black Greek olives, pitted

Button mushrooms marinated in oil and vinegar

Cut the chicken into thin slices. Wrap a slice around an olive, another around a mushroom. Skewer with a toothpick. The delight is in the bite.

TERRINE OF CHICKEN

Serves 8 to 10:

2 pounds of skinned, boned uncooked chicken meat (breasts and thighs are best), coarsely chopped
½ pound of lean boned pork, coarsely chopped
½ pound of ham (with fat), coarsely chopped
½ pound of unsalted fatback (this is labeled in stores as "Pork for cooking beans"), coarsely chopped
2 medium-sized onions, quartered

1 teaspoon of salt
½ teaspoon of Lawry's Seasoned Salt
½ teaspoon of pepper
⅛ teaspoon of cloves
¼ teaspoon of cinnamon
⅛ teaspoon of nutmeg
¼ teaspoon of dried thyme
¼ cup of good brandy
3 eggs, lightly beaten
Butter
1 whole chicken breast, skinned, boned and cut into ½-inch strips

Butter a loaf pan large enough to hold all of the ingredients (or use two smaller pans).

Put the chopped chicken, pork, ham, fatback and onions through the fine blade of a meat grinder or use a food processor. Place the ground meats in a large bowl. Add the salt, seasoned salt, pepper, cloves, cinnamon, nutmeg, thyme, brandy and eggs and mix thoroughly (your hands are the best instruments for this).

Test the mixture for seasoning. Make a small patty and cook it in butter over medium heat until brown on both sides. Taste, then adjust the seasonings.

Lay an even 1-inch layer of the mixture on the bottom of the loaf pan. Arrange 3 strips of the breast down the length of the mixture. Continue layers of the mixture alternating with the strips of breast, ending with a solid top layer. Cover the top snugly with heavy-duty aluminum foil and set in a shallow pan of boiling water (this should come halfway up the baking dish). Bake in a preheated 325°F. oven for 1½ hours, or until the terrine has shrunk from the sides of the dish. Test by inserting a knife blade into the center of the terrine. If it comes out clean the terrine is cooked. Cool.

Leaving the foil on, place a weight on top (a clean brick wrapped in plastic is handy for this) and refrigerate overnight. This terrine will hold in the refrigerator for a week. Cut into ½-inch slices and serve each slice on a lettuce leaf with cornichons (small tarragon French pickles) and hot French bread.

CHINESE CHICKEN WINGS

24 wings:

½ cup of soy sauce
½ cup of brown sugar
¼ cup of dry sherry
2 cloves of garlic, peeled and mashed
¼ teaspoon of ground ginger
¼ teaspoon of cinnamon
¼ teaspoon of pepper
24 chicken wings (use only the larger portion that resembles a small drumstick; save tip portion for soup)

In a large bowl combine all ingredients, blending well. Marinate the wings for 3 hours. (Save the marinade; it keeps well in the refrigerator.) Drain. Broil 5 inches from the heat unit for 3 minutes on each side, or until wings are crisp and tender.

CRISPY WINGS WITH CRANBERRY DIP

24 wings:

24 chicken wings (use only the larger portion that resembles a small drumstick; save tip portion for soup)

Salt
2 teaspoons of dried tarragon
1 stick (¼ pound) of butter
3 tablespoons of olive oil

Dust the wings with salt and tarragon. In a large deep frypan, over medium heat, heat the butter and oil and brown the wings evenly, turning them often, until fork tender (cook in 2 or 3 batches, if necessary). Drain on paper towels and serve hot with the Cranberry Dip.

CRANBERRY DIP

1½ cups of jellied cranberry sauce
1 cup of prepared horseradish

1 tablespoon of sugar
1 teaspoon of salt
½ cup of heavy cream, whipped

Mash cranberry sauce, blend in horseradish, sugar and salt. Chill. Before serving, fold in the whipped cream.

Chapter Two
Chicken Soups

We know an eminently successful photographer who uses a unique method to make his subjects smile when they don't feel like it. It's a simple technique, but it never fails.

"Say soup!" he commands.

Immediately upon uttering the word, eyes light up and lips part in a pleased smile.

The word has that reaction universally. Every nation has a favorite soup that warms the body and the soul, and each of these soups has something in common: Chicken. Practically all of the world's famous soups begin with chicken broth or stock. Plain or fancy chicken soups lead the list of everybody's favorites.

The basis of all soup is broth or stock. There is some confusion regarding the words. Is there a difference?

A stock is the simpler, weaker preparation—water given some body and authority by simmering it with vegetables and/or meat and bones. It is too bland to be eaten by itself, but is excellent for poaching, or as a base for soups or stews.

A stock becomes broth when it is given strength of character by reducing stock by half. Some chefs even add additional fresh bones and vegetables to the stock after it has cooked to give the broth even greater flavor. But if you begin with enough flavorful ingredients, the extra step is unnecessary.

Broth becomes consommé when the stock is again reduced by half. Consommé should be clear and golden. This results from clarifying it with egg white. Clarifying isn't difficult: For 1 quart of consommé you need 2 egg whites, plus 2 crushed eggshells. In a large bowl, combine egg whites and shells. Beat for 1 minute until frothy and about doubled in bulk. Bring the consommé to a boil, reduce the heat to medium, and stir in the egg whites and shells. Raise heat slightly, still stirring the egg whites in the consommé. Let boil until the egg whites rise to the top in a froth. Remove from the heat and let stand for 10 minutes. The impurities will all be collected in the egg white froth; remove that and you have a clear consommé. Some cooks pursue it further by placing a piece of cheesecloth over a bowl and, carefully, ladle by ladle, placing consommé, egg whites and all, into the cheesecloth. Very slowly clarified liquid will then drip into the bowl.

We aren't great consommé fans, liking good, reasonably clear strong chicken broth best for soup, poaching or whatever recipe it may be used in.

There are a number of good commercial chicken broths on the market, but there is nothing like your own, simmered until it is as rich as you like it, then strained and used, or frozen.

Some of the broth can be frozen with nuggets of the chicken meat picked from the bones and added to the broth to produce any number of quick, delicious soups.

CHICKEN BROTH

About 2 quarts:

4 pounds of chicken backs, wings, necks (including 3 or 4 gizzards and hearts)	2 carrots, peeled and chopped
4 quarts of water	3 sprigs of parsley
2 medium-sized onions, each stuck with 2 whole cloves	1 small bay leaf
2 celery ribs, chopped	¼ teaspoon of dried thyme
	8 peppercorns, slightly crushed
	½ tablespoon of salt

Place all ingredients in a soup pot. Cover and bring to a boil, then reduce heat to a simmer, skimming surface scum off when necessary. Remove the cover, and simmer for 2 or 3 hours, or until the liquid is reduced by half and is tasty. Taste for seasoning.

An easy method for clarifying and defatting the broth is to strain it, then store it in a bowl in the refrigerator overnight. Sediment will settle to the bottom, fat will solidify on top.

Remove the fat and discard. Spoon the clear, jellied broth into a bowl. Discard the sediment remaining on the bottom of the bowl.

CHICKEN BROTH WITH ROYAL CUSTARD

Serves 6:

1 whole egg plus 2 egg yolks
¼ cup of heavy cream
¼ cup of chicken broth
Pinch of cayenne
Salt to taste

6 to 8 cups of very rich, very hot chicken broth
2 tablespoons of minced parsley

In a bowl, beat the egg and egg yolks together. Beat in the cream and the ¼ cup broth. Season with cayenne and salt. Pour into a shallow buttered 8-inch-square baking dish. Set in a pan of hot water and bake in a preheated 300°F. oven for 15 minutes, or until the custard is firmly set (do not overcook). Cool and refrigerate.

When thoroughly cooled, cut into small fancy shapes and float on top of the individual cups of hot broth. Sprinkle with a little parsley.

CHICKEN AND CLAM SOUP

Serves 4 to 6:

2 tablespoons of butter
1 celery rib, scraped and chopped
1 medium-sized onion, finely chopped
2 (10½-ounce) cans of cream of chicken soup

2 (10½-ounce) cans of chicken broth
1 (7½-ounce) can of minced clams, with their liquid
2 tablespoons of chopped parsley

In a saucepan, over medium heat, melt the butter. Add the celery and onion and cook until slightly soft, but still crunchy. Stir in the chicken soup and the broth. Mix well and simmer for 3 minutes. Just before serving, add the clams and their liquid and heat through. Serve sprinkled with parsley.

COCK-A-LEEKIE

Serves 6: The prunes in this recipe are a sometime ingredi-ent—including them depends upon your taste for prunes in soup.

1 (3½- or 4-pound)
chicken, with its giblets
1 teaspoon of salt
½ teaspoon of pepper
3½ quarts of water
2 Knorr chicken bouillon
cubes

8 leeks, roots and all but 1
inch of the green part cut
off and discarded, cut
lengthwise, rinsed well and
cut into ½-inch pieces
6 prunes, pits removed (op-tional)
¼ cup of barley, rice or
small pasta (optional)
2 tablespoons of chopped
parsley

Place the chicken, giblets, salt and pepper in a large pot. Add the water and bouillon cubes and bring to a boil. Skim off any scum that rises to the surface. Lower heat, cover and simmer for 1½ hours. Add the leeks and prunes and simmer 30 minutes longer, or until the chicken is tender and the liq-uid has reduced by one-third (if the chicken is cooked before the liquid has reduced sufficiently, remove it). Taste the broth for seasoning.

Remove the skin and bones from the meat. Cut up into small pieces the less choice parts of the bird (reserving the breast and thighs for another meal). Cook the rice, pasta or barley in the broth, add the cut-up chicken, heat through, sprinkle with parsley and serve.

NOTE
If desired, do not add any meat to the soup but serve the whole bird for the main course.

COLD COCHIN CHICKEN SOUP

Serves 4:

3 cups of chicken broth
2 small apples, peeled, cored and coarsely chopped
2 small onions, coarsely chopped
1 cup of shredded coconut

1 cup of medium cream
1 teaspoon of curry powder
Salt and pepper to taste
⅓ cup of chopped salted cashew nuts

Pour the broth into a pot. Add the apples, onion, coconut and bring to a boil. Cover. Lower heat and simmer for 25 minutes, or until the apples and onion are tender. Cool. Place in a blender container and blend until smooth. Push the mixture through a sieve, discarding anything that will not go through. Place in a bowl, blend in the cream and curry powder, mixing well. Taste for seasoning. Add salt and pepper. Refrigerate. Serve chilled sprinkled with cashews.

SPEEDY, COLD, CREAM CHEESE SOUP

Serves 4:

4 cups of chicken broth
½ cup of dry white wine
¼ teaspoon of allspice
½ teaspoon of salt

1 (8-ounce) package of cream cheese, at room temperature
2 tablespoons of chopped watercress

In a blender container, combine the broth, wine, allspice, salt and cream cheese. Blend into a creamy, smooth mixture. Taste for seasoning. Refrigerate. Serve chilled, sprinkled with watercress.

CHICKEN AND CORN SOUP

Serves 6:

2 pounds of chicken backs, wings and necks
3 quarts of water
1 tablespoon of salt
½ teaspoon of pepper
1 onion, peeled and stuck with 1 whole clove
1 celery rib, chopped
1 carrot, cut up
Pinch of thyme

Pinch of tumeric
½ cup of barley
4 ears of corn, cooked and kernels removed or 1 (16-ounce) can of creamed corn
2 hard-cooked eggs, chopped
2 tablespoons of chopped parsley

In a large pot place the chicken, water, salt, pepper, onion, celery, carrot, thyme and tumeric. Simmer for about 35 minutes, or until the chicken is tender. Remove the chicken and when cool, remove the meat from the bones (discard skin and bones) and reserve. Strain the stock, return to the pot with the barley and simmer, partially covered, for 30 minutes, or until the barley is cooked and stock has reduced by one-third. Stir in the reserved chicken meat and corn. Cook for 5 minutes, or until heated through. Serve garnished with the chopped eggs and parsley.

NOTE

This may also be prepared with commercial broth and left-over cooked chicken.

CHICKEN PUREE AND CORN SOUP

Serves 4 to 6:

1 whole chicken breast, skinned and boned
2 egg whites, beaten just until frothy
½ teaspoon of salt
6 cups of rich chicken broth
1 (8-ounce) can of creamed corn

2 tablespoons of cornstarch, mixed with 3 tablespoons of water
2 tablespoons of dry vermouth or sake
2 slices of ham, finely chopped
4 scallions, thinly sliced

Cut the chicken into several pieces. Put it into a processor (or blender) and process until the meat is pureed. Combine the chicken, egg whites and salt, mixing well.

In a saucepan, bring the broth to a boil and stir in the corn. Reduce heat to a simmer, stir in the cornstarch mixture and cook, stirring, until thickened. Stir in the wine and the chicken mixture. Simmer for 2 or 3 minutes, stirring constantly. Serve with the ham and scallions sprinkled on top.

CREAM CONSOMMÉ

Serves 4 to 6:

8 cups of chicken broth

beat together next
    four ingredients
    ¼ cup of dry sherry
    ⅓ cup of heavy cream

1 teaspoon of cornstarch
2 egg yolks

2 tablespoons of chopped
fresh chives

Pour the cold broth into a pot. Blend in the beaten egg mixture. Over low heat, cook, stirring constantly, until the soup is hot (do not boil, or the soup will curdle and separate). Serve sprinkled with chives.

GIBLET SOUP

Serves 6:

½ pound of chicken gizzards
½ pound of chicken livers
1 pound of chicken wings
Flour for dredging
3 tablespoons butter
2 quarts of water
2 Knorr chicken bouillon cubes
Celery leaves from the celery ribs (see below)
1 whole onion, stuck with 2 whole cloves

2 cloves of garlic, crushed
¼ teaspoon of basil
Pinch of thyme
1 small bay leaf
1 teaspoon of salt
¼ teaspoon of pepper
1 large onion, chopped
4 celery ribs, scraped and diced
3 medium-sized carrots, peeled and diced
Lemon wedges
Toasted garlic croutons

Dredge the gizzards, livers and wings with flour. In a large soup pot heat 2 tablespoons of the butter over medium heat. Add the gizzards, livers and wings and brown evenly. Remove the livers and set aside. Add the water, bouillon cubes, celery leaves, whole onion, garlic, basil, thyme, bay leaf, salt and pepper. Bring to a boil and simmer partially covered, for 1 hour, or until the gizzards are almost tender. Add the livers and simmer for 15 minutes longer (the livers should not be overcooked or they will toughen). Strain the stock, reserving the giblets. Heat the remaining butter in the soup pot. Add the chopped onion and cook until soft. Return the strained stock to the pot. Add the celery and carrots. Simmer, uncovered, for 30 minutes, or until the vegetables are crunchy tender. Trim and cut up the gizzards. Remove and cut up the meat from the wings, discarding skin and bones. Cut up the livers. Stir into the soup. Serve with wedges of lemon and the croutons.

CHICKEN SOUP WITH GREENS

Serves 6:

1 cup of canned tomatoes, put through a food mill
8 cups of rich chicken broth
¾ cup of pastine or other very small soup pasta

4 cups of shredded spinach, escarole or romaine lettuce
Salt and pepper to taste

Place the tomatoes and broth in a large saucepan and simmer, uncovered, for 5 minutes. Add the pastine and simmer for 2 minutes, or until it is very *al dente*. Stir in the greens and simmer for 3 minutes, or until the greens are wilted (do not overcook them as they will lose their flavor and fresh green color). Season to taste.

CHICKEN GUMBO SOUP

Serves 6 to 8:

1 (4-pound) chicken
1 whole onion, stuck with 2 cloves
1 carrot, cut up
1 celery rib, with leaves, cut up
1 small bay leaf
1½ teaspoons of salt
¼ teaspoon of pepper
3 quarts of water

2 cups of canned tomatoes, drained and chopped
½ cup of finely chopped green pepper
½ cup of corn kernels
1 medium-sized onion, chopped
½ cup of rice
1 cup of sliced okra

In a large pot, place the chicken, whole onion, carrot, celery, bay leaf, salt, pepper and water. Bring to a boil, lower heat and simmer, partially covered, skimming the scum from the top when necessary, for 1 hour, or until the chicken is tender and the liquid has reduced by one-third. If the bird is cooked before the liquid has reduced sufficiently, remove it, turn up the heat and reduce the liquid quickly. Strain the broth.

Return the broth to the pot and add the tomatoes, green pepper, corn, chopped onion and rice. Simmer for 20 minutes. Add the okra and simmer for 10 minutes longer.

Remove the skin and bones from the chicken and cut the meat into small cubes. Stir into the soup pot and heat through. Taste for seasoning.

LEEK, POTATO AND ZUCCHINI SOUP

Serves 6:

4 medium-large leeks (white part only), cut in half lengthwise, then into ½-inch pieces
1 large carrot, peeled and cut into ¼-inch slices
1 stick (¼ pound) of butter
2 quarts of chicken broth

2 medium-sized potatoes, peeled and cut into ½-inch cubes
1 teaspoon of salt
½ teaspoon of pepper
3 small zucchini, cut in half lengthwise, then into ½-inch pieces
2 tablespoons of chopped fresh dill or parsley

In a large pot, simmer the leeks and carrot in the butter, stirring, until well coated, about 5 minutes. Add the broth, potatoes, salt and pepper. Bring to a boil, lower heat and simmer, covered, for 25 minutes, or until the potatoes are slightly undercooked. Add the zucchini and simmer for 15 minutes longer, or until zucchini and potato are tender. Taste for seasoning. Serve in hot soup bowls with the dill or parsley sprinkled atop.

NOTE

This is also delicious served cold. Cool soup and blend into a puree. Stir in 2 tablespoons of medium cream for each cup of soup.

ABRUZZI CHICKEN LIVER SOUP

Serves 4 to 6:

½ pound of chicken livers, sautéed in butter for 6 minutes, then cut into ¼-inch pieces

1 cup of *maruzzine* (tiny pasta shells), cooked very *al dente* in boiling salted water and drained

7 cups of chicken broth

⅓ teaspoon of leaf sage, crumbled

Salt and pepper to taste

½ cup of grated Asiago or Parmesan cheese

2 tablespoons of minced broadleaf parsley

Prepare the livers and pasta. In a pot, bring the broth to a boil, stir in the livers, the pasta and sage. Simmer for 4 minutes. Season with salt and pepper. Serve very hot, lightly sprinkled with the cheese and parsley.

CREAM OF CHICKEN-CHICKEN LIVER SOUP

Serves 6:

2 tablespoons of butter
3 leeks (use ⅓ of the light green part), chopped
1 celery rib, scraped and chopped
2 tablespoons of flour
Salt and pepper to taste
½ teaspoon of ground cumin
4 cups of rich chicken broth

3 cups of cubed cooked chicken meat
3 chicken livers, simmered in a little chicken broth until just cooked through (do not overcook) and chopped
1 cup of heavy cream
2 tablespoons of chopped broadleaf parsley

In a saucepan, over medium heat, melt the butter. Add the leeks and celery and cook for 5 minutes. Sprinkle on the flour, salt, pepper and cumin and blend. Slowly pour in the broth, stirring constantly, until well blended. Simmer for 10 minutes. Pour the soup in a blender container, blending until smooth. Return the soup to the saucepan. Stir in the chicken cubes, livers and cream. Heat thoroughly, over low heat, but do not boil. Taste for seasoning. Sprinkle with parsley.

CHICKEN SOUP WITH MATZO BALLS AND PASTA VARIATIONS

Serves 4 to 6:

1 (4- to 5-pound) chicken (preferably a stewing chicken), trussed
2 quarts of chicken broth (Water can be used, but for a rich, full-bodied soup, chicken broth is preferred. If you use water, add 2½ teaspoons of salt.)

2 celery ribs, cut into 2-inch pieces
2 carrots, cut into 2-inch pieces
3 onions, halved
½ teaspoon of dill weed

In a 6-quart pot combine the chicken and the broth. Bring to a boil, reduce to medium heat, and cook for 15 minutes, skimming away all froth that floats to the surface. Add the celery, carrots, onions and dill weed. Simmer, covered, for 2 hours, or until chicken is fork tender. Remove chicken and cool. Remove meat from bones, discarding skin and bones. Strain the broth, discarding the vegetables. Save the choice parts of the bird for another use, but add the meat from the wings and drumsticks to the broth.

MATZO BALLS

1 cup of matzo meal	¼ cup of cold water
	½ teaspoon of salt
beaten together in a large bowl	3 eggs

Gradually add the matzo meal to the egg mixture, beating into a smooth, soft dough. Cover and refrigerate for 1½ hours. Shape into walnut-sized balls. Bring a pot of water to the boil, reduce to a simmer, gently drop in the matzo balls and cook for 25 minutes. Drain, then float the balls in servings of piping hot chicken broth.

NOTE

As this is a particularly rich broth (if you have poached the chicken in broth), it is ideal for other soup variations. Instead of the matzo balls, use any of various noodles, or the special little soup pastas such as "stars" and "shells." Cook the amount of pasta according to how thick a soup is desired.

PASQUALE'S MINESTRONE

Serves 8: This is a supper-soup—a meal-in-one—created by our father and father-in-law. It's our Numero Uno *soup.*

2½ quarts of chicken broth (This is the foundation of the soup; poach a chicken to make the broth, or use thighs and backs. It is important to have at least 2 cups of chicken meat nuggets. Make the broth, cut up the chicken and reserve.)

½ cup of dried chick-peas, soaked for 5 hours and drained

½ cup of dried white kidney beans, soaked for 5 hours and drained

3 tablespoons of olive oil

2 white onions, chopped

2 cloves of garlic, minced

1 (1-pound) can of plum tomatoes, broken up

½ cup of chopped cabbage

½ cup of chopped carrot

½ cup of chopped celery

2 or more cups of bite-sized pieces of cooked chicken

½ cup of *ditalini* (little pasta thimbles), cooked *al dente* and drained

1 teaspoon of salt

½ teaspoon of pepper

⅛ teaspoon of crushed, dry hot red pepper flakes

1 cup of grated Asiago or Parmesan cheese

Pour the chicken broth into a large soup pot. Add the chick-peas and beans. Bring the broth to a boil, reduce heat and simmer, covered, for 40 minutes, or until chick-peas and beans are almost tender. In a saucepan, over medium heat, heat the oil and cook the onion and garlic for 4 minutes. Stir in the tomatoes and cook for 15 minutes longer.

In another small pot, over medium heat, cook the cabbage, carrots and celery covered with salted water until crisp-tender. Drain well. Stir these vegetables and the tomato mixture into the broth. Simmer until cabbage is tender. Add the chicken meat, cooked pasta, salt, pepper and red pepper. Stir, and simmer, uncovered, for 10 minutes, or until piping hot. Taste for seasoning. Serve in large heated soup bowls and pass the cheese.

NOTE

You can use canned chick-peas and white kidney beans, if you prefer. Get 1-pound cans. Add them, drained, to the soup pot when you add the cooked chicken.

MULLIGATAWNY

Serves 6:

6 cups of chicken broth
1 large whole chicken breast
4 tablespoons of butter
6 whole scallions, minced
2 celery ribs, scraped and minced
1 tablespoon of curry powder

½ teaspoon of chervil
2 medium-sized very ripe tomatoes, peeled, seeded and chopped
1 teaspoon of salt
½ teaspoon of pepper
1 cup of cooked rice

Pour the broth into a pot. Add the chicken breast, cover, bring to a boil, then reduce heat and simmer for 20 minutes. Cool the breast, discard skin and bones and cut the meat into slivers. Reserve the broth. In a saucepan, over medium heat, melt 2 tablespoons of the butter. Add scallions, celery, curry powder, chervil and tomatoes, blending thoroughly. Cook for 4 minutes. Stir in the reserved chicken broth, salt and pepper, cover and cook over low heat for 45 minutes, stirring occasionally. Add the rice, chicken breast slivers, and the remaining 2 tablespoons of butter. Taste for seasoning. Stir. Bring to a simmer and serve piping hot.

CHICKEN SOUP NAPOLEON

Serves 8:

1 stick (¼ pound) of butter
2 pounds of onions, finely chopped
2 cups of dry white wine
5 cups of chicken broth

8 ounces of Port Salut, Gruyère or Cantal cheese, grated
2 cups of crisp bread croutons
4 tablespoons of minced parsley

In a saucepan, over medium heat, melt butter and cook the onion for 6 minutes, or until tender but not brown. Puree in a blender or food processor. Place onion in a large soup pot, stir in the wine and broth. Cook for 10 minutes, or until the soup is hot but not boiling. Reduce the heat to low, and add the cheese, a spoonful at a time, stirring until the cheese has melted. Place the croutons in a soup tureen, pour in the hot soup and garnish with minced parsley.

OLD-FASHIONED CHICKEN NOODLE SOUP

Serves 6: This is a lusty, economical soup with hefty servings of chicken and noodles.

4 quarts of water
6 chicken backs
2 onions, quartered
2 celery ribs, cut up
2 carrots, halved
1½ teaspoons of salt
½ teaspoon of pepper

1 bay leaf
4 chicken thighs
⅓ pound of medium-broad
   egg noodles, cooked *al*
   dente and drained
Salt and pepper to taste

In a large pot combine water, chicken backs, onions, celery, carrots, salt, pepper and bay leaf. Bring to a boil, then lower heat and simmer, covered, for 1 hour. Remove cover, and over medium-high heat, reduce the broth by one-third. Strain the broth, discarding the vegetables. Remove and reserve the good pieces of meat from the backs, discarding skin and bones. Pour the broth back into the pot and add the chicken thighs. Bring to a boil, lower heat and simmer, uncovered, for 35 minutes, or until the chicken thighs are fork tender. Remove the thighs, cool long enough to be skinned, boned and cut into bite-sized pieces. Place the thigh meat and reserved back meat in the pot. Stir in the noodles, blending meat and pasta well with the broth. Taste for seasoning. Bring to a boil, then a simmer and serve very hot.

EASY ONION SOUP

Serves 6:

3 tablespoons of butter
6 medium-sized onions,
  thinly sliced.
1½ tablespoons of flour
6 cups of boiling rich
  chicken broth
Salt and pepper to taste

12 ½-inch slices of French
  bread sautéed in butter
  until golden on both sides.
1 cup of grated Gruyère or
  Parmesan cheese
Cayenne

In a large saucepan, over medium heat, melt the butter. Add
the onions and cook just until they start to become golden.
Sprinkle on the flour and, stirring constantly, cook until the
onions are slightly browned. Gradually stir in the broth and
simmer, stirring, for 7 minutes. Taste, then season with salt
and pepper.

Ladle the hot soup into individual heatproof bowls. Float 2
slices of the golden bread in each. Sprinkle the bread with the
cheese and a light shake of cayenne. Place under the broiler
until the cheese is bubbling and brown.

CHICKEN AND OYSTER SOUP

Serves 6:

4 cups of chicken broth
1 cup of milk
1 pint of oysters, with liquor
1 cup of slivered cooked
  chicken meat

Salt to taste
Pinch of cayenne
½ cup of heavy cream

In a saucepan bring the broth and milk to a simmer. Add the
oysters with their liquor and cook just until the edges curl.
Stir in the chicken, salt, cayenne and cream. Heat just until
the soup comes to a simmer and the chicken is heated
through. Serve immediately.

PASTA AND SAUSAGE SOUP

Serves 6 to 8: This is a lusty supper soup, a meal when served with crusty bread and a bottle of wine.

3 quarts of chicken broth
½ pound of pea beans, soaked in water to cover for 5 hours and drained
2 tablespoons of olive oil
3 hot Italian sausages, pricked in several places
3 sweet Italian sausages, pricked in several places
3 small potatoes, diced
1 carrot, peeled and chopped
2 medium-sized onions, chopped

2 celery ribs, scraped and chopped
4 medium-sized ripe tomatoes, peeled, seeded and diced
1 teaspoon of salt
½ teaspoon of pepper
1 cup of *cravatte* (small pasta "bowties") or your choice of small soup pasta, cooked *al dente* and drained

Pour 2 quarts of the chicken broth into a large pot. Add the beans, bring broth to a boil, then lower heat and simmer, covered, for 40 minutes, or until the beans are tender. In another pot, over medium heat, heat the oil and evenly brown the sausages. Pour off all but 2 tablespoons of the fat. Add the potatoes, carrot, onion, celery, tomatoes, salt and pepper. Lower heat and simmer, covered, for 15 minutes, stirring occasionally. Remove the sausages and cut them into ¼-inch rounds. Return the sausage to the pot, pour in the remaining quart of chicken broth and simmer, uncovered for 20 minutes. Add the contents of this pot to the bean pot. Stir in the cooked pasta, and simmer, uncovered, for 5 minutes. Taste for seasoning.

SENEGALESE SOUP

Serves 4 to 6:

3 tablespoons of butter
2 medium-sized onions, chopped
2 tablespoons of flour
2 teaspoons of curry powder (or more, if you like a very spicy soup)
6 cups of chicken broth

½ teaspoon of paprika
1½ cups of shredded cooked chicken
1 cup of cream
Salt to taste
2 hard-cooked eggs, chopped
6 green onions, chopped

In a large saucepan, melt the butter over medium heat. Add the onion and cook until transparent. Stir in the flour and curry powder and cook for 2 minutes, stirring constantly. Stir in 2 cups of the broth, a small amount at a time, until you have a smooth mixture. Add the paprika, the remaining 4 cups broth and the chicken. Bring to a simmer, stir in the cream and heat through but do not boil. Taste and add salt, if needed. Serve hot or chilled, garnished with either the chopped egg or green onion.

SUB GUM

Serves 6: There are several variations of this popular Chinese soup. This is our favorite.

1 tablespoon of peanut oil
1 (1-inch-thick) loin pork chop, fat removed and minced
1 whole chicken breast, skinned, boned and minced
1 celery rib, scraped and chopped

2 small carrots, peeled and chopped
6 water chestnuts, chopped
8 cups of hot chicken broth
1 cup of bean sprouts
2 eggs, beaten
Salt and pepper to taste

In a large pot, heat oil and sauté or stir-fry pork for 2 minutes. Add chicken and stir-fry for 1 minute. Stir in celery, carrots, water chestnuts, then stir-fry for 1½ minutes. Pour in the broth and bean sprouts, cover and simmer for 5 minutes. Vegetables should be crunchy. Blend in the eggs. Season with salt and pepper and serve immediately.

TOMATO EGG DROP SOUP

Serves 6: Here's a deliciously different soup.

2 quarts of chicken broth
1 (1-pound) can of stewed tomatoes, mashed into small pieces

2 tablespoons of cornstarch, blended with ¼ cup cold water
3 eggs, beaten
3 whole scallions, chopped

Pour the chicken broth into a pot and bring to a boil. Stir in the tomatoes. When the mixture comes to a boil again, blend in the cornstarch mixture. Reduce heat to low, and cook, stirring, until the soup thickens. As the soup simmers, slowly stir in the beaten eggs. Remove from the heat. Serve in heated soup bowls with the raw, chopped scallions sprinkled on top.

CREAM OF TOMATO SOUP
WITH CHICKEN BALLS

Serves 6 to 8:

2 medium-sized onions, chopped
2 tablespoons of butter
3 medium-sized potatoes, cubed
1 celery rib, scraped and chopped
3 cups of chicken broth

3 large, ripe tomatoes, peeled, seeded and chopped or 1 (1-pound) can of tomatoes, drained and chopped
Salt and pepper to taste
1 cup of cream (reserve this until just before serving)
2 tablespoons of minced parsley

In a saucepan, over medium heat, cook the onion in butter until transparent. Add the potatoes, celery, broth, tomatoes, salt and pepper. Simmer, partially covered, for 20 minutes, or until the potatoes can be mashed against the side of the pan. Put the soup through a food mill, or use a processor or blender to puree. Set aside.

CHICKEN BALLS

1 tablespoon of butter
1 small onion, minced
½ of a whole chicken breast, run through the fine blade of a meat chopper twice, or chopped in a processor

1 slice of sandwich bread, soaked in ½ cup of milk, then squeeze out the milk
1 large egg
½ teaspoon of salt
⅛ teaspoon of cayenne
Flour
2 cups of chicken broth

In a frypan, melt the butter over medium heat. Add the onion and cook until transparent. In a bowl, combine the onion, chicken, bread, egg, salt and cayenne. Beat with a fork to mix thoroughly. Shape the mixture into balls the size of medium-large olives (flouring your hands to do this will help). Lightly dust the balls with flour. Heat the broth to a bare simmer. Lower the balls carefully into the broth with a slotted spoon. Cook for 10 minutes, remove with the slotted spoon and reserve.

Heat the tomato soup (if it is too thick, thin it with some of the broth the chicken balls cooked in to make a medium-thick soup) to a simmer. Stir in the cream. Heat again just to a simmer. Add the chicken balls, heat through and serve sprinkled with the parsley.

ISTANBUL CHICKEN-YOGURT RICE SOUP

Serves 6 to 8:

9 cups of chicken broth
½ cup of long-grain rice
2 cups of diced cooked chicken
2 tablespoons of butter
1½ tablespoons of flour

1 cup of plain yogurt
¼ teaspoon of cumin
Salt and pepper to taste
2 tablespoons of chopped fresh dill

Bring the broth to a boil in a large pot. Stir in the rice, reduce heat and simmer, covered, for 20 minutes, or until the rice is tender but not mushy. Add the chicken to the broth. In a saucepan, over medium heat, melt the butter, stir in the flour and cook, stirring, for 3 minutes. Stir in the yogurt and cumin and simmer for 2 minutes. Add the yogurt mixture to the broth and cook over low heat, stirring, until the soup thickens. Taste for seasoning, adding salt and pepper. Serve with the dill sprinkled on top.

VELVET CHICKEN-VEGETABLE SOUP

Serves 6:

7 cups of chicken broth
4 small carrots, peeled and sliced
2 medium-sized leeks (white part only), sliced
2 medium-sized zucchini, sliced

2 celery ribs, scraped and sliced
1½ teaspoons of salt
½ teaspoon of pepper
1 teaspoon of paprika

Combine all ingredients in a large pot. Bring to the boil, then reduce heat and simmer, uncovered, 20 minutes, or until vegetables are tender. Pour into a blender container or a food processor bowl and blend into a velvety smooth mixture. Taste for seasoning. Reheat and serve piping hot.

CREAM OF CHICKEN SOUP WITH WATERCRESS

Serves 4 to 6:

5 tablespoons of butter
2 tablespoons of flour
6 cups of rich chicken broth
1½ cups of milk
Salt and pepper to taste
2 bunches of watercress, trimmed, washed and drained

1 small white onion, chopped

beaten together
½ cup of heavy cream
2 egg yolks

1 cup of cooked chicken, cut into small cubes

In a large saucepan, over medium heat, melt 3 tablespoons of the butter. Stir in the flour and cook, stirring constantly, until you have a smooth paste. Gradually add 5 cups of the broth and the milk. Cook, stirring, until smooth. Season with salt and pepper and simmer, partially covered, for 10 minutes.

Blanch ½ cup of the watercress leaves in boiling water for 1 minute. Drain and reserve for garnish.

In another saucepan, melt the remaining 2 tablespoons of butter. Add the onion and cook for 2 minutes. Add the remaining watercress and the remaining cup of broth. Cover and simmer for 5 minutes, or until the watercress is limp. Pour into a blender container and puree. Add the puree to the saucepan with the broth-milk mixture. Heat to a simmer. Stir ½ cup of the soup into the egg yolks and cream then return it to the pan. Add the chicken and stir over low heat until slightly thickened (do not boil). Taste for seasoning. Serve garnished with the blanched watercress leaves.

ZUPPA ALLA PAESANA

Serves 6 to 8:

1 pound of dry lentils, rinsed, soaked in water for 5 hours, drained, then cooked, covered, in salted water at a simmer for 45 minutes, or until tender. (Leave them in the liquid and set aside.)
1 tablespoon of olive oil
1 tablespoon of butter
8 anchovy fillets, drained and mashed
2 celery ribs (with leaves), scraped and chopped

1 clove of garlic, minced
1 tablespoon of chopped broadleaf parsley
4 large ripe tomatoes, peeled, seeded and diced
1½ quarts of chicken broth
2 cups of water
½ teaspoon of salt
½ teaspoon of pepper
½ cup of *maruzzine* (small pasta shells), cooked *al dente* and drained
1 cup of grated Asiago or Parmesan cheese

In a large pot, over medium heat, heat the oil and butter. Stir in the anchovies, celery, garlic and parsley. Cook for 4 minutes, or until celery is soft. Add the tomatoes, broth, water, salt and pepper. Bring to a boil, lower heat and simmer, uncovered, for 25 minutes. Add the lentils with their cooking liquid and simmer for 10 minutes. Stir in the pasta shells. Simmer until soup is piping hot. Taste for seasoning. Serve in heated soup bowls and pass the cheese.

Chapter Three

Sauces and Gravies

Probably the most unique aspect of the chicken is that it is superb served plain or fancy. It is very difficult to serve a food more pleasing and satisfying than a roast chicken. But this plain roast bird can also be inventively enhanced with a special sauce or gravy.

Yet, such is the power of the chicken that it seldom can be overwhelmed by any sauce, be it lemon, orange, pineapple, cream, or a savory pan-gravy. The chicken still retains its personality. We remember a chicken that was still recognizable even after it was poached in ginger ale!

Herewith we offer some favorite flavor-enhancers.

ALLEMANDE SAUCE

This is a very rich sauce that the French use with a plain poached or boiled chicken.

To 2 cups of Suprême Sauce (page 64) add 2 beaten egg yolks that have been beaten with ¼ cup of heavy cream. Blend a small amount of the hot Suprême Sauce into the egg yolk mixture before stirring it into the sauce. Do not allow the sauce to boil.

CHICKEN-QUE GEORGIA STYLE

If you enjoy barbecuing, here is a unique sauce from chicken expert J. H. Massey of the University of Georgia's College of Agriculture, together with helpful hints on how to handle chickens over outdoor fires.

CHICKEN-QUE SAUCE

For 6 halves:

¾ cup of vinegar
¼ cup of water
1½ teaspoons of Tabasco or other hot sauce

½ cup cooking oil
1½ tablespoons of salt

Measure the ingredients in a saucepan and bring to a boil. Keep hot on the grill for basting with a cotton mop or pastry brush each time the chicken is turned (a stiff brush will tear the skin).

NOTE

"Sauce with tomato or sugar will burn the chicken and give a very charred appearance. A tomato-based sauce can be used, but it is recommended only for the last 15 minutes of cooking to reduce charring. The above sauce should be used for the first period of cooking.

"The chicken-que sauce is used for large chicken-ques; it can be used in a sprayer. This sauce can be changed to your taste by adding lemon juice, marjoram leaves, Worcestershire sauce, etc; you will be mopping rather than spraying.

"*Charcoal briquettes*—A long-burning briquette is one that is very tight and compact in contrast to a briquette that is very porous.

"*Lighter fluid*—The cheapest and one of the best lighter fluids is mineral spirits, available from some service stations or paint stores. Gasoline is too dangerous to use and kerosene may cause an odor. Do not use any lighter fluid after the fire is started.

"Start with a chicken half that weighs 1 pound. This would be from a 2¼- or a 2½-pound chicken with giblets. The larger the half the longer it takes to cook. Chicken should be placed on the grill with the cut side down after the fire stops blazing. Use tongs for turning as a fork will puncture the skin and allow juices to escape. Turn the chicken by the back as the skin on the breast and legs will tear easily when cooking starts and allow the chicken to dry out. The chicken is better if salted on each side the night before. However, if you are starting with chicken direct from the store, salt both sides before placing on the rack (for large barbecues salt on the skin side when placed on the rack and salt the cut side when first turning). Sauce is basted on the chicken each time it is turned.

"*Controlling the fire* is very important when cooking chicken. You must determine the amount of charcoal to use for your grill. If your grill rack is 10 inches or more from the fire, use about ½ pound of charcoal per half chicken. Reduce the amount, if it is closer than 10 inches. The use of aluminum foil in the bottom of the grill will reflect more heat and reduce the amount of charcoal needed. Sometimes grease will drop on hot charcoal and blaze up. The flame should be put out immediately. This can be done by sprinkling water on the flame.

Caution: Steam will occur, so use a soft-drink bottle with a clothes sprinkler, and never put hands directly over flame."

WEEKENDER CHICKEN-BASTING BARBECUE SAUCE

Makes about 1½ cups:

4 whole scallions, chopped
1 cup of chili sauce
1 teaspoon of dry mustard
⅓ cup of white vinegar
⅛ teaspoon of Tabasco
1 tablespoon of Worcestershire sauce
1 teaspoon of salt
¼ cup of dark brown sugar

Combine all ingredients in a blender container. Blend at high speed until the scallions are minced. Pour into a saucepan and over low heat, simmer, stirring, for 10 minutes.

BLENDER BREAD SAUCE

Makes about 2 cups: For roast chicken

1½ cups of light cream
3 tablespoons of butter
2 small onions, sliced
4 slices of stale bread, in pieces

½ teaspoon of salt
⅛ teaspoon of cayenne
Pinch of ground cloves
Pinch of nutmeg

In a saucepan, combine the cream, butter and onions. Bring to the point just below the boil, stirring. Remove from heat. Combine the bread, salt, cayenne, cloves and nutmeg in the blender container. Blend on high speed for 5 seconds. Gradually blend in the hot cream mixture. Taste for seasoning. Sauce should be served hot.

CRANBERRY SAUCE

Makes about 3 cups:

1 cup of sugar
3 cups of fresh cranberries
1 cup of water

½ teaspoon of grated lemon rind
½ teaspoon of grated orange rind

Combine sugar, berries and water in a saucepan. Bring to a boil, stirring. Reduce heat to low, and cook, stirring, for 6 minutes, or until the berries begin to pop. Remove from the heat and blend in the rinds. Transfer to a bowl and refrigerate for 4 hours.

QUICK CREAM SAUCE

Makes about 1½ cups: Excellent with fried or boiled chicken.

1 (10½-ounce) can of con-
densed cream of chicken
soup
⅓ cup of heavy cream
1 tablespoon of chopped
parsley

1 tablespoon of chopped
chives
1 small clove of garlic,
minced

Combine all ingredients in a blender container and blend into a smooth mixture, about 10 seconds. Pour into a saucepan and cook over low heat, stirring, for 10 minutes.

NOTE

This fast sauce can be varied in interesting ways by using mushroom, celery or cheese soups.

CREAM GARLIC SAUCE

Makes about 3 cups: This sauce adds a nice touch to poached chicken.

2 cups of light cream
12 large cloves of garlic
4 egg yolks, beaten with
⅓ cup of heavy cream

½ tablespoon of fresh lemon
juice
Salt to taste

Pour the cream into a saucepan. Add the garlic and cook over low heat, stirring, for 15 minutes. Beat a small amount of the hot garlic-flavored cream into the egg yolk–cream mixture. Then quickly stir back into the hot cream saucepan. Blend in the lemon juice. Add salt. The sauce should be served hot but do not let it boil or it will curdle. This is usually served with the poached chicken cut into serving pieces, the sauce liberally spooned on top, garlic and all.

CREAM GRAVY FOR FRIED CHICKEN

Makes about 2 cups: This is traditionally served in the South, spooned over the fried chicken.

2 tablespoons of drippings
  from roasting pan
3 tablespoons flour

2 cups of medium "whipping" cream
Salt and pepper to taste

Pour off all but 2 tablespoons of the fat the chicken cooked in. Turn the heat to high, add the flour, scraping up brown particles remaining in the fry pan, stirring and blending well with the fat. Lower heat to medium. Pour in the cream in a thin stream, stirring until it comes to a boil, thickens and is smooth. Turn heat to low and simmer, stirring, for 3 minutes. Season with salt and pepper.

OLD-FASHIONED GIBLET PAN GRAVY

Makes about 2 cups: This is the gravy we all like, made from the residue left in the pan after the chicken has been roasted to a turn.

2 tablespoons of butter
Uncooked giblets from the
  roasting chicken, plus 3
  additional livers, all
  coarsely chopped

3 tablespoons of drippings
  from roasting pan
3 tablespoons of flour
2 cups of chicken broth
Salt and pepper to taste

In a frypan, melt the butter and over medium heat cook the chopped gizzard and heart for 5 minutes, stirring often. Add the livers and cook for 2 minutes. Remove from the heat and set aside.

Place the roasting pan with the drippings on top of the stove over low heat. Stir in the flour, scraping up the browned particles in the bottom of the pan, blending well with the flour and fat. Cook, stirring, for 2 minutes. Gradually stir in the broth, blending into a smooth sauce. Raise the heat to medium and cook, stirring constantly, for 5 minutes. Season with salt and pepper. Stir in the cooked giblets, blending well with the gravy.

NOTE

This simple but tasty gravy can be sparked by adding herbs, dried thyme, rosemary, tarragon (in small amounts as they are potent) just before the chicken broth is stirred into the gravy.

CHICKEN LIVER AND MUSHROOM SAUCE

Makes about 3 cups: Serve this sauce over rice, pasta or other grains.

4 tablespoons of butter
2 medium-sized white onions, finely chopped
¼ pound of cooked ham, coarsely chopped
¼ pound of chicken livers, washed, trimmed and cut into ½-inch cubes
Salt and pepper to taste

¼ teaspoon of dried marjoram
½ pound of small mushrooms, cut into ¼-inch slices
1½ cups of beef broth
4 tablespoons (2 ounces) of Madeira

In a saucepan, over medium heat, melt the butter. Add the onion and ham and cook for 5 minutes, or until the onion is soft. Add the livers, pepper, marjoram and cook for 2 minutes, stirring from time to time. Add the mushrooms and cook for 2 minutes longer. Pour in the broth and wine and simmer, uncovered, for 10 minutes. Taste for seasoning, adding salt and more pepper, if necessary.

ONION GRAVY FOR FRIED CHICKEN

Makes about 2 cups:

4 small onions, thinly sliced
1 tablespoon of the fat that the chicken was fried in
2 tablespoons of flour

2 cups of chicken broth
1 tablespoon of vinegar
½ teaspoon of salt
¼ teaspoon of pepper

In the frypan in which the chicken cooked, add the onions to the reserved 1 tablespoon of fat and sprinkle with flour. Stirring constantly, cook on medium heat for 4 minutes (be careful not to burn). Slowly pour in the broth, continue stirring and cook until the gravy comes to a boil and is smooth and thick. Blend in the vinegar, salt and pepper. Taste for seasoning.

SAUCE PROVENÇALE

Makes about 3 cups: Good over poached or broiled chicken.

3 tablespoons of butter
5 shallots, chopped
3 tablespoons of flour
2 cups of chicken broth
½ cup of dry white wine
3 medium-sized ripe tomatoes, peeled, seeded and chopped

2 cloves of garlic, halved and crushed
3 tablespoons of chopped parsley
Salt and pepper to taste

In a large saucepan, melt the butter over medium heat. Add the shallots and cook for 2 minutes. Stir in the flour and cook for 1 minute. Reduce heat to low and gradually stir in the broth and the wine. Continue stirring until the mixture is thickish and smooth. Blend in the tomatoes and garlic. Simmer, stirring, for 25 minutes. Push through a sieve into a saucepan, then stir in the parsley. Taste for seasoning. Add salt and pepper.

RAISIN-WINE SAUCE FOR ROASTED CHICKEN OR CORNISH GAME HEN

Makes about 1½ cups:

3 tablespoons of drippings from roasting pan

1 teaspoon of flour (enough to bind, but not thicken)

4 tablespoons (2 ounces) of brandy

6 tablespoons (3 ounces) of port

1½ cups of rich chicken broth

1 cup of dry red wine

Salt and pepper to taste

½ cup of raisins, covered with port and soaked for 1 hour, then drained

1 teaspoon of cornstarch, mixed with 1 tablespoon water

In a saucepan, over medium heat, heat the pan drippings. Add the flour and stir until well blended. Pour in the brandy and ignite. After the brandy flames for a few seconds, pour in the port and simmer for 1 minute. Add the broth and red wine and simmer until reduced by one-half. Season with salt and pepper. Blend in the raisins and the cornstarch-water mixture. Heat just to a simmer, stirring until smooth and well blended.

SHALLOT SAUCE

Makes about 1 cup: This is excellent with simple broiled chicken.

4 tablespoons of minced shallots

4 tablespoons of dry white vermouth

½ pound of butter, at room temperature

½ teaspoon of salt

¼ teaspoon black pepper

Place the shallots and vermouth in a saucepan and bring to a boil. Cook over medium heat, stirring, until the liquid evaporates. Remove from heat and cool for 2 minutes. Using a wire whisk, gradually beat in the butter. Still beating, add the salt and pepper. The sauce should be of the consistency of mayonnaise.

Careful: If the pan and shallots are too hot the butter will "curdle."

VELVET SAUCE FOR COLD CHICKEN OR CHICKEN SALAD

Makes about 1½ cups:

1½ cups of mayonnaise
1 celery rib, scraped and chopped
3 whole scallions, chopped
1 small clove of garlic, chopped

1 tablespoon of chopped broadleaf parsley
¼ teaspoon of dried tarragon
1 teaspoon of fresh lemon juice

Combine all ingredients in a bowl, mixing well. Spoon into a blender container and blend on high speed for 8 seconds.

FAST BLENDER WHITE SAUCE

Makes about 2 cups: This is an excellent "base" sauce, with variations.

2 cups of hot milk
4 tablespoons of flour

4 tablespoons of butter
Salt and pepper to taste

Combine the milk, flour and butter in a blender container and blend for 8 seconds. Pour into a saucepan and cook, stirring, over low heat for 4 minutes, or until thickened. Season with salt and pepper.

VARIATIONS

1. For a quick Chicken à la King sauce, add ⅓ cup of heavy cream, 1 tablespoon of sherry and 1 pimiento, sliced.
2. For a quick horseradish sauce for poached chicken, add ⅓ cup of heavy cream and ¼ cup of drained horseradish.

RICH WHITE SAUCE

Makes about 2 cups: Usually white sauce is made with milk, but we like it a bit richer, thus we use light cream.

3 tablespoons of butter	Salt and pepper to taste
3 tablespoons of flour	⅛ teaspoon of nutmeg
2 cups of light cream	

In a saucepan, over low heat, melt the butter. Add the flour and simmer, stirring, into a smooth golden paste, about 4 minutes. Pour the cream in and quickly blend with the roux. (A wire whisk is the best utensil for this.) Raise the heat, stirring constantly, as the sauce comes to the boil. Reduce the heat to low, and cook, stirring occasionally for 10 minutes, or until the sauce no longer has a floury taste, is very smooth and thick enough to coat a spoon. Season with salt and pepper. Blend in the nutmeg.

VELOUTÉ SAUCE

Makes about 2 cups:

3 tablespoons of butter	2 cups of chicken broth
3 tablespoons of flour	Salt and pepper to taste

In a saucepan, melt the butter over medium heat. Add the flour and cook, stirring, until well blended. Gradually stir in the broth. Stirring constantly, cook until the sauce is medium-thick and smooth. Season with salt and pepper.

SIMPLE VARIATIONS ON A VELOUTÉ SAUCE
To a Velouté Sauce (above) add:

1. Butter-sautéed sliced mushrooms
   or
2. Butter-sautéed sliced onions
   or
3. Butter-sautéed minced red or green peppers, for a color and flavor accent.

The amount of each varies with individual tastes.

SUPRÊME SAUCE

Blend ½ cup of heavy cream into the above Velouté Sauce.

PIQUANT SAUCE

Stir the juice of ½ lemon into the above Suprême Sauce. Add a dash of cayenne.

SIMPLE VARIATIONS ON THE SUPRÊME SAUCE

If you have glanced at this sauce chapter, you will know that a Suprême Sauce is simply a Velouté Sauce enriched with heavy cream (above). Ways to further enhance this sauce to serve with or on chicken are many. Here are a few:

CHIVE SAUCE

Add ½ cup of chopped fresh chives to the recipe for Suprême Sauce

DILL SAUCE

Add ½ cup of fresh chopped dill

MUSTARD SAUCE

Add 3 tablespoons of a good mustard such as Dijon

PARSLEY SAUCE

Add ½ cup of fresh chopped broadleaf parsley

TARRAGON SAUCE

Add ½ cup of fresh chopped tarragon, also blending in 2 tablespoons of butter

CHANTILLY SAUCE

To 1 cup of Suprême Sauce blend in ½ cup of whipped cream

Chapter Four

Whole Chickens (Roasting, Poaching, Stuffing, etc.)

We never think of a whole chicken without remembering the first dinner we cooked for Antoine Gilly. Who is Antoine Gilly? He is one of the four greatest living French chefs, who has cooked for a King of England, a Prince of Wales, several Prime Ministers and many other illustrious people. A true genius in the kitchen, he is a friend and mentor, with whom we have worked, in his kitchen and in ours, for well over a decade.

Great chefs like simple food for themselves. Knowing this, when Antoine came to dinner we planned to offer a buttery roast chicken. Of course, we did slide some sliced black truffles under the skin of the breast, and we did stuff the bird with homemade herbed bread crumbs and fresh Chincoteague oysters.

He watched us work on the chicken, then said, "Are you going to truss it?"

We said, "Of course," and proceeded to truss it in our accustomed fashion—with cord pinioning the legs and the wings to the body, compactly, and we thought, neatly.

He shook his head, and said, being our teacher as well as our friend, that that wouldn't do at all. "As the chicken roasts," he explained, "it will shrink somewhat, the cords will loosen and the bird will overcook in some places and undercook in others."

Dinner was late that night. Antoine insisted that we truss, using the French needle system, of which we were unaware. It took us over three hours to find a mattress factory in a

*somewhat distant town, and a mattress needle. It wasn't a
trussing needle but it did the trick, almost a surgical job.
(The technique is relatively simple, once you have learned
it.) That chicken was so beautifully and evenly cooked, so
juicy, that the next day we sent to Paris and got every size
trussing needle the French had created, from quail-sized to a
long turkey trusser.*

*This type of trussing is important because it keeps the
chicken as compact as a clenched fist while it cooks.*

*All the system needs is a little practice; study the illustra-
tion, do it a couple of times and you've got it for a lifetime.
The needles are available in most cookware shops.*

*The long needle draws the cord "through," not around the
bird. There are just two positions, near the tail to truss the
thighs and drumsticks, then through the center of the thighs,
which also ties in the wings and neck skin.*

The needle passes through *the lower carcass, comes back*
over *not through one leg,* through *the tip of the breastbone,
then* over *the second leg. The cord is then tied tightly and
cut, the needle rethreaded.*

*In the second tie, with the new piece of cord, the needle is
pushed through the apex of the second joint (thigh and
drumstick) going right* through *the body and emerging at the
same point on the opposite side. The bird is then turned over,
the wings are folded back and the needle is pushed* through
*one wing. The needle's emerging point catches the loose neck
skin, pins it to the neck, comes up and passes through the
other wing. The cord again is drawn as tightly as possible and
tied. Follow the diagram. And do give it a try. It pays great
flavor dividends.*

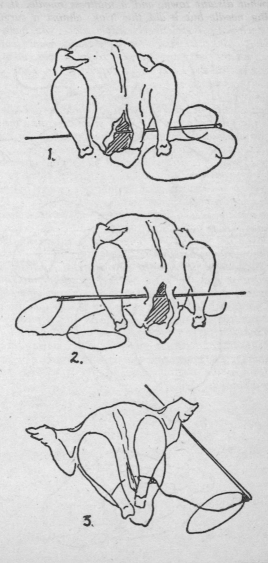

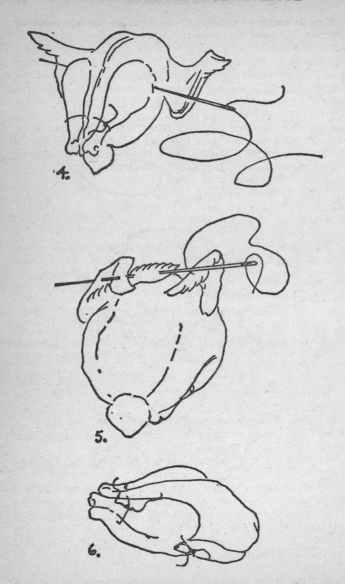

Here is another "needleless" method, we do not think as effective, but good nevertheless.

Use a 3-foot length of cord. With chicken on its back, pull the cord under the legs, then loop it around the legs, crossing it as it is pulled between the legs. Draw the cord around the tail, crossing it beneath it, then tighten the cord which will pull the legs together in a truss.

Draw the cord back, under the drumsticks, hold the cord against the chicken, turn the bird over, pulling the cord through the wings, and draw it across the back. Wings should be tight against the body. Tie the cord tightly and cut off any excess. Fold the neck flap under the tight cord, tucking the wings over the flap.

Any whole chicken should be trussed, no matter what you are going to do with it, roast, poach, broil on a spit, whatever. Trussing definitely improves flavor and helps the bird "cook evenly."

Whole chickens are the most economical, thus the smart buy. If you want them in parts, or separated (as the next chapter will instruct), cut them up yourself and save money.

TESTS FOR DONENESS

The National Broiler Council, a collection of experts representing the entire U.S. chicken industry, offers these tests to determine when a chicken is ready for the table.

• It is ready when a fork can be gently inserted with ease.
• When the thick muscle of the drumstick is soft to the touch.
• When the leg moves readily when lifted or twisted.
• When a meat thermometer inserted into the thickest part of the thigh muscle registers 190°F.
• When the thermometer inserted in the stuffing registers 165°F.

"Fork tender" is a good rule for all chicken except roast chicken. With the roast chicken, we lean heavily toward the chef's rule of thumb: Stick a skewer into the thickest part of the thigh. If clear liquid runs out, the chicken is done; if the liquid is a light pink, cook another 15 minutes. If the liquid is red, the bird has a ways to go.

If there is one fault American cooks commonly share, it is the overcooking of roast chicken. Improper trussing, or not trussing at all, is one of the basic errors; another is cooking too long per pound. But basically the fault lies in the fact that too many of us believe that all there is to roasting a bird is placing it in a pan, shoving it into the oven and turning on the heat. It would be nice if it were that easy.

Roasting is not difficult, but there are rules to follow if the chicken isn't to end up dry and overcooked. The French have a saying, "One can be taught to cook, but must be born with a talent for roasting." Not true, of course, but that belief does point up the fact that there is more to roasting than meets the eye.

There are various systems or techniques, each advocate believing that his is the best.

The high-heat cooks, many of them professionals or semi-professionals, roast at 450°F., claiming that this seals in all the juices and roasts the chicken quickly before it can dry out. They also are basting enthusiasts. The problem is that the juices, when heated this rapidly, become steam. Basting has sealed the skin, locking the steaming juices in. This loosens the skin and puffs it. If served hot (which it shouldn't be—the roast chicken should rest 10 minutes to allow the juices to settle and make carving easier), this is no cosmetic disadvantage. But when the "high-heat" bird cools slightly the skin becomes loose and wrinkled. This is a pity, for a properly roasted chicken is one of mankind's most appealing sights.

Here is how we attain that sight:

First, we have the chicken to be roasted at room temperature. *Second*, we add salt, sometimes seasoned salt, and put something aromatic in its cavity—onion, celery, garlic, also a knob of butter. *Third*, we truss the chicken. As we have stated before, this is important as it insures that the bird cooks evenly. *Fourth*, we smother it with herb butter; this gives the chicken a wonderful flavor. *Fifth*, not always, but often, we pull back the skin, first on one side of the neck, then the other, insert fingers, loosen the skin from the breast, then again using fingers, push herb butter under the skin directly onto the breast. What we are actually doing is giving the bird's breast another inner skin of butter, an herb-butter coat under the outer skin. Next, we pull the skin back into normal position, and place the chicken on a rack in a roasting pan.

The combinations of herb butter are many, depending upon personal taste and imagination. A few: chives, parsley, garlic, shallots, tarragon, thyme, rosemary, lemon butter, ginger, curry (some of these can be combined).

For example, our favorite is a mixture of unsalted butter, minced garlic, salt and pepper, oregano and a couple of stems of dried rosemary (careful, it is an overpowering herb).

In order to mix the herb butter, the butter should not be soft, nor should it be right from the refrigerator. Take it out of the refrigerator 10 minutes before time to prepare it. The herb butter can also be formed into sticks and frozen. Here's our recipe for rubbing a 4- to 4½-pound bird.

OREGANO-ROSEMARY HERB-BUTTER

1 stick (¼ pound) of un-salted butter

½ teaspoon of dried oreg-ano

⅛ teaspoon of dried rose-mary

1 clove of garlic, minced

½ teaspoon of salt

¼ teaspoon of pepper

In a bowl, place the butter and beat it with an electric beater until fluffy. Stir in the remaining ingredients, blending well. Push some herb butter under the skin onto the breast, coat the chicken completely with half of it. Melt the remainder to use in basting the bird.

You can also roast a chicken with just butter. A well roasted, buttery chicken is hard to beat. Use the same method as for herb butter, only use 8 tablespoons of plain, unsalted butter, 4 to coat the bird with, the remainder melted for basting.

Note: Before coating the chicken with butter, rub salt and pepper into it.

Basting the bird every 15 minutes not only insures that it will be evenly colored and juicy, but that it will emerge from the oven with a wonderful buttery flavor. For basting use a pastry brush (just dip it into the melted butter, then "paint" the bird), or a large spoon or bulb baster. We use all three. If a spoon is used, make certain that the chicken is placed in a roasting pan large enough to allow the spoon to be dipped into the pan to scoop up the juices

A note on roasting pans: Chefs advise that the pan not be much larger than the bird, and it should be shallow rather than one with high sides. With such a pan a chicken roasts more evenly, is easier to baste and gets more direct benefit of the heat.

ROASTING

This system of roasting a chicken in a pan without a cover is called "open roasting." It demands frequent basting to keep the bird juicy and the color even.

Preheat the oven to 500°F. Immediately turn the heat down to 375°F. and place the chicken into the oven, breast side up, on a rack in the roasting pan. The rack aids in even distribution of heat. If you have rubbed herb butter or butter onto the chicken's back, the rack needn't be greased; if you haven't, rub the rack lightly with oil before you place the chicken on it.

Cook the chicken by weight: Cook 20 minutes per pound, basting every 15 minutes. If the chicken is stuffed, add 5 minutes per pound to the cooking time. If it weighs over 5 pounds, reduce cooking time by 5 minutes per pound, that is, 15 minutes, rather than 20 per pound.

This is our way, and all factors being equal, the results are excellent. But, in cooking, all factors aren't always equal. We are talking here about roasting a young bird. The age of the bird, its fat content and its size can alter timing. Also, oven temperatures are very often not accurate. With this method, basting often and testing for doneness as already explained, it is difficult not to succeed.

Some cooks offer another test for doneness: Move the leg—if the hip joint is loose, the chicken is cooked. For our tastes, this test proves that the chicken is overcooked.

Another method for roasting a chicken is the "stage" approach. First on one side, then the other, then breast up. The time is the same: 20 minutes on one side, 20 minutes on the other, then 20 minutes, breast up. This technique which its advocates claim is the only way to turn out an evenly cooked chicken, also requires that the chicken be basted often.

Basting can be an art in itself. We have friends who baste roast chickens with a combination of butter-honey-white wine; others who use melted butter and ginger, or butter and lemon.

If asked to name the two most important preparation techniques for roast chicken, we both agree that it is trussing and basting. Trussing pulls the chicken together into one compact whole that helps the bird cook evenly, basting seals and keeps the chicken from drying out.

Methods of cooking a whole bird other than roasting are braising and poaching.

BRAISING

This is a slow method of cooking the chicken in liquid on an aromatic bed of vegetables of your choice. The pot is important: Use one just large enough to hold the chicken so the bird can flavor the liquid and the liquid flavor the bird. It is slow cooking and not recommended for small chickens; they fall apart before the fusion of flavors occurs. Birds 4 pounds or over are best, a 5-pound chicken is perfect.

Truss the bird and rub it with salt and pepper. In a pot, melt 2 tablespoons of butter over medium heat. Brown the chicken evenly and remove it. In the same pot, over low heat, sauté until soft but not brown, coarsely chopped celery, carrots and onion, sprinkled with herbs of your choice. Add enough chicken broth to cover the vegetables, or a combination of broth and wine, and bring to a boil, cooking until the liquid is about evaporated. Place the chicken on top of the vegetables, pour in more broth, or broth and wine, to come halfway up the chicken. Add some fresh uncooked celery, parsley, bay leaf and thyme to the pot. Cover the pot tightly and bake in a preheated 325°F. oven for 1½ hours, or until the bird is fork tender. While the chicken is braising, remove the cover three times and baste well. During the last 15 minutes of cooking time uncover the pot and baste the chicken several times. Serve the chicken whole on a heated platter, surrounded with a selection of vegetables such as carrots, leeks, potatoes, etc., that have been separately cooked in chicken broth. Birds should be cooked 20 minutes per pound.

POACHING

This may be the simplest of all ways to cook a chicken— and some think the best. Covered in barely simmering water or broth, the chicken is cooked 15 minutes per pound for a young chicken, 40 minutes for an old, or a stewing chicken. This old chicken, a "fowl" that has seen its best days, is poached in plain water with a carrot or two, an onion, some celery and a bouquet garni to produce a very rich broth. The old chicken does not make a good "poached" chicken, its meat is mainly good for pies, soups, etc. But its broth is superb, the best of all chicken broths. So-called fowls are not sold in most markets today. Commercial soup companies buy most of them directly from farms and chicken breeders.

Thus, we will concern ourselves with "young" chickens, which can weigh from 3½ to 5 pounds. We even like to poach the large roasting chickens. All chickens, except the hard-to-obtain fowls, should be poached in chicken broth with perhaps 1 cup of white wine added. If the chicken broth is rich, nothing else need be added, although most professional chefs drop in a bouquet garni.

Chickens that weigh under 3 pounds (no matter how careful the cooking and timing) are likely to emerge from the poaching pot on the stringy side. Thus we feel that a 5-pound bird is the perfect specimen for poaching, coming from the pot tender, moist, flavorful, its meat with a fine-grained texture.

The poached chicken can be lifted from the pot whole and served hot with any number of sauces. It can be stuffed and served whole on a hot platter covered with an interesting coating (as it was for the coronation of Edward VII) or it can come in succulent pieces in a soup bowl covered in its own broth garnished with dumplings. Moist poached chicken meat can be used in many ways, from hot pies to elegant cold salads.

One of the most memorable chicken dishes we ever had was one served us in the elegant dining room of the Terminus Hotel in Copenhagen, Denmark. It was poached and accompanied by a creamy horseradish sauce. Moist, tender, full of flavor, it was the perfect poached chicken.

Pitfalls for poaching chicken: As with roast chicken, it is too often overcooked until stringy, flavorless meat literally falls from the bones. Also, if the chicken to be poached isn't competently trussed, it can come from the pot looking like it just lost the chicken fight, legs half off, wings dangling, all overcooked because they were not tied snugly to the body, cooking as a whole, as one.

We have led you into roasting, braising and poaching with detailed explanations of the techniques. Now we shall put theory into practice with recipes for each.

Ahead in this chapter are recipes for a large variety of stuffings. Stuffings are valuable; they add flavor, perfume the chicken, give it double value, stretching the meal. A savory stuffing, crowned with gleaming brown pan giblet gravy, nested beside thick slices of breast and thigh, tells the whole story of why chicken remains the master of meals.

BUTTERY ROAST CHICKEN

Serves 6:

1 stick (¼ pound) of butter
1 (4½- to 5-pound) chicken
2 teaspoons of salt
½ teaspoon of pepper
⅛ teaspoon of dried tarragon
3 cloves of garlic

Divide the butter in half. Rub the inside of the chicken with half of the butter and leave whatever is left inside the bird. Rub the inside of the chicken with half of the salt and pepper, then place the tarragon and garlic inside. Truss it. Generously rub the chicken with the remaining salt and pepper, then the remaining half-stick of butter. Place the chicken on a rack in a roasting pan. Preheat the oven to 500°F. Immediately turn the heat down to 375°F. and cook the chicken, uncovered, for about 1½ hours, or until fork tender, basting with the pan juices every 15 minutes. The bird should emerge from the oven golden-brown and juicy.

NOTE

Before carving, all whole chickens should "rest" for 10 minutes to permit the juices to settle.

BRAISED CHICKEN

Serves 4 to 6: You may want to stuff the bird with one of the many stuffings in this chapter. Braised chicken and stuffing go well together.

1 (4½- to 5-pound) chicken
Salt and pepper
3 tablespoons of butter
1 tablespoon of olive oil
2 small leeks, coarsely chopped
2 celery ribs, coarsely chopped
2 carrots, coarsely chopped
1 cup of dry white vermouth
3 to 6 cups of chicken broth
⅛ teaspoon of dried rosemary
¼ teaspoon of dried tarragon
6 sprigs of broadleaf parsley
2 onions, one stuck with a whole clove

Liberally sprinkle the chicken with salt and pepper inside and out. Truss. In a pot, not much larger than the chicken, heat the butter and oil over medium-high heat and brown the chicken evenly. Remove the chicken. Stir the leeks, celery and carrots into the pot. Cook, over medium heat, until the vegetables are soft, about 5 minutes. Add the vermouth, raise the heat and cook, stirring, until most of the liquid has evaporated. Stir in the broth. Add the chicken. The liquid should come one-third way up the chicken. Add the rosemary, tarragon, parsley and onions. Bring to a boil on top of the stove. Cover with extra-heavy aluminum foil, then the pot's cover. Place in a preheated 325°F. oven and cook for about 20 minutes to the pound (25 minutes for a stuffed bird). Check the pot; the liquid should be just simmering. Baste the chicken every time you check the pot. The danger with a braised chicken (as with a roast bird) is overcooking. So check for tenderness after 1 hour. During the last 20 minutes of cooking, remove the cover and foil and baste frequently.

NOTE
Serve with any of a number of sauces in the sauce chapter, page 53. Suprême Sauce is excellent with braised chicken.

POACHED CHICKEN

Serves 4:

1 (4-pound) chicken,
  trussed
1½ cups of dry white wine
2 quarts (or enough to completely cover the chicken)
  of seasoned rich chicken
  broth

2 tablespoons of butter, at
  room temperature
8 medium-sized whole leeks,
  trimmed
8 medium-sized whole car-
  rots, peeled
4 medium-sized whole potatoes, peeled
kosher salt

Set the chicken in a deep pot slightly larger than it is. Pour in the wine and enough of the broth to cover it. Bring the liquid to a boil. Lower heat, so that the broth barely shimmers in a simmer. Cover the pot. Broth is most efficient in transmitting heat, thus the chicken will probably cook more rapidly than one would think. Depending upon the size and age of the chicken, poaching usually takes about 15 minutes per pound (time after liquid starts simmering). But check for doneness at 45 minutes. Liquid from the thickest part of the thighs should run clear when pricked. Poaching produces a delightfully moist and flavorful result. When cooked, carefully remove the chicken. Let it drain, then rub it generously with butter and keep warm in a 200°F. oven. Add the leeks and carrots to the liquid in the poaching pot and cook over medium heat for 10 minutes. Add the potatoes and cook 15 minutes longer, or until all vegetables are tender. Serve the chicken whole (carve it at the table), surrounded by the vegtables. Pass kosher salt for guests to sparingly sprinkle on the carved chicken and vegetables.

CHICKEN BAKED IN FOIL

Serves 4 to 6:

Salt and pepper
1 (4½- to 5-pound)
  chicken, trussed
6 tablespoons of butter, at
  room temperature

3 whole scallions, chopped
2 celery ribs, chopped
¼ cup of dry vermouth

Generously rub the chicken with salt and pepper. Coat well with 4 tablespoons of the butter. Place the chicken in the center of a large piece of extra-heavy aluminum foil (the foil should be large enough to completely encase the bird). In a saucepan, melt the remaining 2 tablespoons of butter over medium heat and sauté the scallions and celery for 4 minutes. Pour the vermouth around the bird on the foil and spoon the sautéed vegetables over it (you can use herb butter, page 71, to coat the bird and skip the vegetables). Wrap the chicken loosely, drawing the two sides of the foil together across the top of the bird, folding the two edges together, then over again. Fold the ends in the same fashion, pinching together in order to completely enclose the bird.

Place the foil-wrapped chicken on a baking dish or roasting pan and bake, uncovered, in a preheated 375°F. oven for 1½ hours. Slit the foil lengthwise, let the steam puff out, place the chicken on a heated serving dish and spoon the juices in the foil over it. The chicken will have more the flavor and consistency of a steamed bird, rather than a baked one, and is moist, tender and delicious. Carve the whole bird at the table.

CHINESE RED CHICKEN

Serves 4:

2 tablespoons of peanut oil
1 (3½- to 4-pound) chicken, trussed
4 very thin slices of fresh ginger root
4 whole young scallions, cut into 1-inch lengths
3 cloves of garlic, crushed

blended
¼ cup of dry sherry

¼ cup of heavy "black" soy sauce
1 star anise
2 tablespoons of sugar

1 cup of rice wine or sake
1 tablespoon of sesame seeds, crushed and toasted in 2 tablespoons of sesame oil until golden

In a wok or large frypan (with a lid that can cover the pan holding a whole chicken, or use foil to cover) heat the oil over high heat. Quickly sear the chicken evenly, turning until the bird is a gleaming yellow. Remove the chicken. Reduce the heat to medium and stir-fry the ginger, scallions and garlic for 2 minutes. Add the sherry-sugar blend. Bring to a boil, then add the chicken, turning several times to coat well. Pour in the rice wine, cover the pan, reduce the heat to low and cook for 25 minutes. Turn the chicken, cover again and cook for 20 minutes, or until the chicken is fork tender. Remove chicken and drain. Discard the ginger, scallions and garlic but reserve the cooking sauce. Place the chicken on a heated serving dish and remove the trussing cord. Rub well with the sesame oil and sesame seeds. Carve at the table, pouring the cooking sauce over the serving portions.

CHICKEN IN CIDER

Serves 4:

2 tablespoons of butter
1 tablespoon of olive oil
1 (4-pound) chicken, trussed
1½ teaspoons of salt
½ teaspoon of pepper

¼ teaspoon of dried rosemary

blended
½ cup of sweet cider
1 tablespoon of fresh lemon juice

In a casserole, over medium heat, heat the butter and oil. Evenly brown the chicken, seasoning it with salt, pepper and rosemary. Bake, covered, in a preheated 375°F. oven for 1½ hours, basting every 15 minutes with the blend of cider and lemon juice, or until the chicken is fork tender.

CHINESE CLAY POT CHICKEN

Serves 4:

1½ teaspoons of salt
½ teaspoon of fresh
  chopped ginger root
¼ cup of soy sauce

available in specialty shops
  ⅓ teaspoon of Chinese
  Five Spices

⅓ teaspoon of Szechuan
  pepper

1 tablespoon of sesame oil
3 tablespoons of dry sherry
1 (4-pound) chicken

In a large bowl, place all ingredients except the chicken and blend well. Add the chicken and marinate for 4 hours, occasionally turning the chicken and spooning the marinade over it. Remove chicken. With fingers loosen the breast skin near the neck, and run fingers under the skin below the middle of the breast, loosening the skin from the breast. Spoon 2 tablespoons of the marinade under this loosened skin directly onto the breast. Truss the chicken. Soak top and bottom of the clay pot in water to cover for 20 minutes. Remove from water. Drain. Place chicken into the pot, cover and slide into a cold oven. Set heat at 450°F. and cook for 50 minutes.

CHICKEN À LA NAGE WITH SAUCE

Serves 4:

1 (4½-pound) chicken,
  trussed
1 quart of chicken broth
2 cups of white wine
2 teaspoons of salt

½ teaspoon of dried tarragon
½ teaspoon of dried marjoram
½ teaspoon of celery seeds
1 bay leaf

Place all the ingredients in a large pot and cook, covered, at a simmer, until tender, about 1½ hours.

SAUCE

3 tablespoons of butter
3 tablespoons of flour
2 cups of chicken-wine broth
  the chicken cooked in,
  strained

½ cup of heavy cream
2 tablespoons of lemon juice

In a saucepan, melt butter and blend in the flour, stirring into a smooth paste. Gradually add the chicken-wine broth, stirring until smooth. Stir in the cream and lemon juice. Cook for 5 minutes. Do not boil. Taste for seasoning. Remove trussing and carefully carve bird into serving pieces. Serve liberally covered with the sauce.

CLAY POT LEMON CHICKEN

Serves 4: This is one of the oldest forms of cookery. The pot used to be placed in the glowing ashes of a fire. Today the "Roman pot" method of cooking has become very popular producing a chicken moist inside and crusty on the outside.

1 (4- to 4½-pound) chicken
Salt and pepper
1 large lemon, halved

2 large lemons, sliced
1 teaspoon of cornstarch,
  mixed with a little water

Rub the chicken well, inside and out, with salt and pepper. Squeeze the juice of half a lemon into the chicken cavity and add the entire peeled rind of the lemon. Reserve the other half lemon. Truss the chicken. Soak the clay pot and lid in cold water to cover for 20 minutes. Drain. Line the bottom of the pot with the lemon slices. Place the chicken in the pot, cover, and slide into a cold oven. Set the heat at 450°F. and cook for 50 minutes. Remove the top of the clay pot and remove the chicken. Pour the juices from the pot into a saucepan. Discard the lemon slices. Return the chicken to the clay pot and cook, uncovered, in the oven, heat raised to 500°F., for 15 minutes. To the juices in the saucepan, add the juice (strained) of the remaining ½ lemon and the cornstarch. Cook, on medium heat, stirring, for 2 minutes. Spoon this sauce over the lemon chicken after it his been carved into serving portions.

NOTE

Clay pot cookery appears to accentuate flavors, thus much can be done to give the versatile chicken an interesting flavor and texture. For example, without peeling, cut up an apple and an orange and insert them into the chicken's cavity before trussing. A piece of fresh ginger root, 7 or 8 shallots, 6 scallions (tails and all), cut up, all will produce interesting flavors with a whole bird cooked in a clay pot. Use your imagination. A whole, clay pot chicken can also be stuffed. Check out the abundant stuffing recipes in this chapter and give your guests a treat. Perhaps an oriental treat with Eastern Fruit and Rice Stuffing (page 91), or the Almond-Rice Stuffing (page 90).

NOTE

In roasting chickens, if the breast appears to be browning more quickly than the rest of the bird, cover it with foil until the remainder of the chicken catches up in color.

If you have prepared too much stuffing, arrange the overflow on a sheet of aluminum foil, wrap it tightly and place it alongside the roasting chicken. It will supply tasty second servings.

ASIA MINOR STUFFED CHICKEN

Serves 4:

1 tablespoon of olive oil
2 tablespoons of butter
3 scallions, cut into ½-inch pieces
¾ cup of couscous
¼ teaspoon of cinnamon
1 cup of chicken broth
1 medium-sized ripe tomato, skinned, seeded and chopped
½ teaspoon of salt

¼ teaspoon of pepper
½ cup of chopped dried apricots
2 tablespoons of pine nuts
1 (4-pound) chicken
½ cup of honey, mixed with 2 tablespoons of lemon juice, 2 tablespoons of melted butter and ½ teaspoon salt

In a saucepan, over medium heat, heat the oil and butter. Add the scallions and cook for 2 minutes, or until they are just crisp-tender. Stir in the couscous and cook, stirring, for 2 minutes until it is well mixed with the fat. Add the cinnamon, broth, tomato, salt, pepper and apricots. Bring to a boil, cover, remove from heat and allow to set for 10 minutes. Stir in the nuts. Taste for seasoning. Stuff and truss (see "Needle Trussing," page 66) the bird and place in a roasting pan. Rub on or brush entire surface of the bird with the honey mixture. Bake, uncovered, in a preheated 350°F. oven for 1 hour and 15 minutes, or until golden and fork tender, basting often with the remaining honey mixture and pan drippings.

BULGUR-CURRANTS-WALNUT-STUFFED CHICKEN WITH YOGURT SAUCE

Serves 4:

1 cup of chicken broth (approximate)

1½ cups of bulgur (cracked wheat)

5 tablespoons of butter (3 of them soft)

1 tablespoon of olive oil

1 medium-sized onion, finely chopped

Giblets from the bird, chopped (separate the liver)

2 tablespoons of brandy

½ cup of dried currants

¼ cup of coarsely chopped walnuts

Pinch of cinnamon

½ teaspoon of cumin

Salt and pepper to taste

2 tablespoons of lemon juice, mixed with 1 teaspoon of brown sugar

1 (4- to 4½-pound) chicken

1 cup of plain yogurt

In a bowl add enough broth to cover the bulgur. Let it soak for 20 minutes, drain and squeeze dry. Set aside.

In a saucepan, over medium heat, heat 2 tablespoons of the butter and the oil. Add the onion and cook for 2 minutes, or until soft. Add the gizzard and heart and cook for 5 minutes. Add the liver and cook 1 minute longer. Pour in the brandy, ignite and let it burn off. Off the heat, mix in the bulgur, currants, walnuts, cinnamon, cumin, salt, pepper and the lemon juice-brown sugar mixture. Taste for seasoning.

Salt and pepper the inside of the bird, stuff it with the bulgur mixture and truss it (see "Needle Trussing," page 66). Coat the bird with the 3 tablespoons of soft butter. Place in a roasting pan in a preheated 400°F. oven and bake, uncovered, for 15 minutes. Turn oven heat down to 350°F. and cook 45 minutes to 1 hour longer, or until golden and fork tender. Transfer the bird to a heated serving dish and keep warm.

To the pan drippings add the yogurt. Cook, stirring, until heated through but do not boil. Spoon the yogurt sauce over the bird.

GALA CHICKENS

Serves 6:

4 cups of ½-inch bread cubes, sautéed in ½ cup of butter until golden
2 (2¾-ounce) cans of pâté de foie gras
2 tablespoons of minced truffles (if not available, use 4 medium-sized mushrooms, minced and sautéed in 2 tablespoons of butter)
1 teaspoon of grated orange rind
3 shallots, or 1 small white onion, minced

½ cup of chopped parsley
1 cup of chicken broth
Salt and pepper to taste
2 (3-pound) chickens
Soft butter

combined and heated to melt jelly
   Juice and rind of 1 lemon (at least 2 tablespoons of juice)
   ½ cup of black currant jelly
   ¼ cup of Cointreau

In a bowl, combine the bread cubes, pâté, truffles, orange rind, shallots, parsley, broth, salt and pepper, blending well. Salt and pepper the insides of the chickens. Lightly stuff them with the bread cube stuffing and truss (see "Needle Trussing page 66). Rub the outside of the birds with the soft butter and sprinkle with salt and pepper. Bake in a shallow roasting pan, uncovered, in a preheated 350°F. oven for 1 hour. Spoon the currant jelly mixture over the birds and cook 30 minutes longer, or until glazed and fork tender, basting every 10 minutes with the currant jelly glaze.

NOTE
If there is extra stuffing, wrap it in foil and cook it in the pan with the birds.

CHICKEN AU PORTO

Serves 4 to 6:

2 tablespoons of butter
2 shallots, minced
1 celery rib, scraped and chopped
4 chicken livers, washed, dried, trimmed and cut into ½-inch pieces
½ pound of sausage meat, cooked until slightly brown and drained
1½ cups of dried bread crumbs

Salt and pepper to taste
½ teaspoon of mace
7 ounces of port wine
½ cup of light cream
2 (2½- to 3-pound) chickens
6 thin slices of bacon
1 cup of chicken broth
Sprinkle of nutmeg
2 tablespoons of currant jelly

In a frypan, over medium heat, melt the butter. Add the shallots and celery and cook for 1 minute. Add the livers and cook 1 minute longer, or until the livers brown slightly. Remove from the heat and mix in the sausage meat, bread crumbs, salt, pepper, mace, 3 ounces of the port and enough of the cream to hold the stuffing together. Lightly stuff the birds and truss them (see "Needle Trussing," page 66). Arrange the birds in a shallow roasting pan or casserole. Sprinkle with salt and pepper. Lay 3 slices of bacon over each bird.

Pour ½ cup broth and 2 ounces of port around the birds and sprinkle in a few grains of nutmeg. Bake, uncovered, in a preheated 450°F. oven for 15 minutes. Remove the bacon and cook 20 minutes, or until the birds are golden brown and fork tender. Baste frequently during entire cooking period (every 6 or 7 minutes). Transfer the birds to a heated serving dish. Pour off all but 3 tablespoons of the pan drippings. Stir in the 2 remaining tablespoons of port, the remaining ½ cup chicken broth and the currant jelly. Heat on top of the stove, stirring, until it simmers, the sauce is well blended and the jelly melted. Lightly spoon the sauce over the birds.

NOTE

If there is extra stuffing wrap it in foil and cook it in the roasting pan with the birds.

POTATO-SAUSAGE STUFFED ROASTER

To stuff a 5- or 6-pound bird:

3 tablespoons of butter
2 medium-sized onions, chopped
3 medium-sized potatoes, boiled in skins for 8 minutes, dried, peeled and diced
½ pound sausage meat

1½ teaspoons of salt
½ teaspoon of pepper
1 (5- to 6-pound) chicken or capon

blended into a paste
1 teaspoon of dried oregano
3 tablespoons of butter

In a saucepan, over medium heat, melt butter and cook the onion for 2 minutes, or until soft. Add the potatoes, sausage, salt and pepper. Blend and cook for 5 minutes. Stuff the bird and truss (see "Needle Trussing," page 66). Rub the bird well with the butter-oregano paste. Sprinkle with salt and pepper. Place in a roasting pan, and bake, uncovered, in a preheated 375°F. oven for 1½ hours, or until golden and fork tender, basting with pan juices every 15 minutes.

LESBOS RICE STUFFED CHICKEN

Serves 6:

2 tablespoons of butter
1 medium-sized onion, chopped
1 cup of uncooked rice
2 cups of hot chicken broth
½ teaspoon of cumin
¼ teaspoon of dried oregano

Salt and pepper
1½ cups of crumbled feta cheese
2 eggs, beaten
½ cup of chopped raisins
½ cup of pine nuts
1 (5-pound) chicken
Soft butter

In a saucepan, over medium heat, melt the 2 tablespoons of butter. Add the onion and cook for about 2 minutes, or until soft. Stir in the rice and cook for 2 minutes, stirring. Add the hot broth, cumin and oregano. Lightly salt and pepper. Cook covered, for 10 minutes, or until the liquid has been absorbed. Remove from the heat and cool slightly. Stir in the cheese, eggs, raisins and pine nuts. Taste for seasoning.

Stuff the bird (if there is too much stuffing, wrap it in foil and cook it in the pan with the bird). Truss (see "Needle Trussing," page 66) and lightly coat the outside with the soft butter. Sprinkle with salt and pepper. Place in a roasting pan and bake, uncovered, in a preheated 400°F. oven for 15 minutes. Reduce oven heat to 350°F. and, basting the bird every 10 or 15 minutes, cook for 1 or 1½ hours, or until golden and fork tender.

STUFFED BONED CHICKEN

Serving a boned, stuffed chicken is an event.

Writer Christopher Morley once said, "No one is lonely when eating spaghetti." Well, neither is one lonely while boning a bird. It takes all-out concentration. But the result is most satisfying. Once you have boned a couple of birds, you will get the hang of it and enjoy it.

A good practice, when convenient, is to buy a fresh 5-pound chicken, bone it, then freeze it. Then when you are ready for a gala presentation, the bird will be there for you to defrost and stuff.

Here's how:

In boning a bird the main object is to keep the skin intact, not pierce it at any point, as the skin will be the casing for the stuffing and the chicken meat.

Cut the wings off at the second joint (the elbows). Lay the bird on its breast. Using a small, pointed, very sharp knife, cut an incision to the bone, down the middle of the back, from the neck to the tail. Scraping and cutting, keeping the point of the knife next to the bone, work down one side of the chicken, carefully pulling flesh away from the bone as you cut.

When you reach the ball joints, cut through the joint, then continue cutting along the bone of the bird. Reaching the tip of the breastbone, be especially careful, as the skin and bone are very close. Work slowly and attentively against the bone, ever careful not to pierce the skin. Repeat this procedure down the other side of the bird.

Return to the legs. Grip the end of the leg bone tightly (a paper or cloth towel will help prevent it from slipping out of your hand). Scrape down along the leg bone to the end. Now place your hand tightly around the leg meat and pull on the bone, pulling the bone out, turning the leg inside out. Remove the large leg sinews. Any bits of flesh that you scrape off sinew or bone, place back into the bird.

Wing bones can be left in or removed.

The chicken is boned. Now to stuff and reshape it.

BONED STUFFED CHICKEN

Serves 6:

2 tablespoons of butter
1 medium-sized onion, finely chopped
½ pound of lean pork, finely ground
½ pound of veal, finely ground
½ pound of fatback, finely ground
1 (½-inch-thick) slice of cooked ham, weighing not more than ½ pound (cut 3½-inch strips from it and finely grind the remainder)
¼ cup of Marsala or brandy
½ teaspoon of dried thyme
¼ teaspoon of mace
1 teaspoon of salt
¼ teaspoon of pepper
3 tablespoons of shelled pistachio nuts
2 eggs, lightly beaten
Cream
1 (5-pound) chicken, boned
Herb Butter (page 71)

Melt the butter in a frypan over medium heat and cook the onion until soft (do not brown). Combine in a large bowl the onion, pork, veal, fatback, ground ham, wine, thyme, mace, salt, pepper, nuts, eggs and enough cream to slightly moisten the mixture. Make a small patty and cook it in butter to test the seasoning, making any changes necessary.

Lay the chicken flat, skin side down, arranging the chicken flesh so it is rather evenly distributed. Lay one-half of the stuffing on it, stuffing the legs where the bone was removed to reshape them. Lay the strips of ham on the stuffing and put the remaining stuffing on top of the strips of ham. Bring the two flaps of skin on the back of the chicken together and bring back the neck skin and sew with a trussing needle and cord. Mold the bird into shape. Tie cord around the bird in several places, especially the legs to bring them close to the body. Coat the bird with herb butter. Set in a roasting pan on a rack and roast, uncovered, basting often, in a preheated 400°F. oven for 1 hour and 15 minutes, or until tender. If top starts to brown before chicken is cooked, cover lightly with aluminum foil. Serve in slices, hot or cold, with or without a sauce.

If served hot, allow the chicken to set 15 minutes to settle juices so you won't lose them all in the carving. Remove cords before carving.

ANTOINE GILLY'S FRENCH CAPON STUFFING

To stuff a 5- to 6-pound bird:

2 tablespoons of butter
3 medium-sized onions, chopped
2 cloves of garlic, chopped
½ pound of sausage meat
½ pound of lean veal, ground
3 ounces of black truffles or mushrooms, chopped
6 ounces of foie gras
⅛ teaspoon of nutmeg

1 teaspoon of salt
⅛ teaspoon *each* of dried rosemary and dried basil
¼ teaspoon *each* of black pepper and dried thyme
3 eggs, lightly beaten
1 cup of heavy cream
1 cup of bread crumbs
6 tablespoons (3 ounces) of brandy

In a saucepan over medium heat, melt the butter and cook the onions, garlic and sausage for 6 minutes. Cool. In an electric mixer (using the dough mixer) on low speed, add all ingredients, one by one, until the mixture is well blended. Stuff bird and truss (see Needle Trussing, page 66).

ALMOND-RICE STUFFING

To stuff a 4½- to 5-pound chicken:

2 cups of cooked rice
⅓ cup of chopped white
   raisins
½ cup of slivered almonds

2 tablespoons of chopped
   scallions
½ teaspoon of salt
¼ teaspoon of tarragon
3 tablespoons of melted
   butter

Combine all ingredients in a bowl and blend thoroughly. Stuff chicken and truss (see "Needle Trussing," page 66).

CHESTNUT AND PRUNE STUFFING

To stuff a 6- to 8-pound capon or two 3½-pound chickens:

2 tablespoons of butter
1 medium-sized onion,
   chopped
1 celery rib, scraped and
   chopped
2 cups of cooked chestnuts,*
   put through a food mill,
   processor or blender to
   puree

2 cups of bread crumbs
8 plump cooked prunes,
   pitted and quartered
1 teaspoon of Bell's poultry
   seasoning
Salt and pepper to taste
1 egg, beaten
¼ cup of chicken broth

In a frypan, over medium heat, melt the butter. Add the onion and celery and cook for 2 minutes. In a bowl, combine the ingredients in the frypan with all the other ingredients. Mix thoroughly, but lightly (the stuffing should be moist, but not wet; if too dry add more broth). Stuff birds and truss (see "Needle Trussing," page 66).

*If you use the whole chestnuts with the skins on, make a criss-cross in each, place on an oiled baking dish and bake in a 450°F. oven for 10 minutes. Remove shells and skins. Place in a pot with seasoned broth and cook on top of the stove for 30 minutes, or until tender. Drain and put through a food mill or blender or processor to puree. If dried chestnuts are used, soak in water over-night, then cook in broth and proceed as with the whole chestnut.

CORN BREAD STUFFING

To stuff a 5½- to 6-pound bird:

5 tablespoons of butter
8 scallions (white part only), chopped
1 clove of garlic, minced
2 celery ribs, chopped
1 teaspoon of poultry seasoning
4 cups of crumbled corn bread (stale bread is best)

½ cup of grated Asiago or Parmesan cheese
2 tablespoons of chopped broadleaf parsley
2 eggs, beaten
½ cup of rich chicken broth
Salt and pepper to taste
3 tablespoons of butter, melted

In a saucepan, melt the 5 tablespoons of butter and sauté the scallions, garlic and celery for 4 minutes. In a bowl, combine the scallions, garlic and celery in their butter, the poultry seasoning, corn bread, cheese, parsley, eggs, broth, salt and pepper and melted butter. Blend well. Taste for seasoning. If not moist enough, add more broth. Stuff and truss the chicken (see "Needle Trussing," page 66).

NOTE

Commercial corn bread stuffings are available; don't hesitate to use them. They are excellent.

EASTERN FRUIT AND RICE STUFFING

To stuff a 6-pound bird:

2 tablespoons of butter
4 whole scallions, chopped
1½ cups of uncooked rice
2 cups of chicken broth
10 almonds, blanched, skinned and chopped
⅓ cup of sliced dried apricots

¼ cup of sliced dried prunes
¼ cup of chopped watercress or fresh chives
1 teaspoon of salt
½ teaspoon of pepper
¼ teaspoon of cumin
¼ teaspoon of mace

In a saucepan, over medium heat, melt butter and cook the scallions for 3 minutes. Stir in the rice, coating it well with the butter. Add the broth. Cover and cook for 7 minutes. Stir in the remaining ingredients. Simmer, stirring, for 6 minutes, or until most of the liquid has been absorbed. Stuff the chicken or capon, truss (see "Needle Trussing," page 66) and roast.

NORTHERN ITALIAN STUFFING

To stuff a 6- to 8-pound capon or two 3½-pound chickens:

¼ pound of fatback,
  blanched for 5 minutes
  and cut into ½-inch cubes
1 medium-sized onion,
  chopped
1 celery rib, scraped and
  chopped
½ pound of veal, chopped
½ pound of lean Italian
  sausage meat
Hearts, gizzards, livers of
  birds, chopped (keep the
  livers separate)

2 cups of cooked chestnuts,
  coarsely chopped*
1 apple, peeled, cored and
  chopped
½ cup of grated Asiago or
  Parmesan cheese
1 cup of dry bread cubes,
  soaked in milk and
  squeezed almost dry
¼ teaspoon of dried thyme
¼ teaspoon of finely
  crumbled dried leaf sage
Salt and pepper to taste
2 eggs, beaten

In a large frypan, over medium heat, cook the fatback until golden and crisp. Remove with a slotted spoon and reserve. Pour off all but 3 tablespoons of the fat in the pan. Add the onion and celery and cook for 2 minutes. Add the veal, sausage, gizzards and hearts and cook for 8 minutes, stirring. In a bowl, combine the ingredients in the frypan with the chestnuts, apple, fatback cubes, livers, cheese, bread cubes, thyme, sage, salt, pepper and eggs. Mix thoroughly, but lightly (the mixture should be moist but not wet; add a small amount of cream if too dry). Stuff the birds and truss (see "Needle Trussing," page 66).

* See "Chestnut and Prune Stuffing" (page 90) for preparation of chestnuts.

OLD-FASHIONED AMERICAN STUFFING

To stuff a 4½- to 5-pound bird:

3 tablespoons of butter	1½ teaspoons of salt
1 large onion, chopped	½ teaspoon of pepper
2 celery ribs (with leaves), scraped and chopped	½ tablespoon of Bell's poultry seasoning
¼ pound of chicken livers (plus the giblets in the bird), chopped	1 large egg, beaten
	2 cups of dry bread, in cubes (or a commercial bread-cube stuffing)
1 cup of chicken broth	
1 tablespoon of chopped parsley	

In a saucepan, melt the butter over medium heat and sauté the onion and celery for 3 minutes. Stir in the livers and giblets and cook for 2 minutes. Add the broth, parsley, salt, pepper and poultry seasoning, blending well. Remove from heat, cool slightly and blend in the egg and bread cubes, tossing everything together well. Stuff the chicken and truss (see "Needle Trussing," page 66).

OYSTER STUFFING

To stuff a 5-pound bird: (with a chicken liver variation)

2 tablespoons of butter	2 tablespoons of grated Parmesan or Asiago cheese
2 medium-sized onions, chopped	1 tablespoon of chopped parsley
2 celery ribs (with leaves), scraped and chopped	¼ cup of chicken broth
2½ cups of dry, coarse bread crumbs	1 egg, beaten
2 teaspoons of Bell's poultry seasoning	1 pint of fresh oysters, with their liquid
	Salt and pepper (optional)

In a deep saucepan, over medium heat, melt the butter and cook the onion and celery for 4 minutes, or until soft. Remove the pan from the heat and add the remaining ingredients, blending well. Taste for seasoning; however, the poultry seasoning and the oyster liquid should be sufficient without adding salt and pepper. Supreme should be the delicate oyster flavor.

NOTE

This can be varied by substituting for the oysters ½ pound of chicken livers that have been sautéed in butter for 3 minutes, with 2 tablespoons of chicken broth added.

PASTA STUFFING

To stuff a 4- to 4½-pound chicken: Nearly all kinds of pasta make excellent stuffings. One caution: it must be extra al dente *so it isn't too soft.*

1 quart of chicken broth
½ pound of medium-wide noodles
5 tablespoons of butter
¼ pound of mushrooms, thinly sliced
½ cup of grated Asiago or Parmesan cheese
3 tablespoons of heavy cream
1 teaspoon of pepper
Salt to taste

In a pot, bring the broth to a boil; lower heat to medium and cook the noodles for 8 minutes, or until they are less than *al dente,* about two-thirds cooked. They will cook more in the chicken. Drain noodles well. Save broth for future use. In a saucepan, over medium heat, melt the butter and sauté the mushrooms for 2 minutes. Remove from heat. Stir the drained noodles, cheese, cream, pepper and salt into the mushrooms and butter, blending well. Stuff the chicken and truss (see "Needle Trussing," page 66).

PECAN STUFFING

To stuff a 5-pound roasting chicken:

7 slices of stale white bread
  with crusts, cubed
1½ cups of milk
¼ pound of boiled ham,
  chopped
2 hard-cooked eggs, chopped
3 small white onions,
  chopped and cooked in 2
  tablespoons of butter for 4
  minutes (reserve the butter)

2 tablespoons of chopped
  parsley
Salt and pepper to taste
⅛ teaspoon of dried thyme
1 cup of coarsely chopped
  pecans
1½ ounces of brandy
1 egg, beaten

Thoroughly soak the bread in the milk, then squeeze almost
dry. Place the bread in a bowl, blend with the ham, hard-
cooked eggs, onion (with cooking butter), parsley, salt, pepper, thyme, pecans and brandy. Mix well, then blend in the
beaten egg. Stuff and truss the chicken (see "Needle Trussing," page 66) and roast.

RICE, ITALIAN SAUSAGE AND SPINACH
STUFFING

To stuff a 5- to 6-pound bird:

3 sweet Italian sausages,
  casings removed
1 tablespoon of butter
1 medium-sized onion, finely
  chopped
1 celery rib, scraped and
  chopped
1 cup of uncooked rice

Salt and pepper to taste
Pinch *each* of tarragon,
  thyme and oregano
2 cups of hot chicken broth
1 (10-ounce) package of
  frozen, chopped spinach,
  defrosted but not cooked
2 eggs, slightly beaten

In a saucepan, over medium heat, cook the sausage meat in
the butter for 8 minutes, breaking it up with a fork as it
cooks. Remove it with a slotted spoon and reserve. Add the
onion and celery to the pan and cook for 3 minutes, or until
soft. Stir in the rice, mixing well. Season lightly with salt and

pepper, add the herbs and pour in the hot broth. Bring to a boil, lower heat, cover and cook for 10 minutes, or until the liquid had been absorbed. Cool slightly. Stir in the spinach, sausage and eggs. Taste for seasoning. Lightly stuff (if there is too much stuffing, wrap it in foil and cook with the bird) and truss (see "Needle Trussing," page 66) the chicken and proceed as for Lesbos Rice Stuffed Chicken (see page 86).

SAUERKRAUT STUFFING

To stuff a 4- to 5-pound chicken:

3 tablespoons of butter
2 onions, chopped
1 cup of peeled, chopped greening apple
2 cups of sauerkraut, drained

2 teaspoons of caraway seeds
½ teaspoon of salt
½ teaspoon of pepper

In a saucepan, over medium heat, melt the butter and cook the onion for 3 minutes, or until soft. Add the apple and cook for 4 minutes. Stir in the remaining ingredients, blending well. Cook for 4 minutes. Stuff the bird with the mixture and truss (see "Needle Trussing," page 66).

SWEETBREAD STUFFING

To stuff a 4-pound chicken:

3 tablespoons of butter
3 tablespoons of flour
1½ cups of heavy cream
Juice of 1 lemon (at least 2 tablespoons of juice)

¼ teaspoon of nutmeg
Salt and pepper to taste
1 pound of sweetbreads
1½ cups of dry white wine

In a saucepan, over medium heat, melt the butter and blend in the flour, making a smooth golden paste. Add the cream, a small amount at a time, stirring into a smooth sauce. Stir in the lemon juice, nutmeg, salt and pepper. In another saucepan poach the sweetbreads in the wine for 5 minutes. Cool enough so that the membranes can be removed. Discard the wine. Cut the sweetbreads into large cubes and simmer for 5 minutes in the cream-lemon juice sauce. Taste for seasoning. Stuff the bird with the sweetbreads and some sauce (but not too much so that it is runny). Save the remaining sauce to serve hot over the chicken after it is carved.

ABOUT CORNISH GAME HENS

In the recipes that follow we have kept all the Cornish game hens together in their own flock. However, these recipes can be easily adapted for other small chickens, the 1½- to 2½-pound broilers that are so popular, and less expensive than the Cornish game hens. These little Cornish game hens actually are the same chickens we buy as "regular" chickens except that they have been processed at an earlier age to produce a small bird that can be used as an individual serving, which makes them unique. Actually, the 1- to 1½-pound chicken will serve the same purpose—and cost less.

CORNISH GAME HENS AND APPLE CASSEROLE

Serves 4:

4 Cornish game hens
3 tablespoons of butter
1 tablespoon of olive oil
Salt and pepper
6 medium-sized apples, peeled, quartered, cored and sliced

combined and heated together to dissolve sugar
½ teaspoon of brown sugar
3 tablespoons of butter
½ cup of heavy cream

Truss the birds (see "Needle Trussing," page 66). In a frypan, over medium heat, heat the butter and oil. Brown the birds evenly, one or two at a time, adding more butter and oil if needed. Season with salt and pepper. Toss the apples with the cream-butter-brown sugar mixture and, using most of the apple mixture, arrange a layer on the bottom of a casserole just large enough to hold the birds. Arrange the birds on the bed of apples and drop the remaining apples around the birds. Cover and bake in a preheated 375°F. oven for 30 minutes, or until the birds are tender.

NOTE

Potatoes Anna are an excellent accompaniment.

CORNISH GAME HENS WITH BRANDY SAUCE

Serves 4:

4 Cornish game hens
Salt and pepper

blended into a paste
    4 tablespoons of soft butter
    1 clove of garlic, minced
    2 tablespoons of minced parsley
    ½ teaspoon of salt
    ¼ teaspoon of pepper

1 tablespoon of cornstarch mixed with 1 tablespoon of cold chicken broth

3 tablespoons of brandy

simmered together for 5 minutes
    1 tablespoon of butter
    3 tablespoons of currant jelly
    Juice of ½ lemon (at least 2 tablespoons)
    Pinch of cayenne
    ½ cup of chicken broth
    2 whole cloves
    ½ teaspoon of salt

Sprinkle the inside of the birds with salt and pepper. Truss (see "Needle Trussing," page 66). Rub the entire surface of the birds with the butter paste. Place in a shallow roasting pan. Bake, uncovered, in a preheated 450°F. oven for 15 minutes, then in a 350°F. oven for 20 minutes longer, or until tender and golden brown. Baste every 6 or 7 minutes.

Transfer the birds to a heated serving dish. Pour off all but 3 tablespoons of the pan drippings. Stir in the cornstarch. Pour in the brandy and butter-jelly mixture. Stir until well mixed and slightly thickened. Strain the sauce and spoon it over the birds.

CHEESE STUFFED CORNISH GAME HENS

Serves 6:

6 Cornish game hens
Salt and pepper
5 tablespoons of butter (3
    tablespoons softened)
4 celery ribs (including the
    tender leaves), scraped
    and chopped

1 large onion, chopped
1½ cups of chicken broth
6 cups of croutons
¼ cup of melted butter
1½ cups of diced Swiss
    cheese

Lightly sprinkle the birds inside and out with salt and pepper.
In a frypan over medium heat, melt 2 tablespoons of the butter. Add the celery and onion and cook for 2 minutes, stirring. Transfer to a large bowl. Add the broth, croutons,
melted butter, cheese and salt and pepper to taste. Mix well.
Loosely stuff the birds and truss (see "Needle Trussing," page
66). Place the remaining stuffing in a small buttered baking
dish. Rub the entire surface of the birds with the 3 tablespoons of soft butter. Place in a roasting pan just large
enough to hold them and bake, uncovered, in a preheated
350°F. oven for 1 hour, or until tender and golden, basting
frequently. Bake the stuffing at the same time. If the top of
the stuffing gets too brown, cover it loosely with foil.

EASY STUFFING FOR CORNISH GAME HENS

To stuff 4 birds:

4 tablespoons of butter (2
    tablespoons softened)
1 clove of garlic, minced
4 livers from the birds,
    chopped
1 teaspoon of chopped
    parsley
1 teaspoon of chopped
    chives

4 hard-cooked eggs, chopped
2 tablespoons of sour cream,
    mixed with 2 tablespoons
    of heavy cream
Salt and pepper to taste
4 Cornish game hens
½ cup of sour cream

In a frypan, over medium-low heat, melt 2 tablespoons of the
butter. Add the garlic, cook for 1 minute (do not brown).

Add the livers, parsley and chives. Cook for 1 minute. Remove from the heat and mix in the eggs and sour cream-cream mixture. Season with salt and pepper. Divide the stuffing among the four birds and stuff them. Truss the birds (see "Needle Trussing," page 66).

Rub the outside of the birds with the remaining 2 tablespoons of softened butter and sprinkle lightly with salt and pepper. Place in a shallow, roasting pan and bake, uncovered, in a preheated 375°F. oven for 45 minutes, or until tender and golden brown. Arrange the birds on a bed of "Chicken Liver Pilaf" (page 230).

Add the sour cream to the roasting pan. Heat, stirring, on top of the stove and spoon the sauce over the birds.

ROASTED CORNISH GAME HENS WITH SALT PORK

Serves 4:

Salt and pepper
4 Cornish game hens

½ teaspoon of salt
½ teaspoon of pepper

mixed into a paste
2 tablespoons of butter
1 clove of garlic, minced
½ teaspoon of dried oregano

8 thin slices of salt pork with lean streaks
½ cup of chicken broth
2 tablespoons of Madeira

Lightly salt and pepper the insides of the birds. Truss (see "Needle Trussing," page 66). Divide the butter-seasoning paste into 4 parts and rub the outside of the birds with it. Arrange in a shallow roasting pan just large enough to hold them. Place 2 slices of salt pork on each bird. Bake, uncovered, in a preheated 375°F. oven for 45 minutes, or until the birds are fork tender and the salt pork is brown and crisp. Serve with the salt pork on them (it will be a pleasant taste treat). Pour off all but 3 tablespoons of the pan drippings. Add the broth and the Madeira. Heat, stirring, to make a sauce that can be served at the table. Strain and spoon it over the birds after the crisp salt pork has been eaten.

NOTE

Apricots (stewed according to package directions) are a good accompaniment.

CORNISH GAME HENS IN SOUR CREAM

Serves 4:

4 Cornish game hens
4 tablespoons of butter (2 tablespoons softened)
Salt and pepper

1 medium-sized onion, minced
1½ cups of sour cream
½ teaspoon of Hungarian paprika

Truss the birds (see "Needle Trussing," page 66). Rub them with the 2 tablespoons of softened butter and sprinkle with salt and pepper. Place in a casserole just large enough to hold them. Cover and bake in a preheated 400°F. oven for 30 minutes, or until almost tender and golden.

In a frypan, heat the remaining 2 tablespoons of butter, add the onion and cook until soft. Season with salt and pepper. Add the sour cream and paprika, and, stirring, heat through. Pour over the birds in the casserole, cover, reduce oven heat to 350°F. Bake for 15 minutes longer or until birds are tender, basting twice during this time. Serve right from the casserole with white rice. Spoon the sauce over the birds and rice.

CORNISH GAME HENS WITH WINEKRAUT RICE

Serves 4:

4 tablespoons of butter (2 tablespoons softened)
2 shallots, minced
1 small celery rib, scraped and minced
½ cup of wild rice, rinsed several times and drained
Livers of the birds, chopped
1½ cups of chicken broth
½ cup of chopped mushrooms
½ cup of chopped cooked ham
Salt and pepper to taste
2 tablespoons of brandy
4 Cornish game hens
¼ cup of sherry

In a saucepan, over medium heat, melt 2 tablespoons of the butter. Add the shallots and celery and cook for 1 minute. Stir in the rice and livers and cook for 1 minute, stirring. Add 1 cup of the broth, cover and simmer for 10 minutes, or until the broth has been absorbed. Off the heat, stir in the mushrooms, ham, salt (if needed), pepper and brandy. Divide among the four birds and lightly stuff them. Truss (see "Needle Trussing," page 66). Rub the birds with the 2 tablespoons of softened butter and sprinkle with salt and pepper. Place in a shallow roasting pan.

Bake, uncovered, in a preheated 375°F. oven for 40 minutes, or until tender and golden brown. Transfer to a heated serving dish. Pour off all but 3 tablespoons of the drippings in the roasting pan. Pour in the sherry, remaining ½ cup broth and the 2 remaining tablespoons of butter. Heat, stirring, until the butter has melted. Strain the sauce and spoon over the birds.

Optional: The birds in their serving dish may be flambéed at the table by pouring a small amount of brandy (about ¼ cup) over them, then igniting it, but *be very careful* that the dish is large enough and not too close to anyone or anything it might inflame.

CORNISH GAME HENS WITH WINEKRAUT

Serves 4:

4 Cornish game hens
3 tablespoons of butter
2 tablespoons of olive oil
Salt and pepper
2 medium-sized onions, chopped

2 cloves of garlic, minced
1 quart of sauerkraut, drained
1½ teaspoons of caraway seeds
2 cups of dry white wine

Truss the birds (see "Needle Trussing," page 66). In a deep casserole, large enough to snugly hold the birds, heat the butter and oil. Sprinkle the birds with salt and pepper and evenly brown them. Remove and keep warm. Add the onion and garlic to the casserole and cook until soft but not brown. Stir in the sauerkraut, sprinkle with caraway seeds and mix well. Simmer, covered, for 15 minutes. Pour in the wine, blending it well with the sauerkraut. Return the birds to the pot, burying them in the sauerkraut. Cover the pot and bake in a preheated 350°F. oven for 1 hour, or until the birds are fork tender.

Chapter Five

Separated Chickens
(Fricasseeing, Frying, Oven-Browning Pan-Simmering, Sautéing, Stewing)

We showed in the previous chapter the respect that great chefs have for chicken. In this chapter we will put those chefs' respect into recipes for the various parts of the chicken, all of which are held in equal esteem by master chefs. This could be the most helpful and versatile chapter in our book, mainly because it stresses how versatile the chicken is.

Unlike the pig, where it is said that everything is used but the grunt, all parts of the chicken are not utilized in this country for human consumption, as they are in Europe. We will concentrate on the "common" parts and show "uncommon" ways to use them most effectively. But before we get into the complete cut-ups we will discuss the split birds, the broiled chicken.

ABOUT BROILING

Broiled chicken is one of the most popular dishes in this country, so much so perhaps that it may be the reason the group of experts that speak for the entire chicken industry calls itself "The National Broiler Council." Actually, all young chickens today are called broilers, which gives an instant impression of tenderness.

The problem with broiling is correctly judging the amount of heat to use, always remembering that chicken has little fat and does not self-baste. If chicken is broiled too fast, it chars, cooks on the outside, but is underdone inside. If the broiling process is slowed down, the danger is in having the chicken end up too dry.

A major point to remember is that broiling dries. There are ways to compensate for this: basting with butter and/or oil or marinating, both methods designed to give the chicken moisture. The properly broiled chicken is moist inside, crisp outside. Practice is the only way to achieve success.

Start off with a 2- to 2½-pound broiler, and plan to serve ½ bird per person. Try to select broilers that are, as the butchers say, well meated. They should be split, neck and backbone removed. Do it yourself, or ask the butcher to do it. Watch him and do it yourself next time. The backbone should be taken off so the broiler will lie flat and cook evenly. Any chicken to be cooked should always be at room temperature.

Preheat the broiler on high. If using a rack, oil the rack so the chicken won't stick to it. Adjust the broiler pan so that it is 5 inches from the heat, the smaller the chicken, the nearer the heat. For example, if using a 1½- to 2-pound chicken, broil it 4 inches from the heat.

Rub or brush whatever fat, butter or oil, that is being used all over the chicken. Turn often, baste often; that is the rule. Some experienced chefs finish the broiled bird off in a preheated 400°F. oven. The pan juices from the broiler pan should be saved to spoon over the broiled chicken. These birds need this moisture. A basic recipe follows:

SIMPLE BROILED CHICKEN

Serves 4:

1 stick (¼ pound) of butter
4 tablespoons of olive oil
1½ teaspoons of salt
½ teaspoon of pepper

½ teaspoon of Hungarian paprika
2 (2½-pound) broilers, split, necks and backbones removed

Heat the butter and oil and combine in a bowl with the salt, pepper and paprika, blending well. Thoroughly cover the broiler halves with the butter-oil mixture, using a pastry brush. Place, skin side down, on the broiler rack or a shallow baking dish. Broil, 5 inches from the heat, for 4 minutes, basting with the butter-oil mixture. Broil 4 minutes, baste; broil 4 minutes, baste. Turn the chicken pieces and repeat the procedure, making sure that the skin sides do not become charred and black. Toward the end of the cooking time turn all the pieces under the heat several times so they brown evenly, basting with the butter-oil mixture each time. Finish the broilers off by cooking, uncovered, in a preheated 400°F. oven for 8 minutes. This is optional, but some chefs claim this is a certain way to insure that the broilers do not come to the table underdone under that crusty skin. But, if you've overbroiled, it also could dry the chicken out, so experimentation is in order.

That is the most popular way of broiling a chicken. Also try using a tasty baste of melted herb butters (page 71). Another method of broiling chicken is marinating first, then basting with the marinade. Coating them with deviled bread crumbs, after the chicken is first browned, is another tasty alternative.

Broiling outdoors over charcoal is ever popular. Again, in charcoal broiling, the trick is in the timing, not too much heat too fast.

Recipes for these alternative broiling methods follow:

MARINATED BROILED CHICKEN

Serves 4:

1 cup of olive oil
½ cup of dry white vermouth
2 medium-sized onions, chopped
1 clove of garlic, crushed

⅛ teaspoon of dried thyme
1½ teaspoons of salt
½ teaspoon of pepper
2 (2½-pound) broilers, split, necks and backbones removed

In a large bowl or deep dish, combine all ingredients except the chickens, blending well. Marinate the chickens in the mixture for 4 hours, turning from time to time so chickens are entirely coated. Reserve the marinade. Place the broilers on the broiler rack, skin side down, 5 inches from the heat source. Broil for 4 minutes, basting well with the marinade. Broil another 4 minutes, baste, and turn flesh side down.

Broil 4 minutes, baste; broil 4 minutes, baste. Turn the chickens over, broil 4 minutes, baste; turn them again, broil 4 minutes, baste.

BROILERS BRUSHED WITH LEMON MARINADE

Serves 4:

2 (2½-pound) broilers, split, necks and backbones removed

blended well all following ingredients
  ½ cup of fresh lemon juice

1 teaspoon of grated lemon rind
½ cup of peanut oil
1 medium-sized onion, chopped
2 teaspoons of dried tarragon
1 teaspoon of salt

Brush the chickens well with the lemon mixture and place them on the broiler rack, skin side down. Broil 5 inches from the heat source for 5 minutes, brushing well with the lemon mixture. Broil 5 minutes longer, turn flesh side down, baste well and broil for 5 minutes. Baste and broil another 5 minutes.

BROILED BREADED CHICKEN

Serves 4:

2 (2½-pound broilers), split, necks and backbones removed
1½ teaspoons of salt
½ teaspoon of pepper
1½ sticks (12 tablespoons) of butter, melted

blended well
1 stick (¼ pound) of soft butter
2 tablespoons of Worcestershire sauce
1 teaspoon of Tabasco
1 tablespoon of dry mustard
3 cups of bread crumbs

Rub the chickens with salt and pepper, then rub them well with two-thirds of the melted butter. Place in a shallow baking dish, skin side down, and bake in a preheated 400°F. oven for 15 minutes. Oil the broiler rack, place the partially cooked chicken halves on it, flesh side down. Broil 6 inches from the heat source for 5 minutes. Turn over and broil for 5 minutes. Press the bread crumbs mixture firmly onto the skin side of the birds. Broil for 10 minutes, basting with the remaining melted butter twice, watching carefully that the deviled bread crumb mixture doesn't burn.

CHARCOAL BROILED CHICKEN

Serves 4: Read barbecuing advice in Sauce Chapter, page 54.

BARBECUE SAUCE

⅓ cup of peanut oil
1 onion, minced
1 clove of garlic, minced
1 tablespoon of grated
   orange rind
1 tablespoon of dry mustard
2 teaspoons of paprika
1 teaspoon of Tabasco

½ teaspoon of pepper
½ cup of light molasses
½ cup of dark brown sugar
½ cup of wine vinegar
2 (6-ounce) cans of V-8
1 (8-ounce) can of tomato
   sauce

In a saucepan, combine all ingredients, blend well and bring to a boil. Lower heat and simmer, uncovered, stirring often, for 30 minutes.

BROILING

2 (2½-pound) broilers,   ½ cup of peanut oil
   split, necks and backbones
   removed

Key to successful charcoal broiling is medium heat—glowing coals, not a fire that flares. Rub the grill with oil. Brush the broilers on both sides with peanut oil. Place over coals, skin side up, and grill for 10 minutes. Turn, baste with oil, and grill 10 minutes longer. Now brush the barbecue sauce liberally on both sides of the chickens and grill for another 15 minutes, turning often and basting with the barbecue sauce at every turning.

BROILED CHICKEN WITH TARRAGON AND VERMOUTH

Serves 4:

2 (2½-pound) chickens, split
3½ tablespoons of butter (1½ tablespoons softened)
Salt and pepper

blended
½ cup of melted butter
½ cup of dry vermouth

4 tablespoons of chopped fresh tarragon, or 1 tablespoon of dried that has soaked in the vermouth for 1 hour
Juice of ½ lemon (at least 2 tablespoons)

2 chicken livers, cut into ½-inch pieces and lightly dredged with flour
6 medium-sized mushrooms, each cut into 6 pieces
2 tablespoons of chopped parsley

Rub the skin side of the birds with the 1½ tablespoons of softened butter. Sprinkle with salt and pepper. Place on a broiler rack, skin side down, over a drip-pan. Brush inside of chickens with the vermouth mixture. Broil in a preheated broiler, occasionally basting with the vermouth mixture, for 15 minutes on each side, or until fork tender.

In a frypan, over medium-high heat, melt the remaining 2 tablespoons of butter. Add the livers and cook just until outside is brown (inside should be pink). Season to taste with salt and pepper. Add the mushrooms and cook, stirring, for 2 minutes. Transfer the chicken to a heated serving dish. Into the frypan with the livers and mushrooms, pour the drippings from the drip-pan, along with any of the vermouth mixture that remains. Bring to a boil. Taste for seasoning. Spoon over the chicken before serving. Sprinkle with parsley.

SAUTÉING AND PANFRYING

These are other important methods of cooking cut-up chicken (Southern Fried Chicken appears in the Classics Chapter, page 142).

Sautéing is taken from the French *sauter*, meaning "to jump." It probably came from the French method of placing meat or vegetables in a pan over high heat, and making them jump, by turning them often to cook evenly and prevent sticking. Chicken being sautéed is browned over high or medium-high heat, then finished over low heat. The sauté pan has just enough fat or oil in it to keep the chicken from sticking.

SIMPLE SAUTÉ

Serves 4:

1 (3½- to 4-pound) chicken, cut up Salt and pepper	2 tablespoons of butter 1 tablespoon of olive oil

Rinse the chicken but make certain that it is absolutely dry so the sautéing will seal in the juices. Liberally salt and pepper the chicken pieces. In a frypan, over medium-high heat, heat the butter and oil. Add the chicken and sauté, turning the pieces often so that they brown evenly. This sautéing will take about 20 minutes. Lower the heat, cover the pan and cook the chicken for 10 minutes. By this time the breasts and wings will be done. Remove and keep warm. Cook the remainder of the chicken for another 10 minutes. Place the chicken with the breasts and wings in a low oven or warmer. Pour the grease from the sauté pan and deglaze the pan with milk, cream, broth or wine, and prepare a sauce selected from the Sauce Chapter (page 53).

FAST CHICKEN-WINE-SAUTÉ

Serves 4:

1 (3½- to 4-pound)
  chicken, cut up
Salt and pepper to taste
2 tablespoons of butter
1 tablespoon of olive oil
¼ teaspoon of dried tar-
  ragon

⅛ teaspoon of dried rose-
  mary
1 tablespoon of chopped
  fresh chives
½ cup of Chablis

Rinse and dry the chicken pieces thoroughly, then sprinkle
with salt and pepper. In a frypan, over medium-high heat,
heat the butter and oil. Add chicken and sauté quickly, turning it often to brown evenly (this should take about 15
minutes). Lower the heat and sprinkle the tarragon, rosemary
and chives over the chicken. Pour the wine around the
chicken, cover the pan and simmer until tender, about 20
minutes.

NOTE

There are numerous variations, combining sautéed chicken
with special sauces and garnishes, tomatoes, peppers, olives,
leeks, cucumbers. These garnishes add panache, a finishing
touch to sautéed chicken.

EASY PANFRIED-BACON-CHICKEN

Serves 4:

½ pound of bacon
Salt and pepper to taste
1 (3½- to 4-pound)
  chicken, cut up

Flour for dredging
3 tablespoons of flour (for
  the sauce)
2 cups of half-and-half

In a large frypan, over medium heat, cook the bacon until
crisp, drain on paper towels and keep warm. Remove frypan
with bacon fat from heat. Salt and pepper the chicken, then
dredge with flour, shaking off excess. Place pan with bacon
fat over medium-high heat until it is hot enough to almost

instantly brown a cube of bread dropped in (the fat should not be smoking hot). Add the chicken to pan and evenly brown the pieces, turning often. This should take about 15 minutes. Lower the heat, cover the pan and cook for 20 minutes, or until fork tender. Remove the chicken, drain on paper towels and keep warm. Pour off all but 3 tablespoons of fat. Over low heat, blend in the 3 tablespoons of flour, scraping up the browned particles in the pan, blending flour and particles well. Gradually add the half-and-half, stirring constantly until the sauce is smooth and thick. Taste for seasoning, add the necessary salt and pepper. Spoon the sauce over the fried chicken and garnish with the crisp bacon.

These primer points of cooking cut-up chicken are offered to get you into the mood, to show how easy cooking really is.

Following are a medley of other methods with unique recipes still stressing simplicity and versatility.

APPLEJACK CHICKEN

Serves 4:

2 (2½-pound) broilers, split
1½ teaspoons of salt
½ teaspoon of pepper
⅛ teaspoon of dried thyme
4 tablespoons of butter
16 whole shallots, peeled

16 whole baby carrots, peeled
½ cup of applejack
⅓ cup of chicken broth
½ cup of heavy cream
8 crab apples (bought in jars)

Sprinkle the broilers with salt, pepper and thyme. In a top-of-the-stove casserole, over medium heat, melt the butter and evenly brown the broilers. Add the shallots and carrots, then pour the applejack and broth over the birds and vegetables. Cover and bake in a preheated 350°F. oven for 20 minutes, or until the broilers are tender. Transfer the broilers and vegetables to a heated serving dish and keep warm. Place the casserole over medium heat and stir in the cream, blending well. Heat to a simmer, strain and spoon over the broilers. Heat the crab apples in a small amount of their liquid and serve with the broilers.

CHICKEN ASIAGO

Serves 4: If you cannot obtain the aged, nutty Asiago, use Parmesan or even Romano. But Asiago is first choice.

8 chicken thighs

blended
   1½ teaspoons of salt
   ½ teaspoon of pepper
   ½ teaspoon of dried sage

2 eggs, beaten

blended
   1 cup of bread crumbs
   1 cup of grated Asiago
     cheese

5 tablespoons of butter
2 tablespoons of olive oil
⅓ cup of dry vermouth
8 thin lemon slices

Rub both sides of thighs well with the salt-pepper-sage blend. Dip in the beaten egg, then dredge well in the bread crumb-cheese mixture. In a top-of-the-stove casserole, over medium heat, heat the butter and oil and evenly brown the thighs. Remove the thighs. Stir in the vermouth, mixing with particles on bottom of pan. Replace the thighs. Bake, uncovered, in a preheated 350°F. oven for 25 minutes, or until the thighs are tender and crusty. Serve each with a lemon slice on top.

CHICKEN WITH BACON

Serves 4:

1 (3½- to 4-pound)
   chicken, cut up
Salt and pepper
½ teaspoon of ground mace
4 slices of bacon, diced
1 medium-sized onion,
   chopped
1 cup of chicken broth

wrapped in cheesecloth and tied
   1 sprig of parsley
   Rind of ½ lemon
   2 whole cloves
   6 peppercorns

4 tablespoons (2 ounces) of
   Madeira

Sprinkle the chicken pieces with salt, pepper and mace. In a top-of-the-stove casserole, cook the bacon until crisp. Remove with a slotted spoon and drain on paper towels. Add chicken to the casserole and brown evenly. Remove chicken and pour off all but 2 tablespoons of the fat. Add onion and cook for 3 minutes, or until soft. Return the chicken to the pot. Add the broth and packet of seasonings. Cover and bake in a preheated 300°F. oven for 1 hour, or until the chicken is tender. Transfer the chicken to a heated serving dish and keep warm. Strain the sauce and discard the bouquet garni. Return the sauce to the casserole, stir in the Madeira and blend. Simmer for 1 minute. Spoon the sauce over the chicken and sprinkle with the bacon pieces.

BRANDIED BROILERS

Serves 4:

5 tablespoons of butter
2 (2½-pound) broilers, split
1½ teaspoons of salt
½ teaspoon of pepper
¼ cup of brandy, warmed
4 scallions, minced

1 tablespoon of chopped broadleaf parsley
½ tablespoon of chopped fresh thyme or ½ teaspoon of dried
3 egg yolks, beaten with 1½ cups of heavy cream

In a large frypan, over medium neat, melt the butter. Sprinkle the broilers with salt and pepper and evenly brown them. Lower the heat and continue cooking the broilers for 15 minutes, turning frequently. Pour the warm brandy over the broilers. Ignite and when the flame dies, sprinkle in the scallions, parsley and thyme. Cover the frypan and continue cooking over low heat until the broilers are fork tender. Transfer them to a heated serving dish. In the frypan, over low heat, stir in the beaten egg yolk-cream mixture, stirring until the sauce thickens (do not boil). Just before serving pour the hot sauce over the broilers.

CHICKEN WITH A CHEESE CRUST

Serves 4:

3 tablespoons of butter
1 tablespoon olive oil
1 (3½- to 4-pound)
  chicken, cut up
Salt and pepper

1 recipe of White Sauce
  (pages 62, 63)

blended
  ½ cup of bread crumbs
  ½ cup of grated Asiago
    or Parmesan cheese

In a frypan, over medium heat, heat the butter and oil. Sprinkle the chicken with salt and pepper and brown evenly, turning often. This should take about 20 minutes. Cover the pan, lower the heat and simmer the chicken for 20 minutes or until fork tender.

Remove the chicken pieces and place in a shallow baking dish without overlapping. Cover with the white sauce and sprinkle with the mixture of bread crumbs and cheese. Place under the broiler, watching carefully so it doesn't overbrown. It should be a rich crusty-brown.

CHERRY CHICKEN

Serves 4:

1 (4-pound) chicken, quartered
1 teaspoon of salt
2 tablespoons of cooking oil
1 (1-pound) can of pitted sour cherries in water
1 medium-sized onion, chopped
¼ cup of sugar

1 tablespoon of cornstarch
2 tablespoons of butter
⅓ cups of slivered almonds
1 cup of rice, cooked according to package directions
1 tablespoon of grated lemon rind
½ teaspoon of allspice

Season chicken with salt. In a frypan, over medium heat, evenly brown the chicken in the oil. Drain the cherries, reserving the juice. Pour in ½ cup of cherry juice and sprinkle the onion over the chicken. Cover and simmer for 1 hour, or until chicken is tender. Remove chicken from pan and keep warm. Drain the fat, and stir into the pan the cherries, remaining cherry juice, sugar and cornstarch. Stir until thickened and smooth. In a saucepan, melt butter and brown almonds. Blend in the rice, lemon rind and allspice. Serve chicken on mounds of rice, topped with hot cherry sauce.

GOLDEN FRICASSEE OF CHICKEN

Serves 4:

3 tablespoons of butter
1 tablespoon of flour
2 cups of chicken broth
Bouquet garni (2 sprigs of
    parsley, 1 celery rib, pinch
    of thyme, ⅓ bay leaf,
    white part of a leek or a
    quarter of an onion, all
    tied in cheesecloth)

1 (3½- to 4-pound)
    chicken, cut up
Salt and pepper to taste
2 egg yolks, beaten with 1
    tablespoon of lemon juice

In a top-of-the-stove casserole, over medium heat, melt 2 tablespoons of the butter. Stir in the flour and cook, stirring, until smooth and golden. Slowly add the broth, stirring constantly until the sauce is smooth and starts to thicken. Add the remaining 1 tablespoon butter, bouquet garni, chicken, salt and pepper, spooning the sauce over the chicken pieces. Cover the casserole with a piece of aluminum foil, then with its lid, and bake in a preheated 350°F. oven for 40 minutes, or until the chicken is fork tender. Transfer chicken to a heated serving dish. Discard bouquet garni. Set casserole over low heat. Add 3 tablespoons of the sauce to the egg yolk mixture, mix well and stir back into the sauce in the casserole. Taste for seasoning. Spoon sauce over chicken in serving dish. Serve with rice or steamed new potatoes.

POLLO FRITTO MISTO

Serves 6: Here's a party favorite of ours: Italian deep-fried chicken and vegetables.

BATTER

4 eggs, beaten	1 tablespoon of Hungarian
2 cups of beer	paprika
2 cups of flour	2½ teaspoons of salt
	⅛ teaspoon of cayenne

In a bowl, blend the eggs and beer. Sift the flour, paprika, salt and cayenne into the egg-beer mixture. With an electric beater, beat the mixture into a batter that is smooth and medium-thick. Chill for 2 hours. Beat again just before using.

Vegetable oil for deep frying
6 chicken thighs, skinned, boned and cut into 1-inch cubes
3 whole breasts, skinned, boned and cut into 1-inch cubes
1 small cauliflower, separated into flowerets, blanched for 3 minutes and drained

3 medium-sized zucchini, unpeeled and cut into ½-inch-thick slices
12 medium-sized whole mushrooms
1 medium-sized eggplant, peeled and cut into ⅜-inch-thick sticks
6 limes, halved

Using a deep frypan, electric frypan or deep fryer (which is best), heat about 1½ inches of oil (there should be enough to completely immerse the chicken and vegetables) to 380°F. (Use a cube of bread to test the oil. If it browns immediately, the oil is hot enough, but it should not be "smoking" hot.) Dip the chicken and vegetables in the batter, lower into the oil (using a slotted spoon or basket to prevent splashing), a few at a time—do not crowd—and cook for 4 minutes, or until crisply golden brown. Drain on paper towels. Serve immediately. (As you cook the chicken and vegetables, they can be kept warm on a cookie sheet in a 200°F. oven or warmer until the deep frying is completed, but they are at their best if served immediately.) Serve 2 lime halves with each portion, for guests to squeeze over and spark up the *fritto mosto*.

*CHICKEN WITH 25 CLOVES OF GARLIC***

Serves 6:

2 (3-pound) chickens, cut up

25 large whole cloves of garlic, peeled

½ cup of olive oil

½ cup of dry white vermouth

3 leeks (white part only), thinly sliced

8 sprigs of parsley

2 teaspoons of salt

½ teaspoon of pepper

1 teaspoon of dried tarragon

⅛ teaspoon of dried rosemary

Place the chickens and garlic in a large casserole. Pour in the olive oil and vermouth, tossing the chicken pieces well. Add the leeks and parsley. Sprinkle overall with the salt, pepper, tarragon and rosemary. Blend everything thoroughly (the hands are the best instruments for this). Cover the casserole tightly with aluminum foil. Place the top of the pan over the foil, wrap well with another piece of foil and seal around the edges with masking tape. Bake in a preheated 375°F. oven for 1 hour. Serve right from the casserole, dramatically unmasking the dish at the table so the aroma can come wafting out. Surprisingly, the garlic is sweet and delicious, the chicken just nicely scented with it, not at all overwhelmed, as would be expected.

** Fast and Easy

ANTOINE GILLY'S CHICKEN À L'HORIZON

Serves 4: Antoine serves this on thin, heart-shaped toasted slices of bread, also often with rice.

1 (4-pound) chicken, cut into 8 pieces
1½ teaspoons of salt
½ teaspoon of pepper
Flour for dredging
3 tablespoons of butter
12 small white onions, peeled and root ends scored
½ pound of lcan salt pork, cut into small cubes
2 cups of red wine
1 cup of chicken broth
Bouquet garni (2 sprigs of parsley, 2 small bay leaves, pinch of dried thyme, 1 celery rib tied into a cheesecloth bag)
6 tablespoons (3 ounces) of brandy
1 pound of small, fresh whole mushrooms, sautéed in butter for 1 minute

Season chicken with salt and pepper and dredge lightly with flour. In a large, deep frypan, over medium heat, melt the butter and cook the chicken until evenly browned. Add the onion and salt pork and cook for 5 minutes. Cover and simmer for 15 minutes. Pour off all of the fat. Add the wine, broth and bouquet garni. Simmer, uncovered, for 20 minutes. Remove bouquet garni and pour in the brandy, stirring well. Simmer until the sauce is thickened. Stir in the mushrooms and cook for 5 minutes.

HERBED FRIED CHICKEN**

Serves 4:

½ cup of flour
¼ cup of bread crumbs
¼ teaspoon of dried tarragon
⅓ teaspoon of dried rosemary
2 tablespoons minced parsley
½ teaspoon of garlic powder
1½ tcaspoons of salt
½ teaspoon of pepper
1 (3½-pound) chicken, cut up
6 tablespoons of butter
2 tablespoons of olive oil

In a large bowl, blend well the flour, bread crumbs, tarragon, rosemary, parsley, garlic powder, salt and pepper. Dredge the chicken pieces with the flour mixture. In a large frypan, over medium heat, heat butter and oil and fry chicken pieces until golden brown and fork tender, about 20 minutes, turning the chicken frequently so it is browned evenly.

** Fast and Easy

BELGIAN CHICKEN HOTPOT

Serves 6: An elegant, but easy dinner, cooking trademark of the chicken.

2 (3-pound) chickens, cut up
Salt and pepper to taste
Flour for dredging
5 tablespoons of butter
1 tablespoon of olive oil
2 cloves of garlic, minced
1 medium-sized white onion, thinly sliced
3 medium-sized carrots, peeled and thinly sliced

2 cups of dry white wine
1 cup of chicken broth
1 cup of cooked peas
12 small whole Belgian endive, braised until just tender in ½ cup of chicken broth, 3 tablespoons of butter, 1 teaspoon of sugar, salt and pepper
2 tablespoons of chopped parsley

Sprinkle the chicken with salt and pepper and dredge lightly with flour. In a top-of-the-stove casserole, heat the butter and oil and brown the chicken evenly. Remove the chicken. Pour all fat from the casserole. Return the chicken to the pot, add the garlic, onion, carrots, wine and broth. Bring to a boil on top of the stove, cover and transfer to a preheated 350°F. oven and cook for 45 minutes, or until the chicken is fork tender. Transfer the chicken to a heated serving platter. Add the peas and endive to the liquid in the cooking casserole and simmer on top of the stove until heated through. Spoon this sauce with the peas over the chicken pieces on the serving platter and surround them with the hot whole endive. Sprinkle parsley over all.

CHICKEN WITH MUSTARD

Serves 4:

3 tablespoons of butter
1 tablespoon of olive oil
1½ teaspoons of salt
½ teaspoon of pepper
1 (3½-pound) chicken, cut up

blended
   2½ tablespoons of Kosciuski prepared mustard

1 tablespoon of white wine

4 whole cloves of garlic
1 bay leaf
½ teaspoon of dried rosemary
½ cup of white wine
½ cup of heavy cream

In a roasting pan, heat the butter and oil. Salt and pepper the chicken and roll it in the butter and oil, covering it evenly. Place the roasting pan in a preheated 450°F. oven and bake for 5 minutes. Turn the chicken and bake 5 minutes longer.

Rub chicken pieces on both sides with the mustard-wine mixture. Add the garlic, bay leaf, rosemary and wine. Cover tightly. Reduce the oven heat to 375° and bake for 30 minutes, basting frequently. Pour the cream over the chicken. Cover and bake 15 minutes longer, basting every 5 minutes with the cream and pan liquids.

NORMANDY CHICKEN

Serves 4:

1 (4-pound) chicken, cut up
Salt and pepper
Flour for dredging
3 tablespoons of butter
1 tablespoon of cooking oil
1 medium-sized onion, chopped

½ pound of mushrooms, cut into halves if small, or quartered, if larger
3 tablespoons of brandy
1 cup of heavy cream
1 egg yolk

Sprinkle chicken with salt and pepper and dredge lightly with flour. In a frypan large enough to hold the chicken in one layer, over medium heat, heat the butter and oil. Evenly brown the chicken and transfer to a warm dish. Add the onion to the frypan and cook for 3 minutes. Add mushrooms and cook 2 minutes longer. Return the chicken to the frypan, pour on the brandy, lowering the heat. Cook another 10 minutes. Pour in ¾ cup of the cream. Simmer, partially covered, for 15 minutes, or until chicken is fork tender. Taste for seasoning. With a slotted spoon, transfer the chicken, mushrooms and onion to a heated serving dish and keep warm. Beat the egg yolk with the remaining ¼ cup of cream. Stir this into the sauce in the pan and cook, slowly, stirring until thickened (do not boil). Pour over the chicken before serving.

ORANGE-RUM GINGER CHICKEN

Serves 4:

1 whole chicken breast, cut in half, then each half cut in half again crosswise
4 chicken thighs and legs, separated

well blended
  ½ cup of melted butter
  ½ cup of orange juice
  ¼ cup of light rum

1 teaspoon of grated orange rind
1 clove of garlic, minced
½ teaspoon of ground cumin
1 teaspoon of salt
¼ teaspoon of ground ginger

Place the chicken in a large bowl, pouring the butter-rum-spice mixture over it. With your hands, toss the chicken pieces to completely coat. Drain the chicken (reserving the liquid) and place, skin side up, in a shallow baking dish just large enough to hold the pieces in one layer. Bake in a preheated 350°F. oven for 1 hour, or until tender and golden, basting several times with the remaining butter-rum-spice mixture.

SPICY OVEN-FRIED CHICKEN**

Serves 4:

blended well together
½ cup of yellow corn-
  meal
½ cup of flour
1 teaspoon of salt
½ teaspoon of cayenne

½ teaspoon of crushed
  dried oregano leaves

1 (3½ - to 4-pound)
  chicken, cut up
½ cup of milk
6 tablespoons of butter,
  melted

Spread the cornmeal mixture on waxed paper. Dip the chicken pieces in milk, then dredge with the cornmeal mixture. Arrange in one layer in a shallow baking dish. Dribble the butter over the chicken. Bake in a preheated 375°F. oven for 40 minutes, or until tender and crisp.

** Fast and Easy

CHICKEN PAPRIKA WITH YOGURT

Serves 4:

3 tablespoons of butter
1 (3½-to 4-pound)
  chicken, cut up
1 teaspoon of salt
¼ teaspoon of pepper
4 medium-sized onions,
  chopped

1 tablespoon of Hungarian
  paprika
1 cup of chicken broth
1 tablespoon of cornstarch,
  mixed with just enough
  water to dissolve
1 cup of plain yogurt

In a deep frypan, over medium heat, melt butter. Season chicken with salt and pepper and brown evenly. Remove chicken. Stir in the onion and paprika and cook for 5 minutes. Blend in the broth. Return the chicken. Cover and simmer for 40 minutes, or until the chicken is fork tender. Blend the cornstarch mixture with the yogurt. Pour into the saucepan with the chicken. Cook for 5 minutes, or until heated through but do not boil. Serve with buttered broad noodles.

CHICKEN WITH PEPPERS AND TOMATOES

Serves 4:

2 tablespoons of olive oil
2 whole sweet green or red
  peppers
2 tablespoons of butter
1 (3½ - to 4-pound)
  chicken, cut up
2 whole cloves of garlic,
  peeled

2 large, ripe, firm tomatoes,
  peeled, seeded and
  chopped (use canned to-
  matoes, drained, if fresh
  ones are not available)
1 cup of chicken broth
Salt and pepper to taste

In a frypan, over high heat, heat 1 tablespoon of the oil. Add the peppers and cook them, turning, just until the skins blister. Remove and peel. Cut each into 8 strips, discarding the seeds and core.

In a top-of-the-stove casserole, over medium heat, heat the remaining 1 tablespoon of oil and the butter. Add the chicken and garlic, evenly browning the chicken. Discard the garlic. Add the peppers and tomatoes. Cook, stirring, for 2 minutes, Add broth, salt and pepper. Bring to a boil on top of the stove, then place in a preheated 350°F. oven, covered, for about 40 minutes, or until the chicken is fork tender. Taste for seasoning.

DORA RADICCHE'S CHICKEN PERUGIA

Serves 4:

3 tablespoons of olive oil
1 (3½ - to 4-pound)
  chicken, cut up
1½ teaspoons of salt
½ teaspoon of pepper

¼ teaspoon of dried rose-
  mary
1 cup of dry white wine
1 egg, beaten with 2 tablespoons of fresh lemon
  juice

In a frypan, over medium heat, heat the oil. Sprinkle the chicken with salt, pepper and rosemary and brown evenly. Pour in the wine, cover and simmer for 25 minutes, or until the chicken is fork tender. Transfer chicken to a heated serving dish. Over low heat, add the egg–lemon juice mixture to the frypan, stirring constantly until hot (do not boil). Pour the sauce over the chicken on the serving dish.

CHICKEN WITH PRUNES

Serves 4: If you don't like prunes, skip this one. But it is a "different" dish.

1 (3½-pound) chicken, cut up
1½ teaspoons of salt
Flour for dredging
3 tablespoons of butter
2 small onions, chopped
1 clove of garlic, chopped
1 celery rib, scraped and chopped

2 carrots, peeled and chopped
1 cup of dry vermouth
2 tablespoons of wine vinegar
1 cup of chicken broth
20 dried pitted prunes
2 small bay leaves

Sprinkle the chicken pieces with salt and dredge lightly with flour, shaking any excess off. In a large frypan, melt the butter. Brown the chicken evenly, scattering the onion, garlic, celery and carrots over the pieces, stirring to mix. Add the vermouth, vinegar and broth, blending well with the chicken pieces. Scatter the prunes in and add the bay leaves. Cover tightly and cook over medium heat, stirring frequently, until chicken is fork tender, about 40 minutes. Discard bay leaves. This is excellent with buttered broad noodles.

CHICKEN AND RIGATONI GYPSY STYLE

Serves 4:

2 tablespoons of butter
2 tablespoons of olive oil
1 (3½-pound) chicken, cut
  up
½ cup of dry white wine
2 cloves of garlic
⅛ teaspoon of ground sage
⅛ teaspoon of dried rose-
  mary
1 teaspoon of salt
½ teaspoon of pepper

1½ cups of chicken broth
3 anchovy fillets
½ teaspoon of wine vinegar
6 fresh, ripe plum tomatoes,
  peeled and diced, or 1 (1-
  pound) can of plum tomatoes, drained and diced
½ pound of rigatoni, cooked
  al dente and drained
½ cup of grated Asiago or
  Parmesan cheese

In a large, deep frypan, over medium heat, heat the butter
and oil and evenly brown the chicken. Pour in the wine and
cook until it evaporates. Add the garlic, sage, rosemary, salt,
pepper and broth. Cover the pan, lower the heat and simmer
for 30 minutes, or until the chicken is fork tender. Transfer
the chicken to a serving dish and keep warm in a low oven.
Reserve the sauce in the frypan. Soak the anchovies in cold
water to desalt them, drain and crush into a paste in the vinegar. Stir the anchovy-vinegar paste into the sauce in the frypan. Blend in the tomatoes and simmer, uncovered, stirring,
for 20 minutes, or until the sauce is thickened and smooth.
Taste for seasoning. Toss the hot rigatoni with two-thirds of
the sauce. Serve the pasta first, sprinkled with the cheese, and
the chicken as a second course with the remaining sauce
spooned on top.

YOUNG CHICKEN SAN ANTONIO

Serves 4:

Salt and pepper
1 (3½- to 4-pound) chicken, cut up
Flour for dredging
3 tablespoons of butter
2 tablespoons of olive oil
2 medium-sized onions, chopped

3 cloves of garlic, crushed
⅛ teaspoon of cayenne
½ cup of tomato puree
3 tablespoons of chili powder
Pinch of dried rosemary
⅓ cup of red wine

Generously salt and pepper the chicken and lightly dredge with flour. In a frypan heat the butter and oil over medium heat. Add chicken and evenly brown it, turning often. This should take about 20 minutes. Add the onion and garlic and season with cayenne. Cover and cook for 5 minutes. Add the tomato puree, chili and rosemary. Cover, reduce heat to low and simmer for 25 minutes, or until chicken is fork tender. Remove the chicken and keep warm. Raise the heat to medium-high, stir in the wine and cook, stirring, for 7 minutes. Taste for seasoning. Spoon the sauce over the chicken.

CHICKEN AND ITALIAN SAUSAGE PIZZAIOLA

Serves 6:

6 chicken legs and thighs, separated

blended into a paste
  1½ teaspoons of salt
  ½ teaspoon of pepper
  ½ teaspoon of marjoram
  1 clove of garlic, minced
  4 tablespoons of soft butter

2 tablespoons of olive oil
4 Italian sausage links (hot or sweet)
¾ cup of tomato sauce
½ cup of dry red wine
2 small green peppers, cored, seeds removed and cut into ½-inch strips
½ pound of mushrooms, quartered

Rub the chicken with the butter-garlic paste. In a frypan, over medium heat, heat the oil and evenly brown the chicken.

Transfer it to a casserole. In the frypan, cook the sausages for 14 minutes, turning often. Remove and set aside.

Pour off all but 2 tablespoons of the fat in the pan. Pour in the tomato sauce and wine and simmer, stirring for 5 minutes. Pour over the chicken in the casserole. Bake, covered, in a preheated 350°F. oven for 25 minutes. Add the peppers and mushrooms to the chicken pot, cooking until the chicken is almost tender, about 15 minutes. Cut the sausages into ½-inch slices. Add them to the casserole and cook 10 minutes longer, or until the chicken is tender and the sausage heated through.

BRUNSWICK STEW

Serves 4:

1 stick (¼ pound) of butter
1 (4-pound) chicken, cut up
Salt and pepper
1 large onion, chopped
1 green pepper, seeded, cored and chopped
1 (1-pound) can of tomatoes, broken up, including liquid
1 whole onion, stuck with a whole clove

cooked according to package directions
1 (10-ounce) package of frozen kernel corn
1 (10-ounce) package of fordhook limas
1 tablespoon of Worcestershire sauce
2 medium-sized potatoes, cut into ½-inch cubes
Tabasco to taste

In a large pot, heat half of the butter. Add chicken, sprinkle with salt and pepper and brown evenly. Add the chopped onion and green pepper and cook until the onion is soft. Add water to cover, tomatoes and the whole onion. Bring to a boil, cover, lower heat and simmer for 40 minutes, or until chicken is tender. Remove chicken, discard skin and bones, shred the meat and return to the pot. Add corn, limas, the remaining butter and Worcestershire sauce. Cook for 15 minutes. Add potatoes and Tabasco and cook for 15 minutes longer, or until everything is very tender. It all should be rather overcooked. Taste for seasoning. Serve in rimmed soup bowls with corn bread. The flavor is even better if served the following day.

ANTOINE GILLY'S CHICKEN STEW

Serves 4:

2 tablespoons of butter
1 tablespoon of olive oil
1 (4-pound) chicken, cut into 8 pieces
1½ teaspoons of salt
½ teaspoon of pepper
2 ribs of celery, scraped and diced
3 medium-sized onions, sliced

3 sprigs of parsley
½ teaspoon of dried rosemary
1 bay leaf
⅛ teaspoon of mace
⅛ teaspoon of paprika
1 tablespoon of flour, blended with water into a smooth paste
1 cup of red wine

In a large frypan over medium heat, heat butter and oil and brown chicken evenly, seasoning with salt and pepper. Barely cover with hot water. Add the celery, onion, parsley, rosemary, bay leaf, mace and paprika. Cover and simmer for 30 minutes. Remove cover and thicken with the flour-water paste. Stir in the red wine and simmer 15 minutes, or until sauce is smooth and chicken tender. Taste for seasoning and discard bay leaf.

CHICKEN STEW WITH MUSHROOMS AND PEAS

Serves 4:

1 (3½- to 4-pound) chicken, cut up
Salt and pepper to taste
Flour for dredging
4 tablespoons of butter
2 tablespoons of olive oil
1 medium-sized onion, chopped
¼ teaspoon of thyme
3 ounces of dry sherry

½ cup of tomato puree
1 cup of chicken broth
12 medium-sized mushrooms, quartered and cooked in 2 tablespoons of butter for 2 minutes
2 cups of shelled small peas, or 1 (10-ounce) package of frozen small peas, defrosted

Season the chicken pieces with salt and pepper and dredge with flour. In a deep frypan, heat 2 tablespoons of the butter and the oil. Over medium heat, brown the chicken evenly.

Transfer to a warm dish. Add the onion to the frypan and cook for 4 minutes. Stir in the thyme, sherry, tomato puree and broth. Return the chicken to the pan. Cover and simmer for 45 minutes, or until the chicken is fork tender. Add the mushrooms and peas and cook for 5 minutes, or until peas are tender. Taste for seasoning. Stir in the remaining 2 tablespoons of butter and serve.

CHICKEN THIGHS WITH QUICK BROCCOLI MOUSSE

Serves 4:

8 medium-sized chicken thighs	½ teaspoon of pepper
	½ teaspoon of dried tarragon
blended	
1 cup of flour	1 stick (¼ pound) of butter
1½ teaspoons of salt	1 cup of dry white vermouth

Lightly dredge the thighs with the seasoned flour. In a frypan, over medium heat, melt the butter and evenly brown the thighs. Place them in a broilerproof casserole. Pour the vermouth into the frypan in which the thighs cooked, scraping up the browned particles and simmer, stirring, for 4 minutes. Pour over the chicken in the casserole. Bake, uncovered, in a preheated 350°F. oven for 15 minutes. Turn the thighs and baste, then bake another 15 minutes, or until fork tender.

MOUSSE

1 (10-ounce) package of frozen chopped broccoli, thawed	⅔ cup of Hollandaise Sauce (pages 407, 408)
6 whole scallions, minced	¼ cup of grated Asiago cheese
½ teaspoon of salt	

In a saucepan, place enough water to barely cover broccoli and scallions, add salt, stir in the broccoli and scallions. Bring to a boil, cover, reduce heat to a simmer and cook for 6 minutes, or until tender. Drain well, pressing out all water. Purée, using a blender or food processor. In a bowl, combine the cooked broccoli-scallion purée with the hollandaise and blend well.

Spoon a dollop of the mousse evenly on the top of each thigh in the casserole. Sprinkle with the cheese and place under the broiler until bubbly brown.

SPICY POACHED THIGHS**

Serves 4:

1 teaspoon of sugar
¼ cup of dry white vermouth
2 tablespoons of soy sauce
3 cloves of garlic, minced
⅛ teaspoon of cayenne

½ teaspoon of ground ginger
1 cup of chicken broth
8 medium-sized chicken thighs

In a deep frypan large enough to hold the thighs in one layer, combine the sugar, vermouth, soy sauce, garlic, cayenne, ginger and broth, blending well. Add the chicken, turning it several times to coat it thoroughly. Bring to a boil. Cover, reduce heat to a simmer and cook for 15 minutes. Remove cover and again turn chicken several times. Raise the heat to bring liquid to a brisk boil. Cook, turning chicken frequently, until the liquid has evaporated and the thighs are fork tender (about 10 minutes).

** Fast and Easy

ANTOINE GILLY'S CHICKEN IN VELOUTÉ SAUCE

Serves 4:

3 tablespoons of butter
3 tablespoons of flour
2 cups of chicken broth
Juice of 2 lemons (at least 3 tablespoons)

1 (4-pound) chicken, cut into 8 pieces
24 small fresh mushrooms, washed and stemmed
⅓ cup of dry sherry

In a top-of-the-stove casserole, over medium heat, melt the butter, stir in the flour, and then, over low heat, slowly stir in the broth, stirring into a smooth sauce. Stir in the lemon juice. Add the chicken, and bake, covered, in a preheated 350°F. oven for 40 minutes, stirring occasionally so the sauce doesn't stick or scorch. Add the mushrooms and the sherry, and bake, covered, for 10 minutes longer, or until chicken is fork-tender. Mushrooms should be crunchy.

FAST AND FINE VINEGAR CHICKEN**

Serves 6:

2 (3-pound) chickens, cut up
1½ teaspoons of salt
½ teaspoon of pepper

blended
2 cloves of garlic, minced

1½ teaspoons dried oregano
½ teaspoon dried rosemary

½ cup of red wine vinegar

Sprinkle the chicken with salt and pepper. Place on a shallow pan and under a preheated broiler, 4 inches from the heat source. Cook for 5 minutes on each side. Remove from broiler and transfer to a baking dish large enough to hold the chicken in one layer. Sprinkle evenly with the garlic-oregano-rosemary mixture and the vinegar. Bake, uncovered, in a preheated 350°F. oven for 30 minutes (basting every 10 minutes) or until the chicken is fork-tender.

** Fast and Easy

*CRISPY CHICKEN WING TACOS**

Serves 4:

⅓ cup of vegetable shortening
1 cup of flour
2 envelopes of taco seasoning mix

⅓ teaspoon of salt
24 meaty chicken wings
3 eggs, beaten
2 cups of crushed corn chips

In a baking dish large enough to accommodate the wings in one layer, melt the shortening in a preheated 375°F. oven. In a paper or plastic bag, combine flour, taco mix and salt. Place wings in the bag and shake to coat evenly. Dip wings into the egg, then dredge each wing with crushed corn chips, pressing the chips firmly onto the surface of the wings. Place the wings in the melted, hot shortening in the baking dish, turning once to coat. Bake in a preheated 375°F. oven for 40 minutes, or until fork-tender and crisp.

Optional: Serve with Marmalade and Horseradish Sauce (p. 25).

* Especially Inexpensive

Chapter Six
Classics

That French epicure of another century, Jean Anthelme Brillat-Savarin, captured in a single sentence the culinary value of the chicken. "Chicken," he wrote, "is for the cook what canvas is for the painter."

Chefs of every country have proudly "painted" chicken classics, some that have lived for centuries, others, relatively new, that have claimed new converts.

But classics, per se, are those recipes, so imaginative, so well conceived that they have become internationally respected. The French, Japanese, German and Italian dishes, etc., that follow are not cooked only in those countries. They are prepared by chefs and by "cooks" everywhere.

Perhaps you will find a classic here that will become a new favorite, or an old one that you have not experimented with before. Classics, as you will discover, are also fun "to paint on your own canvas."

POLLO CON ARROZ

Serves 6: (Chicken with Rice, Spanish Style)

3 tablespoons of olive oil

¼ pound of fatback (labeled "Pork for beans"), blanched in boiling water for 2 minutes, drained, dried and cut into small cubes

Salt and pepper

2 (3-pound) chickens, cut up

2 medium-sized onions, coarsely chopped

1 large clove of garlic, chopped

2 large fresh, ripe tomatoes, skinned, seeded and chopped, or 2 cups of canned, drained and chopped

¼ teaspoon of powdered saffron

1 teaspoon of powdered cumin

½ teaspoon of powdered coriander

1 small (about 1½ inches) serrano chili, or ⅛ teaspoon of crushed dried red pepper flakes (optional)

1½ cups of rice

3 cups of chicken broth

1 cup of tiny fresh peas, or frozen peas, defrosted

1 canned pimiento, cut into strips

2 tablespoons of chopped fresh broadleaf parsley

In a top-of-the-stove casserole, over medium heat, heat the oil. Add the fatback and cook until golden. Remove with a slotted spoon and set aside. Liberally salt and pepper the chicken pieces and brown them evenly in the casserole. Remove and set aside. Pour all but about 2 tablespoons of the fat from the casserole into a saucepan. Sauté the onion and garlic in the casserole until they are soft. Add the tomatoes, saffron, cumin, coriander and serrano chili and 1 teaspoon of salt. Simmer, uncovered, for 5 minutes.

If the fat you poured out of the casserole into the saucepan does not amount to 2 tablespoons, add some oil. Stir in the rice and over medium heat, sauté the rice until it absorbs the oil, continuing to stir so it does not burn.

Return the fatback cubes and chicken to the casserole with the rice and broth and bake, covered, in a preheated 350°F. oven for 20 minutes, or until the rice and chicken are still slightly underdone. Stir in the peas and continue to cook covered, until rice and chicken are tender and most of the liquid has been absorbed. Taste for seasoning. Serve garnished with the pimiento strips and parsley.

BLANQUETTE OF CHICKEN

Serves 6:

4 large, whole chicken breasts, skinned, boned and cut into 1-inch cubes

8 large chicken thighs, boned and cut into 1-inch cubes

2 medium-sized white onions, peeled and each stuck with 2 cloves

2 carrots, cut up

2 ribs of celery with leaves, cut up

½ teaspoon of dried tarragon

1 bay leaf

Salt and pepper to taste

5 cups of chicken broth (add more, if necessary, to completely cover the chicken)

24 small fresh mushrooms, halved

18 small white onions, root ends scored

3 tablespoons of butter

3 tablespoons of flour

2 egg yolks, mixed with 1 cup of heavy cream and 2 tablespoons of lemon juice

In a large pot, combine the chicken, onions with the cloves, carrots, celery, tarragon, bay leaf, 1 teaspoon of salt and broth. Cover and bring to a boil, then lower the heat and simmer for 20 minutes, or until the chicken is fork tender.

Remove the chicken with a slotted spoon, transfer to a bowl and keep warm. Strain the broth, discarding the vegetables, and return it to the pot. In the broth, cook the mushrooms, covered, for 2 minutes. Remove with a slotted spoon, add to the chicken. Cook the small onions in the broth, covered, for 10 minutes, or until tender. Transfer to the chicken bowl. Raise the heat and reduce the stock to 2½ cups. In a saucepan, over medium-low heat, melt the butter and blend in the flour, stirring into a smooth paste (do not brown). Add the strained warm broth, a small amount at a time, stirring constantly until the sauce is smooth and medium-thick. Season with salt and pepper. Add the chicken, mushrooms and onions to the sauce and place on low heat to heat through. Mix 4 tablespoons of the hot sauce with the egg yolk-lemon juice mixture. Stir it into the sauce, heating gently without boiling.

The classic cacciatore are as varied as the chefs who prepare them, but all have their own unique character. Here are three favorites that we discovered in various regions of Italy.

CHICKEN ALLA CACCIATORI #1

Serves 6:

4 tablespoons of olive oil
2 (3-pound) chickens, cut up
Salt and pepper
3 medium-sized white onions, chopped
2 cloves of garlic, minced

2 medium-sized ribs of celery, scraped and chopped
1 bay leaf
⅛ teaspoon of dried oregano
2 cups of dry white wine

In a large frypan, over medium heat, heat the oil. Season the chicken with salt and pepper and evenly brown (adding more oil, if needed). Transfer to a warm dish. Pour off all but 2 tablespoons of oil. Stir in the onion, garlic and celery and cook for 5 minutes, or until soft. Add the bay leaf, oregano and white wine. Stir, scraping up the brown particles on the bottom of the pan and blending them with the wine and vegetables. Return the chicken to the pan, cover and simmer for 35 minutes, or until the chicken is fork tender. Remove bay leaf. Taste for seasoning. Serve with parsleyed, buttered noodles, lightly spooning the sauce over the chicken and noodles.

CHICKEN ALLA CACCIATORA #2

Serves 4:

2 tablespoons of olive oil
4 tablespoons of butter
1 (3½- to 4-pound) chicken, cut up
Salt and pepper
1 medium-sized white onion, chopped
1 clove of garlic, minced
½ pound of fresh mushrooms (left whole, if small, quartered, if large)

¾ cup of red Chianti
2 tablespoons of brandy
1 cup of chicken broth
4 ripe tomatoes, peeled, seeded and chopped. or 1 (1-pound) can of tomatoes, drained and chopped
½ teaspoon of dried oregano
1 tablespoon of chopped fresh basil

In a deep frypan, over medium heat, heat the oil and 2 tablespoons of the butter. Sprinkle the chicken with salt and pepper and evenly brown. Transfer the chicken to a bowl and keep warm. Pour fat from pan. Add 1 tablespoon of the butter to the pan and cook the onion and garlic, stirring, for 3 minutes, or until soft. Transfer to the chicken bowl. Add the remaining 1 tablespoon of butter and mushrooms and cook for 2 minutes. Transfer to the chicken bowl. Add the wine and brandy to the pan, scraping the bottom to mix in brown particles. Simmer to reduce the liquid by half. Add the broth, tomatoes, oregano and basil and simmer for 15 minutes, covered. Return the chicken, onion, garlic and mushrooms to the pan. Simmer, covered, for 20 minutes, then uncovered for 10 minutes, or until chicken is fork tender. Taste for seasoning. Serve with rice, pasta or plain boiled potatoes.

CHICKEN ALLA CACCIATORA #3

Serves 4:

3 tablespoons of olive oil
1 tablespoon of butter
1 (3½-to 4-pound) chicken, cut up
Salt and pepper
2 medium-sized white onions, thinly sliced
2 cloves of garlic, thinly sliced
1 cup of chicken broth
¾ cup of dry white wine
⅓ cup of white wine vinegar
¼ teaspoon of dried rosemary

1 small bay leaf
12 large black Greek olives (the soft, smooth, oily ones, not the wrinkled ones—actually they are more tan, brown or purplish than black), pits removed and each quartered
6 fillets of anchovy, blotted on paper towel and coarsely chopped
2 tablespoons of chopped broadleaf parsley

In a frypan, over medium heat, heat the oil and butter. Sprinkle the chicken with salt and pepper and evenly brown. Transfer to a bowl. Pour most of the fat from the frypan. Add the onion and garlic and cook until soft. Transfer them to the chicken bowl. To the frypan, add the broth, wine, vinegar, rosemary and bay leaf. Simmer for 4 minutes, scraping the bottom of the pan to mix in brown particles. Return the chicken, onion and garlic to the pan, and simmer, covered, for 25 minutes, or until the chicken is fork tender. Transfer the chicken to a heated serving dish. Cook the liquid in the frypan over high heat until it reduces and thickens a bit. Remove the bay leaf. Stir in the olives, anchovies and parsley and simmer long enough to heat the olives. Taste for seasoning. Spoon over the chicken and serve.

CANTONESE CHICKEN

Serves 4:

2 whole chicken breasts, skinned, boned and medium diced

blended into a marinade
   2 tablespoons of soy sauce
   1½ teaspoons of brown sugar
   2 tablespoons of white wine

1½ tablespoons of cornstarch

1 tablespoon of peanut oil
1 cup of pea pods
½ cup of bamboo shoots
½ cup of bean sprouts
2 tablespoons of soy sauce
1 teaspoon of sugar
3 tablespoons of dry sherry

Marinate the chicken for 2 hours. Drain and discard marinade. In a wok, or large frypan, heat the oil and stir-fry the chicken for 3 minutes. Stir in the remaining ingredients, blending well. Stir-fry for 3 minutes. The vegetables should be crunchy and the chicken not overdone. Serve with plain or fried rice.

CHICKEN CHASSEUR

Serves 4:

1 (3½- to 4-pound)
  chicken, cut up
1½ teaspoons of salt
½ teaspoon of pepper
2 tablespoons of butter
1 tablespoon of olive oil
½ pound of medium-sized
  mushrooms, quartered
3 tablespoons of minced
  shallots
2 tablespoons of flour

1 cup of dry white wine
2 large ripe tomatoes,
  peeled, seeded and
  coarsely chopped
1 cup of chicken broth
1½ tablespoons of chopped
  fresh tarragon or 1
  teaspoon of dried
2 tablespoons of chopped
  fresh parsley

Sprinkle the chicken with salt and pepper. In a deep frypan, over medium heat, heat the butter and oil and evenly brown the chicken. Transfer chicken to a bowl and keep warm. Add the mushrooms to the pan and cook for 2 minutes. Remove with a slotted spoon and keep warm with the chicken. Add the shallots to frypan and cook for 3 minutes. Sprinkle with flour, blending well. Add the wine and simmer for 3 minutes, scraping the bottom of the pan to mix in brown particles. Stir in the tomatoes, broth and tarragon, then simmer for 10 minutes. Return the chicken to the pan, cover and simmer for 10 minutes longer. Add the mushrooms and any juice collected in the bowl and cook 15 minutes longer, or until the chicken is fork tender. Taste for seasoning. Serve the chicken with the mushrooms and sauce spooned over. Sprinkle with parsley.

CHICKEN CORDON BLEU

Serves 4:

4 small whole chicken breasts, halved, skinned, boned and each pounded between sheets of waxed paper until thin (be careful not to put any holes in them)

4 thin slices of prosciutto ham, or any good country ham, slightly smaller than the pounded out breasts

4 thin slices of Swiss cheese the same size as the ham

1 cup of flour seasoned with 1½ teaspoons of salt and ½ teaspoon of pepper

1 egg, beaten with ¼ cup of milk

1½ cups of fine bread crumbs

3 tablespoons of butter

1 tablespoon of olive oil

2 tablespoons of minced shallots

4 medium-sized mushrooms, sliced

3 tablespoons of dry white wine

½ teaspoon of Dijon mustard

2 egg yolks, beaten with 1 cup of medium cream

Salt and pepper to taste

Center a slice of ham on each of 4 "scallops" or "suprême" of breast, then top with a slice of the cheese. Place another scallop of breast on the filling, pressing together and sealing into one, sandwich fashion. Secure with toothpicks, if necessary.

Dredge each "sandwich" with the seasoned flour, dip in the egg-milk mixture, then coat well with bread crumbs. In a frypan large enough to prevent crowding (or use two frypans), over medium heat, heat the butter and oil. Cook the chicken for 10 or 12 minutes, or until evenly browned (do not overcook). Handle carefully to keep filling intact. Drain on paper towels and keep warm on a serving dish in a low oven.

To the frypan in which you browned the chicken, add the shallots (adding more butter, if necessary) and cook for 3 minutes. Add the mushrooms and cook 2 minutes. Stir in the wine and mustard and simmer for 1 minute. Turn the heat to low, stir in the egg yolk-cream mixture and cook, stirring, until the sauce thickens (do not boil or the sauce will curdle). Taste for seasoning. Spoon the sauce over the chicken and serve.

SOUTHERN FRIED CHICKEN

Southern fried chicken is classic American—and confusing. It varies in every Southern state, and, often, with every Southerner. All recipes are simple, as are the best classics. An accompaniment most Southerners agree upon is Southern Corn Fritters (page 457).

A BASIC SOUTHERN FRIED CHICKEN WITH SPECKLED GRAVY

We discovered this recipe in a famous old hotel in Tennessee, with the chef cooperating.

Serves 4:

2 (2½-pound) chickens, cut up

combined and well beaten
  1 cup of milk
  2 eggs

blended
  2 cups of flour
  2 teaspoons of salt
  ½ teaspoon of pepper

1 cup of cooking oil
2 tablespoons of flour
1 cup of milk
1 cup of water
Salt and pepper to taste

Dip the chicken pieces in the milk-egg mixture, then dredge with the seasoned flour. In a large frypan, over medium-high heat, heat the oil and brown the chicken evenly, turning it often, for 20 minutes, or until fork tender. Remove the chicken from the frypan, drain on paper towels and keep warm in a low oven.

Pour all but 3 tablespoons of fat from the frypan. Over high heat, stir in the 2 tablespoons of flour, blending well with the fat and scraping up the browned particles on the bottom of the pan. Gradually blend in the milk, stirring constantly, then the water. Season with salt and pepper and cook, stirring, until thickened. The "specks" are the browned particles from the cooked chicken blended into the gravy.

FRIED CHICKEN MARYLAND WITH CREAM GRAVY

Serves 4:

8 slices of bacon
2 (2½-pound) chickens, cut up

combined in a clean plastic or paper bag and shaken to blend
1½ cups of flour

2 teaspoons of salt
½ teaspoon of pepper

3 tablespoons of butter
2 tablespoons of flour
2 cups of medium cream
Salt and pepper to taste

In a large frypan, fry the bacon until crisp. Remove bacon, drain on paper towels and keep warm, reserving the fat. Shake the chicken pieces in the seasoned flour, coating the pieces evenly. In the frypan, over medium-high heat, heat the bacon fat and the butter. When the fat is bubbling slightly add the chicken and brown evenly. Reduce the heat, cover the frypan and cook the chicken for 20 minutes, or until fork tender. Drain on paper towels, place on a heated serving dish and keep warm in a low oven. Pour all but 4 tablespoons of fat from the frypan. Over medium heat, blend in the 2 tablespoons of flour. Cook, stirring into a smooth paste, about 2 minutes. Gradually stir in the cream, stirring until the gravy is thick and smooth. Season with salt and pepper. Spoon hot gravy over the fried chicken and garnish with the bacon.

CHICKEN À LA HONGROISE

Serves 4:

6 tablespoons of butter
1 tablespoon of olive oil
1 (3½- to 4-pound) chicken, cut up
1 teaspoon of salt
½ teaspoon of pepper
2 tablespoons of Hungarian paprika

3 medium-sized onions, thinly sliced
8 medium-sized mushrooms, thinly sliced
1 tablespoon of flour
1 cup of heavy cream
½ cup of sour cream

In a large frypan, over medium heat, heat 4 tablespoons of the butter and the olive oil. Sprinkle the chicken with salt and pepper and cook in the frypan, skin side down for 15 minutes. Turn the chicken, sprinkle with the paprika and cover with the onion. Cook, covered, for 15 minutes. Add the mushrooms and cook 15 minutes longer, or until the chicken is fork tender. Transfer the chicken to a heated serving dish. Sprinkle the flour over the vegetables in the frypan and blend thoroughly. Slowly stir in the heavy cream, blending well. Stir in sour cream and slowly bring to a simmer. Stir in the remaining 2 tablespoons of butter. Pour the sauce over the chicken in the serving dish.

CHICKEN KIEV

Serves 6: This Russian specialty is a fun dish to serve. If properly prepared, when the diner cuts into the breast, there is an impressive and surprising spurt of butter.

1 stick (¼ pound) of chilled unsalted butter

3 whole large chicken breasts, halved, skinned and boned

Salt and pepper

1 tablespoon of chopped fresh tarragon, or 1 teaspoon dried

1 tablespoon of chopped fresh parsley

1 tablespoon of chopped shallots

½ lemon

Flour for dredging

2 eggs, beaten

1 cup of fine dry bread crumbs

Oil for frying

Shape the butter into six cylinders about ½ inch by 3 inches and freeze. With a mallet, gently pound the breasts between pieces of waxed paper, flattening them to a thickness of about ¼ inch (be careful not to break the flesh). Lay the breasts, boned side up, on a board. Sprinkle each with salt and pepper and one-sixth of the tarragon, parsley, shallots and a few drops of lemon juice. Lay a cylinder of butter near one end of each breast. Roll into packages, first by folding the smaller end of the breast over the butter, then fold in the two sides, and rolling into a neat, tight package.

Dredge the rolled breasts with flour and dip into the beaten egg. Dredge with bread crumbs by patting the crumbs on.

Refrigerate for 3 hours. Heat enough oil in a heavy, deep frypan to cover the breasts. Fry, turning carefully from time to time, for 6 to 8 minutes, or until golden brown. Drain for a second on paper towels and serve immediately on a bed of kasha or rice. The grain will absorb the tasty butter as it spurts out of the chicken breast.

CHICKEN À LA KING

Serves 4: This has become an American classic, and perhaps a partygiver's cliché. But it is tasty and easy to prepare.

5 tablespoons of butter (3 in small pieces)
2 tablespoons of flour
½ cup of chicken broth
1 cup of medium cream
1 teaspoon of salt
2 cups of julienne-cut cooked chicken

8 medium-sized mushrooms, sliced and cooked in butter for 2 minutes
¼ cup of julienne-cut canned pimientos
1 egg yolk, beaten with 2 tablespoons of sherry

In a deep saucepan, melt the 2 tablespoons of butter over medium heat. Stir in the flour, blending into a smooth paste. Gradually blend in the broth, then the cream, stirring into a smooth medium-thick sauce. Add salt and the small pieces of butter, stirring until butter is melted. Add the chicken, mushrooms and pimientos. Cook until heated through. Lower heat and stir in the egg yolk-sherry mixture, blending well (do not boil). This can be served over rice or spooned into crisp, golden patty shells.

CHICKEN MARENGO

Serves 6:

2 (3-pound) chickens, cut up

1 cup of flour seasoned with 1½ teaspoons of salt, ½ teaspoon of pepper and ⅛ teaspoon of allspice

4 tablespoons of butter

2 tablespoons of olive oil

18 small white onions, root ends scored

4 tablespoons (2 ounces) of brandy

1 clove of garlic, minced

1 cup of dry white wine

2 large, ripe tomatoes, peeled, seeded and chopped, or 2 cups of canned, drained and chopped

12 small whole mushrooms, sautéed for 1 minute in 2 tablespoons of butter

12 pitted black Greek olives

2 tablespoons of chopped parsley

Croutons made from 3 slices of bread, quartered and fried in butter until golden on both sides

12 shrimp, cooked in boiling water just until they turn pink (about 1 minute)

6 fried eggs (optional)

Lightly dredge the chicken pieces with the seasoned flour. Over medium heat in a large frypan, heat the butter and oil and brown the chicken pieces evenly. Transfer the chicken to a casserole. Lightly brown the onions in the frypan. Pour the brandy over them, raise the heat and let cook off. Transfer the onions to the casserole. Add the garlic, wine and tomatoes to the casserole, cover and bake in a preheated 350°F. oven for 30 minutes, or until the chicken is almost fork tender. Stir in the mushrooms and olives and cook, uncovered, for 10 minutes, or until the chicken is tender.

Arrange the chicken on a large heated serving dish, spooning over the sauce and vegetables. Sprinkle with parsley and surround with the croutons, shrimp and fried eggs (if used).

BETTY PETER'S CHICKEN MOLLE

Serves 4 to 6:

2 large whole chicken breasts, halved
4 chicken thighs
4 chicken legs
1 large onion, halved and each half stuck with 2 whole cloves
1 rib of celery, cut into 4 pieces
1 carrot, cut into 4 pieces
1½ teaspoons of salt
½ teaspoon of pepper
6 or more cups of water
4 tablespoons of lard or cooking oil
2 medium-sized white onions, finely chopped
2 cloves of garlic, finely chopped
3 tablespoons of flour

finely chopped or run through a food processor
½ cup of toasted almonds
½ square of unsweetened chocolate
1 tablespoon of sesame seeds
1 slice of toasted bread
½ cup of raisins

3 to 6 tablespoons of chili powder (depending on taste)
¼ teaspoon of ground cinnamon
¼ teaspoon of anise seeds
1½ cups of tomato puree
4 cups of the broth the chicken cooked in, strained

In a large pot, place the chicken, the halved onion, celery, carrot, salt and pepper. Pour in at least 6 cups of water (the water should cover the chicken). Poach the chicken until almost tender (do not overcook as it will cook more later).

Oven medium heat, heat the lard in a pot large enough to hold all ingredients. Add the onion and garlic and cook for 5 minutes. Stir in the flour. When it begins to color stir in the chocolate mixture, chili powder, cinnamon and anise seeds. Simmer, stirring, until well mixed. Stir in the tomato puree. Cook, uncovered, until it comes to a simmer. Add the chicken broth and simmer for 10 minutes. Add the poached chicken and cook, gently, just until the sauce thickens. Season with salt, if necessary.

PAELLA

Serves 8: This is not only a Spanish classic, but the national dish of Spain. It is offered in several versions there, depending upon the section of the country: game, fish, pork, but chicken appears to be the favorite. No matter what the version, the dish also always contains fish, shellfish and sausage. It is a spectacular party dinner. We worked on this recipe with the head chef at the famous Botin Restaurant in Madrid. A large circular pan, the paellera *is used, but a fry-pan can be substituted, then the food can be transferred to a casserole and placed in the oven for the last stage. Do not let the long list of ingredients intimidate; the dish is not difficult.*

2 (2½-pound) chickens, cut up (do not use backs or wings; cut the breast into 4 pieces, the thighs in 2)

Salt and pepper

½ cup of olive oil

8 small pieces of haddock

1 large yellow onion, chopped

2 cloves of garlic, minced

1 cup of diced raw lean pork

1 large ripe tomato, peeled, seeded and chopped, or 1 cup of canned, drained

3 cups of uncooked long-grain rice

½ teaspoon of powdered saffron

6 to 7 cups of chicken broth

1 cup shelled fresh green peas, slightly undercooked in salted water, or defrosted frozen ones

4 chorizos (Spanish sausages) or sweet Italian sausages, skins pricked in several places, simmered in water for 10 minutes, drained, sautéed in olive oil until brown, then cut into ¼-inch slices

16 small fresh shrimp, shelled and deveined

16 clams or mussels, or a combination, scrubbed

8 thin strips of pimiento

1 (9-ounce) package of frozen artichoke hearts, cooked according to package directions

Lightly sprinkle the chicken pieces with salt and pepper. Heat one-half of the oil in a paella pan or large casserole over medium heat and evenly brown the chicken. Remove the chicken. Add additional oil, if necessary. Lightly sprinkle the haddock with salt and pepper and sauté for 2 minutes on each side. Remove the haddock.

Add the onion, garlic and pork to the pan and sauté for 10

minutes, or until the pork is brown. Stir in the tomato, rice, saffron and 6 cups of the broth. Simmer for 10 minutes.

Sprinkle the peas over the rice, then arrange the chicken, haddock, sausage slices, shrimp, clams and/or mussels on top of the rice, partially burying them in it. Bring to a simmer on top of the stove, then bake uncovered, in a preheated 350°F. oven for 15 minutes, or until the rice has absorbed all of the broth. Test the rice to see if it is tender. If not, add a small amount of hot broth and return the pan to the oven until the rice is tender (it should not be too soft, but slightly *al dente*).

Garnish with the pimiento strips and artichoke hearts and return to the oven for 5 minutes. Let the paella stand for a few minutes, then serve right from the pan.

ANTOINE GILLY'S POLLO CON ARROZ PERU-VIAN STYLE

Serves 6:

¼ pound of lean salt pork, cut into 1-inch cubes
4 large chicken legs
4 large chicken thighs, each cut in half lengthwise
2 medium-sized onions, sliced
1 cup of sliced green peppers
½ cup of fresh sliced red pimientos
2 cloves of garlic, chopped
2 tablespoons diced celery
2 large ripe tomatoes, skinned, seeded and diced
2 teaspoons of salt
½ teaspoon of cayenne
1 teaspoon of powdered saffron
½ cup of dry white wine
1 quart of chicken broth
Bouquet garni (see "Golden Fricassee of Chicken," page 116)
12 chorizos (Spanish sausages), browned under broiler for 3 minutes on each side
1½ cups of uncooked rice
12 large oysters, shucked
12 large shrimp cleaned
Grated Parmesan cheese

In a large top-of-the-stove casserole, over medium heat, cook the salt pork until crisp. Remove with slotted spoon and reserve. Slowly sauté the chicken in the pork fat for 10 minutes, turning often to cook lightly on all sides. Add the onion, green pepper, pimiento and simmer for 10 minutes, stirring often. Add the garlic, celery, tomatoes, salt, cayenne, saffron, wine, broth and bouquet garni. Bring to a boil, cover, lower heat and simmer for 20 minutes. Add the chorizos, rice and reserved salt pork cubes to the chicken pot. Bring to a boil, cover with aluminum foil *and* lid. Place in a preheated 400°F. oven for 20 minutes, or until the chicken and rice are tender. Add the oysters and shrimp to the pot and cook 5 minutes longer, or until they are just firm. Discard the bouquet garni. Taste for seasoning. Serve cheese separately.

CHICKEN POJARSKI (OR CÔTELETTES)

Serves 8: These are excellent with rice-stuffed tomatoes. They are also good, cold, as picnic fare.

5 slices of white bread, crusts removed, soak in 2 cups of chicken broth in a large bowl, drain, squeeze nearly dry and return to bowl
1 stick (¼ pound) of butter, melted, plus 4 tablespoons of butter

4½ pounds of boned chicken breasts, put through the food processor
4 eggs, lightly beaten
Salt and pepper
6 tablespoons of chopped fresh dill, or 4 tablespoons of dried dill weed
Flour for dredging
1 tablespoon of cooking oil
2 cups of heavy cream

Stir the melted butter into the bowl with the bread. Using a fork, stir in the chicken, eggs, a good sprinkle of salt and pepper (season well) and 4 tablespoons of the fresh dill (or 2 of dill weed). Blend well. Refrigerate 3 hours for easier handling. Make oblong patties about 2 by 3 inches in size. Dredge in flour. In a frypan, over medium heat, heat the 4 tablespoons of butter and the oil. Brown the *côtelettes* evenly (adding more butter, if needed). Place in a single layer in a shallow baking dish, pour on the cream and sprinkle with the remaining dill. Bake, uncovered, in a preheated 350°F. oven for 45 minutes, or until they are cooked through and the cream is bubbling.

BREAST OF CHICKEN SALTIMBOCCA

Serves 6:

3 whole chicken breasts,
  halved, skinned and
  boned
Pepper to taste
12 fresh sage leaves or dried
  sage (see below)

12 slices of prosciutto
6 tablespoons of butter
2 tablespoons of olive oil
¼ cup of Marsala

Cut each half breast in half crosswise (you'll have 12 pieces
of breast). Pound each very thin between sheets of waxed paper and trim into neat 4- or 5-inch squares. Sprinkle each
with pepper. Place a fresh sage leaf (or a pinch of dried
sage) on the center of each, then top with a piece of prosciutto the same size and shape of the flattened chicken breast.
Fasten the prosciutto to the chicken breast with toothpicks
(as you would if pinning two pieces of paper together). Heat
3 tablespoons of the butter and the oil in a large frypan over
medium heat. Brown the chicken, breast side first, then turn
and lightly brown the ham side. Add more oil, if needed. As
you brown them keep them warm on a heated serving plate.
Add the remaining 3 tablespoons of butter and the Marsala
to the pan, mixing well with brown particles. Simmer for 2
minutes and spoon over the chicken-ham scallops. Remove
toothpicks.

CLASSIC TANDOORI CHICKEN

Serves 6 to 8:

3 (2½- to 3-pound) chickens	¼ teaspoon of powdered saffron
1 tablespoon of salt	½ teaspoon of cinnamon
½ cup of lime juice	¼ teaspoon of ground cloves
1 teaspoon of crushed dried red pepper flakes	1 tablespoon of minced ginger root, or 1 teaspoon of ground dried ginger
3 cloves of garlic, coarsely chopped	2½ cups of plain yogurt
1 teaspoon of ground coriander	6 tablespoons of melted butter
1 teaspoon of ground cumin	

Sprinkle the inside of the chickens with salt and truss (see "Needle Trussing," page 66). Cut 3½-inch-deep slits in the legs, breasts and thighs. Combine the salt, lime juice and pepper flakes and rub the outside of the birds with the mixture. Marinate in a bowl or deep nonmetal casserole for ½ hour.

In a blender, or mortar, mix the garlic, coriander, cumin, saffron, cinnamon, cloves, ginger and ¼ cup of the yogurt into a paste. Transfer to a bowl and blend in the remaining yogurt. Coat the chicken with the yogurt mixture. Marinate, covered, overnight in the refrigerator.

Before cooking, bring chickens to room temperature. Arrange in a roasting pan, dribble the melted butter over them and roast in a preheated 375°F. oven for 25 minutes, or until fork tender. Taste for seasoning—if you dare.

Serve garnished with thinly sliced onions, tomato and lime (or lemon) wedges and chunks of cucumber.

SIMPLE CHICKEN TANDOORI

Serves 6:

3 broilers, split in half and skinned

1 quart of natural plain yogurt

¼ cup of fresh lemon or lime juice

3 tablespoons of olive oil

3 large cloves of garlic, crushed

1½ tablespoons of curry powder

¼ teaspoon of ground dried ginger

¼ teaspoon of cumin

¼ teaspoon of coriander

Cut small slits in the chicken halves. Place in a large bowl. Combine the remaining ingredients and mix well. Pour over the chicken halves and marinate for at least 3 hours in the refrigerator. Bring chickens to room temperature before cooking. Discard garlic. Broil slowly, basting with the marinade, for 25 to 30 minutes, turning, or until tender.

CHICKEN TERIYAKI WITH SESAME

Serves 6:

⅔ cup of soy sauce

½ cup of sake or dry white wine

½ cup of sesame seed oil

2 cloves of garlic, crushed

1 tablespoon of fresh minced ginger

2 pounds of boned chicken thighs, cut into ½-inch pieces

⅔ cup of sesame seeds, pan toasted

In a bowl, blend the soy sauce, sake, oil, garlic and ginger. Add the chicken, mixing it with the marinade to coat thoroughly. Marinate for 4 hours, turning the chicken several times. Drain and skewer the chicken pieces on 12 bamboo picks or shish kebab skewers. Broil for 3 minutes then turn and broil another 3 minutes. Roll in the toasted sesame seeds and serve on the skewers (2 skewers per person) on individual dishes atop beds of rice.

BREAST OF CHICKEN VÉRONIQUE

Serves 4:

2 whole chicken breasts,
halved, skinned, and
boned
Salt and pepper to taste
Flour for dredging
5 tablespoons of butter

⅓ cup of Madeira
1 cup of seedless white
grapes
½ tablespoon of currant
jelly

Sprinkle the chicken with salt and pepper. Dredge lightly in flour. In a deep frypan, over medium heat, melt the butter and evenly brown the breasts. Cover, lower heat slightly and simmer for 15 minutes, or until tender. Remove the breasts and keep warm. Pour the fat from the pan, stir in the Madeira, grapes and currant jelly, blending well. Place the breasts in the sauce, cook for 4 minutes. Serve with the sauce and grapes spooned on top.

VIENNESE CHICKEN
(*Wiener Backhendl*)

Serves 4: The Viennese also like this cold on picnics, with salad and crusty bread.

2 (2½-pound) chickens, cut
up
1 cup of flour, combined
with 2 teaspoons of salt
and ½ teaspoon of pepper
2 eggs, lightly beaten

Bread crumbs for dredging
(about 1½ cups)
Shortening or vegetable oil
for frying
1 stick (¼ pound) of but-
ter, melted

Dredge the chicken in the seasoned flour. Dip into beaten eggs and dredge in bread crumbs.

Heat 2 inches of shortening or vegetable oil in a deep, heavy frypan. The fat should be very hot to start, but not smoking. Fry the chicken, a few pieces at a time (do not crowd), turning, until evenly golden, about 10 minutes. Drain on paper towels and transfer to a baking dish. Spoon melted butter over each piece of chicken. Bake in a preheated 350°F. oven for 10 minutes, or until the chicken is crusty and fork tender. Serve immediately.

COQ AU VIN

Serves 6:

½ pound of salt pork, cut into ½-inch dice, blanched for 2 minutes, drained, rinsed under cold water and dried

1½ teaspoons of salt

½ teaspoon of pepper

2 (3-pound) chickens, cut up

Flour for dredging

4 tablespoons of butter

6 tablespoons (3 ounces) of brandy, slightly warmed

18 small white onions, root ends scored

18 medium-sized mushroom caps

2 cups of dry red wine

2 cups of chicken broth

Bouquet garni (1 bay leaf, 3 sprigs of parsley, pinch of thyme, all tied in cheese-cloth)

2 cloves of garlic, chopped

2 tablespoons of chopped parsley

In a deep frypan, over medium heat, cook the salt pork for 3 minutes. Remove the salt pork, reserving it and the fat. Salt and pepper the chicken pieces, then dredge in flour, gently shaking off excess. Add the butter to the pan with the salt pork fat and evenly brown the chicken. Transfer chicken to a casserole. Pour the brandy over the chicken, ignite and baste the chicken until the flame dies. In the frypan in which the chicken browned, cook the onion for 4 minutes. Transfer to the chicken casserole. In the same frypan cook the mushrooms for 1 minute. Remove and reserve. Cook the salt pork in the frypan 10 minutes, or until golden. Transfer to the chicken casserole. Pour off all but about 3 tablespoons of fat from the pan. Pour in the wine and broth, then add bouquet garni and the garlic. Simmer for 5 minutes, stirring and scraping up the brown particles in the bottom of the pan. Pour the wine-broth mixture over the chicken in its casserole. Cover and bake in a preheated 325°F. oven for 35 minutes. Add the mushrooms, cover and cook 15 minutes longer, or until the chicken is fork tender. Discard the bouquet garni. Sprinkle with parsley and serve the chicken in its sauce directly from the casserole.

CHICKEN AU VINAIGRE

Serves 6:

2 (2½- to 3-pound) chickens, cut up
Salt and pepper
4 tablespoons of butter
1 tablespoon of cooking oil
2 medium-sized white onions, chopped
1 clove of garlic, minced
Livers from the chickens, coarsely chopped

½ pound of mushrooms (left whole, if small, quartered, if large)
½ cup of wine vinegar
½ cup of chicken broth
Pinch *each* of dried thyme and tarragon
2 tablespoons of chopped parsley

Sprinkle the chicken with salt and pepper. Heat the butter and oil in a deep, heavy frypan or casserole large enough to accommodate all ingredients. Over medium heat, evenly brown the chicken. Remove chicken. Pour off all but 2 tablespoons of fat, stir in the onion and garlic and cook for 2 minutes. Add the livers and mushrooms and cook 2 minutes longer. Stir in the vinegar, broth, thyme and tarragon. Return the browned chicken to the pan, cover and simmer for 30 minutes, or until the chicken is fork tender. Taste for seasoning. Serve with mushrooms-and-liver sauce spooned over. Sprinkle with parsley.

Chapter Seven
Breasts, "Suprêmes"

Dictionaries define the word "supreme" as the highest quality, paramount, the greatest.

That is what the French call chicken breasts, "suprêmes."

So do we. In fact, the breast is so important, so versatile, of such quality that it deserves its own chapter.

Breasts make the most elegant of dishes. They can also be substituted for other costlier meats. But substitute is not the correct word; stand-in is better, but still not just right, for in many cases the chicken breasts are better than what it passes for. For example, we have used chicken breasts for scaloppine, for schnitzel, for vitello tonnato, all veal dishes. The chicken breasts, in each case, were superior; in fact, they were supreme.

That's what this chapter is all about, superior ways to use these supreme morsels.

CHICKEN ALBERTO

Serves 6:

3 large whole chicken
   breasts, halved
6 tablespoons of olive oil
3 cloves of garlic, halved
½ teaspoon of dried basil
½ teaspoon of dried ore-
   gano
1 bay leaf
⅛ teaspoon of dried rose-
   mary

3 tablespoons of chopped
   broadleaf parsley
1½ teaspoons of salt
½ teaspoon of pepper
Bread crumbs for dredging
   (about 1½ cups)
1½ teaspoons of Hungarian
   paprika

Place all ingredients except the bread crumbs and paprika in a large bowl. Toss well with your hands to thoroughly coat the chicken breasts with the oil and herbs. Marinate for 4 hours. Remove chicken breasts from the bowl, drain and dredge with bread crumbs. Arrange in a large baking dish and sprinkle liberally with paprika.

Bake, uncovered, in a preheated 400°F. oven for 40 minutes, or until golden and tender.

ALMOND CHICKEN

Serves 4:

3 tablespoons of peanut oil
1 cup of blanched whole almonds
2 whole chicken breasts,
  halved, skinned and boned,
  cut into ¾ -inch cubes
2 cloves of garlic, minced
½ pound of fresh
  mushrooms, sliced
2 (6-ounce) packages of
  frozen Chinese pea pods,
  or ½ pound of fresh pods,
  cleaned and blanched for
  1 minute
1 cup diagonally sliced celery
6 scallions (white and green
  parts), cut into 1-inch
  lengths

blended
4 tablespoons of soy sauce
4 tablespoons of dry
  sherry
⅓ cup of water
1½ teaspoons of sugar
½ teaspoon of ground
  ginger
1½ tablespoons of corn-
  starch

Heat the oil in a wok or large frypan over medium-high heat.
Stir in the almonds, tossing and turning, for 1 minute. Stir in
chicken and garlic, tossing, and cook for 2 minutes. Add
mushrooms, pea pods, celery and scallions, stir-frying for 4
minutes, or until just tender-crisp. Pour in the soy sauce mixture, stirring constantly until the sauce thickens and becomes
clear. Serve with mounds of steamed white rice.

APRICOT GLAZED BREASTS

Serves 4:

4 tablespoons of peanut oil

4 small zucchini, halved lengthwise and cut into ¼-inch slices

½ pound of small mushrooms, stems removed

½ teaspoon of salt

4 whole small chicken breasts, halved (do not bone or skin)

1 (6-ounce) package of frozen pea pods, defrosted

blended

½ cup of apricot jam

1 teaspoon of garlic powder

½ teaspoon of powdered ginger

⅛ teaspoon of crushed red pepper

1 tablespoon of white vinegar

1 tablespoon of soy sauce

In a wok, or large frypan, heat 2 tablespoons of the oil over high heat. Lower heat to medium and stir-fry the zucchini and mushrooms for 3 minutes, sprinkling with the salt. Remove and keep warm. Add the remaining 2 tablespoons oil and cook the chicken breasts on medium heat, turning often, for 15 minutes, browning and cooking evenly. Return the vegetables to the pan and blend in the pea pods. Cook over medium heat, stirring and turning the breasts, for 4 minutes, or until almost tender. Spoon the apricot mixture over the breasts. Cook, stirring the vegetables and moving the breasts around so they won't stick, for 4 minutes, or until breasts are fork tender. Serve the breasts surrounded by the vegetables.

BREADED CHICKEN BREASTS WITH CAPER SAUCE

Serves 6:

3 whole large chicken breasts, halved, skinned and boned
Salt and pepper
1 large egg, beaten
Bread crumbs for dredging
5 tablespoons of olive oil

2 cloves of garlic, peeled and crushed
4 tablespoons of butter
2 tablespoons of small capers, drained
¾ cup of chicken broth
2 tablespoons of chopped parsley

Pound breasts between sheets of waxed paper with a mallet until ½-inch thick. Season with salt and pepper. Dip in the beaten egg, then dredge in bread crumbs. Heat the oil in a large frypan over medium heat. Add the breasts and garlic and cook for about 15 minutes, or until the breasts are tender and evenly browned. If the garlic gets too brown, discard it. Drain on paper towels and arrange the breasts on a heated serving dish.

Pour the oil from the pan, add the butter, stir in the capers and broth. Simmer for 4 minutes. Taste for seasoning. Spoon the caper sauce over the browned breasts. Sprinkle with parsley.

CHICKEN BREASTS WITH CHEESE AND MUSHROOMS

Serves 6:

3 whole large chicken breasts, halved, skinned and boned
Flour for dredging
3 tablespoons of butter
1 tablespoon of olive oil
Salt and pepper
½ cup of dry sherry
¾ cup of chicken broth

6 tablespoons of grated Asiago or Parmesan cheese
6 medium-sized mushrooms, cut into ¼-inch slices and sautéed in butter just until brown (about 1 minute, they should be very firm)
2 tablespoons of finely chopped parsley

Between sheets of waxed paper, pound the breasts with a mallet to slightly flatten them (they should not be too thin). Dredge lightly with flour. Heat the butter and oil in a large frypan (or use 2 so as not to crowd the breasts) over medium heat and cook until golden on both sides (about 5 minutes on each side). Sprinkle lightly with salt and pepper. Add the sherry and reduce by one-half. Stir in one-half of the broth. Cover and simmer for 15 minutes (adding more broth, if needed), or until the breasts are almost tender. Sprinkle one-half spoonful of cheese over each breast. Arrange mushroom slices on top of the cheese and sprinkle remaining cheese on top. Spoon a small amount of the sauce over the cheese. Pour in any remaining broth, cover and simmer for 6 minutes, or until the cheese has melted. Sprinkle with parsley.

CHICKEN "CIGARS"

Serves 6:

4 whole chicken breasts, halved, skinned, boned and cut into halves crosswise

mixed into a soft paste
1½-inch cube of salt pork, minced
3 tablespoons of butter
3 tablespoons of minced parsley
1 small clove of garlic, minced
¼ teaspoon of leaf sage, crumbled

blended
½ cup of minced cooked ham
½ cup of coarsely chopped pine nuts
¼ cup of grated Parmesan cheese

Salt and pepper to taste
Flour for dredging
3 tablespoons of butter
1 tablespoon of olive oil
1 medium-sized white onion, finely chopped
12 medium-sized mushrooms, quartered
1 tablespoon of flour
2 tablespoons of brandy
1 cup of broth
¼ cup of heavy cream
2 tablespoons of finely chopped parsley

Between sheets of waxed paper, with a mallet, pound the chicken pieces until quite thin, being careful not to tear the flesh. Arrange on large board or other work area. Divide the salt pork paste into 16 parts, spread one part on each flattened piece of breast, not all the way to the edges. Sprinkle onto each "pasted" breast some of the ham-pine nut-cheese mixture. Season with pepper.

Tightly roll each breast. Tie or use toothpicks so the roll remains secure. Dredge lightly with flour.

In a large frypan, heat the butter and oil over medium heat. Evenly brown the rolls, turning, for about 10 minutes. Remove chicken. Sauté the onion in frypan for 3 minutes. Add mushrooms and sauté 2 minutes longer. Season with salt and pepper. Sprinkle with the 1 tablespoon of flour, blending well. Stir in the brandy, broth and cream, small amounts at a time, stirring into a smooth, medium-thick sauce. Return the chicken "cigars" to the frypan, simmering, spooning sauce over and cook for 4 minutes. Arrange on a hot serving dish, sprinkled with parsley.

CHICKEN CURRY

Serves 6:

¾ cup of flour
2 tablespoons of Hungarian paprika
2 tablespoons of curry powder
⅛ teaspoon of dry mustard
1 teaspoon of salt
½ teaspoon of pepper

3 whole chicken breasts, halved, skinned and boned
5 tablespoons of butter
1 cup of heavy cream
1 cup of dry sherry
1½ cups of chicken broth
1 teaspoon of Worcestershire sauce

Combine flour, paprika, curry powder, mustard, salt and pepper in a bag. Add the chicken and shake well, evenly coating the breasts. In a large frypan, melt the butter over medium-low heat and evenly brown the chicken. Add the cream, sherry, broth and Worcestershire sauce. Cover and simmer, stirring occasionally, for 40 minutes, or until chicken is fork tender.

EASY FINNISH CURRIED CHICKEN AND ASPARAGUS

Serves 4:

2 large whole chicken breasts, skinned, boned and cut into 2-inch squares, ½-inch thick
Salt and pepper
Bell's poultry seasoning
4 tablespoons of butter
2 (10-ounce) packages of frozen asparagus spears, cooked in boiling salted water just until the spears separate

blended until smooth
1 (10-ounce) can of condensed cream of chicken soup
½ cup of light cream
1 teaspoon of curry powder

1 cup of grated Swiss cheese

Lightly sprinkle the chicken pieces with salt, pepper and poultry seasoning. In a frypan, over medium heat, melt the butter. Add the chicken pieces and cook until golden on both sides. Arrange the asparagus spears on the bottom of a buttered, 1½-quart shallow baking dish. Place the chicken squares on top of the asparagus. Spoon the chicken soup-curry powder mixture over the chicken. Sprinkle cheese over the top. Bake in a preheated 350°F. oven for 30 minutes, or until the chicken is tender and top is golden.

CRISP CHICKEN CUTLETS WITH MUSHROOM SAUCE

Serves 4:

2 whole chicken breasts, halved, skinned and boned
Flour for dredging
2 eggs, beaten with 2 tablespoons of milk

1½ cups of crushed shredded wheat
3 tablespoons of butter
1 tablespoon of olive oil
Salt and pepper to taste

Between sheets of waxed paper, with a mallet, pound breasts to a ½-inch thickness. Dredge with flour, dip in the egg-milk mixture, then dredge with the shredded wheat. In a frypan, heat the butter and oil over medium heat and evenly brown the cutlets, cooking for 5 minutes on each side, or until crispy and tender. Season with salt and pepper. Serve with the following Mushroom Sauce.

MUSHROOM SAUCE

2 tablespoons of butter	1 cup of milk
¼ cup of chopped onions	Salt and pepper to taste
1 cup of sliced mushrooms	½ cup of sour cream
1 tablespoon of flour —	

In a saucepan, melt butter and cook onion for 2 minutes. Add mushrooms and cook 2 minutes longer. Stir in the flour, then gradually blend in the milk, salt and pepper. Cook, stirring, until the mixture simmers. Remove from heat and blend in the sour cream. Heat to a simmer (do not boil) and spoon over the hot cutlets.

CHICKEN BREASTS WITH HAM AND CHEESE

Serves 6:

3 whole chicken breasts, halved, skinned and boned	smaller than the breasts after they have been browned
Flour for dredging	6 thin slices of Fontina (or Gruyère) cheese, cut the same as the ham slices
5 tablespoons of butter	
2 tablespoons of olive oil	
Pepper to taste	½ cup of dry vermouth
6 thin slices of prosciutto or other cooked ham, trimmed to a size slightly	¾ cup of chicken broth
	2 tablespoons of chopped parsley

Pound the chicken breasts between sheets of waxed paper with a mallet until about ¼-inch thick. Dredge breasts lightly with flour. In a large frypan, over medium heat, heat 3 tablespoons of the butter and the olive oil. Cook the breasts, 2 or 3 at a time (adding more butter, if needed) for 4 minutes on each side, or until golden brown and cooked through. Sprinkle lightly with pepper. Transfer to a shallow broiler-proof pan. Lay a slice of ham on each breast and top with a slice of cheese. Pour the vermouth and broth into the pan the breasts cooked in and simmer for 5 minutes. Place the breasts under the broiler until the cheese starts to melt.

Just before serving, stir the remaining 2 tablespoons of butter into vermouth-broth sauce, stirring until it has melted. Spoon the sauce over the breasts and sprinkle with parsley.

CHICKEN BREASTS WITH HERBED BUTTER AND VERMOUTH

Serves 6:

blended into herb-butter
- ½ teaspoon of dried leaf sage, crumbled
- ¼ teaspoon of dried rosemary
- 1 clove of garlic, minced
- 6 tablespoons of butter

- 3 whole chicken breasts, halved, skinned and boned
- Salt and pepper to taste
- ⅔ cup of chicken broth
- ⅔ cup of dry vermouth
- 2 tablespoons of chopped parsley

Using two-thirds of the herb butter, coat the chicken breasts (using your hands is the easiest way). Season with salt and pepper. In a large frypan, arrange the breasts and pour ⅓ cup of the broth and ⅓ cup of the vermouth around them. Cover and cook over medium heat for 15 minutes, or until the liquid has cooked off and the breasts are golden. Turn and cook until the other side is golden. Pour in the remaining vermouth and broth and, uncovered, cook until the liquid has reduced by half and breasts are tender. Transfer breasts to a heated serving dish. Add remaining herb butter and parsley to frypan. Heat, stirring, until the butter has melted. Taste for seasoning. Spoon over the hot chicken breasts.

CHICKEN KABOBS

Serves 4: These are excellent served with couscous, which has been cooked in chicken broth, and a crisp green salad, tossed with olive oil and lemon juice.

2 pounds of chicken breasts, skinned, boned and cut into 24 cubes
¼ cup of olive oil
2 tablespoons of grated shallots
3 tablespoons of fresh lemon juice

2 cloves of garlic, minced
½ teaspoon of ground ginger
¼ teaspoon of ground cumin
⅛ teaspoon of cayenne
1 teaspoon of salt
½ teaspoon of pepper

In a large bowl, combine all the ingredients, blending well. Let marinate for 1 hour. Using skewers, place 6 pieces of chicken on each. Preheat broiler. Broil the kabobs, 5 inches from the heat, turning several times so they brown evenly. Do not overcook; 7 minutes should do it.

CHICKEN LEMONAISE

Serves 6:

3 whole chicken breasts, halved, skinned and boned
¾ cup of mayonnaise
Bread crumbs for dredging
5 tablespoons of butter
1 tablespoon of olive oil
Salt and pepper to taste

2 medium-sized onions, chopped
3 tablespoons of flour
1½ cups of chicken broth
4 tablespoons of fresh lemon juice
2 tablespoons of minced parsley

Coat the breasts with ½ cup of the mayonnaise and dredge with the bread crumbs. In a large saucepan, over medium heat, heat 3 tablespoons of the butter and the oil. Add chicken, brown evenly, sautéing until fork tender. Season with salt and pepper. Remove chicken and keep warm. Add the remaining 2 tablespoons butter to the saucepan and sauté the onion for 3 minutes. Stir in the flour, blending well. Gradually add the broth. Simmer, stirring, until the sauce is smooth and well blended. Stir in the lemon juice, the remaining ½ cup mayonnaise and parsley. Simmer until sauce is hot (do not boil). Taste for seasoning. Spoon the sauce over chicken breasts.

CHICKEN BREASTS IN LEMON SAUCE

Serves 6:

3 whole chicken breasts, halved, skinned and boned
Salt and pepper to taste
Flour for dredging
2 tablespoons of olive oil

4 tablespoons of butter
2 shallots, minced
4 tablespoons of lemon juice
3 tablespoons of minced parsley

Pound breasts between sheets of waxed paper with a mallet until ½-inch thick. Season with salt and pepper and lightly dredge with flour. Over medium heat, heat the oil and 2 tablespoons of the butter in a large frypan. Add the shallots and cook for 1 minute. Add the breasts, sauté on both sides until golden and tender (about 7 minutes on each side). Transfer to a heated serving dish and keep warm. Add the remaining 2 tablespoons butter to the frypan. When melted, stir in the lemon juice and parsley. Spoon over the chicken breasts just before serving.

CHICKEN BREASTS WITH LIVER PÂTÉ-CREAM SAUCE

Serves 6:

3 cups of chicken broth
3 whole chicken breasts, halved
1 onion, quartered
7 tablespoons of butter
Salt and pepper to taste

2 cups of heavy cream
2 ounces of Madeira
1 (4¾-ounce) can of liver pâté
1 pound of very fine noodles

Pour the broth into a saucepan. Add the chicken breasts and onion, cover and cook for 20 minutes, or until tender. Drain, then skin and bone the breasts. Over medium heat in a frypan, melt 3 tablespoons of the butter and lightly brown the breasts. Season with salt and pepper. Remove and keep warm. Pour the fat from the pan, pour in the cream and wine and simmer, stirring and scraping the bottom of the pan, for about 3 minutes. Break up the pâté and add it to the pan. Simmer, stirring, until pâté and cream are well blended and the sauce smooth. Taste for seasoning. Return the breasts to the pan with the sauce and keep warm.

Cook the noodles in boiling salted water until *al dente.* Drain well and mix with the remaining 4 tablespoons of butter. Arrange the noodles on a heated serving dish. Arrange the breasts on the noodles and spoon the pâté sauce over them.

SCALOPPINE ALLA MARSALA

Serves 4:

2 whole chicken breasts, halved, skinned and boned
1 teaspoon of salt
½ teaspoon of pepper
Flour for dredging
2 eggs, beaten

Bread crumbs for dredging
3 tablespoons of butter
1 tablespoon of olive oil
½ cup of Marsala
2 tablespoons of fresh lemon juice

Sprinkle the chicken with salt and pepper. Dredge lightly with flour, dip into the beaten eggs, then dredge with the bread crumbs, pressing them on firmly. Refrigerate for 1 hour. In a large frypan, heat butter and oil over medium heat and evenly brown the chicken, turning several times. Remove breasts. Stir in the wine, scraping up the browned particles. Cook for 2 minutes, stirring. Add the breasts. Cook 3 minutes on each side. Dribble lemon juice over them and turn up heat for 1 minute. Serve immediately on heated plates. Parsleyed, buttered noodles are an excellent accompaniment.

CHICKEN BREASTS OREGANO

Serves 4:

4 tablespoons of butter
1 tablespoon of olive oil
4 whole small chicken
   breasts, halved (do not
   bone or skin)
1½ teaspoons of salt

½ teaspoon of pepper
1 tablespoon of dried oregano
3 cloves of garlic
2 tablespoons of dry white
   vermouth

In a large frypan over medium heat, heat the butter and oil. Sprinkle the breasts with salt and pepper and brown evenly, turning several times. Lower the heat and sprinkle the breasts with the oregano. Add the garlic and vermouth, cover, and cook for 30 minutes (turning once or twice), or until the breasts are fork tender.

PROVOLONE-BAKED CHICKEN BREASTS

Serves 4:

2 whole, large chicken
   breasts, each halved and
   skinned (do not bone)
4 (1½-inch by 1½-inch by
   ½-inch) pieces of provolone cheese
1 large egg, beaten

blended
   1 cup of bread crumbs
   1 teaspoon of salt
   ½ teaspoon of pepper
   2 tablespoons of chopped
      fresh chives
   1 tablespoon of Hun-
      garian paprika

4 tablespoons of melted
   butter

Cut a 2-inch incision in the thickest portion of the breasts and bury the cheese in it. Dip the chicken breasts in the beaten egg, then dredge well with the bread crumb mixture. Place in a baking dish in one layer. Dribble half of the butter over the breasts and bake, uncovered, in a preheated 375°F. oven for 20 minutes. Dribble the remaining butter over the breasts and cook 20 minutes longer, or until fork tender.

DUTCH CHICKEN ROLLS

Serves 4:

2 whole chicken breasts, halved, skinned, boned and cut into halves, crosswise
Salt and pepper
8 pieces of Edam or Gouda cheese, cut into 1-inch strips, ½-inch thick and ½-inch wide
Flour for dredging
2 eggs, lightly beaten
Fine bread crumbs for dredging
Vegetable oil for deep frying

Between sheets of waxed paper, with a mallet, pound the chicken pieces to a ¼-inch thickness, being careful not to tear the flesh. Season lightly with salt and pepper. Place a strip of cheese in the center of each. Fold edges over the cheese and roll, envelope fashion, to completely encase the cheese, more or less forming a cylinder. Fasten with a skewer or toothpick. Dredge in flour, dip into the egg, then dredge with crumbs. Allow the chicken rolls to dry for several minutes, then fry in hot oil (325°F.) for about 10 minutes, or until golden brown. Remove skewers or toothpicks before serving.

CHICKEN BREAST ROULADE FRANÇAIS

Serves 6:

3 large whole chicken breasts, halved, skinned, boned and each cut into halves, crosswise
Salt and pepper
12 small, thin slices of ham
12 small chicken livers
Flour for dredging
3 tablespoons of butter
1 tablespoon of cooking oil
6 scallions, cut into ½-inch pieces (use some of the green tails)
1 rib of celery, scraped and coarsely chopped
½ cup of dry white wine
1 cup of chicken broth
½ pound of small mushrooms, cooked in 2 tablespoons of butter until brown but still very firm
2 tablespoons of chopped parsley

Between sheets of waxed paper, pound the chicken breasts with a mallet until thin, but do not break the flesh. Pepper and very lightly salt them. Place a slice of ham on each flattened piece and top with a chicken liver. Roll and tie with cord. Dredge lightly with flour. In a frypan, over medium heat, heat the butter and oil and evenly brown the rolls. Transfer to a casserole that will hold them in a single layer. Add scallions and celery to the frypan and cook for 2 minutes, or until just crisp-tender. Transfer to the casserole with the chicken rolls. Pour the wine and broth into the frypan. Heat to a boil, stirring and scraping the bottom of the pan. Pour into the casserole over the rolls and vegetables. Cover and bake in a preheated 350°F. oven for 30 minutes, or until chicken is tender. Remove cords. Transfer the rolls to a heated serving dish and keep warm. If the liquid in the casserole has not thickened, simmer a minute or two on top of the stove. Mix in the mushrooms and simmer just until the mushrooms are heated through. Taste for seasoning. Spoon sauce and vegetables over the rolls. Sprinkle with parsley.

BAKED CHICKEN SCALOPPINE WITH ARTICHOKE HEARTS

Serves 6:

3 whole chicken breasts, halved, skinned and boned
1 egg, beaten
¾ cup flour, seasoned with 1½ teaspoons salt and ½ teaspoon of pepper
3 tablespoons of butter
2 tablespoons of olive oil
½ cup of chicken broth

2 (9-ounce) packages of frozen artichoke hearts, cooked according to directions, drained, sautéed in 3 tablespoons of butter and seasoned with salt and pepper
½ cup of grated Asiago or Parmesan cheese

Pound breasts between sheets of waxed paper with a mallet to a ½-inch thickness. Dip into the beaten egg, then dredge in the seasoned flour. Over medium heat, in a large frypan, heat the butter and oil. Add the chicken, browning evenly, cooking for 15 minutes, or until almost tender. Arrange them in a shallow baking dish. Drain the oil from the frypan, add the broth and simmer for 1 minute, stirring and scraping the bottom of the pan. Pour this over the chicken breasts. Arrange the artichoke hearts over the breasts, sprinkle with the cheese and bake in a preheated 400°F. oven for 10 minutes, or until the top is golden.

SCALOPPINE OF CHICKEN BREAST WITH CHICKEN LIVERS

Serves 6:

3 whole chicken breasts, halved, skinned and boned
Salt and pepper
Flour for dredging
3 tablespoons of butter
1 tablespoon of olive oil

½ pound of chicken livers, cut into ½-inch cubes
1 ripe tomato, peeled, seeded and chopped
¼ teaspoon of oregano

Pound the chicken breasts between sheets of waxed paper with a mallet until ½-inch thick (they should not be too thin). Season with salt and pepper, then dredge with flour. In a large frypan, over medium-low heat, heat the butter and oil and cook the breasts until golden on both sides and almost tender (about 7 minutes on each side). Dredge the chicken livers lightly with flour. Raise the heat to high, add the livers and cook for 3 minutes, stirring. Add the tomato and oregano and simmer for 5 minutes, or until the breasts are tender. Taste for seasoning. Serve with the chicken liver sauce spooned over the breasts.

CHICKEN SCALLOPS WITH EGGPLANT

Serves 4:

Salt and pepper
3 small eggplants, peeled
    and cut into ½-inch slices
Flour for dredging
2 whole chicken breasts,
    halved, skinned, boned
    and each half cut in half,
    crosswise

3 tablespoons of butter
3 tablespoons of olive oil
8 slices of mozzarella cheese
¼ cup of grated Asiago or
    Parmesan cheese

Salt the slices of eggplant and let them set for 1 hour. Rinse off the salt and dry with paper towels. Flour them lightly. Pound chicken pieces between sheets of waxed paper with a mallet until ½-inch thick. In one frypan, over medium heat, heat the butter and sauté the chicken until tender and golden on both sides (about 5 or 6 minutes on each side), seasoning with salt and pepper.

In another frypan, over medium heat, heat the oil and brown the eggplant on both sides, seasoning with salt and pepper (add more oil, if needed). Remove and drain on paper towels.

In a shallow baking dish large enough to hold the chicken in one layer, arrange the scallops. Place 2 or 3 slices of eggplant overlapping on each scallop, then a slice of mozzarella, then sprinkle with the grated cheese. Place in a preheated 450°F. oven for 10 minutes, or until the cheese has melted and is bubbling and slightly golden.

CHICKEN BREASTS AND SPINACH MORNAY

Serves 4:

2 (10-ounce) packages of fresh spinach or 2 (10-ounce) packages of chopped spinach, defrosted but not cooked
7 tablespoons of butter
2 tablespoons of minced shallots
1 clove of garlic, minced
Pinch of nutmeg
Salt and pepper to taste
1 tablespoon of olive oil

2 whole chicken breasts, halved and boned
2 tablespoons of flour
1 cup of light cream
2 tablespoons of lemon juice
1 egg yolk, beaten with ¼ cup of heavy cream
3 tablespoons of grated Gruyère cheese
3 tablespoons of grated Parmesan cheese

In a large pot, bring 4 quarts of water to a boil. Add the fresh spinach, pushing it down into the water, and bring the water to a boil. Cook 1 minute, pushing the spinach down into the water as it comes to the top. Lift the spinach from the pot with a large fork, drain well and chop. In a frypan, over medium heat, melt 3 tablespoons of the butter. Add shallots and garlic and cook until soft (do not brown). Stir in the spinach, nutmeg, salt and pepper. Leave on the heat just until you have mixed it well. Set aside and keep warm.

In a clean frypan, over medium heat, heat the oil and 2 tablespoons of the butter. Cook the chicken breasts for 7 minutes on each side, or until tender. Remove and discard skins. Salt and pepper the breasts and cut them into ¼-inch slices.

Arrange the spinach in a shallow baking dish, and top with the slices of chicken. Keep warm.

In a saucepan, over medium heat, melt the remaining 2 tablespoons of butter. Stir in the flour and cook, stirring constantly, into a smooth paste. Gradually stir in the light cream, cooking until sauce is smooth and medium-thick. Stir in the lemon juice. Remove from the heat and stir in the egg yolk-heavy cream mixture. Turn heat to low; stir in the Gruyère cheese and cook, stirring, until cheese has melted (do not boil). Season with salt and pepper. Spoon the sauce over the chicken in the baking dish. Sprinkle with the Parmesan and bake in a preheated 400°F. oven for 15 minutes, or until heated through, bubbling and golden on top.

STUFFED CHICKEN BREASTS WITH PEAS

Serves 6:

3 large, whole chicken breasts, halved, skinned and boned (cut each half through the center so they keep their shape but are one-half the original thickness)

1 cup of ground cooked meat (leftover lamb, veal or beef), or use fresh ground meat, cooked until the pinkness has disappeared

3 slices of good bologna

1 egg

¼ cup of bread crumbs

¼ cup of grated cheese (Asiago, Parmesan or Romano)

Pinch of cinnamon

Salt and pepper to taste

¼ cup cream (approximate)

3 tablespoons of butter

1 tablespoon of olive oil

Flour for dredging

2 large, ripe tomatoes, peeled and put through food mill, or use 1 (1-pound) can of tomatoes, drained

1 cup of chicken broth

1 (10-ounce) package of frozen "tiny peas," defrosted

Between sheets of waxed paper, pound chicken breasts with a mallet to flatten them, being careful not to tear the flesh. Put the ground meat and bologna through a meat grinder twice, or use a food processor to mince it. Combine the minced meat, egg, bread crumbs, cheese, cinnamon, salt and pepper in a bowl and mix well. Add enough cream to make a fairly moist but not runny mixture.

Place equal amounts (about 2 tablespoons) of the minced meat mixture on the center of each of the scallops. Roll tightly and tie with cord to keep stuffing intact.

In a frypan large enough to hold the rolls in one layer (use two if necessary), heat the butter and oil over medium-high heat. Lightly dredge the rolls with flour and quickly brown them. Season with salt and pepper. Add the tomatoes and broth, stirring well. Bring to a boil. Lower heat, cover and simmer for 30 minutes, or until the breasts are tender, stirring in the peas during the last 5 minutes of cooking. Remove cords.

CHICKEN BREASTS STUFFED WITH
PROSCIUTTO HAM AND MOZZARELLA CHEESE

Serves 6:

3 large whole chicken
   breasts, halved, skinned
   and boned
12 thin slices of prosciutto,
   cut slightly smaller than
   the chicken breasts
6 ¼-inch-thick slices of
   mozzarella, same size as
   ham
Salt and pepper to taste

Flour for dredging
3 tablespoons of butter
2 tablespoons of olive oil
1 large clove of garlic,
   crushed
½ cup of dry white wine
4 tablespoons (2 ounces) of
   Marsala
⅛ teaspoon of rosemary

Pound the breasts between sheets of waxed paper to a ¼-inch
thickness, being careful not to tear the flesh. Put 2 slices of
prosciutto on one-half of each breast and top with a slice of
cheese. Fold the chicken breast over to enclose ham and
cheese. Pinch the edges closed, using toothpicks to hold it
closed, if necessary. Season with salt and pepper, keeping in
mind that the ham and cheese are salty. Dredge with flour. In
a large frypan heat the butter and oil. Add the garlic and
stuffed breasts. Do not crowd; cook in two batches or use two
pans. Sauté the breasts on both sides until golden brown,
about 10 minutes, adding more butter as needed. If garlic
gets too brown, discard it. Pour in the wines. Add rosemary,
cover and cook over low heat 15 minutes, or until tender. Remove toothpicks, if used. Serve with some of the sauce
spooned over each breast.

CHICKEN TOSCANA

Serves 4:

2 whole chicken breasts,
   halved, skinned and
   boned
Salt and pepper to taste
Flour for dredging
3 tablespoons of butter
1 tablespoon of olive oil

⅓ cup of tomato sauce
⅓ cup of chicken broth

blended
   ½ cup of minced Genoa
     salami
   ½ cup of grated provo-
     lone cheese

Season the breasts with salt and pepper. Dredge with flour. In a top-of-the-stove casserole, heat the butter and oil over medium heat. Evenly brown the breasts. Remove chicken and keep warm. Lower heat and pour the tomato sauce and broth into the casserole, blending well. Return the chicken breasts to the casserole. Cover them with the salami-cheese mixture. Place casserole in a preheated 350°F. oven for 20 minutes, or until the cheese melts and the chicken is fork tender. Serve the breasts with the sauce lightly spooned on top. Milanese rice is an excellent accompaniment.

COLD CHICKEN BREASTS WITH TUNA SAUCE

Serves 6:

4 large whole chicken
   breasts
1 onion, quartered
1 carrot, sliced
1 rib of celery, sliced
1 small bay leaf
½ teaspoon of dried thyme

2 cups of white wine
2 cups of chicken broth
½ rind *each* of orange and
   lemon
1 teaspoon of salt
½ teaspoon of pepper

In a large saucepan, combine all ingredients. Cover and simmer for 45 minutes, or until the chicken is tender (do not overcook). Cool the chicken in the liquid. Make the Tuna Sauce. Then remove the skin and bones from the chicken and slice the meat lengthwise into ⅜- or ½-inch-thick slices. Coat the bottom of a shallow serving dish with some of the tuna sauce. Arrange the chicken slices, slightly overlapping. Coat the slices with tuna sauce. Cover with foil and refrigerate overnight. Before serving, garnish with capers, cornichons, parsley, hard-cooked eggs, or whatever you might find attractive.

TUNA SAUCE

1 cup of good mayonnaise (yours or a commercial one)
1 (3½-ounce) can of tuna, drained

3 anchovy fillets, drained
2 tablespoons of lemon juice
½ cup of the liquid that the chicken poached in, strained

In a blender container, combine the mayonnaise, tuna, anchovy fillets, lemon juice and 3 tablespoons of the poaching liquid. Blend for 30 seconds into a smooth puree. If necessary, add more of the liquid to make a sauce the consistency of medium heavy cream.

EASY CHICKEN CUTLETS VIENNESE

Serves 6:

3 whole chicken breasts, halved, skinned and boned
Salt and pepper
¼ teaspoon of dried thyme
½ teaspoon of garlic powder

2 eggs, beaten with ½ cup of heavy cream
Fine dry bread crumbs for dredging
4 tablespoons of butter

Pound the chicken breasts between sheets of waxed paper with a mallet to a ½-inch thickness. Sprinkle with salt, pepper, thyme and garlic powder. Dip into the egg-cream mixture, then dredge with bread crumbs. In a large frypan over medium-high heat heat the butter. Add the breasts (2 or 3 at a time) and brown on both sides. Cover and cook at slightly lower heat for about 8 minutes (turning once), or until tender. Add more butter, if needed. Keep those that are cooked warm in a low oven until all are cooked.

WILLIAM BAUSERMAN'S WALNUT-ORANGE CHICKEN

Serves 4:

2 tablespoons of butter
½ teaspoon of olive oil
2 whole chicken breasts, halved, skinned and boned
½ (6-ounce) can of frozen orange juice concentrate, thawed
½ teaspoon of Bell's poultry seasoning

¾ teaspoon of salt
¼ cup of water
1 tablespoon of cornstarch, blended with 2 tablespoons water
½ cup of chopped English walnuts
⅓ cup of chopped tender, small scallions

In a frypan, over medium heat, heat the butter and oil and evenly brown the chicken. Stir in the orange juice, poultry seasoning, salt and water. Reduce heat to low, cover the pan and cook the chicken for 30 minutes or until fork tender, basting occasionally with the liquid. Transfer the chicken to a heated serving dish. Keep warm. Over low heat, gradually add the cornstarch mixture, stirring until the sauce is smooth and thickened. Stir in the walnuts and scallions. Pour sauce over the chicken.

Chapter Eight

Casseroles (Meals-in-one)

America is casserole country. Casseroles, generally speaking, are those superb dishes that one can put into the oven, close the door and forget about while conversations and guests are enjoyed.

Casseroles are also those dishes that can be prepared in advance, either refrigerated or frozen and then cooked when one returns from work.

They can be imaginative dishes that combine several ingredients—producing dinners that even master chefs would be proud to serve. In fact, master chefs conceived casseroles. The word is French, meaning food cooked in a covered dish of glass or pottery.

Chicken and casserole cookery are boon companions. They go together like ham and eggs and pork and beans. Better, because chicken successfully combines with more varieties of food than any other meat.

And that is what casseroles are all about. They are a food combination that comprises a complete dinner—if the main ingredient is chicken.

CHICKEN AND ARTICHOKES WITH PROVOLONE CHEESE SAUCE

Serves 4:

1 (9-ounce) package of frozen artichokes, thawed and halved
Salt and pepper
4 cups of bite-sized pieces of cooked chicken
5 tablespoons of butter
3 tablespoons of flour

2 cups of chicken broth
1 cup of grated provolone cheese
⅛ teaspoon of savory
⅛ teaspoon of tarragon
⅛ teaspoon of cayenne
¼ cup of bread crumbs

In a casserole, arrange the artichokes in one layer, then sprinkle lightly with salt and pepper. Arrange the chicken in one layer over the artichokes, sprinkling lightly with salt and pepper. In a saucepan, over medium heat, melt 3 tablespoons of the butter and blend in the flour, stirring into a smooth paste. Lower the heat and gradually add the broth, stirring until the sauce is smooth and medium-thick. Add the cheese, savory, tarragon and cayenne, stirring until the cheese has melted. Pour the cheese sauce over the chicken and artichokes, sprinkle with the bread crumbs and dot with the remaining 2 tablespoons of butter. Bake, uncovered, in a preheated 350°F. oven for 20 minutes, or until bubbling and brown.

FAST CHICKEN AND BISCUITS CASSEROLE*

Serves 4 to 6:

3 tablespoons of butter
3 tablespoons of flour
½ teaspoon of celery salt
1 (10½-ounce) can condensed cream of chicken soup
1 (11-ounce) can of condensed cheddar cheese soup

2 cups of light cream
4 cups of cubed cooked chicken
2 (10-ounce) packages of frozen peas and carrots, defrosted enough to separate
Commercial biscuit mix

* Especially Inexpensive

In a saucepan, melt the butter over medium heat, then blend in the flour and celery salt. Stir in the soups and cream. Cook, stirring, for 8 minutes, or until thick and bubbling. Taste for seasoning. Remove from heat and stir in the chicken and partially thawed vegetables. Turn into a casserole. Bake, covered, in a preheated 400°F. oven for 20 minutes. Uncover, surround with drops of biscuit dough, prepared and dropped according to package directions, and bake for 15 minutes longer.

QUICK CASSOULET OF CORNISH GAME HENS

Serves 4:

3 tablespoons of butter
2 tablespoons of olive oil
½ pound of sweet Italian sausage, cut into ½-inch pieces
2 (1½- to 2-pound) Cornish game hens, split in half
1½ teaspoons of salt
½ teaspoon of pepper
½ teaspoon of garlic powder
4 medium-sized onions, chopped

3 tart apples, peeled, cored and sliced
1 small red pepper, cored, seeded and cut in rings
1 small green pepper, cored, seeded and cut in rings
1 (1-pound 4-ounce) can of white kidney beans (cannellini)
¼ teaspoon of Tabasco
1 teaspoon of Worcestershire sauce

In a large deep frypan, over medium heat, heat the butter and oil and brown the sausages evenly. Remove sausages. Sprinkle game hens with salt, pepper and garlic powder. Brown evenly in the frypan in which the sausages were cooked. Remove game hens. Pour off all but 3 tablespoons of fat and add onion. Cook for 4 minutes. Add apples and peppers, cooking for 5 minutes. Stir in the beans, sausage, Tabasco and Worcestershire and simmer for 2 minutes, blending well. Taste for seasoning. Spoon this bean mixture into four individual casseroles. Place split game hens on top. Cover. Bake in preheated 350°F. oven for 45 minutes, or until game hens are fork tender.

CHEDDAR CHICKEN

Serves 4:

6 large chicken thighs
3 cups of chicken broth
5 scallions (including the green tails), cut in pieces
1 teaspoon of salt
1 cup of *fusilli* (pasta twists), cooked *al dente* and drained
1 cup of shredded sharp Cheddar cheese

⅓ cup of pine nuts
1 (10½-ounce) can of condensed onion soup, blended with 1 cup of the broth the chicken cooked in
⅓ cup of bread crumbs, blended with 1 tablespoon of melted butter

In a large saucepan, combine chicken, broth, scallions and salt. Cover and simmer for 30 minutes, or until chicken is fork tender. Cool slightly, remove and discard skin and bones, then break the chicken meat into chunks just larger than bite-size. Butter a 2½-quart casserole and evenly cover the bottom with the cooked *fusilli*. Sprinkle the cheese over the pasta. Arrange the chicken chunks on top, sprinkle on the pine nuts and pour over the mixture of onion soup and broth. Sprinkle on the buttered bread crumbs and bake, uncovered, in a preheated 375°F. oven for 15 minutes, or until bubbly-brown.

CREOLE CHICKEN

Serves 4:

2 tablespoons of bacon fat
2 tablespoons of butter
1 (3½- to 4-pound) chicken, cut up
Salt and pepper to taste
1 medium-sized onion, minced
1 clove of garlic, minced
1 small green pepper cored, seeded and chopped

4 large ripe tomatoes, peeled, seeded and chopped, or 4 cups of drained canned tomatoes, chopped
2 cups of sliced fresh okra, or 1 package frozen, defrosted and sliced
1 cup of chicken broth
3 tablespoons of chopped broadleaf parsley

In a large frypan, over medium heat, heat the bacon fat and butter. Add the chicken, browning evenly, and seasoning with salt and pepper. Transfer to a casserole. In the same frypan cook the onion, garlic and pepper for 5 minutes. Add the tomatoes and simmer for 10 minutes. Add the okra and the vegetables from the frypan to the chicken casserole, then pour in the broth. Bake, covered, in a preheated 350°F. oven for 25 minutes, then bake, uncovered, until the sauce has thickened and chicken is fork tender. Taste for seasoning. Sprinkle with parsley and serve from the casserole over rice.

CHICKEN DIVAN SUPREME

Serves 6:

1 large bunch (about 1½ pounds) of broccoli, or 3 packages of frozen
2 cups of medium-thick white sauce
¼ teaspoon of nutmeg
½ cup of hollandaise sauce (see "Quick Hollandaise" page 408)
½ cup of whipped cream
3 tablespoons of sherry

1 teaspoon of Worcestershire sauce
1 (5-pound) chicken, poached in water to cover, with 1 onion stuck with a whole clove, 1 carrot, 1 celery rib, salt, pepper and ¼ teaspoon of dried thyme, until tender
1½ cups of grated Parmesan cheese

If fresh broccoli is used, separate the spears and cook in salted water until tender-crisp (if frozen, cook according to package directions, but slightly less than directed).

Prepare the white sauce, then blend in the nutmeg, hollandaise, cream, sherry and Worcestershire sauce. Set aside.

Arrange the cooked broccoli on the bottom of a deep ovenproof serving dish. Sprinkle with ¾ cup of the cheese.

Remove skin from the chicken; take meat from the bones in large pieces, and cut into thick slices. Arrange the slices on the cheese-sprinkled broccoli.

Pour the sauce evenly over the sliced chicken and sprinkle with the remaining cheese. Bake in a preheated 400°F. oven for 20 minutes, or until heated through, then run under the broiler until golden.

CHICKEN AND EGGPLANT

Serves 4:

1 (3½-pound) chicken, cut up
Salt and pepper
3 tablespoons of butter
5 tablespoons of olive oil
2 medium-sized eggplants, peeled and cut into ½-inch dice
½ cup of flour

4 medium-sized onions, chopped
2 cloves of garlic, chopped
⅛ teaspoon of dried rosemary
2 cups of chicken broth
4 pitted black olives, sliced
4 pitted green olives, sliced

Rub the chicken with salt and pepper. In a large frypan, over medium heat, heat the butter and 1 tablespoon of the oil and evenly brown the chicken. Transfer the chicken to a casserole large enough to hold it in one layer. Sprinkle salt and pepper on the eggplant and dredge with flour (reserve any leftover flour). In another frypan, over medium heat, heat the remaining 4 tablespoons of oil and brown the eggplant. Remove with a slotted spoon. In the same frypan, stir in the onions and garlic and cook for 3 minutes over medium heat, stirring. Blend in 2 tablespoons of the reserved flour. Add the rosemary and broth, blending well. Bring to a simmer, stirring constantly. Stir in the eggplant and the olives and pour sauce over the chicken in the casserole. Bake, covered, in a preheated 375°F. oven for 15 minutes. Remove cover and bake for 20 minutes longer, or until chicken is fork tender.

FETTUCCINE WITH CHICKEN

Serves 4:

8 tablespoons of butter
3 cups of cooked chicken, in ¾-inch dice
2 medium-sized carrots, peeled and cut into ½-inch dice
½ cup of cooked fresh peas
8 medium-sized mushrooms, sliced
½ teaspoon of salt

1 pound of fettuccine noodles, cooked *al dente* and drained
1 teaspoon of pepper
1½ cups of heavy cream

blended
⅓ cup of grated Asiago or Parmesan cheese
⅓ cup of grated Romano cheese

Butter a casserole with 1 tablespoon of the butter. In a frypan, over medium heat, melt 3 tablespoons of butter and sauté the chicken and carrots for 5 minutes. Stir in the peas, mushrooms and salt and sauté 3 minutes longer, gently stirring.

Toss the cooked fettuccine with 2 tablespoons of butter, sprinkle with pepper and toss again. Combine the chicken mixture with the noodles. Taste for seasoning. Arrange the chicken and noodles in the buttered casserole. Pour over the cream. Sprinkle with the cheese and dot with the remaining 2 tablespoons of butter. Bake in a preheated 375°F. oven for 15 minutes, or until bubbling and brown.

CHICKEN FRESNO

Serves 4:

Juice of 2 fresh limes
1 (3½-pound) chicken, cut
up

blended
1 teaspoon of salt
½ teaspoon of pepper
1 teaspoon of Hungarian
paprika
3 tablespoons of butter
1 tablespoon of olive oil

12 pitted black California
olives
2 medium-sized onions,
chopped
2 small green sweet peppers,
cored, seeded and sliced
2 small red sweet peppers,
cored, seeded and sliced
1½ cups of fresh orange
juice

Pour the lime juice over the chicken and marinate for 1 hour, turning once or twice during that time. Drain the chicken and sprinkle the salt-pepper-paprika blend over it. In a frypan, over medium heat, heat the butter and oil and evenly brown the chicken. Arrange the chicken in a casserole. Add the olives, onion, peppers and orange juice. Cover and bake in a preheated 350°F. oven for 40 minutes, or until the chicken is fork tender. Taste for seasoning.

CHICKEN FLORENTINE WITH RICE

Serves 6:

1 (5-pound) chicken, poached until tender in water to cover with 1 onion stuck with a whole clove, 1 carrot, 1 rib celery, salt and pepper. Remove the chicken and reduce liquid to one-half of its volume (this can be done the day before)

2 (10-ounce) packages of fresh spinach, tough stems cut off, or 2 (10-ounce) packages of frozen whole leaf-spinach, defrosted, but not cooked

6 tablespoons of butter

1 small onion, minced

Salt and pepper to taste

Pinch of cinnamon

4 tablespoons of flour

3 cups of strained broth (from poaching the chicken)

2 egg yolks, whisked with ½ cup of heavy cream

Juice of ½ lemon (at least 2 tablespoons)

1 cup of rice, cooked in 2½ cups of chicken broth (if you have used all of the broth you cooked the chicken in, use canned broth or bouillon cubes dissolved in hot water)

Remove the skin and bones from the chicken and discard. Cut the chicken meat into large pieces. Bring 3 quarts of water to a boil. Add the fresh spinach, pushing it into the water with a wooden spoon. Bring the water to a boil and cook spinach for 1 minute, pushing it down if it rises above the water. Remove with a large kitchen fork and drain well. In a saucepan, melt 2 tablespoons of the butter, add the onion and cook until soft. Stir in the spinach, sprinkle with salt and pepper and cinnamon.

In another saucepan, over medium heat, melt the remaining 4 tablespoons of butter. Stir in the flour and cook, stirring, into a smooth paste. Gradually stir in the broth and cook, stirring, to make a medium-thick sauce. Season with salt and pepper. Remove from heat. Stir ½ cup of the sauce into the egg yolk-cream mixture. Off heat stir this back into the sauce in the saucepan together with the lemon juice and cook over low heat, stirring, until sauce is smooth and thick (do not boil).

Make a layer of all the rice on the bottom of a buttered, baking dish. Arrange the spinach over it and top with the chicken pieces. Spoon the sauce over the chicken. Bake in a preheated 350°F. oven for 20 minutes, or until heated through, then place under the broiler until golden.

GEORGE HERZ'S CHICKEN AND GREEN NOODLE CASSEROLE

Serves 6:

1 (10-ounce) package of frozen asparagus spears, cooked according to package directions, but cooked only half of the time specified

1 pound of green noodles, cooked *al dente* and drained

1 cup of grated Asiago or Parmesan cheese (reserve ¼ cup for topping)

3 cups of sliced cooked chicken

6 large mushrooms, sliced and cooked for 2 minutes in butter

Salt and pepper to taste

blended (reserve ⅔ cup for top)

1 (10½-ounce) can of condensed cream of chicken soup

1 (10½-ounce) can of condensed cream of celery soup

1 cup of milk

1 tablespoon of butter

In a large casserole, arrange the asparagus in a single layer. Cover with a layer of noodles and sprinkle with cheese. Arrange a layer of chicken slices on this, then a layer of mushroom slices. Season lightly with salt and pepper. Spoon part of the soup mixture over, just covering the mushrooms. Repeat layers of noodles, chicken and mushrooms, sprinkling each lightly with cheese, salt and pepper, and covering with the soup mixture. Spoon the ⅔ cup of soup mixture over the top. Sprinkle with the ¼ cup of cheese and any other cheese that might be left. Dot with butter and bake, uncovered, in a preheated 350°F. oven for 40 minutes, or until bubbling and brown.

CHICKEN HASH WITH POACHED EGGS*

Serves 4:

3 cups of finely diced
   cooked chicken meat
3 cups of finely diced
   cooked potatoes
3 tablespoons of finely
   chopped red bell pepper
3 onions, finely chopped

2 small ribs of celery,
   finely chopped
1 teaspoon of salt
½ teaspoon of pepper
1 cup of chicken broth
4 eggs, poached
1 tablespoon of chives

In a bowl, combine the chicken, potatoes, red pepper, onion, celery, salt and pepper and chicken broth. Blend well. Taste for seasoning. Butter a casserole of sufficient size and evenly spoon in the hash. Cook, covered, in a preheated 375°F. oven for 20 minutes. Remove cover and cook another 20 minutes, or until the top is crusty brown. Arrange the poached eggs on the hash and serve with the chives sprinkled over the eggs.

* Especially Inexpensive

ANTOINE GILLY'S CHICKEN HOTPOT

Serves 4:

1 (4-pound) chicken, cut
   into 8 pieces
1½ teaspoons of salt
½ teaspoon of pepper
Flour for dredging
3 tablespoons of butter
1 tablespoon of olive oil

4 cloves of garlic
4 medium-sized onions,
   sliced
1 cup of dry white wine
½ cup of cooked peas
½ cup of diced cooked carrots

Season chicken with salt and pepper and dredge lightly with flour. In frypan, over medium heat, heat the butter and oil and brown the chicken pieces evenly. Add the garlic, onion and white wine. Cover and simmer for 10 minutes. Remove from the stove top, place in a casserole, cover, and bake in a preheated 350°F. oven for 40 minutes, or until chicken is fork tender. Before serving, stir in the cooked peas and carrots, simmering until heated through.

CHICKEN LOUISIANA

Serves 6:

2 tablespoons of butter
2 tablespoons of olive oil
2 medium-sized onions, chopped
1 medium-sized red pepper, cored, seeded and chopped
2 ribs of celery, scraped and chopped
2 cloves of garlic, minced
Salt and pepper to taste

2 cups of chopped canned tomatoes
3 cups of chicken broth
¼ teaspoon of marjoram
2 cups of uncooked rice
3 cups of cooked chicken, in ½-inch cubes
1 cup of cooked ham, in ½-inch cubes
2 tablespoons of chopped broadleaf parsley

In a heavy casserole over medium heat, heat the butter and oil and sauté onion, pepper, celery and garlic for 3 minutes, or until soft, sprinkling with salt and pepper. Stir in the tomatoes, broth, marjoram and rice. Cover, bring to a boil on top of the stove, then bake in a preheated 350°F. oven for 30 minutes, or until the rice is tender. Remove from oven and stir in the chicken and ham. Return to the oven, uncovered, for 10 minutes, or until the chicken and ham are heated through. Taste for seasoning. Sprinkle with parsley and serve from the casserole.

LOUIS' CHICKEN À LA LYONNAISE*

Serves 4:

1 (3½- to 4-pound)
  chicken, cut up
1½ teaspoons of salt
½ teaspoon of pepper
¾ cup of flour
3 tablespoons of butter

1 tablespoon of olive oil
4 medium-sized onions,
  chopped
3 cloves of garlic, chopped
1½ cups of chicken broth

In a clean plastic or paper bag, place chicken, salt, pepper and flour. Shake well, evenly coating the chicken. Remove chicken from bag and shake off excess flour. In a frypan, over medium heat, heat butter and oil and brown chicken evenly. Transfer to a casserole. Add the onion and garlic to the frypan, cooking for 3 minutes, or until soft. Stir in the broth, blending well. Simmer for 5 minutes. Pour this onion gravy over the chicken in the casserole and cook, uncovered, in a preheated 300°F. oven for 40 minutes, or until the chicken is fork tender. Taste for seasoning.

* Especially Inexpensive

CHICKEN AND MACARONI IN SOUR CREAM

Serves 6:

1 (4-pound) chicken, cut up

blended
  ½ cup of flour
  1 teaspoon of salt
  ½ teaspoon of pepper
  ¼ teaspoon of dried tar-
    ragon

6 tablespoons of butter
1 tablespoon of olive oil

1 pound of elbow macaroni,
  cooked *al dente* and
  drained

blended
  5 shallots, minced and
    sautéed in butter for 2
    minutes
  2 cups of sour cream
  1 (6-ounce) can of to-
    mato puree

Dredge chicken lightly with the seasoned flour. In a frypan, over medium heat, heat 4 tablespoons of the butter and the oil and evenly brown the chicken. Lower the heat, cover the pan and simmer the chicken for 35 minutes, or until just on the point of tenderness. Toss the cooked macaroni with the remaining 2 tablespoons of butter and arrange in a single layer in the bottom of a large casserole. Place the chicken on top of the pasta in one layer, pouring the sour cream mixture over it. Bake, uncovered, in a preheated 375°F. oven for 20 minutes, or until bubbly and the chicken is fork tender.

CHICKEN MOUSSAKA

Serves 6:

3 medium-sized eggplants, peeled and cut lengthwise into ½-inch slices
Salt and pepper to taste
Flour for dredging
Olive oil
2 large onions, chopped
1 clove of garlic, minced
2 pounds of chicken thighs, skinned, boned and coarsely ground

1 (1-pound) can of tomatoes, drained and broken up
¼ cup of dry red wine
½ cup of chopped parsley
½ teaspoon of cinnamon
½ teaspoon of cumin
½ cup of grated Parmesan cheese (to be used when assembling)

Sprinkle the eggplant slices with salt, then lay them in even stacks on paper towels. Place a cutting board on them to cover and put a weight on it (a heavy casserole, or a brick) to allow some of the moisture to drain. Let set at least ½ hour. Dry the slices with paper towels and dredge lightly with flour. Pour 3 tablespoons of olive oil into a frypan and quickly brown the eggplant slices on both sides, a few at a time, then drain on paper towels. Add more oil as needed.

In a clean frypan, heat 3 tablespoons of oil over medium heat. Add onion and garlic and cook until soft. Add the chicken and cook, stirring, until it begins to brown. Add the tomatoes, wine, parsley, cinnamon, cumin, salt and pepper and bring to a boil. Quickly cook, stirring, until most of the liquid in the frypan has cooked off and the meat mixture has thickened. Set aside.

SAUCE

4 tablespoons of butter	Salt and pepper to taste
4 tablespoons of flour	⅛ teaspoon of nutmeg
3 cups of milk	4 eggs, beaten

In a saucepan, melt the butter over medium heat. Add flour, and, stirring, cook into a smooth paste. Gradually add milk, stirring into a smooth, medium-thick sauce. Add salt, pepper and nutmeg. Remove sauce from heat. Stir ½ cup of the sauce into the beaten eggs, then stir this back into the sauce. Cook over medium-low heat (do not boil), stirring, until the sauce becomes quite thick.

To assemble: Arrange a layer of eggplant slices on the bottom of a 9 × 13 × 3-inch baking dish. Sprinkle with 2 tablespoons of grated cheese. Top with the chicken mixture, making a smooth, even layer. Sprinkle with 2 tablespoons of grated cheese. Cover with remaining eggplant slices, sprinkle with 2 tablespoons of grated cheese. Pour on the egg sauce and sprinkle with remaining cheese. Bake in a preheated 350°F. oven for 1 hour, or until the top is golden brown and puffed.

CHICKEN NIÇOISE

Serves 4:

3 tablespoons of butter	2 ounces of dry vermouth
1 tablespoon of olive oil	¾ cup of Greek olives (the
Salt and pepper	dark brown, plump, shiny
1 (3½- to 4-pound) chicken, cut up	ones), cut into halves and pitted
1 large onion, chopped	4 medium-sized potatoes, cut
2 cloves of garlic, minced	into ½-inch slices and
½ teaspoon of dried oregano	quickly browned in butter on both sides (they should
1 (1-pound) can of tomatoes, broken up (use your hands)	not be cooked through)
	2 tablespoons of chopped parsley

In a top-of-the-stove casserole, over medium heat, heat the butter and oil. Salt and pepper the chicken and brown evenly. Transfer chicken to bowl and keep warm. Add the onion and garlic to the casserole (add more butter, if necessary) and cook for about 5 minutes. Add the oregano, tomatoes and vermouth and simmer 5 minutes longer. Return the chicken to the casserole. Add the olives, cover and cook in a preheated 350°F. oven for 15 minutes. Remove cover, add potatoes and cook until potatoes and chicken are tender. Serve sprinkled with parsley.

CHICKEN STEW WITH GREEN OLIVES AND HEART-SHAPED CROUTONS

Serves 4:

1 (2-inch) cube of salt pork, simmered in water for 5 minutes, drained and cut into ½-inch cubes

1 (3½- to 4-pound) chicken, cut up

Salt and pepper to taste

Flour for dredging

2 tablespoons of butter

3 medium-sized white onions, coarsely chopped

12 medium-sized mushrooms (remove, reserve and chop stems), quartered and cooked in 2 tablespoons of butter for 2 minutes

4 tablespoons (2 ounces) of brandy

1 cup of dry white wine

1 cup of chicken broth

Bouquet garni (1 celery stalk, 1 sprig parsley, small bay leaf, pinch of thyme, wrapped in a cheesecloth bag)

2 cloves of garlic, peeled

1 cup of pitted green olives

8 heart-shaped croutons dipped in parsley (see page 197)

Over medium heat, in a top-of-the-stove casserole large enough to hold all ingredients, cook the salt pork cubes until they are golden and crisp. Remove cubes with a slotted spoon and reserve. Season the chicken pieces with salt and pepper and dredge with flour. Combine the butter with the salt pork fat in the casserole, then add the onion and cook for 2 minutes. Add the chicken, browning evenly. Pour off all but 3 tablespoons of fat. Stir in the mushroom stems, brandy, wine and chicken broth. Add the bouquet garni and garlic. Cover and bake in a preheated 400°F. oven for 35 minutes, or until the chicken is fork tender. Stir in the mushrooms and olives and heat through on top of the stove. Discard bouquet garni. Taste for seasoning. Serve right from the casserole, sprinkled with the crisp salt pork cubes. Garnish with the croutons.

HEART-SHAPED CROUTONS DIPPED IN PARSLEY

8 slices of thin bread, trimmed into heart shapes (no larger than 3 by 2 inches)

Butter
Finely chopped parsley

Broil the bread on one side until golden. Butter the other side and broil until golden. Keep warm and just before serving dip each end into the parsley.

CHICKEN CASSEROLE IN RHINE WINE

Serves 4:

1 (3½- to 4-pound) chicken, cut up
Salt and pepper
Flour for dredging
3 tablespoons of butter
1 tablespoon of olive oil
1 tablespoon of flour
1½ cups of chicken broth
1 cup of Rhine wine

1 tablespoon of chopped fresh tarragon, or 1 teaspoon dried
12 shallots, sliced
½ pound of small mushrooms, halved
2 tablespoons of chopped fresh parsley

Sprinkle the chicken with salt and pepper and dredge in flour. In a frypan, over medium heat, heat the butter and oil, add the chicken and brown evenly. Transfer to a casserole that will hold the chicken in one layer. Pour all but 2 tablespoons of fat from the frypan. Stir in the flour. When well mixed with the fat, slowly add the broth and cook, stirring into a smooth, thin sauce. Add the wine and blend. Sprinkle tarragon and shallots over chicken. Pour in the broth-wine sauce. Cover and bake in a preheated 350°F. oven for 30 minutes. Remove cover, add mushrooms and cook 15 minutes longer, or until chicken is fork tender and sauce has thickened. Taste for seasoning. Sprinkle with parsley and serve with hot rice.

ROSEMARY CHICKEN CASSEROLE

Serves 4:

1 (3½- to 4-pound) chicken, cut up
4 small onions, chopped
1 teaspoon of dried rosemary
1 teaspoon of salt
½ teaspoon of pepper

1 (10½-ounce) can of condensed cream of celery soup blended with ⅓ cup of light cream and ¼ teaspoon of Bell's poultry seasoning
⅓ cup of slivered almonds

In a casserole just large enough to hold the chicken in 1 layer, place the chicken pieces, skin side up. Evenly sprinkle the onion, rosemary, salt and pepper over the chicken. Cover with the celery soup-cream-mixture. Bake, uncovered, in a preheated 375°F. oven for 35 minutes, or until chicken is tender. Sprinkle with the almonds and bake for another 10 minutes.

CHICKEN, ITALIAN SAUSAGE AND POTATOES

Serves 6:

1 (4-pound) chicken, cut up
Salt and pepper
2 tablespoons of olive oil

pricked in several places
  3 hot Italian sausages
  3 sweet Italian sausages

4 medium-sized onions, chopped
2 cloves of garlic, minced
4 medium-sized mushrooms, sliced
1 large sweet red pepper, cored, seeded and diced
3 medium-sized potatoes, peeled and cut into ½-inch dice

½ teaspoon of dried basil
½ teaspoon of dried oregano

blended with the tomato sauce below
  ½ cup of chicken broth
  ½ cup of red wine

1 (1-pound, 12-ounce) can of Italian plum tomatoes, broken up, simmered, uncovered, in a saucepan for 30 minutes, seasoned with ½ teaspoon of salt and ½ teaspoon of sugar

Rub the chicken with salt and pepper. In a large frypan, over medium heat, heat the oil. Add the chicken and sausages and cook for 20 minutes, turning often, evenly browning the chicken and sausages. Transfer to a large casserole, alternately arranging the chicken and sausages. Scatter the onion, garlic, mushrooms, pepper and potatoes between and over the chicken and sausages. Sprinkle with the basil and oregano. Pour on the broth-wine-tomato sauce blend. Cover and bake in a preheated 350°F. oven for 30 minutes, or until the chicken, sausage and potatoes are tender.

*SWIFT SAVORY CHICKEN CUT-UP**

Serves 4:

1 cup of uncooked rice
1 (1⅜-ounce) envelope of dehydrated leek soup mix blended with 2 cups of chicken broth

1 (3½- to 4-pound) chicken, cut up
1 (10½-ounce) can of condensed cream of chicken soup
Salt and pepper to taste

In a casserole, place rice and pour in the leek-broth mixture. Arrange the chicken in a single layer on the rice. Evenly spoon the cream of chicken soup over the chicken. Bake, covered, in a preheated 375°F. oven for 15 minutes. Taste sauce and season with salt and pepper. Cook, uncovered, for 45 minutes, or until the sauce is bubbly brown and the chicken is fork tender.

* Especially Inexpensive

CHICKEN AND SPINACH ROQUEFORT

2 tablespoons of butter
2 tablespoons of flour
1 cup of chicken broth
1½ cups of heavy cream
½ teaspoon of Worcestershire sauce
¼ cup of sherry
Good pinch of cayenne
1/16 teaspoon of cinnamon
½ cup of crumbled Roquefort cheese
2 egg yolks, beaten

Salt to taste
2 (10-ounce) packages of frozen leaf-spinach, defrosted
1 (3½- to 4-pound) chicken, poached in water to cover with 1 onion, 1 celery stalk, 1 carrot, salt and pepper until tender, then skin and bones removed

In a saucepan, over medium heat, melt the butter. Add the flour and cook, stirring, into a smooth paste. Gradually add the broth and cream, stirring into a smooth sauce. Stir in the Worcestershire, sherry, cayenne and cinnamon. Lower heat and stir ¼ cup of the sauce and the Roquefort into the egg yolks. Pour egg yolk mixture into the saucepan and beat into the sauce. Cook over low heat (do not boil), stirring, until sauce thickens. Taste for seasoning, adding salt, if needed.

In the bottom of a shallow, buttered baking dish, arrange the spinach. Spoon a little of the sauce over it. Arrange the chicken (in serving pieces) in one layer on the spinach. Cover with the remaining sauce. Bake in a preheated 400°F. oven for 20 minutes, or until thoroughly heated and the top is golden.

CHICKEN TETRAZZINI

Serves 4:

2 tablespoons of butter
1 tablespoon of flour
½ teaspoon of salt
½ cup of heavy cream
1½ cups of milk
2 egg yolks
3 cups of diced cooked chicken
10 small mushrooms, quartered and sautéed in 2 tablespoons of butter until brown, but still firm
¾ pound of narrow fettuccine noodles, cooked *al dente* and tossed with 2 tablespoons of butter
¾ cup of grated Asiago or Parmesan cheese

In a saucepan, melt the butter over medium heat. Stir in the flour and salt, blending well. Pour in the cream and ½ cup of the milk and simmer, stirring, until well blended. Lower heat. Beat egg yolks with remaining 1 cup of milk and blend into the sauce. Cook, stirring, until sauce is slightly thickened (do not boil). This should take about 3 minutes. Stir the chicken and mushrooms into the sauce. Taste for seasoning. Mix one-third of the chicken-mushroom sauce mixture with the noodles. Arrange the noodle mixture in a buttered casserole. Spoon the remaining chicken-mushroom sauce over the noodles, sprinkle with remaining cheese and bake in a preheated 375°F. oven for 20 minutes, or until heated through, bubbling and golden.

CHICKEN THIGHS AND RICE

Serves 4:

6 chicken thighs, skinned, boned and cut into strips
Salt
⅓ cup of cornstarch
3 tablespoons of butter
1 tablespoon of olive oil
¼ teaspoon of dried thyme
¼ teaspoon of dried tarragon
¼ teaspoon of cumin
¼ teaspoon of pepper

5 whole young scallions, chopped
2 cups of chicken broth
½ cup of dry sherry
6 medium-sized mushrooms, sliced
2 medium-sized ripe tomatoes, peeled, seeded and each cut into 8 wedges
1½ cups of rice, cooked in chicken broth

Sprinkle the chicken with salt and dredge in the cornstarch. In a frypan, over medium heat, heat the butter and oil and evenly brown the chicken strips. Blend in the thyme, tarragon, cumin, pepper and scallions. Cook 3 minutes, stirring. Transfer to a casserole, then stir in the broth and sherry. Cover, bring to a boil on top of the stove, then bake in a preheated 350°F. oven for 20 minutes. Stir in the mushrooms and tomatoes and the cooked rice. Cover and bake 20 minutes longer, or until the chicken is tender, gently stirring once. Taste for seasoning.

CHICKEN AND TOMATO RAGOUT

Serves 6 to 8:

¼ cup of olive oil
3 whole chicken breasts, boned and quartered
6 chicken thighs, boned and halved
Salt and pepper to taste
1 medium-sized onion, chopped
1 clove of garlic, minced
4 large, ripe tomatoes, peeled, seeded and coarsely chopped

1 tablespoon of chopped fresh basil or 1 teaspoon dried
Pinch of cinnamon
½ pound of green string beans, in 1-inch pieces
4 very small zucchini (measuring about 1 inch by 4 inches), cut into 1-inch chunks

In a large frypan, over medium heat, heat the oil. Sprinkle the chicken with salt and pepper and evenly brown. Transfer the chicken to a casserole large enough to hold the chicken in one layer. Pour off all but 2 tablespoons of oil from the frypan. Add onion and garlic and cook until soft. Add the tomatoes, basil and cinnamon and simmer for 5 minutes, breaking up the tomatoes as they cook. Layer the string beans over the chicken in the casserole and spoon the tomato sauce over the beans. Bake, covered, in a preheated 350°F. oven for 20 minutes. Add zucchini, spooning the sauce over it, cover and bake for 10 minutes or longer, until the chicken is fork tender. Taste for seasoning.

CHICKEN TRATTORIA

Serves 4: (This is a favorite in those excellent small restaurants in Rome called trattorie.)

4 chicken thighs
2 whole chicken breasts, halved (do not skin or bone)
¾ tablespoon of dried oregano
¾ tablespoon of dried basil
4 cloves of garlic, peeled and halved
1½ teaspoons of salt

½ teaspoon of pepper
6 tablespoons of olive oil
1 cup of bread crumbs
2 teaspoons of Hungarian paprika
4 medium-sized potatoes, peeled, halved and placed in a bowl of cold water to cover

In a large bowl, combine chicken, oregano, basil, garlic, salt, pepper and olive oil. Toss, coating the chicken pieces well. Leave chicken in the bowl, cover with plastic wrap and refrigerate for 4 hours. Spread bread crumbs on a piece of waxed paper. Evenly dredge the chicken pieces in the bread crumbs. Place the chicken in a large casserole and sprinkle liberally with paprika. Drain potatoes and dry with paper towels. Place them in bowl in which chicken marinated, coating with remaining marinade. Arrange the potatoes between the chicken pieces. Bake, uncovered, in a preheated 400°F. oven for 20 minutes. Turn the potatoes and bake another 20 minutes.

CHICKEN-VEGETABLE CASSEROLE

Serves 4:

3 tablespoons of butter
¼ pound of salt pork, chopped
4 medium-sized onions, thinly sliced
3 ribs of celery, scraped and chopped
¼ pound of mushrooms, sliced
Salt

1 (3½- to 4-pound) chicken, cut up
½ pound of parsnips, peeled and sliced
4 small potatoes, peeled and cut into ½-inch slices
1 (1-pound) can of tomatoes, chopped
½ teaspoon of pepper

In a large frypan, melt the butter and over medium heat sauté the salt pork for 5 minutes. Add the onion and celery and cook 3 minutes, then remove with a slotted spoon and evenly spread on the bottom of a casserole. Sprinkle the mushrooms over them. Lightly salt the chicken and evenly brown in the frypan. Arrange the chicken on the mushrooms in the casserole. Layer the parsnips and potatoes over the chicken. Spoon on the tomatoes, sprinkle with 1 teaspoon of salt and the pepper. Cover with foil, then with the lid and bake in a preheated 325°F. oven for 45 minutes, or until chicken and vegetables are tender.

CHICKEN-ZUCCHINI, MEAL-IN-ONE

Serves 4:

4 medium-sized zucchini (about 1½ pounds total weight)
2 tablespoons of butter
2 tablespoons of flour
¾ cup of chicken broth
½ cup of light cream
⅛ teaspoon of mace
1½ teaspoons of salt

½ teaspoon of pepper
¼ pound of Gruyère cheese, grated
2 tablespoons of tender minced scallions
2 cups of cooked chicken, in ½-inch cubes
¼ cup of grated Asiago or Parmesan cheese

Halve the zucchini lengthwise, scooping out most of the pulp. Half-fill a large pot with water, bring to a boil and add the zucchini shells. When the water returns to a boil, remove and drain the zucchini. In a saucepan, over low heat, melt 1 tablespoon of the butter, stir in the flour, blending well, then, small amounts at a time, add the broth and cream, stirring into a smooth sauce. Sprinkle in the mace, salt and pepper. Add the Gruyère cheese, stir and blend until cheese is melted. In another small saucepan, melt the remaining tablespoon of butter and cook the scallions for 2 minutes. Stir in the chicken and one-third of the cheese sauce, mixing well. Taste for seasoning. Place the zucchini in a baking dish and lightly salt the cavities. Fill with the chicken mixture, top with remaining sauce and sprinkle on the grated Asiago cheese. Bake, uncovered, in a preheated 350°F. oven for 15 minutes, or until bubbling and golden.

Chapter Nine

Pies, Livers, Leftover Creations, including Crepes and other Innovations

Chicken potpie is an all-American favorite. In the prestigious Waldorf-Astoria Hotel in New York City, sometimes called New York's official Palace, a place where the great and the near-great from all over the world gather and dine, the chicken pie remains the favorite dish of practically all the guests. Pies are versatile and everyone likes them. Practically all nationalities have their own, unique versions.

And, let's remember, that although chicken livers make great appetizers, chopped, as a pâté, or used as a spread, these delicious, delicate little morsels are also excellent as a meal. Cooked with bacon and onions, or by themselves served with rice, they are a different taste-treat every time, no matter how you cook them. One point to remember though: Do not overcook chicken livers; they should be served slightly pink inside, moist and tender. Overcooking toughens them and diminishes their personality.

Just about every time we cook chicken we purposely prepare more than we need for that meal. Refrigerator-raiders will understand. Is there anything more satisfying than opening the refrigerator door and taking out a tasty drumstick, a wing, a thigh? Leftover chicken paired with spinach, rice and sauce, or with asparagus or broccoli becomes an elegant epicurean original. Mixed with a sauce, mushrooms and ham and folded into a crepe makes leftover chicken a celebration. Tossed with pasta it becomes an event; dipped into beaten egg and rolled in bread crumbs, leftover chicken can become a tasty croquette.

And what about that unique innovation, chicken hash? It is one of our absolute favorites. One great chef even created a unique chicken hash. The only part of the chicken that he used was its crisp skin. We won't, however, go that far. Read on; there could be some exciting discoveries ahead.

CURRIED CHICKEN BALLS

Serves 4:

4 tablespoons of butter
1 medium-sized onion, finely chopped
1 clove of garlic, minced
1 small rib of celery, scraped and minced
1½ pounds of boned, skinned, finely ground chicken breasts
1 cup of fine bread crumbs
1 egg, lightly beaten
1 teaspoon of ground cumin
½ teaspoon of ground coriander
1 teaspoon of grated ginger
1 teaspoon of salt
½ teaspoon of pepper
Flour for dredging
1 tablespoon of vegetable oil
1 tablespoon of curry powder
2 cups of heavy cream
½ cup of dry sherry

In a frypan, melt 2 tablespoons of the butter. Add the onion, garlic and celery and cook 2 minutes. In a bowl, combine the chicken, onion, garlic, celery, bread crumbs, egg, cumin, coriander, ginger, salt and pepper. Blend well. Shape the mixture into balls, about 1 inch in diameter, and lightly dredge in flour.

Heat the remaining 2 tablespoons of butter and the oil in a frypan over medium heat and evenly brown the balls. This will take about 7 minutes. Pour off all but 1 tablespoon of fat. Sprinkle the balls with the curry powder, shaking the pan to distribute it evenly. Cook for 1 minute. Pour in the cream and sherry, stir and simmer for 10 minutes, or until the sauce thickens. Serve with rice.

CHICKEN COQUILLES

Serves 6:

4 cups of cubed cooked
chicken

½ pound of small
mushrooms, sliced and
sautéed in butter

2½ cups of Rich Mornay
Sauce (see page 412)

¾ cup of grated Gruyère
cheese

2 tablespoons of bread
crumbs (approximate)

2 tablespoons of butter

In a bowl, combine the chicken, mushrooms, two-thirds of
the sauce and gently blend. Place in 6 individual scallop
shells or ramekins. Spoon the remaining sauce over the
chicken mixture, sprinkle with the cheese, then bread crumbs
and dot with butter. Place on a baking sheet and bake in a
preheated 375°F. oven for 15 minutes, or until heated
through and the top is bubbly and golden brown.

CHICKEN AND CHEESE CROQUETTES

Serves 4:

2 cups of leftover cooked
ground chicken

4 scallions (white part
only), minced

½ cup of fresh farmer
cheese

¼ teaspoon of dried basil

¼ teaspoon of dried oreg-
ano

1 teaspoon of salt

½ teaspoon of pepper
Flour for dredging
1 egg, beaten

blended
  1 cup of bread crumbs
  2 tablespoons of grated
  Asiago or Parmesan
  cheese

Oil for deep frying

In a bowl, blend well the chicken, scallions, farmer cheese,
basil, oregano, salt and pepper. Shape into any croquette
form desired. Lightly dredge in flour, dip into the beaten egg,
then dredge in the bread crumbs-cheese mixture. Refrigerate
for 2 hours. In a deep frypan or deep fryer, heat enough oil
to completely cover the croquettes to 375°F. Place croquettes

in frying basket, lower into the hot oil and cook for 3 minutes, or until the croquettes are golden. Drain and serve very hot.

CREAMED CHICKEN IN A POPPY SEED NOODLE RING

Serves 4 to 6:

4 tablespoons of butter	1 tablespoon of poppy seeds
4 tablespoons of flour	¾ pound of noodles, cooked
2½ cups of milk	very *al dente*
Salt and pepper to taste	2 tablespoons of minced
½ teaspoon of ground	parsley
cumin	4 cups of cooked chicken,
½ cup of grated sharp	cut into bite-sized cubes
cheese of your choice	

In a saucepan, over medium heat, melt the butter. Stir in the flour and cook, stirring, into a smooth paste. Add the milk, a small amount at a time, stirring into a smooth, medium-thick sauce. Add salt, pepper and cumin. Add 4 tablespoons of the sauce, the cheese and poppy seeds to the noodles. Generously butter a deep 9-inch ring mold. Sprinkle the inside with the parsley. Arrange the noodles evenly in the ring, set in a pan of hot water and bake in a preheated 400°F. oven for 30 minutes, or until top is golden. Carefully combine the chicken with the remaining sauce and heat through. Turn the ring out onto a hot serving dish. Spoon in enough of the chicken mixture to fill it and slightly overflow. Serve the remaining creamed chicken on the side.

CREAMED CHICKEN PRINCESS

Serves 4 to 6:

3 cups of mashed potatoes
(mashed with 1 beaten
egg, 3 tablespoons of butter, 1½ teaspoons salt, ½
teaspoon pepper and 2 ta-
blespoons of heavy cream)
1 cup of small, whole
mushrooms, stems re-
moved
1 small red pepper, seeded,
cored and diced

3 cups of chicken broth
3 tablespoons of butter
3 tablespoons of flour
1 cup of heavy cream
1 teaspoon of salt
⅛ teaspoon of cayenne
1 teaspoon of Tabasco
3 cups of cooked diced
chicken
1 tablespoon of chopped
fresh chives

Line a round ovenproof dish with the mashed potatoes, leaving a well in the center to contain the creamed chicken. Bake
the potatoes in a preheated 350°F. oven for 20 minutes, or
until crusty and golden. In a saucepan, combine the mushrooms, pepper and 2 cups of the broth. Bring to a boil,
then simmer for 8 minutes. Strain and reserve 1 cup of the
broth. In a saucepan over medium-low heat, melt the butter
and stir in the flour, stirring into a smooth paste. Gradually
add the cream and remaining 2 cups of the broth, stirring into
a smooth, thickish sauce. Blend in the drained vegetables,
salt, cayenne, Tabasco and chicken. Taste for seasoning, then
spoon into the well in the mashed-potato-dish. Bake in a preheated 350°F. oven for 15 minutes, or until piping hot.
Sprinkle with the chives.

BASIC STUFFED CREPE RECIPE

Serves 4:

3 cups of finely chopped
cooked chicken
Salt and pepper to taste

1 cup of Velouté Sauce (see
recipe, page 63)
¾ cup of grated Asiago or
Parmesan cheese

In a saucepan, combine the chicken, salt, pepper, 3 tablespoons of sauce and 3 tablespoons of cheese and blend well.

Cook over medium heat until heated through. Lay crepes flat and spoon chicken filling (about 2 heaping tablespoons for each, depending upon the size of the crepe) evenly across the edge of the crepe nearest you. Roll the crepes tightly (but not so tightly that the crepe breaks) and carefully, so that all the filling remains intact. Butter a baking dish or casserole lightly and arrange the crepes, side by side but not touching, seam side down. Spoon the sauce around the crepes (if you want them crisp; if it doesn't matter, spoon the sauce right on the crepes) and sprinkle them with the remaining cheese. Bake in a preheated 400°F. oven for 10 minutes, or until heated through. Run under a broiler until they are golden brown and crisp.

CREPE VARIATIONS

The preceding "Basic Stuffed Crepe Recipe" is the easy method and it works with any filling. Remember that these light, lacy little pancakes can quickly convert chicken and vegetable leftovers into elegant offerings for lunch or supper. (Crepes freeze well, defrost quickly, so have some of the unfilled pancakes on hand in the freezer. Wrapping them in small packages of 4 or 6 makes it easy to pull out any number you need.) Or work with the recipes in this chapter such as Creamed Chicken Princess (page 211) of course, omitting the potatoes) or the Creamy Chicken Hash (page 215). They are ideal crepe fillings.

Leftover asparagus, broccoli, spinach, cauliflower, chopped, mixed with chopped cooked chicken and sauce and sprinkled with cheese (Gruyère, Fontina, Parmesan, Asiago, Blue etc.) are the makings of perfect crepes.

Taste textures can be varied by adding chopped ham and fresh mushrooms, sautéed in butter, with the chicken. Chopped onions, scallions or shallots also spark flavor. Adding sherry (or other wine), a dash of cayenne or Tabasco to Rich White Sauce (recipe page 63) also gives extra flavor.

Rolling crepes around chicken livers is a .unique way to offer those delicious morsels.

CHICKEN LIVER IN ONION CREPES

Serves 6:

12 onion crepes*
4 tablespoons of butter
2 shallots, minced
1 pound of chicken livers,
    cut into small pieces

Pinch of thyme
3 tablespoons of Marsala
1½ cups of Hollandaise
    Sauce (see pages 408,
    409)

Prepare onion crepes. In a frypan, over medium heat, melt the butter. Add the shallots and sauté until soft. Add the chicken livers, thyme and Marsala and cook for 10 minutes, or just until the livers are cooked through (do not overcook or they will toughen). Mix 2 or 3 tablespoons of the hollandaise sauce with the livers. They should be moist but not soupy. Spread the crepes out, and spoon some of the filling onto one end of each. Roll crepes and place, seam side down, side by side but not touching, in a shallow, buttered baking dish. Spoon the remaining hollandaise sauce over the crepes and bake in a 400°F. oven for 10 minutes, or until heated through, then put under a broiler until golden brown.

* To crepe recipe (page 211), add 1 small onion, finely grated

MILANESE CROQUETTES

Serves 4:

1½ cups of finely diced
    cooked chicken
1 small canned lamb tongue,
    finely diced
4 large mushrooms, minced
¼ pound of small elbow
    macaroni, cooked *al dente*
    and drained
¼ cup of grated Asiago or
    Parmesan cheese

1 tablespoon of heavy cream
3 eggs, beaten (beat 2 sep-
    arately for dipping cro-
    quettes)
1 teaspoon of salt
½ teaspoon of pepper
Bread crumbs for dredging
2 tablespoons of butter
2 tablespoons of olive oil

In a bowl, combine the chicken, tongue, mushrooms, macaroni, cheese, cream, 1 beaten egg, salt and pepper, blending well. Shape into croquettes of desired shape and size. Dip them in the remaining beaten eggs, then dredge in bread crumbs. In a frypan, over medium heat, heat the butter and oil and cook the croquettes until golden on both sides. Add more butter and oil as needed. Serve with a sauce of your choice (see Sauce Chapter).

LEFTOVER CHICKEN CURRY

Serves 6:

3 tablespoons of butter
3 medium-sized onions, chopped
1 clove of garlic, minced
1 rib of celery, scraped and chopped
1 medium-sized tart apple, peeled, cored and chopped
3 tablespoons of flour, mixed with 2 tablespoons of curry powder

1 tablespoon of tomato puree
3 cups of chicken broth
½ cup of heavy cream
2 tablespoons of fresh lemon juice
Salt to taste
4 cups of cooked chicken, in 1-inch cubes

In a saucepan, melt the butter over medium heat. Sauté the onion, garlic and celery until soft. Add the apple and cook until it can easily be mashed. Lower heat, stir in the flour-curry mixture and the tomato puree and cook, stirring, into a smooth paste. Gradually add the broth, stirring constantly, until the sauce is smooth and medium thick. Stir in the cream. Strain the sauce, pushing contents through the strainer. Stir in the lemon juice, salt and chicken. Serve over, or with rice.

CHICKEN CUTLETS

Serves 4:

1½ cups of Rich White
  Sauce (page 63)
¼ teaspoon of Tabasco
⅛ teaspoon of leaf sage
1 teaspoon of Worcestershire
  sauce
¼ teaspoon of garlic powder
½ teaspoon of salt

4 cups of chopped cooked
  chicken
Flour for dredging
2 eggs, beaten with 2 tablespoons of water
Crushed cornflakes for
  dredging
Oil for deep frying

In a large bowl, combine the white sauce, seasonings and chicken, blending well. Refrigerate for 2 hours. Shape into cutlets of desired size. Dredge in flour, dip into beaten egg, then dredge in cornflakes. Refrigerate for 2 hours longer. Deep fry in the oil (390°F.) until golden and crisp. Drain on paper towels and serve with a sauce of your choice (see Sauce Chapter).

CREAMY CHICKEN HASH

Serves 4:

1 whole large chicken breast,
  with water to cover, ½
  cup dry white wine, 1 bay
  leaf, 1 celery rib, pinch
  of thyme, 1 teaspoon of
  salt, 1 large onion, stuck
  with 2 cloves poached
  for 20 minutes, or until
  just tender

1½ cups of heavy cream
Salt to taste
Pinch of cayenne
Pinch of nutmeg
4 tablespoons of butter, broken into small pieces
1 egg yolk, beaten with ½
  cup of heavy cream
2 tablespoons of dry sherry

Cool chicken breast. Remove and discard skin and bones and finely dice. In a saucepan, over medium heat, bring the cream to a simmer. Add the chicken, salt, cayenne and nutmeg. Simmer for 5 minutes, uncovered. Stir in the butter. Remove from the heat. Stir 2 or 3 tablespoons of the hot cream mixture into the egg yolk-cream mixture and slowly add it to the chicken hash blending. Stir in the sherry and over low heat, without boiling, cook until the hash thickens. Taste for seasoning. Serve on toast or in patty shells.

ASIAN CHICKEN LIVERS

Serves 4: In India and Pakistan this is served over rice.

3 tablespoons of peanut oil
2 medium-sized onions, chopped
2 cloves of garlic, minced
2 tablespoons of grated fresh ginger or ½ teaspoon of ground ginger
2 teaspoons of cumin

1 teaspoon of coriander
1 teaspoon of chili powder
⅛ teaspoon of crushed red pepper flakes
2 small ripe tomatoes, peeled, seeded and minced
1 pound of chicken livers
Salt to taste

In a large frypan, over medium heat, heat the oil and sauté the onion, garlic and ginger for 5 minutes, or until the onion is soft. Stir in the cumin, coriander and chili powder, and cook, stirring, for 1 minute. Add the red pepper flakes and tomatoes and simmer, covered, for 10 minutes, stirring occasionally. Stir in the chicken livers, sprinkle with salt, cover and cook 10 to 15 minutes longer (do not overcook the livers, they should be slightly pink inside), stirring occasionally.

CHICKEN LIVERS AND BACON

Serves 4:

10 slices of bacon
1 pound of chicken livers
Salt and pepper
10 young scallions (white

part only), coarsely chopped
3 tablespoons of dry sherry

In a large frypan, over medium heat, fry 2 slices of the bacon until brown and crisp. Remove bacon, drain on paper towels, crumble and set aside. In the bacon fat in the frypan, sauté the chicken livers for 5 minutes, or until they are brown on the outside and slightly pink inside. Sprinkle with pepper and lightly with salt. Remove, reserve and keep warm. In the frypan, cook the remaining bacon slices for 10 minutes (until cooked through but not too crisp), turning often. Drain bacon on paper towels and roll each slice. Pour off all but 3 tablespoons of the bacon fat, add the scallions and cook for 5 minutes, stirring. Line the bottom of a broilerproof casserole with the scallions. Alternately arrange the livers and bacon rolls on top and sprinkle with the crumbled bacon. Sprinkle the sherry over all. Run under the broiler for 3 minutes.

CHICKEN LIVERS AND MADEIRA

Serves 4:

5 tablespoons of butter
1 tablespoon of olive oil
2 medium-sized onions, sliced
1 clove of garlic, chopped
4 medium-sized mushrooms, sliced
Salt and pepper to taste

1 pound of chicken livers
Flour for dredging
1 tablespoon of poppy seeds
½ teaspoon of marjoram
¼ cup of Madeira
2 tablespoons of chopped parsley

In a large frypan, over medium heat, heat 2 tablespoons of the butter and the olive oil. Sauté the onion and garlic for 3 minutes, or until onion is soft. Stir in the mushrooms and sauté for 2 minutes. Lightly season with salt and pepper. Remove the onion, garlic and mushrooms with a slotted spoon and reserve. Lightly dredge the livers in the flour and sprinkle with salt and pepper. Heat the remaining 3 tablespoons of butter in the frypan, then add the livers, poppy seeds and marjoram. Turning the livers often, cook for 5 minutes, or until brown on the outside and slightly pink inside. Pour in the Madeira, raise the heat and cook, stirring, until the wine has evaporated. Stir in the onions, garlic and mushrooms and cook, stirring, just until everything is heated through. Sprinkle with the parsley.

CHICKEN LIVERS IN PATTY SHELLS

Serves 4:

4 tablespoons of butter
1 pound of chicken livers, each liver quartered
Salt and pepper to taste
1 small red pepper, cored, seeded, chopped and cooked in butter for 2 minutes, or until crisp-tender

6 shallots, chopped and cooked in butter for 5 minutes
1 (10½-ounce) can of condensed cream of mushroom soup, blended with ⅓ cup of heavy cream
4 commercial patty shells
Hungarian paprika

In a frypan, over medium-high heat, melt the butter and cook the livers for 3 minutes, browning evenly and turning often. Sprinkle with salt and pepper. Add the red pepper and shallots. Stir in the soup-cream blend and when it starts to simmer, lower heat and simmer, stirring, for 7 minutes, or just until the livers are still slightly pink inside. Spoon into the patty shells and sprinkle lightly with paprika.

CHICKEN LIVERS WITH FRESH SAGE

Serves 6: This is a favorite Roman meal, served only in the summer when fresh sage is available. It makes all the difference.

1½ pounds of chicken livers, each cut into 2 or 3 pieces
Salt and pepper to taste
5 tablespoons of butter
2 tablespoons of olive oil
3 thin slices of prosciutto, coarsely chopped
1 cup of Marsala

2 tablespoons of chopped fresh sage
6 large, thick slices of bread, crusts removed, fried in butter on both sides until golden, drained on paper towels and kept warm in a low oven or warmer

Sprinkle the livers with salt and pepper. In a large frypan, over medium heat, heat 3 tablespoons of the butter and the olive oil. Add the livers and brown them evenly. Cook about

4 minutes, stirring. The livers should be slightly pink on the inside (do not overcook). Transfer to a warm dish. Stir the ham into the frypan and cook for 1 minute. Transfer to the liver dish. Pour the Marsala into the frypan, stir in the sage and simmer, stirring, until the liquid has reduced by one-half. Return the livers and ham to the frypan, add the remaining 2 tablespoons of butter. Simmer just long enough to heat the livers and ham through and melt the butter. Stir and taste for seasoning. Serve the livers in their sauce atop the fried bread.

CHICKEN LIVERS AND SOUR CREAM

Serves 4: This is a German favorite.

1 pound of large chicken livers, cut in half	1 medium-sized onion, chopped
Salt and pepper to taste	½ cup of chicken broth
Flour for dredging	⅛ teaspoon of dried thyme
5 tablespoons of butter	¾ cup of sour cream
	2 tablespoons of vinegar

Season the livers with salt and pepper, then dredge lightly in flour. In a large frypan, over medium heat, melt 2 tablespoons of the butter and cook the onion for 3 minutes. Add the remaining 3 tablespoons of butter and evenly brown the chicken livers (do not overcook). Stir in the chicken broth and the thyme. Lower heat, cover, and simmer for 3 minutes, or until the livers are cooked but still slightly pink inside. Stir in the sour cream and vinegar and heat, stirring, to a simmer. Taste for seasoning.

CHICKEN LIVER STUFFED TOMATOES

Serves 4:

4 large ripe, but firm, tomatoes
½ pound of chicken livers,
cooked in 2 tablespoons of
butter for 5 minutes, or
until just slightly underdone, seasoned with salt
and pepper, then minced
1 teaspoon of grated onion

¼ teaspoon of dried basil
1 cup of fine soft bread
crumbs
2 tablespoons of olive oil
½ teaspoon of salt
¼ teaspoon of pepper
1 tablespoon of chopped
parsley

Take a thin slice from the top of each tomato, and carefully spoon out the center pulp and seeds, leaving the tomato shell firm and intact. Chop the pulp and reserve. Turn the tomatoes upside down and drain them for 1 hour. Salt the insides. In a bowl, combine and gently blend the reserved pulp, livers, onion, basil, bread crumbs, olive oil, salt and pepper. Heap the tomato shells with the mixture. Place in a baking dish or pan, and bake, uncovered, in a preheated 350°F. oven for 20 minutes, or until the tops are golden brown and the tomatoes softened. Sprinkle with the parsley before serving.

CHICKEN LIVERS WITH TOMATOES AND MUSHROOMS

Serves 6:

6 tablespoons of butter
3 medium-sized onions,
thinly sliced
1½ pounds of chicken livers
Salt and pepper to taste
½ pound of small
mushrooms, thinly sliced

1 (1-pound) can of toma-
toes, drained and chopped
½ teaspoon of dried basil
1 cup of medium cream
3 tablespoons of chopped
broadleaf parsley

In a large frypan, over medium heat, melt 3 tablespoons of the butter and sauté the onion until soft. Stir in the livers, sprinkle with salt and pepper, adding more butter as needed, and sauté for 5 minutes. Remove livers and set aside. Add the mushrooms and tomatoes and simmer uncovered, stirring for 5 minutes. Stir in the basil and simmer 4 minutes longer. Blend in the cream and simmer for 5 minutes, uncovered. Return the livers to the pan with any remaining butter and simmer, stirring, for 5 minutes, or until the livers are cooked but still slightly pink inside. Sprinkle with the parsley.

VENETIAN CHICKEN LIVERS

Serves 6:

1½ pounds of chicken
   livers, quartered
Flour for dredging
6 tablespoons of butter
2 tablespoons of olive oil
Salt and pepper to taste
2 medium-sized white on-
   ions, thinly sliced

½ teaspoon of dried leaf
   sage, crumbled
½ cup of dry white wine
2 tablespoons of lemon juice
2 tablespoons of minced
   parsley

Lightly dredge the livers with flour. In a large frypan, over medium heat, heat 3 tablespoons of the butter and 1 tablespoon of the oil and brown the livers. Season with salt and pepper. Transfer to a warm bowl.

Add 1 tablespoon of the butter and the remaining table-spoon of oil to the pan and cook the onion until soft. Stir in the sage, return the livers to the pan and cook 4 minutes, turning. The livers should be slightly pink inside. With a slotted spoon transfer the livers and onion to a heated serving dish. Pour the wine and lemon juice into the frypan. Simmer, stirring, for 1 minute. Add the remaining 2 tablespoons of butter, stir and when melted, pour the sauce over the liver and onion. Sprinkle with parsley.

CHICKEN LOAF

Serves about 10: An excellent buffet dish served with a sauce of your choice.

5 cups of minced cooked chicken
3 cups of bread crumbs
1½ cups of cooked brown rice
½ cup of grated Asiago or Parmesan cheese
1½ teaspoons of salt
1 teaspoon of pepper

4 eggs, lightly beaten
1 cup of chicken broth
4 tablespoons of chopped fresh chives
1 teaspoon of dried tarragon
½ teaspoon of Hungarian paprika
¼ teaspoon of Tabasco sauce

In a large bowl, combine the chicken, bread crumbs, rice, cheese, salt and pepper, blending well. Add the remaining ingredients gradually and mix thoroughly. Butter a loaf dish or pan of sufficient size and lightly pack the chicken mixture into it. Bake, uncovered, in a preheated 325°F. oven for 50 minutes, or just until the center of the loaf is set.

HOT CHICKEN MOUSSE

Serves 4:

3 cups of minced cooked chicken (use a food processor or fine blade of a food chopper)
1½ cups of Sauce Suprême (page 64)
3 tablespoons of sherry
4 egg yolks, lightly beaten
1 teaspoon of salt

½ teaspoon of pepper
¼ teaspoon of nutmeg
4 egg whites, stiffly beaten
1 cup of heavy cream, whipped
Garnish with cooked broccoli, seasoned with lemon butter

In a bowl large enough to hold all ingredients, combine the chicken, ½ cup of the sauce, sherry, egg yolks, salt, pepper and nutmeg, mixing well. Fold in the egg whites, then the whipped cream. Spoon into buttered 6-ounce baking dishes (custard cups work well). Set in a pan of hot water and bake in a preheated 325°F. oven for 40 minutes, or until set (insert a knife blade; if it comes out clean, they are ready). Do not overcook. Unmold onto a heated serving dish. Coat each with some of the remaining sauce and serve with the broccoli garnish.

CHICKEN-STUFFED ONIONS

Serves 4: Italians are lovers of "cipolle," onions, using them in imaginative ways. Here is a dish we enjoyed in the north of Italy.

4 cups of chicken broth	1 teaspoon of dried oregano
4 large onions	1 cup of bread crumbs
1 whole chicken breast	½ cup of grated Parmesan
3 tablespoons of butter	cheese
1 tablespoon of olive oil	2 eggs, beaten
2 cloves of garlic, minced	¼ cup of chopped pine nuts
1 carrot, peeled and minced	¼ cup of finely chopped
1 rib of celery, scraped	walnuts
and minced	Salt and pepper to taste

Pour the broth into a large pot and bring to a boil. Add the onions, reduce heat and simmer for 30 minutes, or until the onions can be just pierced with the point of a sharp knife. Remove from the broth and cut into halves, horizontally. Remove part of the center of each half, leaving enough of a shell allowing the onions to stand without collapsing. Chop the onion centers and reserve. In the same broth, at a simmer, poach the chicken breast for 30 minutes, or until fork tender. Remove, cool, discard skin and bones and mince the meat. Reserve the broth.

In a saucepan, over medium heat, heat the butter and oil and cook the garlic for 2 minutes. Stir in the carrot, celery, oregano and chopped onions. Cook for 4 minutes. Blend in the chicken. Remove from the heat and blend in half the bread crumbs, half the cheese, the eggs, pine nuts and walnuts, mixing well. Taste for seasoning, adding salt and pepper. Spoon the chicken-mixture into the onions. Sprinkle with the remaining bread crumbs and cheese. Place in a baking pan, pour in the reserved broth and bake, uncovered, in a preheated 350°F. oven for 30 minutes. Serve 2 half-stuffed onions per person.

CHICKEN IN CREAM WITH OYSTERS

Serves 4:

2 tablespoons of butter
3 shallots, minced
2 tablespoons of flour
2 cups of heavy cream
1 teaspoon of salt
½ teaspoon of pepper

2½ cups of cooked diced chicken
1 pint of fresh oysters
6 tablespoons (3 ounces) of Marsala

In a saucepan, over medium heat, melt the butter and sauté shallots for 3 minutes. Add the flour and stir until well blended. Lower heat and add the cream, a small amount at a time, stirring into a smooth sauce. Season with salt and pepper and stir in the chicken, cooking over medium heat until the sauce bubbles. Add the oysters and Marsala and cook for 2 minutes, or just until the edges of the oysters curl. Serve over pasta or rice or spooned into patty shells.

CORN BREAD, CHICKEN AND OYSTER PIE

Serves 6:

CORN BREAD

2 egg yolks
1 cup buttermilk

sifted together into a large bowl
  ⅔ cup cornmeal
  ⅔ cup flour
  2 tablespoons of sugar

2 teaspoons of baking powder
¼ teaspoon of baking soda
1 teaspoon of salt

3 tablespoons melted butter
2 egg whites, stiffly beaten

Beat the egg yolks with the buttermilk. Add this to the bowl with the cornmeal mixture and beat quickly until well blended. Stir in the melted butter. Fold in the beaten egg whites and pour into a buttered 8-inch-square baking dish. Bake in a preheated 425°F. oven for 25 minutes, or until a toothpick inserted comes out clean and top is golden.

OYSTERS AND CHICKEN

1 pint of oysters and their liquor
4 tablespoons of butter
4 tablespoons of flour
2 cups of chicken broth
2 cups of medium cream
Pinch of cayenne
Salt and pepper to taste

1 tablespoon of lemon juice
8 small mushrooms, sliced and sautéed in butter
4 cups of cooked chicken, cut into bite-sized cubes
2 tablespoons of chopped parsley

Simmer the oysters in their liquor just until the edges curl and oysters are plump (do not overcook). Strain and reserve liquid. Set the oysters aside. In a saucepan, melt the butter over medium heat. Stir in the flour and simmer, stirring, into a smooth paste. Add the broth and cream, small amounts at a time. Simmer, stirring, into a smooth, medium-thick sauce. Stir in ¼ cup of the oyster liquor, cayenne, salt, pepper and lemon juice. Add the mushrooms, chicken, oysters and parsley. Simmer just long enough to heat through.

Heat the corn bread. Cut it into 6 equal pieces, then cut each through the center. Lay the bottom halves on a large hot serving dish, slightly separated. With a slotted spoon, spoon the chicken-oyster mixture over. Lay the top half of each portion of corn bread over the chicken mixture and spoon the sauce on top.

RACHEL'S REGAL CHICKEN PIE

Serves 4: (In our dozen trips around the world, our journals reflect our prime interests. Many entries are recipes. People, mainly, are very kind about sharing recipes. Even professional chefs. This recipe is one of our warmest recollections.)

Driving through Virginia, not planning a place to stop for dinner, we asked at a gas station near Staunton, and were told, "Rachel's. Best place around." A little skeptical, we thought that we would have to "make do." Rachel's was a small, neat red building set back off the road in the midst of several stately oaks, dripping long beards of Spanish moss. The restaurant held only six tables; Rachel, a spry, slender black woman in her seventies, was both chef and waitress. She claimed that chicken pies should contain only chicken. "And eggs is chicken, too." She served individual pies. But this, her recipe, is a supper pie. Make her pastry first.

PASTRY

2 cups of flour, mixed with 1½ teaspoons of salt
⅓ cup of butter
⅓ cup of lard
⅓ cup of cold water

1 egg, beaten with 1 tablespoon of water (egg wash to brush on pastry just before it goes into the oven)

In a bowl, blend the flour, butter and lard, using a pastry cutter (or use a food processor). Add the water and mix well with a fork. Roll into a ball, wrap in waxed paper and refrigerate until ready to roll out.

POACHING THE CHICKEN

1 quart of chicken broth
2 whole chicken breasts
3 ribs of celery, cut in chunks
1 teaspoon of salt
½ teaspoon of pepper
1 recipe of Sauce Suprême (page 64)

8 slightly undercooked, hard-cooked eggs (boil them 1 or 2 minutes less than you usually would, then plunge them in cold water)

Pour the broth into a large pot. Add the chicken breasts, celery and salt and pepper. (Rachel didn't want to "spoil" the delicate flavor of the chicken with anything other than these simple ingredients.) Cover, bring to a boil, reduce the heat and simmer 20 minutes, or until the breasts are tender. Cool in the broth. Use the broth to prepare the Suprême Sauce. Remove and discard the skin and bones and cut the chicken meat into hefty, larger-than-bite-sized chunks.

Remove the whites from the hard-cooked eggs (only the yolks will be used). In a 2-quart shallow baking dish, or one in which contents will come to within ½ inch of the top (a shallow, rectangular Pyrex one works well), arrange the chicken pieces and the egg yolks. Spoon on the sauce to cover. Roll out the pastry to a ¼-inch thickness so it is ¾ inches larger all around than top of baking dish and the same shape as the dish. Moisten edges and mold to edge of the dish. Cut 2 small air holes in the top and prick with a fork in 2 places. Brush the top with the egg wash. Place the pie on a baking sheet in a preheated 450°F. oven for 15 minutes.

Reduce heat to 350°F. and continue baking for ½ hour, or until crust is golden.

And thank you, Rachel!

CHICKEN AND SAUSAGE PIE

Serves 4 to 6:

Prepare pie crust (see Rachel's Regal Chicken Pie, page 225), increasing the recipe by one-half

Make 2 balls from the dough, one slightly larger. Roll out the larger ball between pieces of waxed paper and line a deep 10-inch pie plate.

FILLING

½ pound of sausage meat
1 teaspoon of minced parsley
1 teaspoon of minced chives
1 teaspoon of olive oil
6 tablespoons of butter
2 whole chicken breasts, halved
3 chicken thighs
Salt and pepper to taste

3 cups of chicken broth
6 leeks (white part only), cut into 1-inch pieces
3 tablespoons of flour
¼ cup of heavy cream
⅛ teaspoon of dried tarragon
3 tablespoons of milk, beaten with 1 egg yolk

Combine the sausage, parsley and chives, blending thoroughly, and roll into balls ¾ inch in diameter. In a frypan, over medium heat, heat the oil and evenly brown the balls. Remove, drain on paper towels and set aside. Pour fat from frypan. Melt 3 tablespoons of the butter and evenly brown chicken, cooking until just slightly underdone. Season with salt and pepper. Cool slightly, remove and discard skin and bones and cut the chicken meat into 1-inch cubes. Set aside. In a saucepan, over medium-low heat, pour 1 cup of the broth, add the leeks, bring to a simmer and cook for 5 minutes. Drain leeks, reserving the broth (and leeks). In the chicken frypan, add the remaining 3 tablespoons of butter, stir in the flour and cook over low heat, stirring constantly, into a smooth paste. Gradually add the broth the leeks cooked in, the remaining 2 cups broth and the cream. Cook, stirring, until the sauce is smooth and slightly thick. Blend in the tarragon. Taste for seasoning. Arrange the chicken, sausage balls and leeks on the bottom crust of the pie. Pour in enough sauce to cover. Roll out remaining pastry and cover the pie, sealing edges. Brush the crust with the milk-egg yolk mixture. Cut a hole in the center of the crust and prick with a fork in several places to allow steam to escape. Bake in a preheated 450°F. oven for 15 minutes, then in a 350°F. oven for 15 minutes, or until the crust is golden brown and steam is pouring from the hole in the center. Heat the remaining sauce and pass at the table.

QUICK CHICKEN SWEET POTATO PIE

Serves 4:

5 medium-sized sweet potatoes, cooked and mashed
4 tablespoons of melted butter
⅛ teaspoon of allspice
⅛ teaspoon of nutmeg
1 teaspoon of salt
1 tablespoon of butter
2 medium-sized onions, chopped
2½ cups of diced cooked chicken

1 (10¾-ounce) can of condensed cream of mushroom soup
1 (8-ounce) can of whole kernel corn, drained
1 (8-ounce) can of peas, drained
1 medium-sized tomato, peeled, seeded and chopped

In a bowl, combine the potatoes, melted butter, allspice, nutmeg and ½ teaspoon salt, blending well. Line a 9-inch pie plate with the potato mixture, molding up the edges ½ inch. In a saucepan, melt the tablespoon of butter and over medium heat cook the onion for 4 minutes, or until soft. Blend in the chicken, soup, corn, peas, tomato and remaining ½ teaspoon of salt, mixing thoroughly. Spoon evenly into the potato shell. Bake, uncovered, in a preheated 350°F. oven for 35 minutes.

CHICKEN PILAF

Serves 4 to 6 as an accompaniment:

2 tablespoons of butter
4 small scallions, minced
1 clove of garlic, minced
1 cup of rice
3 cups of chicken broth
⅓ cup of chopped raisins

3 cups of chopped cooked
 chicken
Salt to taste
⅓ cup of pine nuts
2 tablespoons of chopped
 parsley

In a deep saucepan, over medium heat, melt butter and sauté scallions and garlic for 4 minutes. Stir in the rice, blending it with the butter. Add the broth, and simmer, uncovered, over low heat for 15 minutes, stirring occasionally, until most of the liquid has been absorbed. Stir in the raisins, chicken and salt and simmer, stirring, for 10 minutes, or until all liquid has been absorbed and the rice is cooked. Before serving sprinkle with the pine nuts and parsley.

CHICKEN AND CHICKEN LIVER PILAF

Serves 6 to 8 as an accompaniment:

4 tablespoons of butter
1 small white onion, minced
2 cups of rice
3½ cups of hot chicken
 broth
¼ cup of grated Asiago or
 Parmesan cheese
1 whole chicken breast,
 skinned and boned, cut
 julienne

4 chicken livers, cut into
 small pieces
4 small mushrooms, chopped
Salt and pepper to taste
2 large, ripe tomatoes,
 peeled, seeded, chopped
 and cooked in a saucepan
 until most of the liquid
 has evaporated
2 tablespoons of finely
 chopped parsley

In a saucepan, over medium heat, heat 2 tablespoons of the butter. Add the onion and cook for 1 minute. Stir in the rice, coating with butter. Add the broth, cover and cook over low heat until the broth has been completely absorbed and the rice is cooked but slightly *al dente*. Stir in the cheese.

In a frypan, heat the remaining 2 tablespoons of butter

over medium heat. Add the chicken and cook, stirring, for 4 minutes, or until golden. Stir in the chicken livers and mushrooms and cook about 2 minutes longer, so the livers are brown on the outside and slightly pink on the inside. Season with salt and pepper. Stir in the tomatoes and simmer for 1 minute. Stir the tomato-chicken-liver-mushroom mixture into the rice. Simmer 4 minutes, stirring once or twice. Taste for seasoning. Stir in the parsley.

CHICKEN LIVER PILAF

Serves 4 as an accompaniment:

4 tablespoons of butter
3 chicken livers, cut into ½-inch cubes
Salt and pepper to taste
1 medium-sized onion, finely chopped

1 small rib of celery scraped and finely chopped
1 cup of white or brown rice
2 cups of chicken broth
½ cup of slivered almonds, toasted in 2 tablespoons of butter

In a small frypan, over medium heat, melt 2 tablespoons of the butter. Brown chicken livers, but do not overcook (they should be slightly pink inside). Season with salt and pepper. Set aside and keep warm.

Heat the remaining 2 tablespoons of butter in a saucepan. Add the onion and celery and cook over medium heat for 1 minute. Stir in the rice, coating with the butter. Add the broth, bring to a boil, cover, and cook over low heat for 15 minutes, or until the broth has been absorbed and rice is tender. Taste for seasoning. Fluff up with a fork. Just before serving, stir in the chicken livers and almond slivers.

ANTOINE GILLY'S COOKED CHICKEN SALMIS

Serves 4:

Cooked chicken, both white and dark meat, in medium-thick slices, enough to serve four (a 3½ - to 4-pound cooked chicken should be ample)

3 shallots, sliced

Bouquet garni (2 sprigs parsley, 2 small bay leaves, pinch of dry thyme, 1 celery rib tied in cheesecloth)

2 small ripe tomatoes, peeled, seeded and quartered

½ cup of red wine

2 tablespoons of water

⅓ cup of Madeira

1 tablespoon of red currant jelly

1 tablespoon of brandy

8 medium-sized mushrooms, sliced thinly and lightly sautéed in butter

1 tablespoon of flour, blended with water into a smooth thick paste

In a saucepan, place chicken, shallots, bouquet garni, tomatoes, wine and water. Simmer, covered, for 10 minutes. Remove the chicken and the bouquet garni. Stir in the Madeira, currant jelly, brandy and mushrooms. Add the flour paste, stirring over low heat until the sauce is thick and hot. Add the chicken slices and simmer for 10 minutes, or until hot. Serve with rice.

CHICKEN SAUSAGES

Serves 6 to 8:

4 pounds of chicken thighs, boned, skinned and put through the fine blade of a food chopper (or use a processor)

1 teaspoon of cumin

½ teaspoon of cayenne

2 tablespoons of minced parsley

2 tablespoons of minced fresh chives

1 medium-sized onion, minced

4 eggs, beaten

1 teaspoon of salt

½ cup of peanut oil

In a large bowl, combine all ingredients except the oil, blending thoroughly. Make a mini-sausage, cook in a little oil and taste for seasoning, then add whatever it might need. Roll the mixture into sausage shapes, 1 inch wide by 3 inches long, or any desired shape or size. Heat the oil in a frypan over medium-low heat and cook the chicken sausages, browning evenly and turning several times. Drain on paper towels and serve with a Chicken Liver Pilaf (page 230).

FAST CHICKEN-APPLE SCALLOP

Serves 4:

3 cups of cubed cooked
   chicken
1½ tablespoons of Dijon
   mustard
1 (20-ounce) can of pie-
   sliced apples
2 tablespoons of lemon juice
1 teaspoon of salt

blended
   1 (10½-ounce) can of
      cream of mushroom
      soup
   ⅓ cup of heavy cream

blended
   ½ cup of bread crumbs
   2 tablespoons of melted
      butter

Combine the chicken and mustard, blending well. Divide among four small ramekins or individual casseroles. Arrange apple slices evenly on top of each casserole. Sprinkle with lemon juice and salt. In equal portions, pour over the soup and cream blend and top with the buttered bread crumbs. Bake, uncovered, in a preheated 350°F. oven for 25 minutes, or until bread crumbs are crispy brown.

CHICKEN AND SPAGHETTI CAKE

Serves 6:

1 pound of spaghetti (break pieces in half), cooked in boiling, salted water for 10 minutes and drained

5 tablespoons of butter

3 cups of chopped cooked chicken

3 medium-sized onions, finely chopped and sautéed in 2 tablespoons of butter for 4 minutes

6 large mushrooms, sliced

⅓ cup of sliced pimiento-stuffed green olives

⅓ cup of grated Asiago or Parmesan cheese

½ pound of mozzarella cheese, shredded

2 tablespoons of chopped broadleaf parsley

½ teaspoon of salt

¼ teaspoon of pepper

2 eggs, beaten with ¼ cup of cream

½ cup of bread crumbs

In a large bowl, toss the hot spaghetti with the 5 tablespoons of butter. Add the chicken, onion, mushrooms, olives, cheeses, parsley, salt and pepper. Pour in the egg-cream mixture, blending well. Butter a 9-inch springform pan and coat with bread crumbs, reserving 2 tablespoons. Evenly spoon the pasta mixture into the pan. Sprinkle the top with the reserved bread crumbs. Bake, uncovered, in a preheated 375°F. oven for 40 minutes. Let set for 5 minutes. Remove side of pan. Cut wedges from the cake and serve with a tomato or cream sauce and extra grated cheese.

CHICKEN AND SWEETBREADS
IN PATTY SHELLS

Serves 4:

2 whole chicken breasts
4 cups of chicken broth
1 pair of sweetbreads,
   soaked in ice water for 1
   hour, drained and trimmed
   of membranes
4 tablespoons of butter
4 medium-sized mushrooms,
   diced
3 tablespoons of flour
2 tablespoons of Madeira

beaten together
   ⅓ cup of heavy cream
   1 egg yolk
   ½ tablespoon of fresh
      lemon juice

Salt and pepper to taste
4 patty shells (baked at the
   last minute; they should be
   warm and flaky); frozen
   commercial shells are excellent
1 tablespoon of chopped
   parsley

Poach the breasts in the broth, covered, for 25 minutes, or until tender (do not overcook or they will become stringy). Remove the chicken, cool, remove and discard skin and bones. Cube the chicken meat. Place the sweetbreads in the simmering broth and poach for 15 minutes. Remove, cool and cube, reserving the broth. In a saucepan, melt the butter and over medium heat, sauté the mushrooms for 2 minutes. Remove with a slotted spoon. Add the flour to the saucepan and cook, stirring, into a smooth paste. Gradually add 2 cups of the reserved broth and cook, stirring, into a smooth, medium-thick sauce. Lower heat, stir in the wine and cream-egg yolk-lemon juice mixture, stirring into a smooth sauce (do not boil). Add the cubed chicken and sweetbreads and mushrooms to the sauce. Season with salt and pepper. Heat through without boiling. Spoon into the patty shells and sprinkle with the parsley.

CHICKEN TURNOVERS

Serves 4: Easy and excellent for leftover chicken and gravy.

2 tablespoons of butter
1 medium-sized onion, chopped
1 teaspoon of Worcestershire sauce
½ teaspoon of celery salt
¼ teaspoon of pepper

½ teaspoon of paprika
3 cups of finely chopped cooked chicken
2 cups leftover gravy (approximate)
2 cups of biscuit mix
½ cup of cold water

In a frypan, over medium heat, melt the butter. Add the onion and cook until soft. Remove from the heat and stir in the Worcestershire sauce, celery salt, pepper, paprika and chicken, blending well. Add just enough gravy to moisten. Taste for seasoning. Cool.

Blend the biscuit mix with the water according to package directions. Roll dough ¼-inch thin into a 10-inch square. Divide into four 5-inch squares. Place one-fourth of the chicken filling on one-half of each square, then fold over to form triangles. Moisten edges and seal. Place on a baking sheet and bake in a preheated 450°F. oven until browned. Serve with additional gravy and a cranberry relish.

CHICKEN VOL-AU-VENT

Serves 6:

6 tablespoons of butter
6 large chicken thighs
2 cups of chicken broth
½ cup of dry white wine
¾ pound of sausage meat, browned and drained
½ pound of very small mushrooms, sliced

3 tablespoons of flour
1 cup of light cream
Salt and pepper to taste
6 frozen commercial patty shells, thawed
1 egg, beaten with 1 tablespoon of water

In a deep frypan, over medium heat, melt 3 tablespoons of the butter and evenly brown the thighs. Pour in the broth and wine, cover and simmer for 20 minutes. Drain (strain and reserve the liquid) and cool the thighs. Remove the bones, and stuff the thigh cavities with the sausage meat.

In a saucepan, over medium heat, melt the remaining 3 tablespoons of butter. Add the mushrooms and cook for 2 minutes. Stir in the flour, mixing well. Stir in 1½ cups of the reserved liquid and the cream, a small amount at a time, stirring constantly, and cooking until you have a medium-thick smooth sauce. Season to taste.

Roll each patty shell on a floured board into a 6-inch square. Place a stuffed thigh in the center of each square and top with 2 tablespoons of the mushroom sauce. Fold like an envelope, moistening edges and sealing. Place on a shallow baking dish, seam side down. Brush the tops with a little of the egg-water mixture. Bake in a preheated 400°F. oven for 30 minutes, or until golden brown. Serve with the remaining hot sauce.

CHAMPAGNE CHICKEN WINGS WITH HAM AND OLIVES

Serves 4:

4 tablespoons of olive oil
1 tablespoon of butter
8 to 12 (depending on size) meaty chicken wings
Salt and pepper
1½ teaspoons of Hungarian paprika

½-inch slice of cooked ham, diced (should be at least 1 cup)
1 cup of champagne, preferably leftover champagne
¾ cup of pitted Spanish green olives

In a frypan, over medium heat, heat the oil and butter. Sprinkle the wings with salt, pepper and paprika and brown evenly. Remove and reserve wings. Add the ham to the pan and cook, stirring, until slightly browned. Remove and reserve the ham. Pour off any fat in the pan and pour in the champagne. Raise the heat to high and deglaze the pan, stirring to scrape up the browned particles (about 1 minute). Lower the heat, return the wings and ham to the pan. Add the olives, cover and simmer until the chicken is tender.

WINGDING:
CHICKEN WINGS, LIVERS AND WILD RICE

Serves 4:

1 cup of wild or brown rice
⅛ teaspoon of dried thyme
2 tablespoons of chopped
   fresh chives
3 cups of chicken broth

1 stick (¼ pound) of butter
1 pound of chicken livers,
   halved
Salt and pepper
8 meaty chicken wings

In a top-of-the-stove casserole, large enough to hold all ingredients, combine the rice, thyme, chives and broth. Bring to a boil, lower heat, cover the pan and simmer, stirring occasionally, for 15 minutes (rice should not be completely cooked). In a large frypan, melt half of the butter over medium heat and add the chicken livers. Sprinkle lightly with salt and pepper and sauté about 4 minutes, turning, until evenly browned on the outside and still slightly pink on the inside. Remove and reserve the livers. Add two-thirds of the remaining butter to the frypan, add the wings, season lightly, and cook about 10 minutes, turning often and browning evenly. Bury the wings in the rice in the casserole. Dot with remaining butter, cover and bake in a preheated 325°F. oven for 25 minutes, or until the wings are just tender. Push the livers into the rice, remove cover from casserole and cook for 7 minutes.

Chapter Ten
Salads and Sandwiches

Salads. Sandwiches.
Visions. Long summer days. Hot summer nights.
Chilled chicken salads.
Cold (and some hot) chicken sandwiches.
The chicken contests the potato in the salad world.
The chicken runs neck-to-neck with tuna in the sandwich race.
Ask yourself which are the winners.
We're betting on the chicken for its usual talent—versatility.

It is so useful in either salad or sandwich category that it is downright indispensable. A Maryland farmer once remarked, "Chickens, suh," he said, "are the most useful animal there is. You can eat them before they are born and after they have departed."

CHICKEN AND FRESH ASPARAGUS SALAD

Serves 4:

20 asparagus spears, peeled
½   cup of Russian dressing
3   cups of cubed cooked chicken
1   head of Boston lettuce, shredded

⅓   cup of mayonnaise
2   tablespoons of chopped broadleaf parsley
8   pimiento strips
2   hard-cooked eggs, quartered

Cut off the tops of the asparagus in 3-inch pieces. Tie them into 4 bunches. Cut the remaining asparagus into 1-inch pieces and simmer in boiling, salted water until tender-crisp. Drain and set aside. In the same water simmer the asparagus tips until tender-crisp. Drain, cool and marinate the tips in the Russian dressing for 1 hour in the refrigerator. Toss the chicken with the 1-inch pieces of asparagus. Place the shredded lettuce in a salad bowl, center the chicken-asparagus mixture on it. Spoon the mayonnaise over and sprinkle with parsley. Garnish with the asparagus spears, appearing to be tied in bunches with the pimiento strips, and the egg quarters.

CALIFORNIA CHICKEN AVOCADO SALAD

Serves 4:

3 cups of cubed cooked chicken breast

1 cup of finely diced celery hearts

1 cucumber (or enough to yield 1 cup of diced), peeled, quartered lengthwise, seeds removed, diced and drained

1 cup of commercial salad dressing

Juice of 1 fresh lime

Salt and pepper

2 large, ripe avocados, halved, peeled, pitted and rubbed with additional lime juice to prevent darkening

Bibb lettuce leaves

2 fresh limes, quartered

4 teaspoons of drained capers

In a bowl, combine the chicken, celery, cucumber and gently blend with one-half of the salad dressing and the lime juice. Taste and add salt, pepper and additional salad dressing to taste. Heap chicken mixture into the avocado halves and serve in individual salad plates on a bed of Bibb, garnished with the limes, which are to be squeezed over the salad. Sprinkle the capers on top.

CHICKEN, BACON AND EGG SALAD

Serves 4:

4 cups of cubed cooked chicken

8 slices of bacon, crisply fried, drained and crumbled

4 hard-cooked eggs, in thick slices

1 celery rib, scraped and diced

1 tablespoon of chopped fresh chives

1 cup of French dressing

Salt and pepper

2 cups of romaine lettuce, torn into bite-sized pieces

2 cups of Bibb lettuce, torn into bite-sized pieces

8 green olives, chopped

In a bowl, combine the chicken, bacon, eggs, celery, chives and one-half of the dressing. Blend gently. Add salt and pepper to taste. Arrange the greens in a salad bowl. Center the chicken mixture on the greens. Spoon over additional French dressing to taste. Sprinkle with the chopped olives.

CHICKEN SALAD WITH CASHEWS

Serves 4:

½ cup of cashews, separated into halves

1 tablespoon of butter

4 cups of cubed cooked chicken

4 tender celery ribs, scraped and diced

8 medium-sized mushrooms, sliced

blended into a smooth dressing

⅔ cup mayonnaise

½ cup of buttermilk

½ cup of sour cream

½ teaspoon of cumin

¼ teaspoon of cayenne

2 tablespoons of lemon juice

Salt to taste

Crisp Boston lettuce leaves

2 tablespoons of chopped parsley

Sauté the cashews in the butter, stirring, until golden and crisp. Cool. Combine the cashews, chicken, celery and mushrooms in a bowl with one-half of the dressing and gently blend. Taste and add additional dressing, if desired. Serve on Boston lettuce leaves with the parsley sprinkled over the top.

CORN AND CHICKEN SALAD

Serves 4:

3 cups of cooked cubed
chicken

3 ears of corn, cooked and
kernels cut off, or 1 (10-
ounce) package of frozen
corn kernels, cooked ac-
cording to package direc-
tions

2 scallions (white part
only), minced

1 small red pepper, seeded,
cored and chopped

1 medium-sized ripe tomato,
peeled, seeded and
chopped

blended into a dressing
¾ cup of mayonnaise
3 tablespoons of chili
sauce
3 drops of Tabasco

Salt and pepper to taste
Tender romaine lettuce
leaves
3 hard-cooked eggs, each
quartered

Combine chicken, corn, scallions, pepper, tomato and two-
thirds of the dressing. Taste for seasoning. Add salt, pepper
and additional dressing to taste. Blend well. Line a salad bowl
with the lettuce. Spoon in the salad and garnish with the
quartered eggs.

CURRIED CHICKEN SALAD

Serves 4:

3 cups of ½-inch cubes of
cooked chicken

2 cups of cooked couscous
(cooked in chicken broth
and drained)

1 cup of chopped scallions
(white part only)

blended into a dressing
1½ cups of commercial
salad dressing
½ teaspoon of salt

¼ teaspoon of pepper
2 teaspoons of curry pow-
der
2 tablespoons of lemon
juice

Lettuce leaves
3 small, ripe tomatoes,
peeled and quartered
¼ cup of chopped scallions
(green part only)

In a bowl, combine the chicken, couscous, scallions (white part) and one-half of the blended dressing. Mix gently but well. Taste and add more dressing, salt and pepper, if desired. Heap on crisp lettuce leaves on individual salad plates. Garnish with the tomato quarters and sprinkle scallions (green part) on top.

CHICKEN SALAD ELEGANTE

Serves 4:

3 cups of cubed cooked chicken

2 cups of diced cooked shrimp

2 large cucumbers, peeled, quartered lengthwise, seeded, cubed and drained

blended into a dressing
  1½ cups of mayonnaise
  2 tablespoons of lemon juice

1 teaspoon of Worcestershire sauce

⅛ teaspoon of cayenne

½ teaspoon of salt

Bibb lettuce leaves

½ cup of chopped macadamian nuts

2 hard-cooked egg yolks, put through a potato ricer

In a bowl combine the chicken, shrimp, cucumbers and one-half of the dressing. Mix gently but well. Taste and add additional dressing, if desired. Arrange the lettuce on a salad dish and heap the chicken mixture on it. Sprinkle with the macadamian nuts and egg yolks.

CHICKEN WITH ENDIVE SALAD

Serves 4:

4 heads of Belgian endive, quartered lengthwise

4 cups of julienne-cut cooked breast of chicken

2 cups of julienne-cut Gruyère cheese

blended into a dressing
½ cup of mayonnaise
½ cup of whipped cream

½ tablespoon of Dijon mustard

2 tablespoons of fresh orange juice

Grated rind of one navel orange

1 teaspoon of salt

Navel orange sections, membranes and skin removed

Arrange the endive on a salad dish, spoke fashion. Alternate the chicken and cheese strips between the endive. Spoon the mayonnaise mixture overall and garnish with the orange sections.

HOT CHICKEN SALAD

Serves 4:

2 tablespoons of lime juice

2 tablespoons of Dijon mustard

½ teaspoon of cumin

½ teaspoon of sugar

½ teaspoon of salt

8 whole young scallions, chopped

⅓ cup of chicken broth

4 cups of cubed cooked chicken

3 cups of shredded hearts of escarole

2 tablespoons of toasted, crushed sesame seeds

In a frypan, combine the lime juice, mustard, cumin, sugar, salt, scallions and broth. Cook, stirring, over medium heat for 3 minutes. Stir in the chicken, and cook, stirring, until the chicken is thoroughly heated through. Spoon over the escarole on individual salad plates. Sprinkle sesame seeds on top.

MARDI GRAS CHICKEN SALAD

Serves 6:

4 cups of cubed cooked
chicken

1 cup of crumbled blue,
Roquefort or Gorgonzola
cheese

1 (10-ounce) package of
frozen tiny peas, cooked
until barely tender and
drained

1 cup of cooked small pasta
shells

1 tablespoon of minced onion

2 celery ribs, scraped and
finely chopped

1 small sweet red pepper,
cored and finely chopped

blended into a dressing
⅔ cup of sour cream
⅔ cup of mayonnaise
1 teaspoon of dried thyme
1 teaspoon of salt

2 cups of bite-sized pieces of
crisp, tender spinach
Cherry tomatoes

In a bowl, combine the chicken, cheese, peas, pasta, onion,
celery, red pepper and one-half of the blended dressing. Mix
gently but thoroughly. Taste and add more dressing, if
desired. Chill for 2 hours. Arrange the spinach on a serving
dish. Spoon the chicken mixture over it and garnish with the
cherry tomatoes.

CHICKEN-MUSHROOM SALAD

Serves 4:

1 (3-½ to 4-pound) chicken,
poached in water to cover
with 2 teaspoons of salt, 1
teaspoon of pepper, 2 on-
ions, halved, 2 celery ribs
with leaves, 2 carrots, and
2 cloves garlic for 1 hour,
or until tender

½ pound of fresh button
mushrooms

1 tablespoon of drained
capers

½ cup of mayonnaise (or to
taste)

2 tablespoons of lemon juice
Lettuce leaves

2 hard-cooked eggs, sliced

1 tablespoon of chopped
parsley

Remove the chicken from the broth (reserving the broth)
and cool. Remove and discard skin and bones and cut

chicken into bite-sized cubes. Transfer to a bowl. Place mushrooms in a small saucepan, cover with broth from the poached chicken and cook for 3 minutes. Drain, cool and combine with chicken. To the chicken add capers, mayonnaise and lemon juice, blending and tossing well. Serve on lettuce leaves, garnished with the eggs slices and parsley.

CHICKEN NIÇOISE WITH VINAIGRETTE SAUCE AND CHAPONS

Serves 6 to 8:

2 cups of bite-sized pieces of Boston lettuce

2 cups of bite-sized pieces of chicory

4 scallions (white part only), sliced

1 small cucumber peeled, sliced

2 medium-sized ripe tomatoes, peeled and cut into wedges

12 Greek olives, halved and pitted

3 cups of cubed cooked chicken

2 cups of tiny new red potatoes, cooked in their skins

Vinaigrette Sauce (see below)

4 anchovy fillets, soaked in white vinegar to cover, drained and each cut in half lengthwise

2 tablespoons of chopped broadleaf parsley

In a large salad bowl, combine the greens, scallions, cucumber, tomatoes, olives, chicken, potatoes, two-thirds of the vinaigrette sauce and the *chapons* (see below). Mix gently but well. Taste and add more sauce, if desired. Garnish with the anchovy strips and sprinkle with parsley.

CHAPONS

6 slices of French bread, toasted, rubbed with garlic, sprinkled with 2

teaspoons of olive oil, then quartered

VINAIGRETTE SAUCE

½ teaspoon of dry mustard
¾ teaspoon of salt
¼ teaspoon of pepper
⅔ cup of olive oil

3 tablespoons of wine vinegar
1 tablespoon of chopped fresh basil
1 clove of garlic, crushed

In a bowl, combine the mustard, salt and pepper. Pour in just enough oil to make a smooth paste, gradually stirring in and blending well the remaining oil and vinegar. Blend in the basil and garlic.

COLD PAELLA CASSEROLE

Serves 6:

5 tablespoons of butter
1 tablespoon of olive oil
2 whole chicken breasts, halved
3 chicken thighs
Salt and pepper
6 tablespoons (3 ounces) of sherry
3 cups of chicken broth (approximate)
24 medium-sized shrimp, shelled and deveined
1 medium-sized onion, chopped
1 clove of garlic, minced

1 cup of rice
¼ teaspoon of powdered saffron
½ cup of cooked peas
1 cup of cubed cooked ham
1 lobster, cooked and cubed (optional)
3 medium-sized ripe tomatoes, peeled and sliced
1 canned pimiento, cut into 6 or more strips
½ cup of green stuffed olives
Mayonnaise-Caper Sauce (see below)

In a large frypan, over medium heat, heat 3 tablespoons of the butter and the oil. Sprinkle the chicken with salt and pepper and brown evenly. Pour in the sherry and 2 cups of the broth and simmer, covered, for 10 minutes or until the chicken is barely tender. Add the shrimp, cover and cook for 1 minute, or just until they turn pink (do not overcook). Remove shrimp and set aside. Remove the chicken, discard skin and bones and cut the meat into slices. Set aside. Strain the pan juices into a large measuring cup.

In a saucepan, heat the remaining 2 tablespoons butter,

add the onion and garlic and cook just until soft. Stir in the rice and saffron, mixing well. Add enough of the remaining chicken broth to the measuring cup with the pan juices to make 2 cups. Pour this liquid into the saucepan with the rice, cover and simmer for 15 minutes, or until the liquid has been absorbed and the rice is tender, but still slightly firm.

In a large bowl, combine the rice, chicken slices, shrimp, peas, ham and lobster (if used) and gently mix. Cool. Rim a serving dish with the tomato slices. Spoon the rice mixture into the center, just covering the edges of the tomatoes. Garnish with the pimiento strips and olives. Serve with the Mayonnaise-Caper sauce.

MAYONNAISE-CAPER SAUCE

Blend thoroughly 1 cup of mayonnaise, 2 tablespoons of lemon juice, 1 tablespoon of sherry and 1 tablespoon of drained capers.

PIQUANT CHICKEN SALAD

Serves 4:

1 large whole chicken breast	½ teaspoon of salt
2 cups of chicken broth	½ pound of bean sprouts
4 slices of fresh ginger root	3 scallions, chopped

In a deep saucepan, combine the chicken, broth, ginger root and salt. Bring to a boil, cover, lower heat and simmer for 15 minutes, or until chicken is tender. Drain (reserve the broth for some other use) and cool chicken. Remove skin and bones and shred the chicken. Blanch the bean sprouts and scallions in boiling water for 6 seconds, stirring. Rinse in cold water, drain and squeeze dry.

SAUCE

blended

1 teaspoon of cider vinegar
1 tablespoon of soy sauce
1 teaspoon of sesame oil
2 teaspoons of hot pepper oil

In a bowl, combine the chicken, bean sprouts, scallions and sauce, blending well.

PLAIN CHICKEN SALAD

Serves 4:

4 cups of cubed cooked
  chicken breast
Salt and pepper

blended into a dressing
  ¾ cup of mayonnaise
  2 tablespoons of finely
    chopped sour pickles

2 tablespoons of finely
  chopped stuffed green
  olives

8 crisp lettuce leaves
Radishes for garnish

In a bowl, place the chicken, lightly sprinkle with salt and
pepper and toss with one-half of the mayonnaise mixture.
Add more dressing to taste. Arrange lettuce leaves on a salad
dish, spoon on salad and garnish with the radishes.

CHICKEN RELLEÑO

Serves 6:

2 cups of diced cooked
  chicken
2 tablespoons of minced
  jalapeño pepper
1 tablespoon of minced
  parsley
1 tablespoon *each* of minced
  onion, celery and carrot

1 teaspoon of salt
½ teaspoon of pepper
½ cup of mayonnaise
3 medium-sized ripe avocados, peeled, halved and
  pitted
Boston lettuce leaves

SALAD DRESSING

blended
  1 cup of sour cream
  1 cup of mayonnaise

½ teaspoon of curry pow-
  der
2 tablespoons of chopped
  cilantro or parsley

In a bowl, combine the chicken, jalapeño pepper, parsley, onion, celery and carrot, salt, pepper and the one-half cup of
mayonnaise, blending thoroughly. Heap the chicken mixture
onto the avocado halves. Arrange the avocados on lettuce
leaves on a serving dish. Spoon half of the salad dressing over
them and pass the remaining dressing at the table.

SIMPLE RED CHICKEN SALAD

Serves 4:

3 cups of cubed cooked
    chicken
1 cup of cubed boiled pota-
    toes
1 cup of sliced cooked beets
1 cup of diced celery hearts

blended into a dressing
  1½ cups of mayonnaise

2 tablespoons of minced
    parsley
3 radishes, finely diced

Salt and pepper
Lettuce leaves
Red onion rings
2 tablespoons of chopped
    fresh dill

In a bowl, combine the chicken, potatoes, beets, celery and
one-half of the dressing. Mix gently but thoroughly. Taste
and season with salt, pepper and additional dressing, if
desired. Mound on the lettuce leaves on a salad plate. Garnish with the onion rings and sprinkle with the dill.

SUMMER CHICKEN SALAD WITH GRAPES AND WALNUTS

Serves 4:

4 cups of julienne-cut
    cooked chicken breast,
    lightly salted
½ cup of canned white
    grapes
⅔ cup of halved walnuts

Assorted salad greens (water-
    cress, Bibb, spinach, etc.),
    in bite-sized pieces
Michele Sauce (see below)
Grapefruit sections, skin and
    membranes removed

Combine the chicken, grapes and walnuts. Place on a bed of
the salad greens, spoon over the Michele Sauce and garnish
with the grapefruit sections.

MICHELE SAUCE

1½ cups of mayonnaise
2 shallots
1 tablespoon of capers
1 small celery rib, scraped and chopped

1 small clove of garlic
⅛ teaspoon of dried marjoram
2 tablespoons of chopped broadleaf parsley

Combine all ingredients in a blender container and blend for 7 seconds.

CHICKEN-RICE SUMMER SALAD

Serves 6:

1 cup of long-grain rice (cooked according to package directions), chilled
3 cups of cubed cooked chicken
1 tablespoon of grated onion
1 small, tender sweet red pepper, seeded, cored and cut julienne
2 small carrots, peeled and thinly sliced

3 celery ribs, scraped and thinly sliced
¾ cup of mayonnaise
Salt and pepper to taste
Boston lettuce leaves
2 temple oranges, peeled and cut into sections, removing all seeds and the membranes dividing the sections

In a bowl, combine all the ingredients except the lettuce leaves and orange sections. Add more mayonnaise, if necessary. Chill. Serve on the lettuce leaves, garnished with the orange sections.

SWEET-AND-SOUR CHICKEN SALAD

Serves 8:

2 cups of elbow macaroni,
  cooked *al dente* and
  drained
4 cups of bite-sized pieces of
  cooked chicken
2 cups of honeydew melon
  balls
1 (20-ounce) can of un-
  sweetened pineapple
  chunks, drained, reserving
  ¼ cup of the juice

blended into a dressing
  ¼ cup of mayonnaise
  ½ cup of sour cream
  ¼ cup of pineapple juice
    (see above)
  1 teaspoon of salt
  ½ teaspoon of paprika
  1 tablespoon of chopped
    fresh chives
  1½ teaspoons of dry
    mustard

Boston lettuce leaves

In a bowl combine the macaroni, chicken, melon balls and 1 cup of the pineapple chunks. Pour on the blended dressing and mix gently but thoroughly. Place on a bed of lettuce leaves on a salad plate and garnish with the remaining pineapple chunks.

CHICKEN SALAD IN TOMATO CUPS

Serves 4:

3 cups of diced cooked
  chicken
1 cup of diced artichoke bottoms
½ cup of diced boiled potatoes
Salt and pepper

*blended into green mayon-
  naise*
  1 cup of mayonnaise

¼ cup of minced water-
  cress leaves
½ cup of minced broad-
  leaf parsley

4 large ripe tomatoes,
  peeled, tops sliced off with
  seeds and center pulp
  scooped out leaving a firm,
  hollow tomato cup
Lettuce leaves

In a bowl, combine the chicken, artichoke bottoms and potatoes. Sprinkle lightly with salt and pepper and toss gently.
Add three-fourths of the green mayonnaise and blend gently

but thoroughly. Heap into the tomato cups and place on lettuce leaves on a salad plate. Garnish tops with the remaining
green mayonnaise.

CHICKEN SALAD VESUVIO

Serves 6:

2 bunches of watercress,
  trimmed and separated
4 cups of julienne-cut
  cooked chicken (preferably breast meat)
1 large head of fennel,
  thinly sliced
2 cucumbers, peeled, cut in
  quarters lengthwise,
  seeded, cut julienne and
  drained
6 radishes, quartered
2 large ripe tomatoes,
  peeled, seeded, quartered
  and drained

1 (2-ounce) can of anchovy
  fillets, drained, then
  soaked to cover in white
  vinegar, drained again and
  each cut into 3 pieces
Salad dressing (see below)
6 green olives, pitted and
  halved
6 Italian black olives, pitted
  and halved
3 hard-cooked eggs, quar-
  tered

In a salad bowl make a base of the watercress. In another
bowl combine the chicken, fennel, cucumbers, radishes, tomatoes and anchovies. Blend gently but thoroughly. Add to the
bowl with the watercress and toss with half of the dressing.
Taste and add more dressing, if necessary. Garnish with the
olives and quartered eggs.

SALAD DRESSING

3 tablespoons of chicken
  broth
1 tablespoon of prepared
  mustard

¾ cup of olive oil
3 tablespoons of lemon juice
Pepper to taste

In a bowl, beat the chicken broth with the mustard. Gradually beat in the oil, until the dressing has thickened, then beat
in the lemon juice and pepper.

PITA CHICKEN-AVOCADO SANDWICHES

Serves 8:

1 ripe avocado, pitted,
  skinned and cubed
½ cup of sour cream
1 tablespoon of lemon juice
2 whole scallions, diced
1 small ripe tomato, skinned,
  quartered and seeded

4 cups of finely cubed
  cooked chicken (breast is
  best, but any cooked
  chicken will do)
8 individual pita breads,
  warm and cut in half so
  they can be opened to
  form pockets

In a blender container, combine the avocado, sour cream, lemon juice, scallions and tomato. Blend into a smooth, creamy mixture. Spread this on one side of the pita pocket, spoon some of the chicken over it and close the now "stuffed" pita bread sandwiches.

HOT BURGER CHICKEN

Serves 4:

3 cups of chopped cooked
  chicken breast
3 tablespoons of mayonnaise
3 tablespoons of grated Asiago or Parmesan cheese

¼ teaspoon pepper
4 hamburger buns, split and
  bottom half buttered

In a bowl, blend well the chicken, mayonnaise, cheese and pepper. Spread on the buttered half of the bun, place under broiler 2 minutes or until golden. Cover with bun top.

CHICKEN BURGER VARIATION

Serves 4:

4 cups of finely ground dark
  and white meat of chicken
1 tablespoon of minced onion
1 teaspoon of salt

½ teaspoon of pepper
6 tablespoons of butter
4 hamburger buns, split and
  bottom half buttered generously

In a bowl, combine the chicken, onion, salt, pepper and 1 tablespoon of butter, blending well. Form into 4 thickish, firm patties. In a saucepan, over medium heat, melt the remaining 5 tablespoons of butter and sauté chicken patties for 5 minutes on each side, or until evenly browned and cooked to taste. Place on buttered bun half, and cover with the bun top. Pass condiments, such as catsup, mustard, relish, etc.

CLUB SANDWICH

Serves 1:

3 slices of bread, toasted slightly (not hard or crusty) and each slice buttered

Slices of chicken breast to generously cover 1 slice toast

Mayonnaise
Salt and pepper to taste
Lettuce
2 slices of ripe tomato
2 slices of bacon, fried (but not so crisp that it will crumble) and drained

Place chicken on 1 slice of toast, cover lightly with mayonnaise, and sprinkle lightly with salt and pepper. Cover with second slice of toast, buttered side up. Place a lettuce leaf on the second slice, then the tomatoes. Sprinkle lightly with salt and pepper and spread lightly with mayonnaise. Top with bacon, cover with the third slice of toast, buttered side down. Fasten sides together at corners with toothpicks, cut into triangles.

VARIATIONS ON THE "CLUB SANDWICH"

Using the same 3-slices-of-toast, Double-Decker technique, substitute baked ham for the bacon and tomato.

* * *

Substitute sliced tongue for the bacon.

* * *

Place the lettuce leaf on the first slice, then the chicken, covered with tomato. Pair any number of cheeses with the bacon instead of the tomato, Swiss, crumbled Roquefort, creamy Munster, etc.

* * *

Substitute slices of hard-cooked egg for bacon. Or Genoa salami. Or slices of dark meat of chicken.

* * *

Substitute roasted pepper for tomatoes.

* * *

Place the bacon and tomato on the first slice, cover the double-decker slice with chicken, then cucumbers sprinkled with black pepper.

* * *

Best variation: Your imagination plus appetite.

CHICKEN, COLESLAW WITH RUSSIAN DRESSING

Serves 4:

Slices of cooked chicken
    breast to generously cover
    4 slices of the bread
8 slices of Jewish rye bread,
    buttered
Salt and pepper to taste
1 medium-sized, solid head
    of cabbage, cored, finely
    shredded, dropped into
    boiling salted water; when

it comes to a second boil,
drain well and toss with 1
teaspoon of celery seeds

blended into a Russian
dressing
  1 cup of mayonnaise
  ⅓ cup of chili sauce
  1 tablespoon of fresh
     lemon juice
  1½ teaspoons of sugar

Arrange the chicken slices on 4 slices of the bread. Lightly sprinkle with salt and pepper. Toss the coleslaw with the Russian dressing. Arrange it on the chicken and cover with the remaining 4 slices of bread.

CHICKEN-CREAM CHEESE-CRANBERRY SPREAD

Use amounts according to the number of sandwiches desired.

Cream cheese
Mayonnaise
Alfalfa sprouts

Chicken breasts, sliced
Cranberry-orange relish

Soften the cheese by working it with the mayonnaise with a fork. Spread on the bread, cover with sprouts, then the chicken, then lightly with the cranberry relish. Cover with a second slice of bread, press together firmly, cut in half.

CHICKEN CROQUE MONSIEUR

Serves 4:

8 slices of white bread,
   crusts trimmed and generously buttered
Slices of cooked chicken
   breast to cover 4 slices of
   the bread

4 slices of ham
1 cup of grated Gruyère
   cheese
Pepper to taste
4 tablespoons of butter

Arrange the chicken slices on 4 slices of the bread. Top with a ham slice and sprinkle with the cheese and pepper. Cover with second slices of bread, press firmly together. In a frypan, over medium heat, melt 2 tablespoons of the butter and fry sandwiches until golden-brown on one side. Add the remaining 2 tablespoons butter and brown sandwiches on the other side.

CURRIED CHICKEN SANDWICHES

Makes 12 half sandwiches:

2 cups of finely chopped
  cooked chicken
1 small, tender celery rib,
  scraped and minced
2 scallions (white part
  only), minced
½ teaspoon of celery seed
Curry powder to taste (start
  with ¼ teaspoon)

Salt and pepper to taste
1 teaspoon of lemon juice
¾ cup mayonnaise
Butter
12 very thin slices of bread,
  white, whole-wheat or
  pumpernickel, crusts
  trimmed
1 cup of minced parsley

In a bowl, combine the chicken, celery, scallions, celery seed, curry powder, salt, pepper, lemon juice and one-half of the mayonnaise, blending well. Add more mayonnaise to taste. Lightly butter the bread and spread 6 slices evenly with the chicken mixture. Cover each with a second slice of bread and cut into halves. Spread the edges of the sandwiches lightly with mayonnaise and dip in the parsley, so each sandwich has a green frame. Serve with tiny gherkins or fat Greek olives.

DOUBLE-DECKER CHICKEN AND EGG SALAD SANDWICH

Serves 1:

3 slices of bread, lightly
  toasted (not hard or
  crusty) and each slice buttered

Sliced cooked chicken breast
  to generously cover 1 slice
  of toast
Egg salad to cover 1 slice of
  toast, not sloppily

Place the chicken slices on 1 slice of toast, cover with another toast slice, buttered side up. Spread egg salad on the second slice and cover with the third toast slice, buttered side down. Fasten together at corners with toothpicks, cut into triangles and garnish with your own selection of potato chips, olives, pickles, etc.

CRISPY HOT CHICKEN SANDWICHES

Makes 4 sandwiches:

2 cups of chopped cooked
chicken
1 celery rib, scraped and
finely chopped
1 tablespoon of minced onion
2 tablespoons of finely
chopped chutney
2 small sweet gherkins,
finely chopped

⅓ cup of mayonnaise
Salt and pepper to taste
8 slices of white bread
2 eggs, beaten with ½ cup of
milk
2 cups of crushed shredded
wheat (approximate)
4 tablespoons of butter

In a bowl, combine the chicken, celery, onion, chutney, gherkins and mayonnaise, blending well. Taste and season. Add
more mayonnaise, if needed. Divide the mixture into four
parts and spread on 4 slices of bread. Cover with the remaining 4 slices. Dip sandwiches in the egg-milk mixture to completely coat. Then dredge completely in the crushed shredded
wheat. In a heavy frypan, over medium heat, melt butter and
brown sandwiches on both sides, adding more butter, if
needed.

EASY HOT CHICKEN SANDWICH

Serves 6:

2 cups of diced cooked
chicken
1 cup of diced Cheddar
cheese
3 hard-cooked eggs, chopped
3 scallions (white part
only), minced

2 tablespoons of minced
sweet red pepper
½ cup of mayonnaise
6 hamburger rolls, split and
buttered
Aluminum foil

In a bowl, combine all the ingredients, except the rolls, blending thoroughly. Spread the mixture evenly on the rolls, wrap
in foil and bake in a preheated 350° F. oven for 25 minutes.

FRENCH FRIED CHICKEN SANDWICHES

Serves 4:

8 slices of pumpernickel
  bread, buttered and one
  side spread with mustard
Slices of cooked chicken
  breast to generously cover
  4 slices of bread

4 thin slices of Muenster
  cheese, to cover the
  chicken

beaten together
  2 eggs, beaten
  1 cup of medium cream

4 tablespoons of butter

Arrange the chicken and cheese on 4 slices of bread. Cover each with a second slice and press firmly together. Dip the sandwiches into the egg-cream mixture. In a frypan, over medium heat, melt the butter and fry the sandwiches, turning until they are golden-brown and the cheese is beginning to melt. Don't overcook or they'll be a gooey mess with the cheese dribbling out.

CHICKEN AND HAM SANDWICH FILLING

Makes about 3 cups of filling:

1 cup of minced cooked
  chicken
1 cup of minced cooked
  ham
½ cup of finely chopped celery
1 teaspoon of celery seed

½ cup of chopped sweet
  pickles
½ teaspoon of fresh grated
  horseradish (if not available, use processed)
½ cup of mayonnaise

In a bowl, combine the chicken, ham, celery, celery seed, pickles, horseradish and one-half of the mayonnaise. Blend well, adding additional mayonnaise to taste. Spread on a bread of your choice.

SAUTÉED CHICKEN-HAM SANDWICH

Serves 1:

2 slices of white bread
Softened Roquefort cheese
1 slice of cooked ham
Slices of cooked chicken
  breasts, enough to cover
  the ham

1 egg, beaten with 2 tablespoons of milk
Butter

Spread the bread with the Roquefort cheese. Make a sandwich with the ham and chicken slices. Dip the sandwich in
the beaten egg mixture. Heat 1 tablespoon of butter in a
small frypan. Brown sandwich on both sides, adding more
butter if needed.

CHICKEN AND TOMATO HERO

Serves 4:

1 loaf of French bread
Butter
2 medium-sized ripe toma-
  toes, peeled and sliced
Salt and pepper to taste
Slices of cooked chicken to
  generously cover the bread

when cut in half length-
wise
8 anchovy fillets, soaked in
  wine vinegar and drained
1 small red onion, sliced
  thinly
Shredded lettuce

Cut the bread in half lengthwise, not cutting all the way
through. Butter one side. Arrange the tomato slices the length
of the bread. Sprinkle with salt and pepper. Arrange the
chicken slices on the tomato slices, then the anchovy fillets on
the chicken, the onion slices on the anchovy and the lettuce
on the onion. Close the sandwich and cut into 4 portions.

A PICKLED CHICKEN HERO

Serves 4:

4 hero rolls, cut down the center lengthwise (do not cut through) and buttered
Slices of cooked chicken to generously cover one side of the rolls

8 sweet pickled peppers, halved and seeded
24 slices of pickled beets
Olive oil
Shredded lettuce

Cover one side of each of the rolls with the chicken slices. Arrange the pickled peppers on the chicken, the pickled beets on the pickled peppers. Dribble with olive oil. Cover with lettuce, close the sandwich and eat immediately.

CHICKEN-LIVER-PÂTÉ OPEN-FACE SANDWICH

Makes 4 sandwiches:

½ pound of butter
4 shallots, minced
1 pound of chicken livers, each cut into 6 pieces
3 tablespoons of brandy
¼ teaspoon of allspice
½ teaspoon of salt
¼ teaspoon of pepper

¼ cup of heavy cream
1 hard-cooked egg, chopped
2 scallions (white part only), minced
4 slices of rye bread
4 Boston lettuce leaves
2 hard-cooked eggs, sliced

In a frypan, over medium heat, melt 3 tablespoons of the butter. Add the shallots and cook for 1 minute. Add the livers and cook 4 minutes. Add brandy, allspice, salt and pepper and cook 2 minutes longer, or until the livers are brown on the outside and slightly pink inside (add more butter, if needed). Transfer contents of frypan to a blender container. Add the cream and blend until smooth.

Melt remaining butter, add to blender and blend until well mixed. Spoon contents of blender container to a bowl, add the chopped egg and scallions and mix well. Taste for seasoning. Pack into a small rectangular mold and chill. When cool, slice for sandwiches. Spread a slice of rye bread with mayonnaise or butter, lay a lettuce leaf on it, then a slice of pâté, then hard-cooked egg slices with a small dab of mayonnaise on each slice.

OPEN-FACE CHICKEN SALAD SANDWICH

Makes 4 sandwiches:

2 cups of chopped cooked chicken
½ cup of finely chopped water chestnuts
1 scallion (white part only), minced
1 tablespoon of lemon juice
1 tablespoon of olive oil
Pinch of cayenne

½ cup of mayonnaise
Salt and pepper to taste
4 Boston lettuce leaves
4 slices of oatmeal, whole-wheat or other hearty bread, toasted and buttered
4 teaspoons of chopped tarragon

In a bowl, combine the chicken, water chestnuts, scallion, lemon juice, olive oil, cayenne and half of the mayonnaise, blending thoroughly. Add more mayonnaise to taste. Taste for seasoning.

Lay a leaf of the lettuce on each slice of toasted bread. Heap one-fourth of the salad on each and sprinkle with the tarragon.

CHICKEN SALAD SANDWICH

Serves 4:

1 cup of finely shredded garden red lettuce

1 large ripe tomato, diced and drained

4 whole young scallions, diced

blended into a salad dressing
   3 tablespoons of olive oil
   2 tablespoons of wine vinegar
   ½ teaspoon of salt

¼ teaspoon *each* of pepper, sugar, dried oregano and dried basil

8 slices of buttered rye, pumpernickel or whole-wheat bread

Slices of cooked chicken breast to generously cover 4 slices of the bread

4 slices of Monterey Jack cheese to cover the chicken

In a bowl, combine the lettuce, tomato, scallions and dressing, tossing well. Place the chicken slices on 4 slices of bread, then the cheese on the chicken. Cover with the "salad" and top with a second slice of bread.

CHOPPED CHICKEN AND SHRIMP ON BUNS

Serves 4:

4 hamburger buns with sesame seeds, toasted and buttered

blended
   2 cups of chopped cooked chicken
   ⅛ teaspoon of Tabasco
   2 tablespoons of mayonnaise

blended
   4 tablespoons of chopped water chestnuts
   1 tablespoon of mayonnaise

blended
   2 cups of chopped shrimp
   ½ teaspoon of pepper
   2 tablespoons of heavy cream

1 cup of watercress leaves
Salt to taste

On the bottoms of the buns spread a layer of the chicken mixture, then a thin layer of the water chestnut mixture, then a layer of the shrimp mixture. Arrange watercress on top of the shrimp mixture. Salt to taste. Cover with bun tops.

HOT CHICKEN STEAK SANDWICHES

Serves 4:

2 whole breasts from 2 (2½-pound) chickens halved, skinned, boned and pounded lightly with a meat mallet between sheets of waxed paper
Salt and pepper

⅛ teaspoon of dried tarragon
4 tablespoons of butter
1 tablespoon of olive oil
4 long hard-crusted steak rolls, cut into halves and both sides buttered

Sprinkle the breasts with salt, pepper and tarragon. In a large frypan, over medium heat, heat the butter and olive oil. Sauté the chicken "steaks," turning them often and browning evenly. It should take about 12 minutes. The chicken should be cooked, but still soft and moist (do not overcook; breasts dry out easily). Place the chicken steaks on one-half of each roll, sprinkle with pepper and cover with the roll tops—cross beef steak sandwiches off your list! Delicious!

TANGY CHICKEN SANDWICH SPREAD

This makes a unique and delicious sandwich.
Makes about 2½ cups:

2 cups of cubed cooked chicken
⅓ cup *each* of almonds and walnuts
2 small onions
2 hard-cooked eggs

½ cup of mayonnaise
2 tablespoons of brandy
⅛ teaspoon of cayenne
½ teaspoon of salt
¼ teaspoon of pepper

Put chicken, nuts, onion and eggs through a food chopper. In a bowl, blend them well with the mayonnaise, brandy, cayenne, salt and pepper. Chill overnight. Before spreading, taste for seasoning. Spread on rye bread, topped with crisp, tender Boston lettuce leaves.

Chapter Eleven

Microwave Magic

This is not a microwave cookbook (we have already written one, Mastering Microwave Cooking, also published by Bantam), so we will only touch upon some microwave cooking points that we consider important to chicken cookery, and offer two recipes as a guide.

Chicken does extremely well under the microwaves. It cooks food in one-fourth of the time, and microwaves use 75 percent less energy than an electric or gas stove. But the most important fact for a cook is that the chicken emerges from the waves juicy and delicious—if cooked properly.

Most microwave books state that chicken should be cooked 7 minutes to the pound. We disagree. We cook ours perfectly at 6 minutes to a pound. Why? Heat equalization in microwave cookery must always be taken into consideration. (Internal temperature can rise as much as 40 degrees in 20 minutes.)

This is called "carryover" cooking, which means that the cooking will continue after you have removed the chicken from the oven, wrapped it in foil and let it set. This "setting" period in foil also gives the juices time to settle, making it more moist and easier to carve.

Trussing is equally important (see Chapter IV, "Whole Chickens," for method) because protruding legs, thighs, wings, anything "akimbo" will be quickly dried out by the superfast microwaves.

After trussing, we like to rub the chicken with herb butter. The flavor is superb.

HERB BUTTER

½ pound of butter
1 teaspoon of fresh lemon juice
½ teaspoon of soy sauce
½ teaspoon of Worcestershire sauce

1 teaspoon of Dijon mustard
1 tablespoon of chopped fresh parsley
½ teaspoon of pepper
¼ teaspoon of dried tarragon
¼ teaspoon of dried thyme

Place butter from the refrigerator in a 2-cup glass measuring cup. Heat it in the microwave oven for 15 seconds, or just until it begins to soften. Blend in all of the remaining ingredients, working into a smooth mixture. Shape into two sticks. Wrap in plastic wrap, then in aluminum foil and freeze. To use, simply slice off the amount needed and let soften at room temperature.

In cooking the perfect whole chicken under microwaves, we also place small strips of aluminum foil on protruding wing tips and legs and on part of the breast adjacent to the cavity. These are "shields" protecting those areas that will dry out quickly if not so shielded.

Do not salt any chicken or large piece of chicken unless it is covered with sauce. We offer both examples as a guide. Salt draws moisture to the surface, forming a crust that slows microwave penetration.

The chicken should also be placed on an inverted saucer, or nonmetal trivet to elevate it above the juices that will flow off the bird as it cooks.

In addition, liquid that accumulates should be spooned or basted off. Liquid attracts microwaves and will upset timing. If the liquid isn't taken from the oven, the bird could emerge undercooked, even with the later carry-over cooking.

The chicken must also cook evenly. The best way to accomplish this is to *turn* the bird. Start it off on one side, then breast down, then the other side, then breast up.

Chicken parts should be cooked with the thicker portions toward the outside, where the waves strike first, the slender portions nearer the center.

To prevent splattering, cover the chicken loosely with waxed paper.

Chicken will vary in cooking time according to age, size, diet and length of time it was frozen or stored. Microwave cooking is, especially at first, an exercise in "testing." You experiment and learn.

For example, if you like cooking chicken on an outdoor grill, the microwave can be your helper. Precook the chicken pieces in minutes under microwaves, then later bring them to crisp perfection over charcoal. The chicken will be evenly cooked; too often charcoal-barbecued chicken is very crisp and brown on the outside but underdone inside.

Chicken is done in the microwave when it is fork tender. But we remove the bird before this point, wrap it in aluminum foil and let the carry-over cooking time finish it off, then try for fork-tenderness. We do the same with the meat thermometer, testing the thickest part of the thigh after the chicken has rested in aluminum foil for 10 minutes. If it is done, the temperature will read 170°F. The breast will read 180°F.

Another test: Pierce the thigh with the point of a sharp knife or fork prongs. The emerging liquid should be clear, not pink. For "show me" cooks, make a test slice between the leg and the body of the bird to see if it is cooked to your satisfaction. On a whole chicken the leg joints should move easily, flexibly, and the meat of the thigh should be soft to the touch or squeeze.

It also is a simple matter to adapt a favorite chicken recipe for the microwaves. The microwave oven cooks most foods in one-fourth of your regular oven time. Thus, if a regular recipe calls for a cooking time of 2 hours, the microwaves will do it in 30 minutes.

But, remember the carry-over cooking time. Cook the chicken for 25 minutes, wrap it in foil and let it set for 10 minutes. You can undercook and correct the cooking time. But if you overcook you've had it, the damage cannot be undone.

So use caution on all recipes, undercook until you have mastered microwave timing. And always remember, the more food items you put into the microwave oven, the longer the time. Two Cornish game hens will take longer than one, three longer than two.

ROAST BUTTERY CHICKEN

Serves 4: (Cook Full-Power 18 minutes)

1 (3½-pound) chicken
Lawry's seasoned salt
1 large onion, cut into quarters

¼ pound of soft unsalted butter
½ teaspoon of pepper

Liberally sprinkle the cavity of the bird with seasoned salt. Add the onion and truss the chicken. Coat it well with butter and sprinkle with pepper. Cover the ends of legs and wings with small strips of aluminum foil, also the breast-tip at the cavity. Place the chicken on its side on an inverted saucer in a glass baking dish. Cover loosely with waxed paper. Cook in the center of the oven for 4 minutes. Baste, and siphon or spoon off any liquid. Turn the chicken breast down and cook for 6 minutes. Baste. Spoon off collected liquid. Turn the chicken onto its other side, cook 4 minutes longer. Baste. Turn it breast side up and cook 4 minutes. Remove from oven, wrap in foil and let set for 10 minutes. Prick the thigh; if the juices run pink it will need another 3 minutes in the microwave oven. The bird now will be golden brown. Season to taste with salt. If you want it browner and crisper, place it under the broiler of your conventional oven.

THYME CHICKEN IN TOMATO SAUCE

Serves 4: (Cook Full-Power 14 minutes)

2 large whole chicken breasts, halved and boned
1 small green pepper, cored, seeded and cut into thin strips
1 medium-sized onion, thinly sliced

Salt and pepper to taste
¼ teaspoon of dried thyme
1 (10½-ounce) can condensed tomato soup
2 tablespoons of red wine vinegar

Place the chicken breasts in a glass casserole, skin side down, in one layer, thicker parts toward the edge of the dish. Arrange the pepper strips and the onion slices around the chicken. Sprinkle lightly with salt. Sprinkle with pepper and thyme. Blend the tomato soup and the vinegar and pour over the chicken. Cover with waxed paper. Cook 7 minutes, rotating the dish one-half turn after 4 minutes. Turn the breasts over. Spoon the sauce over them and cook 7 minutes, rotating the dish one-half turn after 4 minutes. Cover the dish tightly with aluminum foil and let set for 5 minutes. Test for tenderness and seasoning. This is an excellent dish served with rice, the sauce lightly spooned over the rice.

These are sample recipes, test recipes. Try them, then try the other chicken recipes in this book that appeal to you, adapting them to your microwave oven as we have suggested.

Part Two

1978-1979 WINNERS OF THE NATIONAL CHICKEN COOKING CONTEST

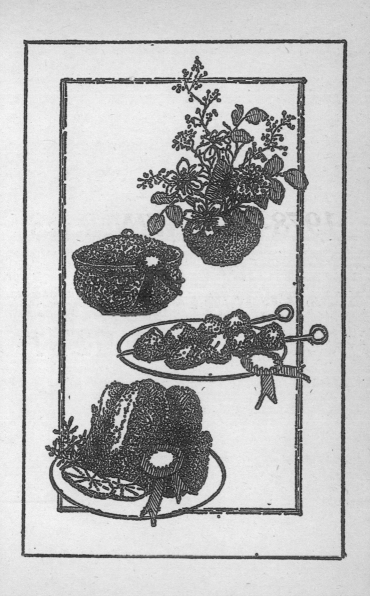

Book Bonus! Here are the winning recipes of 102 of America's best chicken cooks from every state and the District of Columbia.

The National Chicken Cooking Contest *is the nation's oldest annual cooking competition, dating back to 1949. Held each year in a different poultry-producing state to encourage innovative ways to cook and serve chicken, it has, from the first contest, attracted talented cooks nationwide.*

Those who compete in the national cook-off are winners of state contests and approved by the National Broiler Council, *sponsor of the national contest and spokesman for the entire U.S. chicken industry.*

The winner receives the first prize of $10,000; four other winners divide another $10,000.

All contestants cook their winning recipes in 51 mini-kitchens, in an impressive affair that begins with state flags flying, a parade of states, a military band and a military escort for each contestant.

Recipes are judged by a panel of ten nationally known food experts.

The male author of this book served as one of those judges in the 1979 national cook-off in Charleston, South Carolina.

Through the courtesy of officials of the National Chicken Cooking Contest *and the* National Broiler Council *we herewith not only present all of the excellent recipes of that 1979 contest but of the previous 1978 national cook-off.*

NOTE

Those of you who are proud of your chicken cooking talent and would like to try for the $10,000 first prize, or the runner-up prizes, should write to Susan Orr, Director, National Chicken Cooking Contest, 1155 - 15th Street, N. W., Washington, D. C. 20005. Mention that you read of the contest here in *The Chicken and The Egg Cookbook.*

273

ALABAMA

CHINESE SWEET AND SOUR CHICKEN

Serves 4:

2 whole broiler-fryer chicken breasts
3 cups water
¼ cup soy sauce
½ cup plus 2 tablespoons granulated sugar
1 egg
⅔ cup of milk
1 cup sifted flour
2 teaspoons baking powder
½ teaspoon salt

¼ cup cooking oil
¼ cup butter
⅔ cup pineapple chunks, juice reserved
½ cup chopped green onion
1 green pepper, seeded and diced
2 tomatoes, cut in wedges
1 cup vinegar
½ cup brown sugar
½ cup cornstarch

In deep saucepan place chicken, 2 cups of the water, soy sauce and the 2 tablespoons granulated sugar. Cover and simmer for about 1 hour or until fork tender. Remove chicken, and cool. Discard skin and remove meat from bones. Cut chicken in ¾-inch cubes. In a bowl beat the egg. Add milk and mix well. Add flour, baking powder and salt, stirring constantly. Dip chicken cubes in this mixture. In a frypan, heat oil to medium temperature. Add chicken and cook, turning, until brown on all sides. Remove chicken and keep warm. In the frypan melt butter over medium heat. Add pineapple, onion and green pepper and sauté for about 5 minutes, or until onion and pepper are tender. Add tomatoes and sauté 1 minute longer.

In small saucepan place the remaining 1 cup water, vinegar, brown sugar and the ½ cup granulated sugar. Bring to boil; then remove from heat. In bowl combine cornstarch and pineapple juice . Add to vinegar mixture in saucepan, stirring constantly. Bring to boil again and continue to cook, stirring, about 4 minutes longer, or until sauce is thick and clear. Serve over white rice, placing chicken and vegetables on rice and pouring sauce over all.

Sheila R. Eckman, Auburn, Alabama

ALASKA

BASQUE CHICKEN

Serves 4:

½ cup butter
1 broiler-fryer chicken, cut
   into parts
1 teaspoon salt
¼ teaspoon pepper
¾ cup olive oil
1 onion, chopped

6 tomatoes, peeled and cut
   into eighths
1 cup slivered almonds
¾ cup mixed large green and
   black olives, pitted and
   sliced
¾ cup dry vermouth

In a large shallow baking pan, heat the butter in the oven until butter is melted. Arrange chicken in pan, skin side down,
in a single layer, and sprinkle with salt and pepper. Bake,
uncovered, in a 375° F. oven for 30 minutes. Turn chicken
and bake about 15 minutes longer, or until chicken is golden
brown and fork tender. In frypan heat oil to medium. Add
onion and sauté about 3 minutes, or until golden. Add tomatoes, almonds, olives and wine. Pour tomato mixture over
chicken and return to oven for 5 minutes, or until heated
through.

Margit Muntzert, Fairbanks, Alaska

ARIZONA

LEMONY GREEK CHICKEN EN SAUSSE

Serves 4:

2 whole broiler-fryer chicken
   breasts, halved
1 teaspoon salt
¼ cup cooking oil

3 egg yolks, well beaten
Juice of 2 lemons
⅔ cup water
Grated rind of 1 lemon

Sprinkle chicken with salt. In a frypan heat oil to medium
temperature. Add chicken and cook, turning, about 10
minutes, or until brown on all sides. Cover and simmer for
about 35 minutes, or until fork tender. Remove from frypan
and cool slightly. Discard skin and remove meat from bones.

Cut chicken into bite-sized pieces. Drain fat from pan. Return chicken to frypan, cover and keep warm. In the top of a double boiler, place egg yolks. Add lemon juice and water, slowly, beating constantly. Heat over slowly boiling water for about 10 minutes, or until thickened (do not boil). Add chicken pieces and heat through. To serve place chicken on hot pasta. Pour lemon-egg mixture over all. Sprinkle lemon rind on top.

Ruth Ann Folk, Tucson, Arizona

ARKANSAS

SKILLET CHICKEN

Serves 4:

¼ cup butter	¼ cup dry white wine
2 whole broiler-fryer chicken breasts, halved	½ cup red currant jelly
	½ cup sour cream

In frypan melt butter over medium heat. Add chicken and cook, turning, for about 10 minutes, or until brown on all sides. Add wine, cover and simmer for 35 minutes. Remove cover and add currant jelly. Cook, uncovered, over low heat, turning and basting frequently, for about 30 minutes, or until fork tender. Remove chicken to serving platter. Add sour cream to mixture remaining in frypan. Heat through and pour over chicken.

George P. Bilheimer, Jr., Little Rock, Arkansas

CALIFORNIA, 1ST PRIZE 1978

CHICKEN PIZZA

Serves 4:

1 package (8 rolls) refrigerated crescent rolls
¼ cup cooking oil
2 whole broiler-fryer chicken
  breasts, halved, skinned,
  boned and cut into 1-inch
  pieces
1 large onion, sliced into
  thin rings
1 large green pepper, cored,
  seeded and cut into thin
  rings

½ pound fresh mushrooms,
  sliced
½ cup sliced pitted ripe olives
1 (10½-ounce) can pizza
  sauce with cheese
1 teaspoon garlic salt
1 teaspoon oregano
¼ cup Parmesan cheese
2 cups shredded mozzarella
  cheese

Unroll crescent dough into 8 triangles. Press dough onto a
lightly oiled 12-inch pizza pan, especially at perforations, to
seal. In frypan heat oil to medium temperature. Add chicken,
onion, green pepper, mushrooms and olives and cook, stirring, about 5 minutes or until fork tender. Spread pizza sauce
over crust. Spoon chicken mixture evenly over sauce.
Sprinkle garlic salt, oregano and Parmesan cheese on all. Top
with mozzarella cheese. Bake, uncovered, in 425° F. oven for
20 minutes, or until crust is done. Cut into wedges to serve.

Mary G. Cerami, Ojai, California

COLORADO PRAIRIE CHICKEN

Serves 4:

4 tablespoons butter
1 broiler-fryer chicken, cut into parts
1½ teaspoons salt
¼ teaspoon dry mustard
⅛ teaspoon pepper
¼ cup chopped onion
2 cloves garlic, crushed

¼ cup water
1 (16-ounce) can tomatoes, drained and juice reserved
3 cups sliced zucchini
1 (10-ounce) package frozen chopped spinach, defrosted
1½ tablespoons cornstarch

In frypan melt butter over medium heat. Add chicken and cook, turning, about 10 minutes, or until brown on all sides. In bowl mix together salt, mustard and pepper. Sprinkle mixture over chicken. Add onion, garlic and water to chicken. Cover and simmer for about 1 hour, or until fork tender. Remove chicken from pan. In frypan combine tomatoes, zucchini, spinach and one-half of the reserved tomato juice. Cover and simmer for 5 minutes. In a bowl combine cornstarch and the remaining tomato juice, stirring constantly. Pour cornstarch mixture into frypan slowly, stirring constantly. Cook, uncovered, stirring, for about 3 minutes, or until slightly thickened. Return chicken to frypan. Cover and simmer about 8 minutes longer, or until heated through. Place vegetables around chicken on platter to serve.

Vivian Jeanette Neville, Colorado Springs, Colorado

POULET À LA ROUMAINE

Serves 4:

3 tablespoons chicken fat
1 large onion, chopped
1 clove garlic, minced
½ teaspoon parsley
2 bay leaves
¼ cup teriyaki sauce
¼ cup dry red wine
1 tablespoon soy sauce

1 teaspoon salt
¼ teaspoon pepper
Juice from ½ lemon
2 whole broiler-fryer chicken breasts, halved, skinned, boned and cut into 1-inch square pieces

In a frypan melt chicken fat over medium heat. Add onion and cook about 3 minutes, or until golden brown. Add garlic, parsley, bay leaves, teriyaki sauce, wine, soy sauce, salt and pepper. Stir to mix well. Simmer about 5 minutes. Remove from heat and add lemon juice, stirring. Place about 6 pieces of chicken on each of 8 skewers. Brush sauce on chicken. Place skewers on grill over hot coals about 8 inches from heat. Cook, turning and brushing with sauce, about 5 minutes, or until fork tender. To serve, place chicken on skewers on rice and pour remaining sauce over all.

Marilen Hoette, Farmington, Connecticut

PICNIC PEANUT CHICKEN

Serves 4:

1 broiler-fryer chicken, cut into parts
1 teaspoon salt
¼ teaspoon pepper
¾ cup flour
1 egg, beaten

1 cup orange marmalade
1 teaspoon dry mustard
2 cloves garlic, crushed
1½ cups ground salted peanuts

Sprinkle chicken with salt and pepper. Put flour in a bag. In shallow dish blend eggs, marmalade, mustard and garlic. Put peanuts in another shallow dish. Shake chicken, one piece at a time, in bag to coat, dip in egg mixture and then roll in peanuts. In a large shallow baking pan place chicken, skin side up, in single layer. Bake in a 375°F. oven for about 40 minutes, or until fork tender.

Betty Calvert, Clayton, Delaware

DISTRICT OF COLUMBIA

COUNTRY FRENCH BAKED CHICKEN

Serves 4:

1 whole broiler-fryer chicken	2 tablespoons butter
2 teaspoons salt	12 small white onions, peeled
1 teaspoon ground thyme	
2 celery tops with leaves	12 small potatoes, peeled
1 yellow onion, cut in half	¼ cup dry sherry
6 sprigs parsley	

Sprinkle inside of chicken with 1 teaspoon of the salt and thyme. Place celery tops, yellow onion and parsley in cavity of chicken. Tie chicken legs together, then to tail. Put chicken in a large shallow baking pan, and dot with butter. Cover tightly and bake in a 375°F. oven for 30 minutes. Add white onions and potatoes. Pour sherry over chicken. Sprinkle remaining 1 teaspoon salt over all. Cover and bake 30 minutes longer. Uncover and bake, basting, for 10 minutes, or until chicken is fork tender and vegetables are brown and tender.

Jerry M. Mallick, Washington, D. C.

FLORIDA

CHICKEN BANGELASH

Serves 4:

¼ cup flour
1½ teaspoons salt
¼ teaspoon pepper
1 broiler-fryer chicken cut into parts
⅓ cup cooking oil
1 onion, sliced
½ cup sliced celery
1 clove garlic, crushed

2 (8-ounce) cans tomato sauce with bits
1 cup water
2 teaspoons curry powder
3 cups hot cooked rice
¼ cup seedless raisins
¼ cup chopped salted peanuts

In shallow dish combine flour, 1 teaspoon of the salt and pepper. Add chicken, one piece at a time, turning to coat. In frypan, heat oil to medium temperature. Add chicken and cook, turning, for about 10 minutes, or until brown on all sides. Add onion, celery and garlic and cook until soft. Drain off fat. Add tomato sauce, water, curry powder and the remaining ½ teaspoon salt. Cover and simmer for about 45 minutes, or until fork tender. Serve on rice tossed with raisins. Sprinkle with nuts.

Carl Victor Helm, Neptune Beach, Florida

GEORGIA

OBAA-CHAN'S CHICKEN

Serves 4:

2 eggs, beaten
⅓ cup flour
1 broiler-fryer chicken, cut into parts

1 pint cooking oil (approximate)
1 cup sugar
½ cup soy sauce

In bowl place eggs. In shallow dish place flour. Dip chicken in eggs, then in flour, one piece at a time, turning to coat. In deep fryer, place oil, filling utensil no more than one-third full. Heat to medium-high temperature (about 360°F.). Add chicken a few pieces at a time and cook about 15 minutes, or until golden brown and fork tender (test piece removed from oil). In saucepan mix together sugar and soy sauce and bring to boil. Dip chicken in soy sauce mixture while still hot. Drain on rack. Place rack in a 350°F. oven and bake about 5 minutes, or until crispy and crunchy.

Teru F. Sasaki, Ft. Benning, Georgia

HAWAII, 2ND PRIZE 1978

KOREAN PUPU CHICKEN

Serves 4:

⅓ cup flour
8 broiler-fryer chicken thighs
1 pint cooking oil (approximate)
½ cup soy sauce

6 tablespoons sugar
1 clove garlic, minced
1 green onion (green and white parts), chopped
1 small red chili pepper*

In a shallow dish, place flour. Add chicken, turning to coat. In deep fryer place oil, filling utensil no more than one-third full. Heat to medium-high temperature (about 360°F.). Add chicken, a few pieces at a time, and cook about 15 minutes, or until golden brown and fork tender. In bowl make sauce by mixing together soy sauce, sugar, garlic, onion and chili pepper. As soon as chicken is removed from deep fryer, roll in sauce, turning over twice.

* If fresh chili pepper not available, use ⅛ teaspoon dried chili pepper.

Patricia Hinau, Honolulu, Hawaii

IDAHO

POULET MOUTARDE

Serves 4:

⅓ cup flour
2 whole broiler-fryer chicken
  breasts, halved, skinned
  and boned
2 tablespoons butter
2 tablespoons olive oil

½ cup heavy cream
⅛ teaspoon paprika
1/16 teaspoon curry powder
2 teaspoons prepared
  mustard
1 egg yolk

In shallow dish place flour. Add chicken, one piece at a time, turning to coat. In frypan melt butter and heat oil to medium temperature. Add chicken and cook, turning, about 10 minutes, or until brown on both sides. Cover and simmer, turning occasionally, for about 10 minutes, or until fork tender. Remove from heat and let stand, covered, for 10 minutes. In saucepan combine cream, paprika, curry powder and mustard. Heat, stirring, but do not boil. In bowl add small amount of cream mixture to egg yolk, mixing well. Gradually add egg yolk back to cream mixture, stirring constantly, until sauce thickens. Pour over chicken.

Fay Petersen, Pocatello, Idaho

ILLINOIS

CHICKEN VEG-A-SKILLET

Serves 4:

⅓ cup flour
1 teaspoon salt
1 teaspoon paprika
¼ teaspoon ground sage
¼ teaspoon pepper
1 broiler-fryer chicken, cut
  into parts
¼ cup shortening

1 teaspoon sugar
1 (13¾-ounce) can chicken
  broth
1 tablespoon lemon juice
1 cup sliced carrots
1 onion, sliced
2 tablespoons chopped
  parsley

In plastic bag combine flour, salt, paprika, sage and pepper. Add chicken, a few pieces at a time, and shake to coat. Reserve excess flour mixture. In frypan melt shortening over medium heat. Add chicken and cook, turning, for about 10 minutes, or until brown on all sides. Remove chicken from frypan. Add reserved flour mixture and sugar to pan drippings and stir well. Add broth. Cook, stirring, for about 5 minutes, or until thick and bubbly. Add lemon juice, carrots, onion and parsley. Stir. Place chicken on top of vegetable mixture. Cover and simmer, stirring occasionally, for about 40 minutes, or until vegetables are tender and fork can be inserted in chicken with ease.

Judith Wyatt, Noble, Illinois

INDIANA

KASEY'S TIPSY CHICKEN

Serves 4:

¼ cup butter	¾ teaspoon onion salt
½ teaspoon chopped fresh parsley	¼ teaspoon celery salt
¼ teaspoon garlic powder	⅛ teaspoon pepper
⅛ teaspoon salt	¼ teaspoon poultry seasoning
2 tablespoons sherry	1 whole broiler-fryer chicken

*Place butter in an 8-ounce glass measuring cup. Microwave on high for 1½ minutes, or until melted. Add parsley, garlic powder, salt and sherry. Microwave on high for 3 seconds to blend flavors. Set aside for basting. In bowl combine onion salt, celery salt, pepper and poultry seasoning. Sprinkle mixture on inside and outside of chicken. On microwave roasting rack in large shallow glass baking dish place chicken, breast side down. Microwave, uncovered, on high for 12 minutes.

* For a conventional oven melt butter in saucepan. Add parsley, garlic powder, salt and sherry and let stand until needed for basting. Follow procedures for chicken as listed. Cover and roast in a 400°F. oven for 30 minutes. Remove cover. Drain off juices. Spoon basting mixture over chicken. Roast, basting, about 15 minutes longer, or until lightly browned and fork tender.

Turn breast side up and microwave, uncovered, on high for 10 minutes. Brush basting mixture on chicken. Microwave on high 5 minutes longer, or until fork tender. Remove chicken from oven, cover with foil and let stand about 5 minutes before serving.

Elizabeth J. Laws, Brownsburg, Indiana

IOWA

EASY CHICKEN WELLINGTON

Serves 4:

¼ cup mayonnaise
1 teaspoon crushed rosemary leaves
2 teaspoons chopped freeze-dried chives
1 teaspoon salt
½ teaspoon white pepper
2 whole broiler-fryer chicken breasts, halved, skinned and boned

1 (8-ounce) can refrigerated crescent dinner rolls
1 egg, beaten
1 tablespoon flour
1½ tablespoons white wine
1 (4-ounce) can sliced mushrooms, liquid reserved
3 tablespoons cream

In frypan melt mayonnaise over very low heat. Add rosemary and chives. Sprinkle salt and pepper on both sides of chicken pieces. Place in frypan and cook, uncovered, over medium heat for 3 minutes. Turn chicken and cook about 3 minutes longer, or until fork tender. Separate dough into 8 triangles. Place 4 of the triangles on large baking tray. Remove chicken from frypan and place a piece of chicken on each triangle. Place a second triangle on top of each piece of chicken. Stretch dough to cover, sealing around chicken. Brush generously with egg. Bake, uncovered, in a 375°F. oven for about 15 minutes, or until golden brown. Stir flour into pan drippings and bring to boil over medium heat. Reduce heat and add wine, liquid from mushrooms and cream, stirring constantly. Add mushrooms. Pour over chicken in dough when serving.

Martha Barclay, Mason City, Iowa

KANSAS

CHICKEN AND STUFFING PIE

Serves 4:

1 broiler-fryer chicken, cut into parts, with giblets
4 cups water
½ cup plus 1 tablespoon margarine
1 (8-ounce) package herb seasoned stuffing mix
1 egg, beaten
¼ cup plus 2 teaspoons flour
1 (4-ounce) can mushrooms, drained and liquid reserved

½ cup chopped onion
1 cup frozen peas, thawed
2 tablespoons diced pimiento
1 tablespoon parsley flakes
1 teaspoon Worcestershire sauce
½ teaspoon thyme
4 slices Cheddar cheese, each slice cut into 4 strips

In dutch oven place chicken and giblets. Add water. Cover and simmer for about 30 minutes, or until fork tender. Cool, reserving broth. Discard skin and separate meat from bones. Cut chicken in bite-sized pieces, and chop giblets. In saucepan place ¾ cup of the reserved broth. Add ½ cup of the margarine and heat until melted. Remove from heat. Add stuffing and egg, mixing well. Press stuffing mix mixture into pie plate to form a bottom crust. In bowl place the ¼ cup flour and add 5 tablespoons broth, stirring constantly. In saucepan place 1½ cups broth. Add flour mixture to broth in saucepan, stirring. Cook over medium heat for about 10 minutes or until thick. Add giblets. In bowl place the 2 teaspoons flour and add mushroom liquid, stirring constantly. In frypan place remaining 1 tablespoon margarine. Add mushrooms and onion and sauté for about 3 minutes, or until onion is soft but not brown. Add giblet mixture, mushroom liquid mixture, chicken, peas, pimiento, parsley flakes, Worcestershire and thyme. Heat through. Place in crust. Bake in a 375°F. oven for 20 minutes. Place cheese in lattice design on pie. Bake about 5 minutes longer, or until cheese is melted.

Mildred Eichman, Westmoreland, Kansas

SWEDISH HEIRLOOM CHICKEN

Serves 4:

1 broiler-fryer chicken, cut into parts
2 cups water
¼ cup butter
⅓ cup chopped onion
¼ cup flour
1 teaspoon salt
½ teaspoon white pepper
1 cup light cream

1 (5-ounce) can water chestnuts, drained and sliced
2 cups cooked rice
1 cup shredded Cheddar cheese
1 cup milk
2 tablespoons chopped pimiento
2 tablespoons lemon juice

Place chicken in a deep saucepan. Add water. Cover and simmer for about 45 minutes, or until fork tender. Cool. Discard skin and separate meat from bones. Cut chicken in bite-sized pieces. In frypan melt butter over medium heat. Add onion and sauté for about 3 minutes, or until soft but not brown. Add flour, salt and pepper. Cook about 5 minutes, or until bubbly. Gradually add cream, stirring until smooth. Cook about 5 minutes longer, or until thick. Remove from heat. Add water chestnuts, rice, ½ cup of the cheese, milk, pimiento and lemon juice. Stir until blended. In greased large shallow baking pan, place chicken. Place rice mixture on top of chicken. Sprinkle remaining ½ cup cheese on top. Bake in a 325°F. oven for about 15 minutes, or until heated through.

Eva Duncan, South Shore, Kentucky

DUCY'S BAKED CHICKEN AND YAMS

Serves 4:

1 broiler-fryer chicken, quartered	3 tablespoons water
1 tablespoon salt	1 cup fine dry bread crumbs
1 teaspoon pepper	4 medium yams, cooked and peeled
2 eggs, beaten	½ cup butter, melted

Sprinkle chicken with salt and pepper. Combine eggs and water in a shallow dish and beat. Place crumbs in another shallow dish. Dip chicken, one piece at a time, first in crumbs then in egg mixture, then in crumbs again, turning to coat. In greased large shallow baking pan place chicken and yams. Pour in ¼ cup of the melted butter. Bake, uncovered, in a 350°F. oven, basting with remaining ¼ cup butter, for about 1 hour, or until fork tender.

Marine H. Dupas, Moreauville, Louisiana

OVEN FRIED PINEAPPLE CHICKEN

Serves 4:

1 broiler-fryer chicken, cut into parts	¼ cup margarine
¼ cup soy sauce	1 (1-pound 4-ounce) can pineapple chunks
1 tablespoon finely chopped onion	2 tablespoons lemon juice
½ teaspoon ground ginger	1 teaspoon grated lemon rind
½ cup cornstarch	

Place chicken in a large bowl. Add soy sauce, onion and ginger and let stand 30 minutes, turning frequently. Remove chicken, reserving sauce. Place cornstarch in a shallow dish. Add chicken, one piece at a time, turning to coat. In large shallow baking pan melt margarine in a heated oven. Place chicken, skin side down, in single layer, in pan with margarine. Bake, uncovered, in a 350°F. oven for 30 minutes. Turn chicken. To soy sauce mixture in bowl add pineapple with juice, lemon juice and rind. Pour over chicken. Bake, uncovered, about 15 minutes longer, or until fork tender.

Ruthada Campbell, Caribou, Maine

MARYLAND

CHICKEN SALAD SUPREME

Serves 4:

2 whole broiler-fryer chicken breasts
2 broiler-fryer chicken thighs
2 broiler-fryer chicken drumsticks
2½ cups water
2 teaspoons salt
½ teaspoon pepper
3 celery tops
1 small onion, sliced
½ bunch green onions, minced
1 cup finely chopped celery
½ cup chopped English walnuts
¼ cup finely chopped fresh parsley
1 tablespoon orange juice
¾ cup plus 2 tablespoons mayonnaise
½ pound romaine lettuce, shredded
2 hard-cooked eggs, sieved
1 (4-ounce) jar pimiento

In deep saucepan place chicken. Add water, 1 teaspoon of the salt, ¼ teaspoon of the pepper, celery tops and sliced onion. Cover and simmer for about 45 minutes, or until fork tender. Remove chicken from broth, and cool. Remove skin. From one whole chicken breast cut meat in slices and set aside. Separate meat from bones of remaining pieces. Cut chicken in bite-sized pieces and place in large mixing bowl. Add green onion, chopped celery, the remaining 1 teaspoon salt, and ¼ teaspoon pepper, nuts and parsley. In bowl combine orange juice with ¾ cup of the mayonnaise, then stir into chicken mixture. On serving platter arrange lettuce. Spoon chicken mixture on lettuce. In bowl mix eggs with remaining 2 tablespoons mayonnaise. Spread egg mixture over chicken mixture. Place chicken slices on top, evenly spaced. Place pimiento between slices.

Ruth Dykes, Beltsville, Maryland

MASSACHUSETTS

LEMON CHICKEN PATRIKIS

Serves 4:

2 lemons, cut in thin slices
  and seeded
1 broiler-fryer chicken, cut
  into parts

2 cups chicken broth
1 tablespoon oregano
1 teaspoon salt
¼ teaspoon pepper

In large shallow baking dish place half of lemon slices. Place chicken, skin side up, in single layer on top of lemon. Pour in broth. Sprinkle on oregano, salt and pepper. Place remaining lemon slices on top of chicken. Bake, uncovered, in a 375° F. oven for about 1 hour, or until fork tender.

Peter C. Patrikis, Cambridge, Massachusetts

MICHIGAN

CHICKEN KEBAB

Serves 4:

½ cup cooking oil
Juice of 1 lemon
6 cloves garlic, crushed
1 teaspoon salt
¼ teaspoon nutmeg
¼ teaspoon allspice

¼ teaspoon pepper
2 whole broiler-fryer chicken
  breasts, halved, skinned,
  boned and cut in 1-inch
  chunks
1 pound fresh mushrooms

In bowl mix together oil, lemon juice, garlic, salt, nutmeg, allspice and pepper. Add chicken and marinate for 1 hour. Remove chicken, reserving marinade. On each of 4 skewers arrange alternating pieces of chicken and mushrooms. Place skewers on grill over hot coals about 8 inches from heat. Cook, turning and basting with marinade, for about 30 minutes, or until fork tender. To serve place chicken on skewers over rice pilaf.

Suzy Tazian, Birmingham, Michigan

MINNESOTA

DILLY GRILLED CHICKEN

Serves 4:

⅓ cup dill pickle liquid
2 tablespoons orange juice
¾ cup mayonnaise
1 tablespoon grated onion
½ teaspoon pepper

½ teaspoon nutmeg
1 broiler-fryer chicken, cut
  into parts
8 slices dill pickle

In bowl mix together dill pickle liquid, orange juice, mayonnaise, onion, pepper and nutmeg. Dip chicken, one piece at a time, in mayonnaise mixture. Place on grill over hot coals about 8 inches from heat. Cook, turning and basting every 15 minutes, or until fork tender. To serve, place a pickle slice on each piece of chicken.

Bonna Paulson, Hackensack, Minnesota

MISSISSIPPI

CHEESY CHICKEN

Serves 4:

⅓ cup flour
¼ pound margarine
2 whole broiler-fryer chicken
  breasts, halved
1¼ cups evaporated milk

1½ cups grated cheese
1 (10¾-ounce) can cream of
  mushroom soup
1 teaspoon salt

In shallow dish place flour. In large, shallow, baking pan melt margarine in a heated oven. Dip chicken, one piece at a time, in flour, turning to coat, then place, skin side down, in margarine in baking pan. Bake, uncovered, in 425°F. oven for 30 minutes. Turn chicken and bake for 15 minutes longer. In bowl mix together milk, cheese, soup and salt and pour over chicken. Reduce oven heat to 325°F. Cover and bake for 15 minutes longer, or until fork tender.

Willodean Hanson, Hamilton, Mississippi

MISSOURI

CHICKEN BREASTS ROCKEFELLER

Serves 4:

½ teaspoon seasoned salt
⅛ teaspoon paprika
2 whole broiler-fryer chicken breasts, halved, skinned, boned and flattened
1 (10-ounce) package frozen, chopped spinach, thawed and well drained
½ cup minced green onion

1 cup shredded sharp Cheddar cheese
1 (10¾-ounce) can cream of chicken soup
2 tablespoons light cream
1 tablespoon Worcestershire sauce
2 tablespoons toasted, buttered bread crumbs

* Sprinkle seasoned salt and ⅛ teaspoon paprika on chicken. In a bowl mix spinach and onion. Place 1 tablespoon spinach mixture on each chicken breast half, topping with 1 tablespoon cheese. Roll chicken, jelly-roll fashion, and secure with wooden picks. In large shallow glass baking dish combine soup, cream, Worcestershire, remaining cheese and remaining spinach mixture. Microwave at high for 2 minutes. Stir and microwave about 2 minutes longer, or until cheese is melted. Place chicken breast rolls in glass dish in soup mixture. Spoon soup mixture over chicken, and top with crumbs. Sprinkle additional paprika on top of crumbs. Cover with waxed paper. Microwave, turning dish every 5 minutes, for about 20 minutes, or until fork tender. Let stand, covered, for 5 minutes.

Betty Staufenbiel, Affton, Missouri

* For conventional oven, combine sauce ingredients in saucepan and cook, stirring, over medium heat about 5 minutes, or until cheese is melted. Follow procedures with chicken as listed. Bake, uncovered, in a 350°F. oven for about 50 minutes, or until fork tender.

MONTANA
CHICKEN ELEGANTE

Serves 4:

4 whole broiler-fryer chicken
  breasts, halved, skinned
  and boned
1 (10¾-ounce) can cream
  of mushroom soup

½ cup dry white wine
½ pound fresh mushrooms,
  sliced
1 cup sour cream
⅛ teaspoon paprika

In a large shallow baking pan place chicken. In a bowl combine soup, wine and mushrooms. Pour over chicken. Bake in a 350°F. oven for about 1 hour, or until fork tender. Remove chicken to heated serving dish. Add sour cream to liquid in baking pan. Heat, stirring constantly (do not boil). To serve, place chicken on hot fluffy rice and pour sauce over all. Sprinkle paprika on top.

Debra Rowse-Eagle, West Yellowstone, Montana

NEBRASKA, 5TH PRIZE 1978
CHICKEN HAWAIIAN

Serves 4:

1 broiler-fryer chicken, cut
  into parts
1 teaspoon salt
1 egg, beaten
⅓ cup frozen pineapple-
  orange juice concentrate,
  thawed

1 cup cornflake crumbs
½ cup shredded coconut
½ teaspoon curry powder
¼ cup butter, melted

In large dish place chicken and sprinkle with salt. In bowl combine egg and juice. Pour over chicken and marinate for 1 hour, turning pieces once. In shallow dish mix together crumbs, coconut and curry. Remove chicken from marinade and drain slightly. Dip chicken, one piece at a time, in coconut mixture, turning to coat. In large shallow baking pan place chicken, skin side up, in a single layer and dribble over melted butter. Bake, uncovered, in a 350°F. oven for about 1 hour, or until fork tender.

Alice Albertsen, Wayne, Nebraska

NEVADA

CHICKEN PUFF

Serves 4:

1½ cups flour	½ cup shortening
2 teaspoons salt	3 eggs, beaten
½ teaspoon pepper	2½ cups milk
1 broiler-fryer chicken, cut into parts	¼ cup butter, melted
	1 teaspoon baking powder

In a shallow dish combine ½ cup of the flour, 1 teaspoon of the salt and ¼ teaspoon of the pepper. Add chicken, one piece at a time, turning to coat. Reserve remaining flour mixture. In frypan melt shortening over medium heat. Add chicken and cook, turning, for about 10 minutes, or until brown on all sides. In a bowl make batter by blending eggs, 1½ cups of the milk and butter. Add remaining 1 cup of flour, baking powder and remaining 1 teaspoon of salt. Beat until smooth. In greased large shallow baking pan pour batter. Arrange chicken on top of batter, skin side up, in single layer. Sprinkle with the remaining ¼ teaspoon pepper. Bake, uncovered, in a 350°F. oven for about 1 hour, or until fork tender. Make a gravy by adding reserved flour mixture to drippings in frypan. Stir. Add remaining 1 cup milk, stirring constantly. Cook, stirring, about 5 minutes, or until smooth and bubbly. To serve, pour gravy over chicken in batter.

Sue Gould, Reno, Nevada

NEW HAMPSHIRE, 4TH PRIZE 1978

FARMER BROWN'S CHICKEN CASSEROLE

Serves 4:

1 tablespoon cooking oil
1 tablespoon butter
1 broiler-fryer chicken, cut into parts, with giblets
6 small onions, peeled
2 cups sliced fresh mushrooms
4 medium potatoes, peeled
4 large carrots, peeled, sliced lengthwise and cut into 1-inch chunks

3 ribs celery, cut into 1½-inch lengths
1 cup chicken broth
1 teaspoon salt
¼ teaspoon pepper
4 small garlic buds
½ cup heavy cream
1 tablespoon lemon juice
2 tablespoons flour

In frypan heat oil and melt butter over medium temperature. Add chicken and cook, turning, for about 10 minutes, or until brown on all sides. Remove chicken to large, shallow baking pan. Add onions, mushrooms and giblets to frypan and sauté for about 5 minutes, or until lightly browned. Add to chicken in baking pan, together with potatoes, carrots, celery, broth, salt and pepper. Cover and bake in a 350°F. oven for about 1½ hours. Add garlic and bake 30 minutes longer, or until fork tender. Remove garlic buds. Place chicken and vegetables on platter. Drain liquid from baking pan into a saucepan. Add cream and lemon juice. Stir in flour. Cook, stir constantly, until thickened. Pour sauce over chicken and vegetables.

Robert A. Brown, Pittsfield, New Hampshire

NEW JERSEY

CHICKEN SESAME

Serves 4:

1 egg white, slightly beaten
1 tablespoon dry white wine
1 teaspoon salt
⅛ teaspoon white pepper
⅓ cup sesame seeds
2 whole broiler-fryer chicken breasts, halved, skinned, boned and cut in 2-inch pieces
1½ teaspoons cornstarch
1 tablespoon sugar

½ cup chicken broth
¼ cup white vinegar
Juice of 1 lemon
½ cup mandarin oranges, drained and juice reserved
½ cup pineapple chunks, drained and juice reserved
Grated rind of 1 lemon
1 pint cooking oil (approximate)

In a shallow dish combine egg white, wine, salt and pepper. In another shallow dish place sesame seeds. Add chicken, a few pieces at a time, first in egg white mixture, then in sesame seeds, turning to coat. In a saucepan combine cornstarch and sugar. Stir in broth, vinegar, lemon juice and reserved juices. Simmer for 3 minutes, stirring. Add lemon rind, oranges and pineapple. Keep warm. In deep fryer place oil, filling utensil no more than one-third full. Heat to medium-high temperature (about 360°F.). Add chicken, a few pieces at a time, and fry for about 3 minutes, or until golden brown and fork tender in a test piece removed from oil. Drain on paper towels. To serve, place chicken on lettuce leaves. Pour fruits in sauce over chicken.

Dee Kwok Wang, Tenafly, New Jersey

NEW MEXICO

CHICKEN ZAMBOANGA

Serves 4:

8 broiler-fryer chicken thighs
1 (10½-ounce) can cream of mushroom soup, undiluted
2 ounces whipped cream cheese

2 tablespoons chopped ripe olives
1 teaspoon grated ginger root
1/16 teaspoon curry powder

In a shallow baking pan place chicken, skin side up, in single layer. In a bowl combine soup, cream cheese, olives and ginger. Spread mixture evenly on chicken and sprinkle with curry. Bake, uncovered, in a 350°F. oven for about 1 hour, or until fork tender. To serve, place chicken on rice and pour soup mixture over all.

Winifred Berry, Los Alamos, New Mexico

NEW YORK

POTTED PAPRIKA CHICKEN

Serves 4:

¼ cup paprika
1 teaspoon garlic powder
1 teaspoon salt
½ teaspoon pepper
1½ cups water
1 broiler-fryer chicken, quartered and skinned

1 tablespoon cooking oil
1 onion, chopped
4 large carrots, peeled and sliced
4 large potatoes, peeled and cut in cubes

In a shallow dish combine paprika, garlic powder, salt, pepper and ½ cup of the water. Add chicken, one piece at a time, turning to coat. In a Dutch oven heat oil to medium temperature. Add onion and sauté for about 3 minutes, or until lightly brown. Add chicken and cook, turning, for about 10 minutes, or until lightly brown on both sides. Add carrots, potatoes and remaining 1 cup water. Simmer, covered, for about 1½ hours or until vegetables are done and chicken is fork tender.

Mira Kass, Brooklyn, New York

NORTH CAROLINA

CHICKEN BREASTS WITH HONEY-WINE SAUCE

Serves 4:

1 cup dry white wine
4 tablespoons soy sauce
¼ teaspoon garlic powder
4 whole broiler-fryer chicken breasts, halved, skinned, boned and cut in chunks

¼ cup flour
¼ teaspoon salt
¼ teaspoon pepper
4 tablespoons cooking oil
½ cup of honey

In a bowl combine wine, soy sauce and garlic powder. Add chicken and marinate for 1 hour. Drain chicken, reserving marinade. In a shallow dish combine flour, salt and pepper. Add chicken, one piece at a time, turning to coat. In a fry-pan heat oil to medium temperature. Add chicken and cook, turning, about 10 minutes, or until brown on all sides. Add honey to marinade mixture and pour over chicken. Simmer, covered, for about 20 minutes, or until fork tender. Spoon sauce over chicken when serving.

John H. Maddry, Chapel Hill, North Carolina

NORTH DAKOTA
CHINESE SMOKED CHICKEN

Serves 4:

¼ cup cooking oil
1 whole broiler-fryer chicken
1 orange, peeled and separated into segments
2 green onions (white and green parts), cut into 1-inch pieces

¼ cup soy sauce
2 tablespoons honey
Juice of 1 orange
Grated rind of 1 orange
¼ cup minced onion
1 clove garlic, minced
¼ teaspoon ground ginger

Brush oil on inside and outside of chicken. Place orange segments and green onion in cavity of chicken. Tie wings and legs together. In a bowl make sauce by combining soy sauce, honey, orange juice and rind, minced onion, garlic and ginger. Place chicken on spit and baste with sauce. Cook, turning, over hot coals about 8 inches from heat, basting with soy sauce mixture, for 1 hour. Add wet hickory chips to briquettes.* Continue to cook, turning and basting, for about 30 minutes longer, or until fork tender.

* Instead of using wet hickory chips, the contestant used 1 teaspoon liquid smoke in the soy sauce mixture.

Mary Kay Rethke, Minot, North Dakota

OHIO
CHEDDAR PUFF CHICKEN BREASTS

Serves 4:

2 whole broiler-fryer chicken breasts, halved, skinned and boned
¼ cup sweet-and-sour sauce
¼ pound sharp Cheddar cheese, grated

3 slices bacon, ground
¼ cup chopped green onion (white and green parts)
4 slices canned pineapple, well drained

Rub chicken with sauce. In a large shallow baking pan place chicken in single layer. Bake, uncovered, in a 375°F. oven for about 45 minutes, or until fork tender. In a bowl combine cheese, bacon and onion. Place chicken and pineapple on broiler rack in single layer with pineapple beside chicken. Set temperature control at broil or 450°F. Arrange rack so chicken is about 6 inches from heat. Spread cheese mixture on chicken. Broil about 5 minutes, or until cheese bubbles and puffs and edges are golden. To serve, place pineapple on chicken.

Anita Atoulikian, Parma, Ohio

OKLAHOMA, 3RD PRIZE 1978

COOKOUT BARBECUED CHICKEN

Serves 4:

1 broiler-fryer chicken, quartered	1 tablespoon Worcestershire sauce
½ cup margarine, melted	1 tablespoon vinegar
1 cup catsup	1 teaspoon salt
1½ cups water	1 teaspoon celery salt
2 tablespoons lemon juice	⅛ teaspoon Tabasco
1 tablespoon soy sauce	3 tablespoons honey

*Add wet hickory chips to briquettes in charcoal grill. Brush both sides of chicken with margarine. Place chicken, skin side up, on grill over hot coals, about 8 inches from heat. Cook, turning and basting with margarine, for about 30 minutes, or until chicken is lightly browned. In saucepan combine catsup, water, lemon juice, soy sauce, Worcestershire, vinegar, salt, celery salt and Tabasco. Boil 5 minutes. Brush chicken with catsup mixture and continue to cook, turning and basting every 5 minutes, for 30 minutes longer. Add honey to catsup mixture. Brush on chicken and cook about 10 minutes longer, or until fork tender. Heat remaining sauce and pour over chicken when serving.

June R. Grayson, Enid, Oklahoma

* Instead of using wet hickory chips, the contestant used 1 tablespoon liquid smoke in the catsup mixture.

PARTY CHICKEN SALAD

Serves 4:

2 whole broiler-fryer chicken breasts, halved
1 (6-ounce) can water chestnuts, drained and sliced
1 cup mayonnaise
1 tablespoon soy sauce

Place chicken in a large shallow baking pan. Cover and bake in a 375°F. oven for about 1 hour, or until fork tender. Cool chicken. Discard skin, separate meat from bones and cut chicken into bite-sized pieces. In a bowl combine chicken and water chestnuts. Refrigerate for about 1 hour. In another bowl blend mayonnaise and soy sauce. Add chicken and chestnuts. Mix well. Serve on lettuce.

Virginia McGoldrick Brane, Newport, Oregon

CREAM PUFF TOPPED CHICKEN PIE

Serves 4:

2 whole broiler-fryer chicken breasts, halved, skinned, boned and cut into 1-inch chunks
1 teaspoon salt
¼ teaspoon white pepper
3 tablespoons butter
1 cup chicken broth
1½ cups frozen mixed vegetables
¼ cup water
2 tablespoons cornstarch
3 tablespoons cooking sherry
⅓ cup sour cream
¾ cup shredded Cheddar cheese
Cream Puff Topping (recipe below)

Sprinkle chicken with salt and pepper. In frypan melt butter over medium heat. Add chicken and sauté, stirring, for about 8 minutes, or until chicken is opaque and fork tender. Add broth and vegetables. Cover and simmer for 10 minutes. In a bowl mix water and cornstarch, stirring to blend. Add cornstarch mixture to chicken. Stir in sherry and sour cream. In a deep baking pan place chicken mixture, sprinkling cheese on top. Drop cream puff topping by the teaspoonful in mounds on chicken mixture. Bake, uncovered, in a 425°F. oven for 20 minutes. Reduce heat to 350°F. and bake about 15 minutes longer, or until puffs are done and brown.

CREAM PUFF TOPPING

In a saucepan combine ½ cup water, ¼ cup butter and ⅛ teaspoon salt. Bring to boil, reduce heat and add ½ cup flour all at once. Beat until dough forms a ball and leaves sides of pan. Remove from heat and beat in 2 eggs, one at a time, until mixture is smooth and glossy.

Judy Reynolds, Edinboro, Pennsylvania

RHODE ISLAND

CHICKEN PICASSO

Serves 4:

1 broiler-fryer chicken, cut into parts
4 ripe tomatoes, chopped
½ cup chopped black olives
½ cup chopped pimiento-stuffed green olives

Place chicken, skin side down, on broiler rack. Set temperature control at broil or 450°F. Arrange rack so chicken is about 6 inches from heat. Broil 20 minutes, then turn chicken. Broil about 15 minutes longer, or until fork tender. To drippings in broiler pan add tomatoes and cook on top of stove over medium heat for 5 minutes. Add olives and cook 2 minutes longer. To serve, place chicken on platter and top with olive-tomato mixture.

Jean Fontaine, Providence, Rhode Island

BUENOS DIAS CHICKEN FRICASSEE

Serves 4:

8 broiler-fryer chicken thighs
1 teaspoon seasoned salt
¼ cup cooking oil
½ cup white wine
½ cup tomato sauce with mushrooms
½ cup cream of shrimp soup

¼ cup diced hot green chilies
1 small onion, finely chopped
1 clove garlic, finely chopped
½ cup chopped cashew nuts

Sprinkle chicken with salt. In frypan heat oil to medium temperature. Add chicken and cook, turning, about 10 minutes, or until brown on both sides. In bowl combine the remaining ingredients and pour over chicken. Cover and simmer for about 50 minutes, or until fork tender. Remove chicken to platter and pour sauce over.

Elizabeth Webster, Columbia, South Carolina

CHICKEN MALAYSIA

Serves 4:

1 broiler-fryer chicken, cut into parts
2 cloves garlic, crushed
1 teaspoon paprika
1 teaspoon salt
½ teaspoon pepper
⅓ teaspoon poultry seasoning.
½ cup flour plus 1 tablespoon
⅓ cup butter

¼ cup cooking oil
½ cup chopped onion
½ (10½-ounce) can chicken broth
½ cup dry white wine
1 (10-ounce) package frozen cut green beans, thawed and drained
½ cup salted, roasted peanuts

Rub chicken with garlic. In a shallow dish combine paprika, salt, pepper and poultry seasoning. In another shallow dish place ½ cup of the flour. Place chicken, one piece at a time, first in paprika mixture then in flour, turning to coat. In frypan melt butter and heat oil over medium temperature. Add chicken and cook, turning, for about 10 minutes, or until brown on all sides. Remove chicken. Drain all but 2 tablespoons fat from frypan. Add onion and sauté about 3 minutes, or until golden. Stir in the remaining 1 tablespoon flour, and cook for 1 minute. Add broth and wine, stirring to loosen browned bits from pan. Cook about 3 minutes, or until mixture boils and is thick. Add chicken, cover and simmer for about 20 minutes. Add green beans. Cook, covered, for 10 minutes longer, or until fork tender. To serve, sprinkle peanuts on chicken.

Thomas W. King, Aberdeen, South Dakota

TENNESSEE

HUNGARIAN CHICKEN

Serves 4:

½ cup flour	½ teaspoon salt
1 broiler-fryer chicken, cut into parts	⅛ teaspoon pepper
	1 cup sliced onion
2 tablespoons cooking oil	1 cup chicken broth
1½ tablespoons paprika	½ cup sour cream

Put flour in a shallow dish and add chicken, one piece at a time, turning to coat. In frypan heat oil to medium temperature. Add chicken and cook, turning, for about 10 minutes, or until brown on all sides. Sprinkle paprika, salt and pepper on all sides of chicken until actually coated with paprika. Remove chicken from frypan. Add onion and cook 3 minutes, stirring occasionally. Return chicken to frypan. Add chicken broth, cover and simmer for 30 minutes, or until fork tender. Arrange chicken on heated platter. Strain liquid into saucepan and boil over high heat for 3 minutes. Reduce heat and add sour cream. Cook, stirring, until heated through and well mixed (do not allow to boil). Pour sauce over chicken.

Christine Harris, Nashville, Tennessee

TEXAS

QUILTED CALICO CHICKEN

Serves 4:

4 slices bacon
½ cup flour
2 teaspoons garlic salt
2 whole broiler-fryer chicken breasts, halved and skinned
½ cup cooking oil

¼ cup tomato sauce with mushrooms
1½ cups shredded Swiss cheese
2 tablespoons finely diced green pepper
1 tablespoon chopped pimiento

Cook bacon until crisp. Remove, drain and crumble. In a shallow dish combine flour and garlic salt. Add chicken, one piece at a time, turning to coat. In a frypan heat oil. Add chicken and cook, turning, about 15 minutes, or until brown on all sides. Reduce heat, cover and cook about 15 minutes longer, or until fork tender.

Place chicken in a large shallow baking pan. Slit a pocket in each breast. Brush inside of pockets and top of chicken with tomato sauce. Combine cheese, bacon, green pepper and pimiento. Place 2 tablespoons of cheese mixture in each pocket and sprinkle remaining cheese mixture on top of chicken. Broil about 5 minutes, or until cheese begins to bubble.

Beverly A. Sebastian, Fort Worth, Texas

UTAH

JEAN'S PRIDE AND JOY CHICKEN

Serves 4:

2 cups wheat germ
1 teaspoon garlic salt
2 oranges

8 broiler-fryer chicken
  thighs, boned
8 slices bacon

In a shallow dish combine wheat germ and garlic salt. In another shallow dish squeeze juice from one of the oranges. Dip chicken, one piece at a time, first in juice, then in wheat germ, turning to coat. In a large shallow baking pan place chicken, open side up, in single layer. Peel the remaining orange and separate into 8 sections. Wrap 1 slice of bacon around each orange section. Place into cavity of each piece of chicken. Bake, uncovered, in a 350°F. oven for about 60 minutes, or until fork tender.

Madeline Grow, Ogden, Utah

VERMONT

CHEESY LEMON CHICKEN

Serves 4:

⅓ cup flour
½ teaspoon salt
10 broiler-fryer chicken
  thighs
¼ cup cooking oil

1 (8-ounce) container lemon
  yogurt
½ cup soy sauce
½ cup white wine
2 tablespoons grated Parmesan cheese

Combine flour and salt in a bag, shaking to mix. Add chicken, a few pieces at a time, and shake to coat. In frypan heat oil to medium temperature. Add chicken and cook, turning, about 10 minutes, or until brown on all sides. Drain on paper towels. In bowl blend yogurt, soy sauce, wine and cheese. In a large shallow baking pan place chicken, skin side up. Pour yogurt mixture over chicken. Bake, uncovered, in 350°F. oven, basting occasionally, for about 45 minutes, or until fork tender.

Cathy M. Ladd, Shoreham, Vermont

VIRGINIA

LEMON-PEPPER CHICKEN

Serves 4:

2 tablespoons cooking oil
1 whole broiler-fryer chicken breast, halved
2 broiler-fryer chicken thighs
2 broiler-fryer chicken drumsticks
2 tablespoons prepared mustard

1 large onion, sliced
½ cup chicken broth
1 lemon, thinly sliced and seeded
1 green pepper, seeded and sliced in rings

In frypan heat oil to medium temperature. Add chicken and cook, turning, about 10 minutes, or until brown on all sides. Spread mustard over each piece of chicken. Add onion and broth. Reduce heat to low, cover and cook for 20 minutes. Add lemon and green pepper and cook about 5 minutes longer, or until fork tender.

Winifred Gilliam Martin, Norfolk, Virginia

WASHINGTON

GOURMET CHICKEN LIVERS IRAN

Serves 4:

8 tablespoons butter
1 onion, chopped
1 pound chicken livers
1 teaspoon salt
1 teaspoon cinnamon
½ teaspoon freshly ground
  black pepper

¼ teaspoon nutmeg
2 cups water
4 cups diced celery
1 cup chopped parsley
3 tablespoons lemon juice

In a deep saucepan melt 4 tablespoons of the butter over
medium heat. Add onion and sauté for about 3 minutes, or
until soft but not brown. Stir in livers, salt, cinnamon, pepper
and nutmeg. Add water, cover and simmer about 10 minutes,
or until fork tender. In a frypan melt the remaining 4 tablespoons butter over medium heat. Add celery and parsley and
sauté 10 minutes. Add celery-parsley mixture and lemon juice
to livers. Simmer for 15 minutes. Serve over hot rice.

Shirlie M. Byam, Lynnwood, Washington

WEST VIRGINIA

CHARIOT CHICKEN

Serves 4:

2 whole broiler-fryer chicken
  breasts
2 cups water
2 teaspoons salt
½ teaspoon freshly ground
  pepper
2 tablespoons butter
1 onion, sliced into thin
  rings

1 (5.3-ounce) can evapo-
  rated milk
1 teaspoon caraway seeds
1 orange
1 (8-ounce) package cream
  cheese
2 ounces pimiento, sliced
  into strips

In a deep saucepan, place chicken, water, 1 teaspoon of the
salt and ¼ teaspoon of the pepper. Cover and simmer for

about 1 hour, or until fork tender. Cool. Discard skin and separate meat from bones. Cut chicken into chunks. In a frypan melt butter over medium heat. Add onion and cook, stirring, about 5 minutes, or until tender. Add chicken, milk, caraway seeds, the remaining 1 teaspoon salt and remaining ¼ teaspoon pepper. Simmer for 10 minutes. In bowl mix juice and pulp from orange with cream cheese. Add to the chicken and simmer 10 minutes longer. Add pimiento and simmer for 5 minutes. Serve over toasted bread.

Fred Annie, Bluefield, West Virginia

WISCONSIN

SHARON'S LEMON CHICKEN

Serves 4:

2 tablespoons cornstarch
1 tablespoon sugar
1 teaspoon ground ginger
2 tablespoons soy sauce
2 tablespoons dry sherry
2 whole broiler-fryer chicken breasts, halved, skinned, boned and cut into thin slices

2 tablespoons cooking oil
½ fresh lemon, shredded
¼ pound fresh mushrooms, thinly sliced
1 teaspoon salt
¼ teaspoon pepper
2 green onions, shredded

In a bowl, combine cornstarch, sugar and ginger. Stir in soy sauce and sherry. Add chicken and marinate for 30 minutes. In a frypan heat oil to medium temperature. Stir in lemon. a few pieces at a time, and cook about 5 minutes, or until brown and fork tender. Add mushrooms, salt and pepper and cook, stirring, for 2 minutes. Add green onions.

Sharon Burns, Madison, Wisconsin

WYOMING

PINEAPPLE FRIED CHICKEN

Serves 4:

1 broiler-fryer chicken, cut
  into parts
2 cups water
1 cup pancake mix
½ teaspoon salt

¼ teaspoon paprika
⅛ teaspoon nutmeg
¾ cup pineapple juice
1 pint cooking oil (approximate)

In a deep saucepan place chicken and water. Cover and
simmer for 20 minutes, then drain. In bowl make batter by
combining pancake mix, salt, paprika and nutmeg. Add
pineapple juice and stir well. Dip chicken, one piece at a
time, in batter. Drain well on rack over waxed paper. In deep
fryer place oil, filling utensil no more than one-third full.
Heat to medium temperature (about 360°F.). Add chicken,
a few pieces at a time, and cook about 5 minutes, or until
golden brown and fork tender, a test piece removed from oil.
Drain.

Jane B. Norman, Moorcroft, Wyoming

ALABAMA

GREEK CHICKEN FILO PIE

Makes 12 4-inch squares

1 broiler-fryer chicken, cut
  into parts
5 cups water
1 (10-ounce) package
  frozen chopped onion
1½ teaspoons salt
1 pound butter, melted, plus
  4 tablespoons

6 tablespoons flour
4 eggs, beaten
⅛ teaspoon nutmeg
⅛ teaspoon white pepper
¼ cup grated Romano
  cheese
1 (1-pound) package frozen
  filo dough, defrosted

Put chicken in a deep saucepan. Add water, onion and 1
teaspoon of the salt. Cover and simmer for about 45 minutes,
or until fork tender. Cool. Remove chicken from broth, re-

serving the broth. Separate meat from bones, discarding bones and skin. Cut chicken in bite-sized pieces. Mash onions in blender or with potato masher. In Dutch oven, heat 4 tablespoons of the butter over medium temperature. While butter is melting, add flour, beating with wire whisk until thoroughly blended. Stir in 3 cups of the reserved, hot chicken broth. Continue beating with a whisk until smooth. Slowly add eggs, nutmeg, the remaining ½ teaspoon salt, pepper and cheese. Cook, stirring, over low heat for about 3 minutes, or until thick. Add chicken and onion. Set aside to cool. Brush bottom and sides of a 12-×-17-inch baking pan with the melted butter. Layer 10 sheets of the dough in pan, brushing each sheet individually with butter, using about half of the melted butter. Spread chicken mixture evenly over the dough. Fold sides of dough over chicken. Layer remaining sheets of dough on top of chicken, brushing each layer with butter, using remaining melted butter. With scissors, cut through top sheets of dough into about 4-inch squares. Bake, uncovered, on the lowest rack of a 375°F. oven for 45 minutes. Move pan to middle rack of oven and bake 20 minutes longer. Let stand for 10 minutes. Cut through bottom sheets of dough before serving.

Sophia Clikas, Mobile, Alabama

ALASKA

YOGURT COATED OVEN-FRIED CHICKEN

Serves 4:

1 cup plain low-fat yogurt
1 teaspoon celery salt
1 teaspoon paprika
¼ teaspoon pepper
1 teaspoon lemon juice
1 teaspoon Worcestershire
 sauce

4 slices whole-wheat bread,
 dried and made into
 crumbs
1 broiler-fryer chicken, cut
 into parts
4 tablespoons margarine,
 melted

In a shallow dish, combine yogurt, celery salt, paprika, pepper, lemon juice and Worcestershire. In another shallow dish, place crumbs. Dip chicken, one piece at a time, first in yogurt mixture, spreading thoroughly over chicken with spatula; then dip in crumbs, turning to coat. In a large shallow baking pan, place chicken, skin side up, in single layer. Pour margarine on chicken. Bake, uncovered, in a 400°F. oven for about 45 minutes, or until fork tender.

Mary Crawford, Fairbanks, Alaska

ARIZONA

DELICIOUS CHICKEN DINNER

Serves 4:

1 (28-ounce) can whole
  peeled tomatoes
1 cup chopped onion
1 cup chopped celery
½ cup water
1 (0.6-ounce) package Italian salad dressing mix

2 teaspoons salt
⅟₁₆ teaspoon pepper
⅟₁₆ teaspoon garlic powder
1 broiler-fryer chicken, cut
  into parts
2 cups cooked rice

In a large shallow glass baking dish combine tomatoes, onion, celery, water, salad dressing mix, salt, pepper and garlic powder. Add chicken, skin side up, in single layer. Cover and microwave on high for 5 minutes. Turn chicken to skin side down. Cover and microwave on simmer for about 15 minutes. Remove from oven. Let stand, covered, for 5 minutes before testing for doneness. Return to oven for additional cooking if not fork tender. Cool. Remove chicken from broth, leaving broth in baking dish. Separate meat from bones, discarding bones and skin. Add rice and chicken to broth in baking dish. Cover and microwave on simmer for 3 minutes. Let stand, covered, 3 minutes longer.

Sandra Jean Banks, Tempe, Arizona

ARKANSAS

CHICKEN THIGHS FROM ON HIGH

Serves 4:

1 (4½-ounce) can deviled ham

12 dried apricot halves, chopped

2 tablespoons fine bread crumbs

2 tablespoons chopped slivered almonds

1½ teaspoons dried minced onion

1½ teaspoons parsley flakes

¾ teaspoon salt

8 broiler-fryer chicken thighs, boned

1 cup sour cream

¾ cup apricot jam

2 tablespoons Dijon mustard

In bowl, mix together 2 tablespoons of the deviled ham, apricots, bread crumbs, almonds, onion, parsley flakes and salt. Divide in 8 portions and place 1 portion in center of each thigh. Close with wooden toothpicks. In a greased large shallow baking pan, place chicken, skin side down, in a single layer. Cover and bake in a 350°F. oven for about 40 minutes, or until fork tender. In a saucepan, make sauce by combining sour cream, apricot jam, mustard and remaining deviled ham (heat but do not boil). To serve, place chicken on rice and pour sauce over all.

Faye N. Suitt, Little Rock, Arkansas

CALIFORNIA

CHICKEN MICRO-NESIA

Serves 4:

¼ cup brown sugar
2 tablespoons cornstarch
1 cup orange juice
2 tablespoons lime juice
1 (8-ounce) can crushed
   pineapple
¼ cup diced green pepper

¼ cup diced pimiento
1 tablespoon soy sauce
½ cup butter, melted
1 cup flour
2 teaspoons seasoned salt
1 broiler-fryer chicken, cut
   into parts

In a glass bowl or glass saucepan, make sauce by combining sugar, cornstarch and juices, stirring until blended. Add pineapple, green pepper, pimiento and soy sauce. Microwave on high, stirring every 2 minutes, for about 6 minutes, or until clear and thick. Set aside. In a shallow dish, place melted butter. In another shallow dish, mix flour and seasoned salt. Dip chicken, one piece at a time, first in butter; then in flour mixture. In large shallow glass baking dish, place chicken, skin side up, in single layer, placing meatier pieces to outside. Cover with waxed paper. Microwave on high for 10 minutes. Turn dish one-half turn and microwave on high for 10 minutes longer. Remove from oven and let stand, covered, for 5 minutes before testing for doneness. Return to oven for additional cooking if not fork tender. Return sauce to microwave and microwave on high for 2½ minutes. To serve, pour sauce on chicken.

Leah L. Nosek, Torrance, California

SPICY CHICKEN FIESTA

Serves 4:

¼ cup flour
2 teaspoons prepared chili
 mix
½ teaspoon taco seasoning
 mix
½ teaspoon salt
¼ teaspoon freshly ground
 pepper

8 broiler-fryer chicken thighs
¼ cup cooking oil
2 tablespoons finely chopped
 onion
½ cup beer
8 teaspoons tomato sauce

In a shaker combine flour, chili mix, taco mix, salt and pepper. Sprinkle on both sides of chicken. In an ovenproof frypan, heat oil to medium. Add onion and sauté, stirring, for about 5 minutes, or until soft. Add chicken and cook, turning, for about 15 minutes, or until brown on both sides. Pour beer on chicken. Put 1 teaspoon tomato sauce on each piece of chicken. Cover and bake in a 350°F. oven for 45 minutes, or until fork tender.

Esther Mae Chinn, Grand Junction, Colorado

CONNECTICUT, 3RD PRIZE 1979

SHIRLEY'S CHICKEN AND MACARONI

Serves 4:

½ cup flour
2 teaspoons seasoned salt
1 broiler-fryer chicken, cut
into parts
½ cup cooking oil
5 green onions, (green and
white parts), chopped
1 cup chopped green pepper
1 pound mushrooms, sliced
1 (28-ounce) can tomatoes,
drained and coarsely
chopped, liquid reserved

¼ cup sherry
1 tablespoon salt
1 teaspoon freshly ground
black pepper
2 tablespoons prepared
grated horseradish
1½ teaspoons dry mustard
½ teaspoon tarragon
2 chicken bouillon cubes
1 cup water (approximate)
2 cups uncooked macaroni

In a bag combine flour and seasoned salt. Add chicken, a few pieces at a time, and shake to coat. In a frypan, heat oil over medium temperature. Add chicken and cook, turning, for about 15 minutes, or until brown on all sides. Remove chicken and set aside. Add onion and green peppers to frypan, and sauté for about 5 minutes, or until soft. Add mushrooms and sauté 2 minutes. Stir in tomatoes, sherry, salt, pepper, horseradish, mustard and tarragon. Remove from heat. Dissolve bouillon cubes in 1 cup water, then add to tomato mixture. Place reserved tomato juice in a measuring cup, add water to measure 2 cups and add to tomato mixture. Spread macaroni in large shallow pan. Arrange chicken, skin side up, in single layer on macaroni. Pour tomato mixture over all. Cover and bake in a 350°F. oven for about 40 minutes, or until fork tender.

Shirley Miska, Weston, Connecticut

DELAWARE

FLIPOVER CHICKEN

Serves 4:

1 broiler-fryer chicken, cut
  into parts
2 cups water
1 whole onion plus 2 tablespoons chopped onion
1 rib celery, cut in half,
  plus ¼ cup chopped celery
2¾ teaspoons salt
3 tablespoons butter
2 tablespoons chopped green
  pepper
3 tablespoons flour

¾ cup milk
1¼ cups shredded sharp
  Cheddar cheese
2 tablespoons chopped pi-
  miento
1 tablespoon sauterne
¼ teaspoon paprika
¼ teaspoon thyme
1 teaspoon parsley flakes
¼ teaspoon pepper
2 (8-ounce) packages re-
  frigerated crescent rolls

In a deep saucepan, place chicken. Add water, whole onion, celery rib and 2 teaspoons of the salt. Cover and simmer for about 45 minutes, or until fork tender. Cool. Remove chicken from broth and separate meat from bones, discarding bones and skin. Cut chicken in bite-sized pieces. In saucepan, melt butter over medium heat. Add chopped onion, chopped celery and green pepper, and sauté for about 3 minutes, or until onion is soft. Stir in flour. Gradually add milk, stirring, and cook about 5 minutes, or until mixture is thick and bubbly. Add ½ cup of the cheese, pimiento, wine, paprika, thyme, parsley flakes and remaining salt and pepper. Stir until blended, then stir in chicken. Unroll a package of rolls on an ungreased baking sheet. Press together perforated edges to make one piece of pastry. Spread chicken mixture on pastry. On waxed paper, unroll dough from remaining rolls and press perforated edges to make one piece of pastry. Flip second piece of pastry over chicken mixture. Seal edges of pastry together. Sprinkle remaining ¾ cup cheese on top. Bake, uncovered, in 375°F. oven for about 20 minutes, or until golden brown. Let stand 5 minutes before serving.

Janielle L. Sherkey, New Castle, Delaware

DISTRICT OF COLUMBIA

FAST AND FANCY CHICKEN

Serves 4:

1 (12-ounce) package
   frozen spinach soufflé,
   thawed and diced
½ cup sour cream
½ cup mayonnaise
1 tablespoon finely chopped
   onion
¼ teaspoon nutmeg
3 tablespoons butter
1 teaspoon paprika

½ teaspoon sage
½ teaspoon thyme
½ teaspoon garlic powder
2 whole broiler-fryer chicken
   breasts, halved, skinned
   and boned
2 tablespoons lemon juice
½ teaspoon salt
¼ teaspoon pepper

Place spinach in a large shallow baking pan. In a bowl, combine sour cream, mayonnaise, onion and nutmeg. Stir into the spinach and spread mixture over bottom of baking pan. In frypan, melt butter over medium heat. Add paprika, sage, thyme and garlic powder. Cook, stirring for about 3 minutes, or until hot and frothy. Add chicken and cook, turning once, for about 5 minutes, or until brown on both sides. Remove chicken from pan and arrange on top of spinach mixture. Pour drippings from pan onto chicken. Sprinkle 1 tablespoon of the lemon juice on chicken, then salt and pepper. Cover and bake in a 350°F. oven for about 25 minutes, or until fork tender. Sprinkle remaining 1 tablespoon lemon juice on chicken before serving.

Frank Mullin, Washington, D.C.

CHICKEN CACCIATORE BLANC

Serves 4:

2 tablespoons cooking oil	1 teaspoon chopped parsley
1 broiler-fryer chicken, cut into parts	½ teaspoon salt
1 medium onion, sliced	$\frac{1}{16}$ teaspoon freshly ground black pepper
2 tablespoons butter	½ cup dry sherry
1 cup sliced fresh mushrooms	½ cup water

In frypan, heat oil to medium temperature. Add chicken and cook, turning, for about 20 minutes, or until brown on all sides. Add onion and sauté about 5 minutes, or until onion is soft. Drain oil from pan and add butter, mushrooms, parsley, salt and pepper. Sauté for 3 minutes, then add wine and water. Simmer until slightly thick. Transfer chicken to a serving platter and pour sauce over it.

Camilla Jane Muntz, Fort Lauderdale, Florida

BOB'S ORANGE GLAZED CHICKEN

Serves 2 generously:

1¼ teaspoons salt	1 tablespoon prepared mustard
¼ teaspoon pepper	2 teaspoons cornstarch
1 broiler-fryer chicken, halved	1 teaspoon grated orange zest
¼ cup butter, melted	½ teaspoon oregano
¾ cup orange marmalade	⅓ cup toasted pecans
½ cup orange juice	
¼ cup vinegar	

Sprinkle 1 teaspoon of the salt and pepper on chicken. Place chicken in a large shallow baking pan, skin side up, in a single layer. Brush with butter. Bake, uncovered in a 400°F. oven for 45 minutes, basting every 15 minutes with drippings.

In a saucepan, make a glaze by combining marmalade, orange juice, vinegar, mustard, cornstarch, zest, oregano and the remaining ¼ teaspoon salt. Cook, stirring, for about 5 minutes, or until thick. Add pecans. Brush glaze on chicken and continue baking and glazing about 15 minutes, or until chicken is fork tender.

Robert English, Savannah, Georgia

HAWAII

CRUNCHY CHICKEN DELIGHT

Serves 4:

12 broiler-fryer chicken thighs, boned
1½ teaspoons salt
¼ teaspoon pepper
1 cup flour
1 egg, beaten
¾ cup ice water
1 clove garlic, grated
1 (7-ounce) package bread crumbs

1 pint cooking oil (approximate)
3 tablespoons catsup
2 tablespoons soy sauce
1½ tablespoons vinegar
2 teaspoons sugar
1/16 teaspoon hot pepper sauce

Sprinkle chicken with 1 teaspoon of the salt and the pepper. In a bowl make batter by combining flour, remaining ½ teaspoon salt, egg and water. Stir in garlic. Put bread crumbs in a shallow dish. Dip chicken first in batter, turning to coat evenly, then in bread crumbs, rolling to coat. In a large frypan, place oil, filling utensil to ½-inch depth. Heat to medium temperature. Add chicken, a few pieces at a time and cook for about 15 minutes, or until golden brown and fork tender when a test piece is removed from oil. Drain chicken. In bowl, make sauce by blending catsup, soy sauce, vinegar, sugar and hot pepper sauce. Cut each chicken thigh in 4 pieces and serve with the sauce.

Bobbiette Tamura, Honolulu, Hawaii

IDAHO

ITALIAN CHICKEN SUPREME

Serves 4:

⅓ cup flour
1 broiler-fryer chicken, cut into parts and skinned
2 tablespoons cooking oil
1 teaspoon salt
¼ teaspoon pepper
1 tablespoon margarine
2 ribs celery, thinly sliced on the diagonal

2 tablespoons chopped onion
1 clove garlic, finely chopped
½ pound fresh mushrooms, sliced
½ cup dry white wine
2 cups commercially prepared spaghetti sauce

Put flour in a shallow dish. Add chicken, one piece at a time, dredging to coat. In Dutch oven, heat oil to medium temperature. Add chicken and cook, turning, for about 15 minutes, or until brown on all sides. Sprinkle with salt and pepper. In frypan, melt margarine over medium heat. Add celery, onion, garlic and mushrooms and sauté for about 5 minutes, or until onion is soft. Add wine, cover and simmer for 5 minutes. Add this sauce to chicken in Dutch oven. Cover and simmer for about 30 minutes, or until fork tender. Serve with rice.

Lucille Kavanaugh, Nampa, Idaho

ILLINOIS

CHICKEN WITH ROSEMARY

Serves 4:

2 tablespoons cooking oil
1 broiler-fryer chicken, cut into parts
1 small onion, chopped
1 clove garlic, chopped
3 sprigs parsley, chopped

1 rib celery, chopped
1 teaspoon rosemary
½ teaspoon basil
⅓ cup sherry
1 tablespoon wine vinegar
¼ cup pecan halves

In frypan, heat oil to medium temperature. Add chicken, onion, garlic, parsley and celery. Cook, turning and stirring, for about 15 minutes, or until chicken is brown on all sides. Add rosemary, basil, wine and vinegar. Cover and simmer for about 30 minutes, or until fork tender. To serve, place chicken on rice, add pecans and pour liquid over all.

Florence Edmunds, Bloomington, Illinois

INDIANA

CHICKEN NORMANDY

Serves 4 generously:

7 tablespoons flour	½ cup diced onion
1 teaspoon salt	½ teaspoon tarragon
¼ teaspoon pepper	1 (10¾-ounce) can chicken
2 whole broiler-fryer chicken breasts, halved	broth
	1 cup cider
4 broiler-fryer chicken thighs	½ lemon, squeezed
2 tablespoons butter	½ cup whipping cream
2 tablespoons cooking oil	

In a bag, combine 4 tablespoons of the flour, salt and pepper. Add chicken, a few pieces at a time, and shake to coat. In frypan melt butter and heat oil to medium temperature. Add chicken and cook, turning, for about 15 minutes, or until brown on all sides. Add the remaining 3 tablespoons flour, onion and tarragon. Sauté for 5 minutes, turning chicken pieces several times to coat well. In a saucepan, blend broth, cider and lemon juice and heat. Add to chicken in frypan. Cover and simmer for about 25 minutes, or until fork tender. Remove chicken from frypan. To contents of frypan, gradually add cream, stirring constantly. To serve, pour cream mixture over chicken.

Beatrice F. Langer, Bloomington, Indiana

IOWA

SPECIAL OCCASION CHICKEN

Serves 4:

6 tablespoons butter
2 whole broiler-fryer chicken
   breasts, halved and
   skinned
¾ cup sauterne

½ medium onion, chopped
1 cup sour cream
1 teaspoon salt
¼ teaspoon white pepper

In a frypan, melt 4 tablespoons of the butter over medium heat. Add chicken and cook, turning, for about 15 minutes, or until brown on both sides. Pour ½ cup of the wine on chicken. Cover and simmer for about 20 minutes, or until fork tender. In a saucepan, melt the remaining 2 tablespoons butter over medium heat. Add onion and sauté for 3 minutes, then stir in remaining ¼ cup wine and sour cream. Remove from heat, and pour sour cream mixture on chicken. Add salt and pepper. Heat slightly until sauce is warm. To serve, place chicken on rice and pour sour cream mixture over all.

Marla René Ament, Lawton, Iowa

KANSAS

HOEDOWN BARBECUED DRUMSTICKS

Serves 4:

¼ cup butter
8 broiler-fryer chicken
   drumsticks, skinned
1 cup chopped green onion
   (white and green parts)
⅔ cup beer
1 (1⅜-ounce) envelope dry
   onion soup mix

¾ cup pineapple preserves
½ cup catsup
2 tablespoons steak sauce
1 tablespoon prepared
   mustard
2 teaspoons prepared horseradish
⅓ cup slivered almonds

In a frypan, melt butter over medium heat. Add chicken and green onion and cook, turning and stirring, for about 15 minutes, or until chicken is brown on all sides. Remove chicken and place in single layer in a large shallow baking pan. Pour in beer and sprinkle one-half of the soup mix on chicken. Turn chicken and sprinkle with remaining soup mix. Bake, uncovered, in a 350°F. oven for 30 minutes. In the same frypan make barbecue sauce by blending preserves, catsup, steak sauce, mustard and horseradish. Simmer, uncovered, stirring occasionally, for 10 minutes. Pour barbecue sauce on chicken and sprinkle almonds on top. Bake, uncovered, for about 20 minutes, or until fork tender.

Kathleen R. Stubler, Kansas City, Kansas

KENTUCKY

CHICKEN AND RICE OLÉ

Serves 4:

½ cup margarine, melted
1 (11-ounce) can condensed cheddar cheese soup
1 (10¾-ounce) can condensed tomato soup
⅔ cup water
1 (1.25-ounce) envelope taco seasoning mix
1 (4-ounce) can green chilies, seeded, drained and chopped

2 medium tomatoes, drained and coarsely chopped
⅔ cup long-grain rice
1 egg, beaten
½ cup flour
½ cup yellow cornmeal
1 broiler-fryer chicken, cut into parts
1 onion, sliced

Coat the bottom and sides of a large shallow baking pan with 2 tablespoons of the margarine. In bowl combine soups, water, all except 1 tablespoon of the taco mix, chilies, tomatoes and rice. Pour into baking pan. In a shallow dish, mix egg and remaining margarine. In another shallow dish, blend flour, cornmeal and remaining taco mix. Dip chicken first in egg mixture, turning to coat, then in flour mixture, dredging well. Place chicken, skin side up, in single layer, larger pieces toward outside, on top of rice mixture. Cover and bake in a 350°F. oven for 30 minutes. Remove cover and continue baking about 1 hour longer, or until fork tender. Separate onion into rings. Dip first in remaining egg mixture, then in remaining flour mixture. Place onion slices in single layer on an ungreased baking sheet. Bake, uncovered, in a 350°F. oven for 30 minutes. To serve, arrange onion slices on chicken.

Timothy E. Troendle, Lexington, Kentucky

LOUISIANA

CHICKEN SAN JOAQUIN

Serves 4:

2 whole broiler-fryer chicken breasts, halved, skinned, boned and cut in strips
¼ teaspoon garlic powder
1 teaspoon salt
¼ teaspoon pepper
3 tablespoons butter
1 cup sliced green onion (white and green parts)

1 (4-ounce) can sliced mushrooms, drained and liquid reserved
¼ cup dry sherry
2 tablespoons cornstarch
⅓ cup chicken broth
2 tomatoes, peeled and chopped
½ cup sour cream

Sprinkle chicken with garlic powder, salt and pepper. In a frypan, melt butter over medium heat. Add chicken and cook about 2 minutes. Add onion and mushrooms, cooking about 5 minutes, or until onion is soft. Stir in wine. In a small bowl, blend cornstarch, mushroom liquid and broth, stirring until smooth. Pour cornstarch mixture in chicken mixture. Cook, stirring constantly, for about 5 minutes, or until thick. Stir in tomatoes and sour cream. Cook for about 3 minutes, or until heated through (do not boil). Serve over rice.

Mary Menard, Breaux Bridge, Louisiana

MAINE

DAVE'S SPECIALTY CHICKEN

Serves 4:

2 tablespoons margarine
2 whole broiler-fryer chicken breasts, halved, skinned, boned and cut in bite-size pieces
½ pound Chinese cabbage*
½ pound fresh mushrooms, sliced
1 cup sliced green onion (white and green parts)

¼ cup soy sauce
1 clove garlic, finely chopped
1½ cups chicken broth
2 tablespoons cornstarch
½ teaspoon sugar
1 (6-ounce) package Chinese pea pods

In a frypan, melt margarine over medium heat. Add chicken and cook, turning, for about 5 minutes, or until brown. Add cabbage, mushrooms, onion, soy sauce and garlic, stirring lightly to coat vegetables with soy sauce. Cover and cook, stirring occasionally, for about 15 minutes, or until barely tender. Add ½ cup of the broth and simmer about 5 minutes longer, or until chicken is fork tender. In a small bowl, combine cornstarch and sugar. Stir in the remaining 1 cup broth. Pour cornstarch mixture into chicken mixture and stir. Add pea pods. Cook, stirring constantly, for about 5 minutes, or until heated through and sauce is thick. Serve on fluffy rice.

Linda Giasson Breau, Augusta, Maine

* If Chinese cabbage is not available, regular cabbage may be substituted.

MARYLAND, 4TH PRIZE 1979

CHICKEN MUSHROOM DINNER

Serves 4:

1 whole broiler-fryer chicken
1 teaspoon salt
4 slices bacon
4 tablespoons margarine
½ pound fresh mushrooms, sliced
½ teaspoon monosodium glutamate
¼ teaspoon white pepper

2 tablespoons finely chopped parsley
3 tablespoons flour
1 teaspoon paprika
1 teaspoon oregano
1 teaspoon caraway seeds
2 medium potatoes, skinned and cut into thick slices
½ cup white cooking wine
1 cup chicken broth

Rub chicken with salt and set aside. Cook bacon until crisp, drain and crumble. In a saucepan, melt margarine over medium heat. Add mushrooms, monosodium glutamate and pepper. Cook, stirring, for 5 minutes. Add parsley, then remove from heat and cool. Add 2 tablespoons of the flour and the bacon, stirring well. Stuff the chicken with mushroom mixture. Place chicken in ovenproof frypan and sprinkle with paprika, oregano and caraway seeds. Arrange potatoes around chicken. Add wine and ½ cup of the broth. Bake, uncovered, in a 350°F. oven, basting occasionally, for 1 hour, or until leg moves freely when lifted or twisted. In small bowl, place the remaining 1 tablespoon flour. Add the remaining ½ cup broth, stirring well. Add to chicken and potatoes in frypan. Bake 5 more minutes longer.

Barbara M. Zollikofer, Towson, Maryland

MASSACHUSETTS

CURRIED CHICKEN À LA HILL

Serves 4:

3 tablespoons peanut oil
1 clove garlic
2 whole broiler-fryer chicken breasts, halved, skinned, boned and cut into bite-size pieces
1 cup chopped onion
2 chicken bouillon cubes
2 cups hot water
2 tablespoons chunk-style peanut butter
1 cup milk

1 tablespoon cornstarch
1 tablespoon curry powder
½ teaspoon ground cinnamon
¼ teaspoon ground ginger
¼ teaspoon ground coriander
¼ teaspoon ground cloves
¼ teaspoon salt
2 tablespoons lemon juice
1 teaspoon hot pepper sauce

In a wok, heat oil to medium temperature. Place wooden pick in the garlic and cook in the oil for 1 minute. Remove garlic and discard. Add chicken to oil and sauté, stirring, for about 3 minutes, or until fork tender. Remove chicken and keep warm. Sauté onion in the wok for 3 minutes, or until golden and soft. Remove onion from wok and mix with chicken. In a small bowl dissolve bouillon cubes in water. In another bowl, combine peanut butter, and ¼ cup bouillon, mixing well. In wok, place remaining bouillon, peanut butter mixture and milk. Heat, stirring, over medium heat until simmering point is reached. In another bowl, combine cornstarch, curry powder, cinnamon, ginger, coriander, cloves and salt. Pour ¼ cup liquid from wok into bowl of mixed spices. Stir until smooth and return to wok. Add chicken and onion mixture. Simmer, stirring, for about 5 minutes, or until thoroughly warmed and slightly thick. Add lemon juice and hot pepper sauce just before serving.

H. B. Hill III, Brighton, Massachusetts

MICHIGAN

CURRIED BARBECUE CHICKEN

Serves 2 generously:

1 broiler-fryer chicken, halved lengthwise
2 cups water
1 cup tomato sauce
½ cup dry vermouth
½ cup olive oil
2 teaspoons crushed rosemary
2 teaspoons curry powder
1½ teaspoons salt

Place chicken in a deep saucepan, add water, cover and simmer for 15 minutes. In a saucepan, make barbecue sauce by combining the remaining ingredients. Simmer for 5 minutes. Place chicken on grill, skin side up, about 8 inches from heat. Cook, turning and basting with sauce about every 8 minutes, for about 25 minutes, or until fork tender.

Mrs. Genie Perkins, Grand Rapids, Michigan

MINNESOTA

CHICKEN 'N SPIRITS

Serves 4:

2 whole broiler-fryer chicken breasts, halved, skinned and boned
2 tablespoons cooking oil
1 (8-ounce) package fresh mushrooms
1 cup finely chopped green pepper
1 cup finely chopped onion
1 cup dry white wine
1 tablespoon brown sugar
1 tablespoon lemon juice
1 tablespoon soy sauce
1 teaspoon garlic powder
½ teaspoon thyme
½ teaspoon oregano
¼ teaspoon pepper
¼ teaspoon paprika

In a large shallow baking pan place chicken in a single layer. In a frypan, heat oil to medium temperature. Add mushrooms, green pepper and onion. Sauté for about 5 minutes, or until onion is soft. Add wine, sugar, lemon juice, soy sauce, garlic powder, thyme, oregano, pepper and paprika, stirring to mix. Pour on chicken. Cover and bake in a

375°F. oven for 60 minutes. Remove cover and bake about 30 minutes longer, or until chicken is golden brown and fork tender.

Bette Svendsen, St. Paul, Minnesota

MISSISSIPPI

SKEWERED CHICKEN THIGHS

Serves 4:

1 cup olive oil	2 teaspoons salt
½ cup soy sauce	2 bay leaves
Juice of 1 lemon	1 small onion, sliced
¼ cup honey	8 broiler-fryer chicken thighs
1 tablespoon red wine vinegar	½ cup chicken broth

In large bowl, combine oil, soy sauce, lemon juice, honey, vinegar and salt. Beat with wire whisk. Add bay leaves and onion, whisking to bruise onion slightly. Add chicken, turning to coat. Marinate at room temperature for 1 hour. Drain and reserve marinade. Remove bay leaves. Place 4 pieces of chicken on each of 2 skewers with bones at right angles to skewers. In a broiling pan, place skewered chicken, skin side up, in single layer 6 inches from heat. Broil for about 5 minutes, or until skin is brown and crisp. Turn chicken and move broiling pan 8 inches from heat. Broil about 10 minutes longer, or until fork tender. In a saucepan, place reserved marinate. Add broth and heat until warm. To serve, place chicken on rice; place onion on top of chicken; pour marinade over all.

Charlotte S. Paul, Jackson, Mississippi

MISSOURI

CHICKEN DIANE

Serves 4 generously:

¼ cup flour
4 whole broiler-fryer chicken breasts, halved, skinned and boned
¼ cup butter
1 small tomato, chopped
3 tablespoons lemon juice

3 tablespoons Worcestershire sauce
2 tablespoons chopped onion
2 teaspoons chopped green pepper
½ teaspoon salt
2 teaspoons catsup
1 teaspoon prepared mustard

Put flour in a shallow dish. Add chicken, one piece at a time, dredging to coat. In a frypan, melt butter over medium heat. Add chicken and cook, turning, about 25 minutes, or until light brown and fork tender. Transfer chicken to a serving platter and keep warm. Pour fat off juices in frypan. Add the remaining ingredients, stirring to blend. Simmer, uncovered, for 2 minutes. To serve, pour mixture from frypan onto chicken.

Fay Gillerman, University City, Missouri

MONTANA

ORANGY BARBECUE CHICKEN

Serves 4:

1 broiler-fryer chicken, cut into parts
1 cup catsup
6 whole cloves
1 medium onion, chopped
1 clove garlic, finely chopped
2 tablespoons butter
2 tablespoons steak sauce
2 tablespoons Worcestershire sauce

1 tablespoon cooking oil
1 tablespoon vinegar
1½ tablespoons prepared mustard
½ teaspoon hot pepper sauce
¼ teaspoon salt
¼ teaspoon pepper
Juice of 1 orange
Rind of ½ orange, cut into small pieces

On a rack in a large shallow baking pan, place chicken, skin side up, in a single layer. Bake, uncovered, in a 350°F. oven for 40 minutes. Turn chicken to skin side down and bake about 40 minutes longer, or until fork tender. In a large saucepan, make sauce by combining the remaining ingredients. Cook, stirring, until mixture boils. Cover and simmer for 40 minutes. Pour sauce on chicken and bake, uncovered, for 15 minutes. Turn chicken to skin side up; pour on sauce and bake, uncovered, for 15 minutes longer. Serve with reheated remaining sauce.

Nancy Carlson, Hamilton, Montana

NEBRASKA

CHICKEN NORWEGIAN

Serves 4:

⅓ cup flour
1 teaspoon salt
¼ teaspoon pepper
1 broiler-fryer chicken, cut into parts
2 tablespoons butter
2 tablespoons cooking oil

1 tablespoon caraway seeds
⅛ teaspoon rosemary
⅛ teaspoon marjoram
⅛ teaspoon thyme
¾ cup hot water
1 cup sour cream

In a bag combine flour, salt and pepper. Add chicken, a few pieces at a time, and shake to coat. In a frypan, melt butter and heat oil over medium temperature. Add chicken and cook, turning, for about 15 minutes, or until brown on all sides. Add caraway seeds, rosemary, marjoram, thyme, water and ¼ cup of the sour cream. Cover and cook over low heat for about 40 minutes or until chicken is fork tender. Remove from heat and let stand, covered, for 20 minutes. Pour the remaining ¾ cup sour cream over chicken and return frypan to heat. Cook over medium temperature for about 10 minutes, or until hot.

Frieda Kaufman, Lincoln, Nebraska

NEVADA

CHICKEN IN HILTON SAUCE

Serves 4:

2 whole broiler-fryer chicken breasts, halved and skinned
1 medium green pepper, chopped
1 large onion, chopped
1 clove garlic, finely chopped
2 whole cloves
2 cups tomato sauce

1¾ cups water
2 (0.1875-ounce) packages granulated chicken bouillon
2 teaspoons chili powder
½ teaspoon salt
¼ teaspoon hot pepper sauce
4 teaspoons unsweetened cocoa
2 teaspoons cornstarch

In non-stick frypan, place chicken and cook, turning, over medium heat for about 15 minutes, or until brown on both sides. Remove chicken and set aside. Add green pepper, onion and garlic to the frypan and sauté about 5 minutes, or until onion is soft. Add cloves, tomato sauce, 1 cup of the water, bouillon, chili powder, salt and hot pepper sauce. In a small bowl, combine cocoa and ½ cup of the water, stirring to mix. Add to contents of frypan. Return chicken to frypan, cover and simmer for about 30 minutes, or until fork tender. In small bowl, blend cornstarch and the remaining ¼ cup water, stirring until smooth. Add cornstarch mixture to contents of frypan. Cook, stirring, over medium heat for about 5 minutes, or until thick. To serve, place chicken on rice and pour mixture over all.

Jonelle Hilton, Reno, Nevada

NEW HAMPSHIRE

SMOTHERED SAGEBRUSHED CHICKEN

Serves 4:

1 cup flour
1 teaspoon ground sage
1 teaspoon salt
⅛ teaspoon pepper
1 broiler-fryer chicken, cut
    into parts

¾ cup cooking oil
½ cup chopped onion
¼ cup chopped green pepper
½ teaspoon celery seed
2 cups tomato juice
2 teaspoons soy sauce

In shallow dish, combine flour, sage, salt and pepper. Add chicken, one piece at a time, dredging to coat. In a frypan, heat oil to medium temperature. Add chicken, a few pieces at a time, and cook, turning for about 5 minutes each side, or until brown. Remove all but 3 tablespoons oil from pan. Add the remaining ingredients. Cover and cook about 25 minutes, or until chicken is fork tender. To serve, place chicken on rice and pour pan juices over all.

Orrin J. Willson, Rochester, New Hampshire

NEW JERSEY

GOLDEN DELIGHT JACKETLESS CHICKEN

Serves 4:

¼ cup flour
½ teaspoon salt
⅛ teaspoon pepper
⅛ teaspoon parsley flakes
⅛ teaspoon garlic powder
1 broiler-fryer chicken, cut
    into parts and skinned
½ cup cooking oil

1 (16-ounce) can sliced
    peaches, drained and juice
    reserved
3 tablespoons prepared
    mustard
3 tablespoons maple syrup
½ cup chicken broth
2 tablespoons chopped pi-
    miento

In a paper bag combine flour, salt, pepper, parsley flakes and garlic powder. Add chicken and shake to coat. In frypan, heat oil to medium temperature. Add chicken and cook, turning, for about 15 minutes, or until brown on all sides. Drain. In a large shallow baking pan, place chicken, in single layer, skin side up. In a bowl, mix together reserved peach juice, mustard, maple syrup and broth. Pour over chicken. Cover and bake in a 350°F. oven for about 40 minutes, or until fork tender. Place peaches and pimiento on top of chicken and bake, uncovered, about 15 minutes longer, or until brown.

Sister Mary Agnes Toscano, Trenton, New Jersey

NEW MEXICO
ORIENTAL CHICKEN AND ASPARAGUS

Serves 4:

3 tablespoons cornstarch
2 cups chicken broth
3 tablespoons soy sauce
¾ teaspoon ginger
½ teaspoon dry mustard
4 tablespoons cooking oil
2 cups ¼-inch diagonally sliced asparagus
¾ cup ¼-inch diagonally sliced celery
1 whole broiler-fryer chicken breast, halved, skinned, boned and cut into 1-inch cubes
4 broiler-fryer chicken thighs, skinned, boned and cut into 1-inch cubes
¾ cup 1-inch roll-cut sliced green onion (white and green parts)
2 cloves garlic, finely chopped
1 cup sliced mushrooms

In a bowl, blend cornstarch with ¼ cup of the broth, stirring until smooth. Add remaining broth, soy sauce, ginger and mustard, stirring to mix. Set aside. In a wok, place 2 tablespoons of the cooking oil and swirl. Heat over medium-high heat for 30 seconds. Add asparagus and stir-fry for 2 minutes. Add remaining 2 tablespoons cooking oil, then add celery and chicken. Stir-fry for 2 minutes. Add green onion and garlic and stir-fry 1 minute. Pour broth mixture gradually down side of wok, stirring to blend. Add mushrooms. Simmer, stirring often, for about 3 minutes, or until thick. To serve, pour over rice.

Toni Rehkopf, Albuquerque, New Mexico

OVEN FRIED CHICKEN WITH LEMON BARBE-CUE SAUCE

Serves 4:

½ cup flour
2¼ teaspoons salt
½ teaspoon pepper
2 teaspoons paprika
1 broiler-fryer chicken, cut into parts
½ cup butter, melted

¼ cup lemon juice
1 tablespoon chopped onion
2 tablespoons cooking oil
1 clove garlic, finely chopped
¼ teaspoon poultry seasoning

In a bag, combine flour, 2 teaspoons of the salt, ¼ teaspoon of the pepper and paprika. Add chicken, a few pieces at a time, shaking to coat. In a large shallow baking pan, place chicken, skin side down, in single layer. Pour butter on chicken. Bake, uncovered, in a 350°F. oven for 30 minutes. In a bowl, make sauce by blending lemon juice, onion, oil, garlic, poultry seasoning, remaining ¼ teaspoon salt and remaining ¼ teaspoon pepper. Turn chicken to skin side up. Pour sauce on chicken. Bake, uncovered, about 30 minutes longer, or until fork tender.

Regina Potwora, Niagara Falls, New York

ROAST CHICKEN WITH ORANGE GLAZE

Serves 4:

½ cup chopped cranberries
2½ tablespoons sugar
1½ cups cornbread stuffing mix
1½ cups seasoned croutons
1 teaspoon salt
¼ teaspoon pepper
1 egg, beaten

¼ cup margarine, melted
½ cup chopped pecans
½ cup chopped fresh orange sections
6 tablespoons orange juice
1 whole broiler-fryer chicken
½ cup orange marmalade

In small bowl, combine cranberries and sugar. In a large bowl make stuffing by mixing together stuffing mix, croutons, salt and pepper. Add egg and margarine and toss lightly. Add cranberries, pecans, orange sections and 4 tablespoons of the orange juice. Place stuffing in cavity of chicken. Roast, uncovered, on rack in a large shallow baking pan in a 325°F. oven for 1¼ hours. In a small bowl, combine marmalade and the remaining 2 tablespoons orange juice. Spread mixture on chicken. Roast, basting frequently, about 15 minutes longer, or until leg moves freely when lifted or twisted.

Mildred K. Crawford, Greensboro, North Carolina

NORTH DAKOTA
SWEET AND SOUR CHICKEN

Serves 4:

¾ cup catsup
½ cup soy sauce
½ cup wine vinegar
¼ cup sugar
¼ cup honey

2 cloves garlic, mashed
1 teaspoon dry mustard
1 broiler-fryer chicken, cut into parts

In bowl, make sauce by blending catsup, soy sauce, vinegar, sugar, honey, garlic and mustard. Place chicken in single layer in a baking pan and pour sauce over. Cover and bake in a 325°F. oven, turning frequently, for about 1½ hours, or until fork tender.

Melinda R. Curl, Bismarck, North Dakota

OHIO

CREAM CHICKEN NEPTUNE

Serves 4:

¾ cup crushed wheat crackers

1 teaspoon salt

2 tablespoons butter

2 whole broiler-fryer chicken breasts, halved, skinned and boned

1 (10¾-ounce) can New England-style clam chowder

⅓ cup milk

In a shallow dish, combine cracker crumbs and salt. Reserve 2 tablespoons. Put butter in a shallow glass dish. Microwave on high for about 1 minute, or until melted. Dip chicken, one piece at a time, first in butter, then crumb mixture, turning to coat. In a large, shallow glass baking dish place chicken in single layer. Cover with waxed paper. Microwave on high 8 minutes. Place soup in blender container. Add milk and blend about 15 seconds, or until creamy. Remove chicken from microwave. Pour soup mixture on chicken. Sprinkle reserved crumb mixture over soup. Cover chicken and return to oven; microwave on high 2 minutes. Remove from oven and let stand, covered, for 5 minutes before testing for doneness. Return to oven for additional cooking, if fork cannot be inserted in chicken with ease.

Kathleen Dean, Fredericktown, Ohio

OKLAHOMA

MICROWAVE BARBECUED CHICKEN

Serves 4:

1 broiler-fryer chicken, cut into parts

¾ cup bottled hickory smoke flavored barbecue sauce

½ cup drained, crushed pineapple

1 green onion (white and green parts), finely chopped

2 tablespoons honey

½ teaspoon ground ginger

In a large shallow glass baking dish, place chicken, skin side down, with meaty pieces toward outside. In a bowl, combine remaining ingredients and pour over chicken. Cover dish with plastic wrap, pricking with a fork to allow steam to escape. Microwave on high for 12 minutes. Turn chicken pieces to skin side up. Cover. Microwave on high 12 minutes longer. Remove from oven and let stand, covered, for 5 minutes before testing for doneness. Return to oven for additional cooking, if fork cannot be inserted in chicken with ease.

Carol R. Blackburn, Edmond, Oklahoma

OREGON

INDIA CHICKEN

Serves 4:

⅓ cup flour
1½ teaspoons salt
1 teaspoon paprika
½ teaspoon freshly ground pepper
2 whole broiler-fryer chicken breasts, halved and boned

3 tablespoons butter
2 tablespoons dark brown sugar
½ teaspoon ground ginger
1 cup red wine
2 tablespoons soy sauce
⅓ cup toasted sesame seeds

In a paper bag, combine flour, salt, paprika and pepper. Add chicken, a few pieces at a time, shaking to coat. In a frypan, melt butter over medium heat. Add chicken and cook, turning, for about 15 minutes, or until brown on both sides. Transfer chicken to a shallow baking pan, arranging in a single layer. In the frypan, blend brown sugar, ginger, wine and soy sauce. Bring to a boil, stirring. Pour over chicken. Sprinkle sesame seeds on top. Cover and bake in 350°F. oven for about 1 hour, or until fork tender.

J. Maxine Curde, Salem, Oregon

PENNSYLVANIA

CHICKEN WITH CHICKEN LIVER SAUCE

Serves 4:

4 tablespoons butter
2 tablespoons olive oil
1 broiler-fryer chicken, cut into parts
2 teaspoons salt
½ teaspoon freshly ground pepper
1 clove garlic, mashed

2 tablespoons chopped chives
½ cup dried mushrooms
1 cup dry white wine
½ cup chicken broth
¼ pound chicken livers, each liver cut in half

In a frypan, melt 2 tablespoons of the butter and the oil. Add chicken and cook, turning, for about 15 minutes, or until brown on all sides. Sprinkle 1 teaspoon of the salt and ¼ teaspoon of the pepper on chicken. Add garlic, chives, mushrooms, wine and broth. Cover and simmer about 30 minutes, or until fork tender. In another frypan, melt the remaining 2 tablespoons butter. Add livers and sauté for about 5 minutes, or until very little pink remains. Add remaining 1 teaspoon salt and ¼ teaspoon pepper. Pour liver mixture on chicken. Cover and cook for 5 minutes.

Jo Ann Dunlevy, Lancaster, Pennsylvania

RHODE ISLAND

HERB GARDEN CHICKEN SALAD

Serves 4:

2 whole broiler-fryer chicken breasts, halved
3 quarts water
16 small new potatoes, halved
2 cups chopped celery
1 cup chopped green onion (white and green parts)
⅔ cup cooking oil

⅓ cup vinegar
1 tablespoon lemon juice
2 teaspoons basil
2 teaspoons dill weed
2 teaspoons dried mint leaves
1 teaspoon sugar
1 teaspoon salt

Put chicken in a Dutch oven, add water, cover and simmer for 10 minutes. Add potatoes. Cover and simmer about 20 minutes longer, or until fork tender. Cool and drain. Separate meat from bones, discarding bones and skin. Cut chicken in bite-sized pieces. In large bowl, combine chicken and potatoes. Add celery and onion. In a bowl blend the remaining ingredients and pour over chicken mixture. Refrigerate for about 2 hours, or until well chilled, tossing once.

William Arthur Drew, Providence, Rhode Island

SOUTH CAROLINA 2ND PRIZE 1979

GINGERED PEAR CHICKEN AND WALNUTS

Serves 4:

3 tablespoons margarine
2 whole broiler-fryer chicken breasts, halved and skinned
¼ teaspoon salt
1 (16-ounce) can pear halves, drained, each half cut in 2 wedges and juice reserved

¾ cup ginger ale
¼ cup brown sugar
3 tablespoons soy sauce
2 teaspoons cornstarch
¼ cup water
¼ teaspoon powdered ginger
¼ cup coarsely broken walnuts

In a frypan, melt margarine over medium heat. Add chicken and cook, turning, about 10 minutes, or until brown on both sides. Sprinkle with salt. Measure pear juice, adding water to make ¾ cup, if necessary. In bowl, blend pear juice, ginger ale, brown sugar and soy sauce. Pour over chicken. Cover and cook over medium heat, turning occasionally, for 25 minutes, or until fork tender. Transfer chicken to a large shallow baking pan, in a single layer. Place pear wedges around chicken. In small bowl, combine cornstarch and water, stirring until smooth. Stir in ginger then add to liquid remaining in frypan. Cook, stirring, for about 5 minutes, or until thick. Pour thickened mixture over chicken and pears. Sprinkle walnuts on top. Bake, uncovered, in a 350°F. oven for about 10 minutes, or until pears are heated through.

Fran C. Foster, Easley, South Carolina

SOUTH DAKOTA

ORANGE CHICKEN ORIENTAL

Serves 4:

⅓ cup flour
1 teaspoon salt
½ teaspoon ground ginger
½ teaspoon pepper
1 broiler-fryer chicken, cut into parts
1 cup cooking oil
Juice of 2 oranges

⅛ teaspoon grated orange rind
1 tablespoon sugar
2 tablespoons soy sauce
2 teaspoons Worcestershire sauce
½ cup slivered almonds
2½ cups water
1 tablespoon cornstarch

In a shallow dish combine flour, salt, ginger and pepper. Add chicken, one piece at a time, dredging to coat. In a frypan heat oil to medium temperature. Add chicken and cook, turning, for about 25 minutes, or until brown on all sides. In a bowl, blend orange juice and rind, sugar, soy sauce. Worcestershire and almonds. Remove chicken from frypan, and drain off oil. Add orange juice mixture to pan drippings. Bring to a boil and add 2 cups of the water. Return chicken to frypan, cover and simmer for about 30 minutes, or until fork tender. In a small bowl, blend cornstarch with the remaining ½ cup water, stirring until smooth. Add cornstarch mixture to frypan. Cook, stirring, over medium heat for about 5 minutes, or until thick. Pour over chicken when serving.

David Charles Nagle, Chamberlain, South Dakota

COMPANY'S A COMIN' CHICKEN BREASTS

Serves 4:

¼ cup flour
2 teaspoons salt
1 teaspoon paprika
3 whole broiler-fryer chicken
  breasts, halved and
  skinned
¼ cup butter
¼ cup water

2 teaspoons cornstarch
1½ cups half-and-half
¼ cup sherry
2 teaspoons grated lemon
  rind
2 tablespoons lemon juice
1 cup grated Swiss cheese

On waxed paper, combine flour, salt and paprika. Add chicken, one piece at a time, dredging to coat. In a frypan, melt butter over medium heat. Add chicken and cook, turning, for about 15 minutes, or until brown on all sides. Add water. Cover and simmer for about 30 minutes, or until fork tender. In a large shallow baking pan, place chicken in single layer. In a small bowl, blend cornstarch and ¼ cup of the half-and-half, stirring until smooth. Add cornstarch mixture to pan drippings. Stir in the remaining 1¼ cups half-and-half, wine, lemon rind and lemon juice. Cook, stirring, for about 5 minutes, or until thick. Pour over chicken in baking pan. Bake, uncovered, in a 300°F. oven for 10 minutes. Sprinkle cheese on chicken.

Dorothy W. Schmittou, Clarksville, Tennessee

TEXAS

CHICKEN DALLAS

Serves 4:

3 tablespoons butter
1 cup chopped onion
1 cup diced celery
½ cup chopped green pepper
1 large clove garlic, finely
   chopped
1 broiler-fryer chicken, cut
   in parts with giblets
¾ cup brown sugar
¾ cup cream sherry

½ cup orange juice
¼ cup catsup
1 tablespoon vinegar
1 tablespoon Worcestershire
   sauce
1 tablespoon Dijon mustard
1 teaspoon salt
½ cup Parmesan cheese
1 tablespoon flour

In large shallow baking pan, melt butter on top of the stove over medium heat. Add onion, celery, green pepper and garlic, distributing evenly in bottom of pan. Arrange chicken and giblets on top of vegetables. In bowl, blend brown sugar, wine, orange juice, catsup, vinegar, Worcestershire sauce, mustard and salt. Pour over chicken. Sprinkle cheese on chicken. Bake, uncovered, in a 350°F. oven for about 1½ hours, or until fork tender. Transfer chicken to a warm serving platter. Remove excess grease from pan. In small bowl combine flour and ¼ cup of liquid from baking pan, stirring until smooth. Add flour mixture to contents of baking pan. Cook, stirring, over medium heat for about 5 minutes, or until thick. Pour on chicken when serving.

Richard W. Kraetke, Dallas, Texas

UTAH

SPRING CHICKEN

Serves 4:

⅓ cup flour
½ teaspoon paprika
¾ teaspoon salt
1 broiler-fryer chicken, cut into parts
1 tablespoon olive oil
4 tablespoons butter
1 (8½-ounce) can artichoke hearts, drained and cut in bite-size pieces

2 (10-ounce) packages frozen chopped spinach, cooked according to package directions and drained
1 (8-ounce) package cream cheese
4 tablespoons milk
¼ teaspoon garlic powder
⅓ cup grated Parmesan cheese

In a shallow dish, combine flour, paprika and ½ teaspoon of the salt. Add chicken, one piece at a time, dredging to coat. In a frypan, combine the oil and 2 tablespoons of the butter. Add chicken and cook, turning, for about 15 minutes, or until brown on all sides. Remove chicken and place in large shallow baking pan. Place artichokes on top of chicken, covering with a layer of spinach on top. In bowl, blend cream cheese and remaining 2 tablespoons butter. Stir in milk, garlic powder and remaining ¼ teaspoon salt. Spread cream cheese mixture on top of spinach, and sprinkle Parmesan cheese on top. Cover and bake in a 350°F. oven for about 40 minutes, or until fork tender. Remove cover and bake 15 minutes longer, or until topping is brown.

Ann Greenlee, South Ogden, Utah

VERMONT

COMPANY CHICKEN IN SHRIMP SAUCE

Serves 4:

8 broiler-fryer chicken
   thighs, skinned
2 tablespoons flour
4 tablespoons butter
1 medium green pepper,
   seeded and cut into ¼-inch
   squares

10 pimiento stuffed green ol-
    ives, quartered crosswise
1 (10¾-ounce) can con-
   densed cream of shrimp
   soup
⅓ cup dry sherry
½ teaspoon salt
½ teaspoon hot pepper sauce

Place flour in a shallow dish. Add chicken, one piece at a
time, dredging to coat. In a frypan, melt butter over medium
heat. Add chicken and cook, turning, for about 15 minutes,
or until brown on both sides. Transfer chicken to a large
shallow baking pan, skin side up in a single layer. In the frypan, sauté green pepper for 3 minutes. Add olives, soup,
wine, salt and pepper sauce. Simmer, uncovered, for 5
minutes. Pour mixture over chicken. Bake, uncovered, in a
400°F. oven for about 30 minutes, or until fork tender.
Brown slightly under broiler just before serving.

Elizabeth B. Dern, Dorset, Vermont

VIRGINIA, 5TH PRIZE 1979

WILLIAMSBURG CREOLE CHICKEN

Serves 4:

¼ cup flour
1 teaspoon salt
½ teaspoon thyme
¼ teaspoon paprika
2 whole broiler-fryer chicken
   breasts, halved
⅓ cup cooking oil
1 medium onion, chopped

1 medium green pepper,
   chopped
1 (28-ounce) can whole tomatoes
¼ teaspoon hot pepper sauce
1 bay leaf, crumbled
¼ cup chopped parsley

In shallow dish, combine flour, salt, thyme and paprika. Add chicken, one piece at a time, dredging to coat. In a frypan, heat oil over medium temperature. Add chicken and cook, turning, for about 10 minutes, or until brown on all sides. Remove chicken from frypan. Add onion and green pepper and sauté about 3 minutes, or until onion is soft. Add tomatoes, pepper sauce and bay leaf, stirring to break tomatoes apart slightly. Cover and simmer 30 minutes. Add parsley and chicken. Cover and simmer for 30 minutes, or until chicken is fork tender. Serve over rice.

Kathryn F. Meyers, Williamsburg, Virginia

WASHINGTON

CHICKEN WITH SHERRY

Serves 4:

1 broiler-fryer chicken, cut into parts	1 teaspoon grated orange rind
1 onion, sliced	1/16 teaspoon nutmeg
4 tablespoons chopped green pepper	1½ teaspoons salt
1 cup sliced mushrooms	¼ teaspoon pepper
1 tablespoon flour	1 cup orange juice
2 teaspoons chopped parsley	½ cup water
	3 tablespoons dry sherry

In a large shallow baking pan, place chicken, skin side up, in single layer. Add onion, green pepper and mushrooms. In saucepan combine flour, parsley, orange rind, nutmeg, salt and pepper. Add orange juice, water and wine. Simmer, uncovered, over medium heat for about 5 minutes, or until thick and bubbly. Pour over chicken. Bake, uncovered, in a 375°F. oven, basting occasionally, for about 1 hour, or until fork tender. Skim fat from juices in pan. To serve, pour juices on chicken.

David A. Berger, Seattle, Washington

WEST VIRGINIA

CHICKEN BREASTS IN RICH WINE SAUCE

Serves 4:

¼ cup flour
1 teaspoon salt
¼ teaspoon pepper
2 whole broiler-fryer chicken breasts, halved and skinned
3 tablespoons cooking oil
¼ cup chopped onion

2 (8-ounce) cans tomato sauce
¾ cup Burgundy
¼ cup applesauce
¼ cup water
½ teaspoon sugar
½ teaspoon basil
¼ teaspoon rosemary

In a paper bag combine flour, salt and pepper. Add chicken, a few pieces at a time, and shake to coat. In a frypan, heat oil to medium temperature. Add chicken and onion and cook, turning, for about 15 minutes, or until brown on both sides. In bowl, blend the remaining ingredients and pour over chicken. Cover and simmer for about 45 minutes, or until mixture is thick and chicken is fork tender.

Rachel Mae Chapman, South Charleston, West Virginia

WISCONSIN

BAKED STUFFED CHICKEN

Serves 4:

2 teaspoons salt
⅜ teaspoon pepper
1 whole broiler-fryer chicken
2 tablespoons butter
¾ cup chopped celery
½ cup chopped onion
½ pound chicken livers, chopped
2 tart apples, chopped
⅓ cup raisins

¼ cup chopped almonds
1 teaspoon chopped parsley
½ teaspoon poultry seasoning
¼ teaspoon rosemary
¼ teaspoon mace
¼ teaspoon finely chopped garlic
¹⁄₁₆ teaspoon ground cloves
¼ cup water

Sprinkle 1 teaspoon of the salt and ¼ teaspoon of the pepper on the chicken. In a frypan, melt butter over medium heat. Add celery and onion and sauté over very low heat for 30 minutes. Make stuffing by adding livers, apples, raisins, almonds, parsley, poultry seasoning, rosemary, mace, garlic, cloves, and remaining teaspoon of salt and pepper. Cook over low heat for 15 minutes, then place in cavity of chicken. Place chicken in large shallow baking pan. Pour water around chicken. Bake, uncovered, in a 375°F. oven, turning and basting several times, for 1½ hours, or until leg moves freely when lifted or twisted.

Erna Voss, Neenah, Wisconsin

WYOMING, 1ST PRIZE 1979

BARBARA LONG'S CURRIED CHICKEN ROLLS

Serves 4:

2 whole broiler-fryer chicken breasts, halved, skinned and boned
½ teaspoon salt
⅛ teaspoon pepper
1 tablespoon margarine
½ onion, finely chopped
¾ cup cooked rice
¼ cup raisins
1 tablespoon chopped parsley

1 teaspoon curry powder
½ teaspoon poultry seasoning
1 teaspoon brown sugar
1/16 teaspoon garlic powder
1 tablespoon cooking oil
½ cup white wine
1 teaspoon granulated chicken bouillon

On hard surface with meat mallet or similar flattening utensil, pound chicken to ⅜-inch thickness. Sprinkle salt and pepper on chicken. In frypan, make stuffing by melting margarine over medium heat. Add onion and sauté for about 3 minutes, or until soft. Add rice, raisins, parsley, curry powder, poultry seasoning, brown sugar and garlic powder. Stir until well mixed. Divide stuffing into 4 portions. Place one portion on each piece of chicken. Roll and fasten with wooden picks. In another frypan, heat oil to medium temperature. Add chicken rolls and cook, turning, for about 15 minutes, or until brown on all sides. Add wine and bouillon. Cover and simmer about 30 minutes longer, or until fork tender.

Barbara Long, Laramie, Wyoming

Part Three

THE INCREDIBLE
EDIBLE EGG

Foreword

We would not like to try to determine which has the larger following, the chicken or the egg. Egg devotees are convinced that theirs is the most versatile food, and they also maintain, with much justification, that the egg was an appreciated food centuries before the chicken was even considered. Man plundered the nests of birds, especially seabirds, and ate their eggs long before he learned to capture the wily Red Jungle Fowl, the ancestor of our domestic chicken.

The authors of this book prize the pair equally (the best chicken pie we know couples chicken and cooked egg yolks); both the chicken and the egg have our total culinary respect.

Moreover, we believe that eggs deserve a better break than they are getting. Although most of us appear to like them, proving it by a per capita consumption of 273 yearly, we seem to eat eggs more from habit than desire. When we sit down to a make-do meal of scrambled eggs, or a routine breakfast of eggs and bacon, many of us seem unaware of what we are eating.

We take for granted what many nutritionists consider to be our most nourishing food, and we do not seem to fully appreciate one of nature's remarkable accomplishments. Coming from that shell is one of the purest and most perfectly packaged of all foods with no chemicals or preservatives added, its contents untouched by human hands until cracked for cooking, and containing an astonishing variety of vitamins and nutrients.

The ordinary egg has such a high-quality protein that it often is used as a standard of comparison for other proteins. Egg protein is amazingly complete, with all of the essential *amino acids, those building blocks necessary for growth that are not produced by the body.*

Also packaged in that shell are all of the vitamins, except C. The rare "sunshine" D, a growth vitamin, in eggs is second only to that in fish liver oils. Thirteen minerals are there, too, including that important trio, iron, phosphorus and magnesium.

Despite the egg being such a powerhouse of nutrition, it is not only misunderstood but maligned by those concerned with the prevention of heart disease. But not by all. Dr. Michael DeBakey, one of America's most knowledgeable cardiologists, comments: "Most of the dietary advice about how to prevent heart disease is just so much bunk. The people who take strong positions on food—who even want to have laws about it—are absolutely unreasonable. Eggs are a wonderful food."

Those of us who cook as a hobby or as a profession have always known that. We may not be aware of all of the nutritional facts, but we do regard the egg as probably the most versatile food. That was illustrated as long ago as 1919, when Chef Adolphe Meyer wrote a book, Eggs in a Thousand Ways.

Joe Famularo in his book, The Festive Famularo Kitchen, *eloquently speaks for most of us. "We couldn't cook without them," he enthused. "Eggs combine magnificently with other foods and are responsible for performing culinary miracles. They whip into Italian zabaglione, French mayonnaise and American baked Alaska. They are indispensable as lightening, thickening, binding and enriching agents. They are necessary for cutlets, fritters and custards; in garnishing, salads and dressings; in sauces and soups. They clarify liquids. They become main dishes. They scramble, fry, boil, poach and bake. In addition to this remarkable versatility, the egg is special because it can be turned into a meal on only a few minutes notice."*

The egg is special also because it stirs the imagination. We'll never forget a dish served at a friend's home in Nice. Centered on a warm plate were boat-shaped shells of puff pastry the French call barquettes *filled with minced, sautéed, fresh mushrooms, known as* duxelles. *Nesting on these beds were lightly poached pullet's eggs crowned with creamy hollandaise.*

A French chef friend poaches eggs in red wine, another sometimes serves a dramatic first course in summer of cold soft-poached eggs buried in aspic. When we want to make an impression at dinner we often serve as a first course a puffy golden soufflé. Eggs never looked so good.

Among experts, eggs can hold their own with the world's most expensive food—sturgeon's eggs. Gerd Kafer, one of Germany's most famous restaurateurs and caterers, when asked by Gourmet *magazine (March 1978) what food was his favorite, said, "I love the simple things. An egg, evenly cooked underneath and above, served on a slice of bread, and topped with cold, fresh caviar."*

For centuries eggs have been the subject of legends and myths, respected as good luck charms, have been worshipped and used to tell fortunes. They have been used in fertility rites, sacrificed and sometimes feared. The early Phoenicians believed that the egg was formed in ancient waters, then split, with one half becoming heaven, the other earth. The Chinese thought that an egg dropped from heaven eventually hatched Man. The Hindus claimed that the unknown universe formed into a giant egg, eventually breaking to become the sky and earth, the fluids the oceans. American Indians were certain that mysterious waters produced a golden egg containing the Great Spirit who shattered the shell, emerging to create their world. Even today, the egg, usually hard-cooked and pastel-colored is a symbol of rebirth in the Christian faith.

Modern man, however, is a realist, respecting the egg as a convenience in a busy world, a supper-in-a-shell. But with today's inflation, the egg is much more than a quick, convenient meal. Consider, for example, what other item of food can provide a healthful meal for 15 cents, the price of two large eggs? In addition, those two eggs supply about 30 percent of our minimum daily requirements of protein, necessary fat and vitamins.

American Egg Board experts say that although the price of eggs is affected by grade and size, the nutritive value is the same for all. Grades AA and A are the most frequently sold and used. Grade B eggs, not strictly fresh, are best for scrambling and used with other ingredients.

What is the difference in grades? Grade refers to cleanliness and soundness of shell, thickness of albumen and size of air cells. However, neither the shell's size nor color affect quality. Brown eggs come from brown hens, white from white hens.

Grade AA have very small air cells, a large amount of thick white and a firm upstanding yolk. When broken out of the shell, AA eggs cover a small area; grade A spread a bit more, as the white is not so thick and high. Grade B eggs cover a wide area, have much thinner whites and flatter yolks. In other words, if that yolk doesn't stand up proud and erect and isn't rather tightly surrounded by the white, the egg isn't AA, or "fancy fresh." To quickly test an egg for freshness without breaking the shell, drop it in a pan half full of water. If fresh, the egg will sink.

The cord-like formation in some egg whites, that thick twining of egg whites, which grows on either side of the yolk while the egg is developing, is called the chalazae. It anchors the yolk in the center, and is a sign that the egg is of high quality. As eggs grow stale, the chalazae disappears.

If the white sticks to the inside of the raw egg shell, it does not mean it isn't fresh. In fresh eggs the white is thicker and more difficult to extract from the shell. The fresh white will also be cloudy. Beware if the white is crystal-clear; that is an aging egg.

How fresh is "fresh" and how long can eggs be stored and still be edible? First, they must be stored properly. Experts do not recommend storing eggs in the egg-shelf or tray on the refrigerator door. The frequent opening and closing exposes eggs to air, which helps hasten the loss of carbon dioxide. This creates larger air cells that flatten yolks and thin whites, decreasing flavor. Eggs in an open tray can also absorb refrigerator odors. The best method is to keep the eggs, large end up, in the container in which they were bought, stored on the bottom shelf, the coldest in the refrigerator.

With proper storage, eggs remain grade AA for about one week after they are laid, and then become grade A for slightly more than a month. Eggs kept at room temperature, 72°–80°F., lose more quality in one day than they would in a week if refrigerated. Thus, it makes sense to buy only a week's supply of fresh eggs.

Size dictates price, based on minimum weight per dozen. Jumbos, at 30 ounces a dozen, are the most expensive; next come the 27-ounce Extra Large, 24-ounce Large, 21-ounce Medium, 18-ounce Small and the pullet's Pee Wees at 15 ounces.

Most popular are Jumbo, Extra Large and Large. Recipes usually call for Large. When buying, however, it is wise to consider eggs by weight. If, for example, Large eggs sell for 60 cents a dozen, and Medium for 57 cents, this means that the Large cost 40 cents a pound, and Medium, 43 cents. Thus, the Large are the better buy.

Buying rule of thumb, according to the Department of Agriculture: If there is less than a 7-cent price spread per dozen eggs between one size and the next smaller size in the same grade, the best buy is always the larger size. Do not buy "cracked" eggs thinking that you are getting a bargain. They may contain bacteria that could cause food poisoning.

Sound, fresh eggs at any size may be our best buy, and remain the least inflated in price of any comparable food. For example, in 1940, eggs retailed at 33.1 cents a dozen. Today, 40 years later, that same dozen eggs costs 84.1 cents. Compare that rise of 51 cents with the other food in the Meat Group, in which eggs are officially listed. What did a T-bone steak cost in those days? Today? Consider also that eggs not only put character into a meatless meal, but contain no bone, no waste (except the shell) and there is no shrinkage if cooked properly. Few, if any, other foods have such assets.

In addition to being a good-taste-bargain, eggs are also that rarity that can be included in the diet of almost everyone. One of the first solid foods given infants, they also aid rapid growth in children and teenagers. Their nutritive strength makes them valuable for adults, and because they are easily digested, eggs often are the first semi-solid diet for the ill and the convalescent, and an excellent, easy-to-eat meal for the elderly.

This remarkable food is also prized by informed weight watchers. A large egg at only 80 calories offers more protein and less calories than other protein foods. One hundred grams of egg (2 Large eggs) has only 160 calories, contrasted with the same grams of ham, 397 calories, Cheddar cheese, 398, hamburger, 364, even salmon with 203 calories.

Even those of us who aren't fans eat eggs in more ways than we realize. According to the U.S. Department of Agriculture, many commercial foods wouldn't be possible without eggs. About one out of every ten eggs is used to produce such products as bread, cake, cookies and pies, noodles, macaroni, salad dressings, mayonnaise, hollandaise, confections, ice cream and the quick convenience food mixes such as breads, doughnuts, waffles, cakes, frostings and puddings.

The amazing egg is also a tool of medical science, as it is an effective vaccine-growing medium. During America's swine flu scare, an alarming delay in producing the vaccine *was caused because the egg industry wasn't given sufficient notice.*

The egg industry has come a long way from the days two decades ago when eggs were irregularly collected from small farms and held in cold storage for a month or more. Unless bought at a farm, or from a rural roadside stand, really fresh eggs then were the exception, not the rule. Most city people didn't know what a fresh egg tasted like.

Although eggs, produced from hens brought from England, were introduced in America as early as 1609, large-scale production didn't start for many years. The first poultry show was held in Boston in 1849, but it wasn't until 1873 that the American Poultry Association was created to establish breeding standards. A year later the first "Standard of Perfection" was printed.

It was a fits-and-starts industry, carried on by hobbyists and people who just liked chickens. We were two of them, sometimes selling a few eggs to help pay for the feed. Not until 1932 was "An Approved Buying Guide for Eggs" adopted, then only in the Midwest. As late as 1945, eggs were still being laboriously washed by hand. Finally, in 1959 the Fresh Fancy Grade was established, but not until 1970 did Congress pass the Egg Products Inspection Act.

Recently we took a close look at what has happened to the egg industry in our home state of Connecticut, visiting a cooperative, a scientific breeding complex, a producer, and a distribution center, where eggs are packaged and sent to market. First, the hen is no longer called a hen or even a chicken. It is an "egg-machine." Today, we have more of these machines than people, about 280 million.

Emanuel Hirth, General Manager of the Central Connecticut Co-op Farmers' Association in Manchester, pointed out that about 25 years ago "backyard-flocks" were still very much in vogue, and a 500-bird flock was considered large. Today, a "flock" of 70,000 is small.

Buying feed by train carloads, thereby getting a better price for members, this Co-op delivers carefully-blended nutritious chicken feed, the single most important item in egg production. The Co-op also stays on top of the nationwide market situation, packaging and selling the members' eggs at the best current price under various labels to chain stores throughout the state and other sections of New England. Eggs go from farm to market in 24 hours, an average of 48,000 dozen daily, five days a week.

"A drop in the bucket," Hirth told us, *"considering that 64 billion, 540 million eggs are produced in this country every year."*

The bible of the industry, the Poultry Tribune, *recently took a census of America's egg producers, concentrating on those operators who maintained 1 million, or more, bird-flocks. They discovered that 34 "farms" with a total of 69,650,000 layers, own about 25 percent of the country's egg-machines.*

From a standpoint of total output, Cal-Maine Foods, Inc., of Jackson, Mississippi, with 11 million layers in 13 states, is the number one egg producer. The Tribune points out that just 22 companies the size of Cal-Maine could supply all of the egg needs of the United States.

The largest producer under one roof is Julius Goldman, with his *"Egg City"* 3.1 million flock in California.

Because of the work of such farms the production of eggs has had an amazing upsurge. For example, In 1930, a laying hen produced 121 eggs a year. Today the average is 235 eggs per bird, and some strains produce more.

Less than 20 years ago, dual-purpose hens weighed five and three quarters pounds and consumed almost nine pounds of food to produce a dozen eggs. Today, trim specialists (the White Leghorn is the acknowledged egg-laying champion) weigh one third less and eat half the amount of food to produce the same number of eggs. With these efficient egg-machines, inflation has been turned around for the benefit of us all.

We visited a farm at North Westchester, Connecticut, where two buildings housed 70,000 layers, a flock that maintains a 90 percent production record. Although this farm is considered small in the industry the buildings cost three quarters of a million dollars, the birds in each building $100,000.

This is a typical egg operation, with several birds in one wire cage. Water and feed are supplied six times daily, automatically motivated by an electric time clock. Eggs are collected on a continuously moving conveyor belt. The *"egg-machines"* are spurred into laying at about 12 weeks of age (becoming soup chickens at about a year) by a gradual increase of artificial lighting, a total of 16 hours of *"springtime"* light every 24 hours.

Eggs are washed and oiled before they are delivered to the Co-op's packaging and distribution center. Spraying the eggs with a thin coat of a harmless, tasteless, odorless oil seals the egg shell pores and helps maintain freshness.

At the Co-op automated distribution center, mass candling (strong electric lighting detects blood spots and other defects), cleaning, oiling, grading, sorting and packaging are all done by conveyor belts and machinery that eliminates almost all human handling. The purpose of this speed is to get the eggs into refrigerated trucks and to the consumer quickly as possible.

Is science developing new "egg-machines" to increase production? Every geneticist in the egg industry was aware of history being made in 1957 when an English bird laid 353 eggs in one year, and two Japanese White Leghorns each laid 361 eggs in the same period.

Several scientists in this country are hoping to better these impressive records. For example, Harold Beillier of the University of Missouri is attempting to develop a strain of chickens that will lay one egg every day, one third more than the average.

As a final word on "nature's masterpiece," we quote a notable French chef, Monsieur Stacpoole:

"The egg, is the cement that holds all the castle of cookery together."

Chapter One
Appetizers and Salads

It has been said that if the chicken hadn't laid the egg it would have been invented; for without the egg, not only the American appetizer tray, but the entire dining scene would be much poorer. Consider: Epicures claim that there are almost as many ways to stuff a hard-cooked egg as there are days in a year—What they are really saying is that the hard-cooked egg is a challenge to the imagination. There are cocktail offerings of eggs stuffed with shrimp, anchovies, olives, prosciutto, mushrooms, curry-stuffed eggs, pickled red eggs, Chinese tea eggs, pickled spiced eggs. There are egg puffs, egg and clam balls.

The egg may be the answer to many a question you have on what to serve at that upcoming cocktail party.

HARD-COOKED EGGS

Professionals never called these eggs "hard-boiled" as most of us do. They are always "hard-cooked," and to play upon words, for many of us they are indeed hard to cook. Too often the yolks are too dark, the whites rubbery—cooked too hard. As with any aspect of cookery, there are several schools of thought on how to properly hard cook an egg.

First, no egg should be cooked on high heat, especially in hard-cooking eggs do not have the water boiling throughout the cooking period. Eggs should be covered with cold water, by at least 1 inch over the eggs, the water brought to the boil on high heat, then immediately the heat should be lowered so the water just simmers. Continual boiling toughens the egg.

Our method is to cook the eggs exactly 10 minutes after

the water comes to the boil and the eggs are simmering. At the end of that time plunge them immediately into cold water. With this method we always produce hard-cooked eggs with a soft, creamy white, cooked, but not cooked to a rubbery consistency. The yolk is also slightly soft, not darkened.

Another method that many suggest: After the water comes to the boil, remove the pan from the heat, cover it and let it set for 20 minutes. Then cover with cold water.

Another method: Some suggest that 10 minutes isn't enough. Time it at 13 minutes, splitting the difference, making certain that the eggs are hard enough to suit all tastes.

Always have the eggs to be cooked at room temperature.

They should be as fresh as possible.

Don't crowd too many eggs in the cooking pot.

If the eggs are difficult to peel, peel under cold running water. Tap the large, blunt end of the hard-cooked egg. That contains the air sac, and peeling from that end at the start makes the job easier.

Store hard-cooked eggs in the refrigerator, especially if they have been shelled. If left at room temperature for any length of time, the yolks darken. To avoid crumbling the yolk when slicing an egg, first dip a sharp knife in cold water.

Commercial egg-slicers, with the thin wire cutters, are inexpensive and worth having, slicing the whole egg at one time without crumbling the yolk.

EGG AND ANCHOVY COCKTAIL SANDWICHES

24 small sandwiches:

1 (2-ounce) can of anchovies
5 tablespoons of butter (3 softened)
2 tablespoons of mayonnaise
4 hard-cooked eggs, coarsely chopped
2 tablespoons of minced fresh dill, or 2 teaspoons of dill weed
1 whole scallion, minced
Pepper to taste
12 very thin slices of bread, crusts trimmed
1 tablespoon of cooking oil

Drain anchovies and pat dry between paper towels. In a bowl, combine and mash the anchovies, the 3 tablespoons of softened butter, mayonnaise, eggs, dill, scallion and pepper. Divide the anchovy-egg mixture among 6 slices of the bread and spread smoothly. Cover each with a second slice and press together. In a large frypan, over medium heat, heat the remaining 2 tablespoons of butter and the oil. Add sandwiches and brown on both sides. Add more butter and oil as needed. Drain on paper towels. Cut each sandwich into 4 squares or triangles. Serve hot.

INDIVIDUAL BEEF TARTARES

Serves 6:

2 pounds of lean top round
6 egg yolks
2 tablespoons of minced onion
2 tablespoons of capers, well drained
2 tablespoons of chopped parsley

6 lemon wedges
2 (2-ounce) cans (anchovy fillets), drained
Salt and pepper to taste
Small slices of rye bread, buttered

Trim the beef. Put into a food processor (or food chopper with a fine blade) and process until the beef is minced (this should not be done too far in advance as the meat may darken). Make 6 thick patties of the beef. Set each on a plate. Make a depression in the center of each and drop an egg yolk into it. Around the meat arrange 1 teaspoon each of onion, capers and parsley, in small mounds, and a lemon wedge. Place the anchovy fillets (3 for each serving) spoke-fashion on the beef, with the egg yolk centered.

At the table, guests will blend the beef, egg yolk, onion, capers, parsley and anchovy, adding salt and pepper to taste. Serve with the rye bread.

COCKTAIL CHEDDAR CHEESE SHELLS

Makes about 3 dozen small shells:

1 cup of water
½ cup of butter
¼ teaspoon salt
1 cup sifted flour
4 eggs

1 cup of grated sharp Cheddar cheese
⅛ teaspoon of cayenne
Sesame seeds

In a saucepan, combine the water, butter and salt and bring to a boil. Lower heat, add the flour all at once, stirring constantly until mixture forms a ball, pulling away from the sides of the pan. Remove from heat and cool slightly. Add the eggs, one at a time, and beat until smooth after each addition. Beat in ¾ cup of the cheese and the cayenne.

Drop the cheese dough onto a greased baking sheet by the tablespoonful, leaving a space of at least one inch between each. Sprinkle with the remaining cheese and sesame seeds. Bake in a preheated 375°F. oven for 35 minutes, or until the pastry has puffed and is golden brown, crisp and firm.

Cocktail Cheddar Cheese Shells can be filled by cutting part way into the shell (as you would a hamburger roll) and spooning in a small amount of filling, then closing the shell. Fill with mixtures listed below or make up your own.

FILLINGS FOR COCKTAIL CHEDDAR CHEESE SHELLS

1. Chopped hard-cooked egg, mayonnaise, lemon juice, curry powder or chives

2. Shredded crabmeat mixed with mayonnaise, fresh minced dill, cayenne

3. Crumbled blue cheese, minced celery, brandy, cream

4. Minced ham, mayonnaise, mustard

5. Cream cheese, sour cream, watercress

ROQUEFORT CHEESE MOUSSE

Makes about 2 cups:

1½ tablespoons of gelatin (1½ envelopes)	½ pound of Roquefort cheese, pressed through a fine sieve
⅓ cup of cold water	
3 eggs separated	Parsley or watercress for garnish
1½ cups of heavy cream	
1 teaspoon of cognac	Toast rounds

In a measuring cup, stir the gelatin into the cold water to soften. In a bowl beat the egg yolks until light. Add ¼ cup of the heavy cream, cognac, cheese and mix well. Melt the gelatin over hot water until transparent. Add it to the egg yolk-cheese mixture, beating to blend well. Place in the refrigerator until it just begins to set. Beat the egg whites until stiff and whip the remaining 1¼ cups cream. Fold into the egg yolk-cheese mixture. Pour into an oiled mold and chill for 3 hours, or until firmly set. Unmold on a serving dish, garnish with parsley or watercress and serve on rounds of toast.

HAM AND EGG ROLLS IN ASPIC

Serves 2 or 4:

4 poached eggs, drained, trimmed and cooled

4 thin lean slices of prosciutto or other good ham

Pepper

2 cups of aspic (see "Tomato Stuffed-with-Stuffed-Egg Salad," page 372 for recipe), cool but still liquid

2 tablespoons of mayonnaise, mixed with 1 teaspoon prepared mustard

4 slices of a crisp sweet pickle

Set a poached egg on each slice of prosciutto. Sprinkle it lightly with pepper. Carefully roll the ham around the egg envelope fashion. Arrange on a serving plate seam side down. Spoon over half of the aspic. Refrigerate until the aspic has set. Spoon over the remaining aspic (if it has set, heat it just enough to liquefy and allow to cool). Refrigerate until set. Just before serving garnish the ham rolls by spooning ½ tablespoon of the mayonnaise-mustard mixture on top of them, then a slice of pickle. Garnish with anything else that pleases, slices of foie gras radishes, olives, etc.

MARINATED EGGS

Serves 6:

1 cup of wine vinegar	1 tablespoon of sugar
⅔ cup of water	1½ teaspoons of salt
2 celery ribs, chopped	6 hard-cooked eggs, shelled
2 garlic cloves, crushed	

In a saucepan, combine the vinegar, water, celery, garlic, sugar and salt. Bring to a boil, then simmer, uncovered, for 10 minutes. Strain and cool. In a small, but deep bowl place the eggs and pour in the cooled marinade to cover them. Refrigerate for 2 days. Drain. Slice and serve on rounds of toast or on cucumber slices, sprinkled with a little chopped parsley or paprika.

ARTICHOKES AND EGG SALAD

Serves 4 to 6:

6 hard-cooked eggs, quartered	*mixed into a sauce*
1 (9-ounce) package of frozen artichoke hearts, cooked according to package directions, cooled and quartered	1 teaspoon of chopped fresh tarragon
	1 teaspoon of chopped broadleaf parsley
	¼ cup of vinegar
	½ cup of olive oil
2 medium-sized new potatoes, cooked in their skins, peeled and cubed	½ teaspoon of dry mustard
	Salt and pepper to taste

Lettuce leaves

Combine the eggs, artichoke hearts and potatoes in a large bowl. Pour on one-half of the sauce, mixing gently. Taste and pour on additional sauce to taste. Serve on lettuce leaves.

BACON, BEAN SPROUTS AND EGG SALAD

Serves 4 to 6:

4 hard-cooked eggs, coarsely chopped

6 slices of bacon, cooked crisp, drained and crumbled

1 head of crisp Boston lettuce, broken into bite-sized pieces

1 cup bean sprouts, crisped in cold water and drained

1 (8-ounce) can of water chestnuts, thinly sliced

Salad dressing (see below)

Place all ingredients except dressing, in a large salad bowl. Mix well with enough of the salad dressing to moisten thoroughly.

SALAD DRESSING

1 cup of olive oil

1 teaspoon of sugar

⅓ cup of red wine vinegar

1 tablespoon of Worcestershire sauce

1 medium-sized onion, minced

Salt and pepper to taste

Place all of the ingredients in a jar and shake well, or use a blender. Refrigerate leftover dressing.

EGG AND SWISS CHEESE SALAD

Serves 6:

½ pound of Swiss cheese, cut julienne

6 hard-cooked eggs, reserve 2 yolks and coarsely chop the remainder

blended into a salad dressing
⅓ cup of sour cream

⅓ cup of mayonnaise

½ teaspoon of Dijon mustard

Salt and pepper to taste

1 teaspoon grated onion

1 teaspoon of celery seed

6 Boston lettuce leaves

Combine the cheese strips and chopped eggs and gently blend with salad dressing to taste. Line a salad bowl, or 6 salad dishes, with lettuce leaves and spoon the salad onto the lettuce leaves. Push the reserved egg yolks through a fine sieve over the salad.

SLICED HARD-COOKED EGG SALAD WITH GARLICKY SAUCE

Serves 6:

Boston lettuce leaves
6 hard-cooked eggs, sliced
 with an egg slicer

blended into a sauce
 1 clove of garlic, minced
 4 anchovy fillets, minced
 1 teaspoon of capers,
  rinsed, drained and
  minced

⅛ teaspoon of cayenne
2 tablespoons of lemon
 juice
5 tablespoons of olive oil
Salt to taste

2 tablespoons of chopped
 parsley

On individual plates, arrange the egg slices, slightly overlapping, on a lettuce leaf. Top with sauce and sprinkle with parsley.

NIÇOISE SALAD

Serves 6 to 8:

4 medium-sized new pota-
toes, cooked in skins just
until tender, cooled, peeled
and cut into bite-sized
cubes

¼ pound of green beans,
cooked until crisp-tender
and cut into 1-inch pieces

½ cup of Greek black olives
(the plump, shiny ones),
pitted

½ cup of green stuffed olives

6 hard-cooked eggs, 4 cut
into quarters, 2 coarsely
chopped

blended into a salad dressing
½ teaspoon of Dijon
mustard
¼ teaspoon of dry mus-
tard

¼ teaspoon of sugar
1 cup of olive oil
3 tablespoons of white
wine vinegar
1 egg yolk, beaten
½ teaspoon of celery seed
Salt and pepper to taste

1 (7-ounce) can of solid
white tuna, broken into
bite-sized chunks

Boston lettuce leaves to line
salad bowl

6 to 8 anchovy fillets

1 canned pimiento, cut into
6 to 8 strips

3 small ripe tomatoes, peeled
and quartered

2 tablespoons of chopped
parsley

In a large bowl, combine the potatoes, green beans, olives,
chopped eggs and ½ cup of the salad dressing. Mix well and
let stand for 1 hour. Carefully mix in the tuna. Taste and add
more dressing, if desired. Line a salad bowl with the lettuce
leaves and spoon in the mixed ingredients. Garnish with the
anchovy fillets, egg quarters, pimiento strips and tomato
wedges. Dribble a little salad dressing over the ingredients
used for garnish and sprinkle with the parsley.

JIM ANELLI'S EGG AND ORANGE SALAD

Serves 6: This is an old Sicilian dish, introduced to us by the talented Vincenzo "Jim" Anelli. It is deliciously different.

12 ¼-inch-thick center slices of fresh, juicy oranges that have been peeled (with a knife) and all the white portion removed along with any seeds
Salt and pepper to taste

Garlic powder to taste
3 hard-cooked eggs, sliced (use an egg slicer)
6 anchovies, drained, rinsed of oil and salt
2 tablespoons of olive oil

On 6 salad dishes center 2 slices of orange overlapping them. Sprinkle lightly with salt, pepper and garlic powder. Arrange the egg slices on the orange slices. Place 1 anchovy fillet over the egg slices and sprinkle lightly with olive oil.

EGG AND PIMIENTO SALAD

Serves 6:

4 hard-cooked eggs, coarsely chopped

combined and well blended for a dressing
    4 tablespoons of mayonnaise
    2 tablespoons of olive oil

2 tablespoons of white wine vinegar
Salt and pepper to taste
4 tablespoons of chopped parsley
6 canned whole pimientos
6 leaves of Boston lettuce

Combine the eggs with one-half of the dressing and 2 tablespoons of the parsley. Stuff the pimientos with equal amounts of the egg mixture. Place each stuffed pimiento on a lettuce leaf and pour over the remaining dressing. Sprinkle with the remaining 2 tablespoons of parsley.

EGG AND SPINACH SALAD WITH CREAMY DRESSING

Serves 6 to 8:

2 (10-ounce) packages of fresh spinach, tough stems removed and discarded, washed thoroughly and dried

8 slices of lean bacon, cooked crisp, drained and crumbled

4 hard-cooked eggs (reserve one whole yolk), coarsely chopped

3 scallions, finely chopped

Creamy Dressing (see below)

In a large salad bowl, combine the spinach, bacon, chopped eggs and scallions. Serve mixed with the Creamy Dressing.

CREAMY DRESSING

Makes about 1¾ cups:

½ cup *each* of mayonnaise, buttermilk and sour cream

2 tablespoons of wine vinegar

1 tablespoon of Dijon mustard

2 tablespoons of grated onion

1 teaspoon of ground cumin

½ teaspoon of celery seed

2 shakes of Worcestershire sauce

Salt and pepper to taste

Combine all ingredients, mix well and refrigerate for 4 hours. Just before serving the spinach salad, mix in ½ cup of the dressing. Mix well and taste. Add more dressing to taste. Push the reserved egg yolk through a sieve over top of salad.

TOMATOES STUFFED-WITH-
STUFFED-EGG SALAD

Serves 4:

8 small ripe tomatoes, peeled
Salt and pepper to taste
¼ cup of mayonnaise
4 hard-cooked eggs, shelled
   and cut in half widthwise
½ cup of chopped cooked
   chicken
½ cup of chopped cooked
   ham
1 scallion (white part only),
   minced

3 tablespoons of olive oil
1 tablespoon of white wine
   vinegar
24 to 32 capers, rinsed and
   drained
Lettuce leaves
16 asparagus spears, peeled
   and cooked tender-crisp
2 cups of aspic (optional—
   see below)

Cut a slice off the top of each tomato. Scoop out the seeds and center pulp, leaving the pulp on the sides and bottom. Lightly salt and pepper the inside. Smooth ½ tablespoon of mayonnaise on the bottom of each tomato. Remove yolks from eggs, keeping white shells intact. In a bowl, combine the egg yolks, chicken, ham, scallion, olive oil, vinegar, salt and pepper, blending well. If too dry, add more oil and vinegar. Spoon or pipe the chicken-ham-egg yolk stuffing into the egg white shells. Set a stuffed egg half on the mayonnaise in each tomato. Place 3 or 4 capers on each stuffed egg. Arrange lettuce leaves on a serving dish, then the tomatoes on the lettuce and garnish with the asparagus.

If you do not use the aspic, sprinkle a little vinaigrette sauce on the asparagus.

If you use the aspic, chill the stuffed tomatoes. Chill the aspic until it begins to thicken. Spoon aspic over the stuffed tomatoes and asparagus. Allow to cool and set. Spoon 1 or 2 more layers of aspic on the salad, allowing each layer to cool and set before applying another.

QUICK CHICKEN ASPIC

Makes about 3 cups:

3 cups of rich clarified
chicken broth
¼ cup of dry white wine
½ teaspoon of celery salt

3 envelopes of gelatin, dissolved in ¼ cup of cold
water

Heat the broth and wine to the boiling point. Stir in the celery salt and dissolved gelatin. Cool. If aspic sets before you
can pour it, heat slightly to liquefy, then cool.

SALMON MOUSSE SERVED WITH HORSERAD-
ISH-CREAM STUFFED TOMATOES

Serves 4:

1 pound of fresh poached
salmon, saving ½ cup of
the liquid it cooked in, or
1 (1-pound) can of
salmon, reserving ½ cup
of the liquid and removing
skin and bones
3 scallions (white part
only), chopped
2 tablespoons of lemon juice
¾ cup of heavy cream
3 whole eggs, plus 1 egg
yolk
½ teaspoon of salt
¼ teaspoon of pepper

½ teaspoon of Dijon mus-
tard
1 tablespoon of chopped
fresh parsley
1 cup of Quick Mousseline
Sauce (page 408), mixed
with 1 tablespoon of fresh
grated horseradish (or a
good commercial one)
1 tablespoon of minced fresh
dill
4 small ripe tomatoes; peel
and scoop a small hole out
of the center, removing
seeds

Combine the salmon, liquid, scallions, lemon juice, cream,
eggs and yolk, salt, pepper, mustard and parsley into a
blender jar and blend until smooth. Pour into an oiled 4-cup
mold, or 4 individual molds. Set in a pan. Pour in enough hot
water to come halfway up the molds. Bake in a preheated
375°F. oven for 30 minutes, or just until firmly set (do not
overcook). Remove from water and cool.

To serve, unmold the mousse onto lettuce leaves. Spoon ½

tablespoon of the Mousseline sauce over each, if individual, or 2 tablespoons if cooked in one mold. Sprinkle with a small amount of the dill. Garnish with the tomatoes. Spoon the remaining sauce into the scooped-out tomatoes, sprinkle the remaining dill on top.

GREEN SPINACH PIE
(SPANAKOPETA)

Serves 6 for an appetizer or 4 for lunch:

12 sheets of commercial phyllo pastry
2 tablespoons of olive oil
2 tablespoons of butter
1 cup of finely chopped scallions (including ⅓ of the tender green tail)
2 pounds of spinach (stems cut off and discarded), washed, dried and chopped
1 tablespoon of flour
3 tablespoons of milk

½ cup of chopped broadleaf parsley
2 tablespoons of chopped fresh dill, or 2 teaspoons of dill weed
½ cup of pine nuts
⅛ teaspoon of cinnamon
½ teaspoon of salt
¼ teaspoon of pepper
½ pound of feta cheese, crumbled
4 eggs, beaten
1 cup of melted butter

If frozen phyllo is used, defrost it for 2 hours before using and keep covered with a damp cloth as it dries out quickly.

In a frypan, heat the oil and butter. Add the scallions and cook until soft. Add the spinach, cover and cook for 3 minutes. Remove cover and cook, stirring, until most of the liquid has evaporated. Sprinkle with the flour, stir well, then stir in the milk. Cook 1 minute, shaking pan. Stir in the parsley, dill and pine nuts, cinnamon, salt and pepper. Transfer to a bowl, cool, then stir in the cheese and eggs.

Butter a shallow 9- × -12-inch baking dish. Line with 1 sheet of phyllo pastry and brush with melted butter. Repeat procedure with 5 more sheets, buttering each. Spoon the spinach mixture onto the last sheet of pastry, spreading it evenly. Top with the remaining 6 sheets of pastry, brushing each with butter. Bake in a preheated 350°F. oven for 45 minutes, or until pastry is crisp and golden.

Cut into squares to serve. It can be served hot or slightly cooled.

EGG AND BLUE CHEESE SPREAD

Makes 20 canapés:

4 ounces of blue cheese (or Roquefort or Gorgonzola)	Salt and pepper to taste
2 hard-cooked eggs	10 slices of "party size" rye bread, toasted, buttered and halved
3 hard-cooked egg yolks	
2 scallions (including ⅓ of the green tails), minced	2 tablespoons of chopped parsley
½ cup of mayonnaise	

In a bowl, combine the cheese, eggs and yolks, scallions and one-half of the mayonnaise and mash until smooth. Add more mayonnaise, if mixture seems to dry. It should not be runny, just moist. Taste and season. Lavishly spread on the bread, garnishing each with a pinch of parsley.

OTHER HARD-COOKED EGG MIXES FOR CANAPÉS

Each makes about 1 cup:

1. 3 hard-cooked eggs
    5 tablespoons of mayonnaise
    Anchovy paste to taste
    2 drops of Tabasco
    Capers for garnish

2. 3 hard cooked eggs
    2 tablespoons of minced onion
    5 tablespoons of mayonnaise
    ½ teaspoon of Dijon mustard
    1 tablespoon minced parsley
    Sliced radishes or gherkins for garnish

3. 3 hard-cooked eggs
    5 tablespoons of mayonnaise
    ½ teaspoon of ground cumin
    1 teaspoon of curry powder
    Chopped chives for garnish

With each of the above, blend all ingredients, except the garnish, in a blender until smooth. Add additional mayonnaise, if necessary. Spread on rounds of toast and garnish with whatever is designated for that mix or anything else you may like: anchovy fillet, small shrimp, chopped cucumbers, etc.

4. 4 hard-cooked egg yolks   Melted butter to moisten
    ½ cup of minced cooked   Salt and pepper to taste
      lobster meat   Chopped fresh dill

Put the egg yolks through a sieve. Combine with the lobster meat, butter, salt and pepper. Spread on toast and garnish with dill.

5. 3 hard-cooked eggs   ½ teaspoon paprika
    ¼ cup of minced shrimp   5 tablespoons of mayon-
    1 teaspoon of lemon   naise
      juice   Cucumber slices, seeds
    Salt and pepper   removed

Mash eggs. Mix well with shrimp, lemon juice, salt, pepper, paprika and mayonnaise. Lay a slice of cucumber on a round of toast and fill the cavity (made by removing the seeds) with the mixture.

6. 3 hard-cooked eggs   1 teaspoon of poppy
    3 tablespoons of grated   seed
      Parmesan cheese   3 tablespoons of mayon-
    1 (3-ounce) package of   naise
      cream cheese   Salt and pepper to taste

Mash eggs and combine with other ingredients. Spread on toast rounds.

STUFFED EGGS

The deviled or stuffed egg is perhaps the most versatile of appetizers or cocktail offerings. It can be stuffed with everything from anchovy to zucchini. The hard-cooked mashed or riced yolk is delicious simply mixed with mayonnaise; add a little mustard to that mayonnaise and up comes a new taste texture. Add to that mayonnaise whipped heavy cream or sour cream and it's an exciting new offering. The alphabet can almost be recited with ingredients that can convert a hard-cooked egg into an epicurean delight. Minced cheese, ham, shrimp, a dab of horseradish, some chopped chives. Imagination is the key here.

Cut the hard-cooked egg lengthwise, or straight across to vary shape; use the new-laying pullet's small pee-wee eggs for a new look in stuffed eggs.

We offer a few recipes to put you on the road, then you can zoom merrily along on your own.

ANCHOVY AND CAPER STUFFED EGGS

For 12 egg halves:

6 hard-cooked eggs
2 teaspoons of capers, minced
2 scallions, minced
6 anchovy fillets, drained and minced

2 to 3 tablespoons of olive oil
Pepper to taste
Chopped parsley or fan-sliced cornichons (or other small pickle)

Cut eggs into halves widthwise. Cut a very thin slice off of each end so they will sit up. Remove the yolks, and, in a bowl, blend with the capers, scallions, anchovies, olive oil and pepper into a smooth thick paste. Stuff the whites with this mixture. Sprinkle or garnish the top of each with parsley or a cornichon.

CHICKEN STUFFED EGGS

For 16 egg halves:

8 hard-cooked eggs, shelled, cut in half widthwise and yolks removed (cut a tiny slice off the bottom of the whites so they sit up)
½ cup of minced cooked chicken
4 medium-sized mushrooms, cooked and minced

2 tablespoons of minced sweet pickle
2 tablespoons of tomato juice
1 cup mayonnaise
Salt and pepper to taste
16 slices of radish (from small radishes)
Chopped chives

In a bowl, combine the egg yolks, chicken, mushrooms, pickle, tomato juice and one-half of the mayonnaise and blend well, mashing the yolks. Taste for seasoning, adding salt and pepper. If mixture seems too dry, add additional mayonnaise. Pipe or spoon the stuffing into the egg whites. Chill slightly. Place a slice of radish with a pinch of chives on top of each stuffed egg and serve.

EGGS STUFFED WITH LUMPFISH CAVIAR

For 16 egg halves:

8 hard-cooked eggs, cut in half crosswise and yolks removed
½ cup of mayonnaise
1 teaspoon of Dijon mustard

¼ teaspoon of Tabasco
2 tablespoons of black lump-fish caviar
Caviar for garnish

In a bowl, combine the egg yolks, one-half of the mayonnaise, mustard and Tabasco, mashing until smooth. Add more mayonnaise, if too dry. Fold in the caviar. Spoon or pipe into the egg whites. Garnish with additional caviar.

STUFFED EGGS ROMANOV

For 16 egg halves:

8 hard-cooked eggs, cut in half crosswise, yolks removed

⅔ cup of crumbled blue cheese (or Roquefort or Gorgonzola)

1 tablespoon of chopped chives

¼ cup of soft butter

2 tablespoons of lemon juice

Pinch of cayenne

Heavy cream (if necessary to moisten)

2 tablespoons of red salmon caviar

Caviar to garnish

In a bowl, combine the egg yolks, cheese, chives, butter, lemon juice and cayenne and mash until smooth. Add a small amount of cream, if too dry (it should not be runny, just moist). Fold in the caviar. Spoon or pipe the mixture into the egg whites. Garnish with additional caviar.

SMOKED SALMON STUFFED EGGS

For 16 egg halves:

8 hard-cooked eggs, cut in half widthwise, yolks removed (cut a tiny slice off the bottom of the egg white so it will sit up)

1 cup of chopped smoked salmon

½ cup of mayonnaise

½ cup of sour cream

Chopped fresh dill

In a bowl, combine the egg yolks, salmon, one-half of the mayonnaise and one-half of the sour cream. Mash and blend well. If mixture seems too dry, add additional mayonnaise. Pipe or spoon into the egg whites. Top with a dab of the remaining sour cream and a pinch of the dill.

POACHED EGGS IN ASPIC

Serves 4:

2 cups of aspic, cool but still in liquid form (see "To-matoes Stuffed-with-Stuffed-Egg Salad," page 372 for recipe)

4 poached eggs, drained, trimmed and cooled

4 anchovy fillets, cut in half lengthwise

8 very thin strips of canned pimiento

mix in a blender to make a smooth puree

or

mash with a fork, then push through a sieve

¼ cup of soft butter

⅔ cup of minced cooked chicken

1 teaspoon of lemon juice

2 tablespoons mayonnaise

Pour ½ inch of cool aspic into the bottom of 4 individual soufflé dishes. Refrigerate and when set place a poached egg in the center on the aspic. Then spoon on enough of the remaining aspic (if it has set, heat slightly just to liquefy it and allow to cool) to just cover the eggs. Arrange the anchovy and pimiento strips crisscross on top of the aspic, trimming if too long. Refrigerate until aspic has set then pipe the butter-chicken mixture around the edges of the soufflé dishes in small twirls or rosettes.

QUICHES

One of the culinary glories of the egg is, without question, the quiche. For years these unique custard appetizer, luncheon or supper pies seemed to be the exclusive property of fine French restaurants.

Today their popularity has brought them everywhere—in many offerings.

Here we have recipes for quiches that we think make especially elegant appetizers. Others will appear in the Meal Chapter (page 414).

ASPARAGUS QUICHE WITH ANCHOVY FILETS

Serves 6 for an appetizer or 4 for lunch:

3 eggs
1½ cups of medium cream
1 shallot, minced
¼ cup of grated Asiago or
   Parmesan cheese
¾ cup of grated Swiss cheese
½ teaspoon of salt
¼ teaspoon of pepper
Pinch of nutmeg
½ pound of fresh asparagus,

cooked until just tender,
cut into bite-sized pieces,
or use 1 (10-ounce) pack-
age of frozen, cooked ac-
cording to package
directions but only one-
half of the time specified
1 (9-inch) partially baked
pastry shell
6 anchovy fillets

In a bowl, combine the eggs, cream, shallot, Asiago cheese, ½ cup of the Swiss cheese, salt, pepper and nutmeg and beat until well blended. Arrange the asparagus pieces on the bottom of the pastry shell and spoon the egg-cream mixture over them. Sprinkle over the remaining ¼ cup Swiss cheese and arrange the anchovy fillets, spoke-fashion, on top. Place on a baking sheet and bake in a preheated 375°F. oven for 30 to 40 minutes, or until set, puffed and golden. If top starts getting too brown before quiche sets, cover lightly with aluminum foil. Serve immediately.

CLAM QUICHE

Serves 6 for an appetizer or 4 for lunch:

4 slices of bacon
1 medium-sized white on-
   ion, minced
1 (8-ounce) can minced
   clams, drained and liquid
   reserved
1 tablespoon of minced
   parsley
1 tablespoon of minced
   chives

4 eggs
1½ cups of medium cream
1 tablespoon of flour
½ teaspoon of salt
¼ teaspoon pepper
9-inch partially baked pastry
   shell
¼ cup of freshly grated
   Asiago or Parmesan cheese

Cook bacon until crisp, but not too brown. Drain well and reserve the fat. Cut bacon into ½-inch squares. In a frypan, using 2 tablespoons of the bacon fat, sauté the onion until soft (do not brown). Off the heat, add the bacon, clams, parsley and chives to the frypan, mixing with the onion. In a bowl, beat the eggs, cream, flour, salt, pepper and the reserved clam juice (not exceeding ½ cup). Distribute the bacon-clam mixture over the bottom of the pastry shell. Carefully pour in the cream-egg mixture. Sprinkle with the cheese. Place on a baking sheet in a preheated 375°F. oven and bake for 30 minutes, or until set, puffed and golden. Do not overcook. If top starts getting too brown before quiche sets, cover lightly with aluminum foil. Serve immediately.

LOBSTER QUICHE

Serves 6 for an appetizer or 4 for lunch: An equal amount of crabmeat, shrimp, salmon or tuna can be substituted for lobster.

3 tablespoons of butter
4 tablespoons of minced shallots, or 1 white onion
2 (5-ounce) cans cooked lobster meat, cut into ½-inch cubes
9-inch partially baked pastry shell
½ cup plus 2 tablespoons of grated Gruyère cheese

2 whole eggs plus 2 egg yolks
1½ cups of medium cream
Pinch of nutmeg
1 tablespoon of flour
3 tablespoons of sherry
1 teaspoon salt
¼ teaspoon of pepper

In a frypan, over medium heat, melt 2 tablespoons of butter. Sauté the shallots until soft (do not brown). Combine the shallots with the lobster meat and evenly distribute over the bottom of the pastry shell. Sprinkle with the ½ cup of cheese. In a bowl, beat together the eggs and yolks, cream, nutmeg, flour, sherry, salt and pepper. Pour carefully over the contents of pastry shell. Sprinkle with the remaining 2 tablespoons of cheese. Dot with the remaining 1 tablespoon of butter. Place on a baking sheet in a preheated 375°F. oven and bake for 30 minutes, or until set, puffed and golden (do not overcook). If top starts getting too brown before quiche sets, cover lightly with aluminum foil. Serve immediately.

MUSHROOM QUICHE

Serves 6 for an appetizer or 4 for lunch:

3 tablespoons of butter
3 scallions (including ⅓ of the green tails), minced
½ pound of mushrooms, sliced
½ teaspoon of salt
3 whole eggs plus 1 egg yolk

2 cups of medium cream
3 tablespoons of sherry
½ cup of grated Swiss cheese
¼ cup of grated Asiago or Parmesan cheese
1 (9-inch) partially baked pastry shell

In a frypan, over medium heat, melt 2 tablespoons of the butter. Add scallions and cook for 1 minute. Add the mushrooms and salt and cook, covered, for 4 minutes. Remove cover, raise heat and cook until all liquid has evaporated.

Beat the eggs, yolk and cream in a bowl. Stir in the sherry, ¼ cup of the Swiss cheese, the Asiago and the mushroom mixture. Pour into the pastry shell. Sprinkle the top with the remaining ¼ cup Swiss cheese and dot with the remaining 1 tablespoon butter. Place on a baking sheet and bake in a preheated 375°F. oven for 30 to 40 minutes, or until set, puffed and golden. If top browns too quickly, cover lightly with foil.

ONION QUICHE
(appetizer or luncheon)

Serves 6 as an appetizer or 4 for lunch:

4 tablespoons of butter
4 cups of thinly sliced onion
½ cup of white wine
1 tablespoon of flour
Pinch of dried thyme
1 teaspoon of salt
¼ teaspoon of pepper
2 whole eggs plus 2 egg yolks

1 cup of light cream
¾ cup of grated Gruyère or Parmesan cheese
6 slices of lean bacon, cooked until barely crisp, drained on paper towels and diced
9-inch partially baked pastry shell

In a large frypan, over medium heat, melt 3 tablespoons of the butter. Add the onion and cook until soft and transparent. Add the wine and cook until most of the liquid has evaporated and the onion is slightly golden. Sprinkle on the flour, thyme, salt and pepper, stir and cook 1 minute. Remove from the heat.

In a bowl, beat the eggs, yolks, cream and ½ cup of the cheese. Stir in the onion. Sprinkle the bacon pieces over the bottom of the pastry shell. Pour in the onion-egg-cream mixture. Sprinkle the top with the remaining ¼ cup cheese and dot with the remaining 1 tablespoon butter. Place on a baking sheet and bake in a preheated 375°F. oven for 30 minutes, or until quiche has set and is puffed and golden brown.

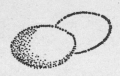

Chapter Two

Soups

Here, in a number of recipes, the chicken teams with the egg to produce an outstanding soup. The chicken makes the broth possible, the egg is the flavor enhancer. (See page 31 for a broth recipe.)

Those who appreciate fine food believe that soup is an appetite clarifier, settling taste buds, alerting them for the taste sensations that will follow in the meal to come.

But for many people, soup is much more. It is a meal in itself, a lunch, a supper. Many nationalities have egg soup specialties, Greek Egg-Lemon Soup, Italian Stracciatella, Jewish Egg-Matzo Ball soup, French Egg-Custard.

The English poet Lord Byron called soup "A soul satisfier." He had to be talking about egg soups.

Can you imagine how satisfied that clever Chinese cook must have been when he or she first dropped egg, accidentally, or deliberately, into bubbling chicken broth to produce Egg Drop Soup?

ABRUZZI EGG SOUP

Serves 4:

4 tablespoons of olive oil
1 clove of garlic, chopped
4 scallions (white part only), minced
4 ripe tomatoes, peeled, seeded and chopped
7 cups of hot chicken broth
5 medium-sized mushrooms, thinly sliced

Salt and pepper to taste

well beaten together
    3 eggs
    2 tablespoons of light cream
    ½ cup of finely crumbled Gorgonzola cheese
Chopped parsley

In a large saucepan, over medium heat, heat the oil and sauté the garlic and scallions for 3 minutes, or until the scallions are crisp-tender. Add the tomatoes and cook for 10 minutes. Add the broth and cook, uncovered, for 15 minutes, stirring occasionally. Add the mushrooms, salt and pepper and cook 5 minutes. Place the egg-cheese mixture in the bottom of a soup bowl or tureen. Pour in the very hot soup, stirring, until well blended. Serve immediately, sprinkled with parsley.

AVGOLEMONO SOUP

Serves 6:

8 cups of rich chicken broth
⅓ cup of uncooked rice
3 eggs, separated

Juice of 1 lemon (about 3 tablespoons)
Salt and pepper
Thin lemon slices

In a saucepan, bring the broth to a boil. Add the rice. Cover and cook for 15 minutes, or until the rice is *al dente*. Remove from the heat. In a bowl, beat the egg yolks until light and lemon-colored. Beat in the whites, then the lemon juice, beating constantly. Still beating, add 1 cup of the chicken broth (free of rice). Then gradually beat in another cup of the broth. When well mixed, slowly pour into the saucepan with the remaining broth, stirring. Reheat slowly (do not allow to boil). Taste for seasoning, adding salt and pepper. Serve immediately, garnished with lemon slices. Buttered toast may be served on the side.

EGG-CREAM BARLEY SOUP

Serves 4:

3 tablespoons of butter
2 tablespoons of flour
5 cups of chicken broth
4 tablespoons of pearl barley, cooked until tender in chicken broth

beaten together
  3 egg yolks
  ¾ cup of milk

¼ cup of heavy cream
Salt and pepper to taste
1 cup of shredded watercress leaves

In a large saucepan, over medium heat, melt the butter and blend in the flour stirring into a smooth golden paste. Lower heat and add the broth, stirring until slightly thickened. Stir in the barley. Stir the egg yolk-milk mixture into the soup and simmer (do not boil), stirring, for 3 minutes. Stir in the cream and season with salt and pepper. Serve piping hot, sprinkled with the watercress.

EGG BROCCOLI SOUP

Serves 4 to 6:

1 (10-ounce) package of frozen chopped broccoli, cooked according to package directions (cook slightly less than instructed) and well drained
7 cups of chicken broth

beaten together
  2 egg yolks
  1½ cups of heavy cream

⅛ teaspoon of nutmeg
½ cup of grated Gruyère cheese

In a large saucepan, bring the broth to the boil. Add the broccoli and simmer for 5 minutes. Puree small amounts at a time in a blender. Return to the saucepan. Bring soup to a simmer and stir in the egg yolk-cream mixture. Add the nutmeg. Cook, stirring constantly, for 2 minutes (do not boil). Serve in individual hot soup bowls with the cheese sprinkled on top.

VARIATION

Add a small cooked soup pasta just before serving.

CABBAGE, POTATO AND TOMATO SOUP

Serves 6 to 8:

3 tablespoons of butter
3 medium-sized potatoes, cubed
2 cups of shredded cabbage
4 medium-sized leeks, chopped
2 quarts of chicken broth
1 (1-pound) can of tomatoes

⅛ teaspoon of thyme
Salt and pepper to taste
3 egg yolks, blended with ½ cup of chicken broth
Chopped fresh dill
Garlic croutons (see Puree of Vegetable Soup, page 399)

In a large pot, over medium heat, melt the butter. Add potatoes, cabbage and leeks and cook for 2 minutes, stirring, or until vegetables are well coated with butter. Add the broth, tomatoes and thyme and cook, uncovered, for 30 minutes, or until the potatoes can be mashed against the side of the pot. Season with salt and pepper. Cool slightly and puree in a blender, a small amount at a time. Return to the pot and heat to a simmer. Mix the egg yolk-broth mixture with 1 cup of the hot soup. Pour back into the soup pot and heat, stirring, about 2 minutes (do not boil). Sprinkle with dill and pass the croutons.

CREAM OF CARROT SOUP

Serves 6:

3 tablespoons of butter
8 carrots, peeled and sliced
2 medium-sized white on-
   ions, chopped
3 celery ribs, scraped and
   sliced
1 quart of chicken broth
1 teaspoon of dried tarragon

1 tablespoon of chopped
   fresh parsley
Salt and pepper to taste

beaten together
   3 egg yolks
   1 cup heavy cream

1 tablespoon of chopped
   fresh chives

In a large saucepan, melt the butter over medium heat. Add the carrots, onion and celery and cook for 2 minutes, stirring, or until well coated with butter. Stir in the broth, tarragon and parsley and simmer until the carrots can be mashed against the side of the pot. Cool slightly and puree in a blender, a small amount at a time. Return to the pot, season with salt and pepper. Heat just to a simmer and stir in the egg yolk-cream mixture. Heat, about 2 minutes, stirring, but do not boil. Serve sprinkled with chives.

CREAM OF CAULIFLOWER SOUP

Serves 6:

1 medium-sized very white
   cauliflower, trimmed and
   flowerets separated
1 quart of chicken broth

2 egg yolks, beaten with 1
   cup of medium cream
2 tablespoons of butter, in
   small pieces
Salt and pepper to taste

In a large saucepan, cook the cauliflower in boiling, salted water until soft but still intact. Drain and reserve 1 cup of the cooking water. Break into very small bits (about the size of a small fingernail) ½ cup of the flowerets and reserve. Push the remaining cauliflower through a sieve. Return it to the saucepan with the reserved cup of water and the broth. Simmer for about 15 minutes, or until it begins to thicken. Remove from heat and slowly stir in the egg yolk-cream mixture. Over low heat, add the butter and stirring constantly, cook until the soup is heated through (do not boil or the eggs will curdle). Season with salt and pepper and stir in the reserved cauliflower bits.

VELVET CELERY SOUP

Serves 4 to 6:

8 medium-sized ribs of celery, scraped and chopped
4 medium-sized onions, chopped
8 cups of chicken broth
2 tablespoons of butter
2 tablespoons of flour

beaten together
   3 egg yolks
   1 cup of light cream

Salt and pepper to taste
Minced fresh chives

In a large saucepan, combine the celery, onion and broth. Bring to a boil, then reduce to a simmer and cook until the celery is soft. Puree in a blender, a small amount at a time. In another large saucepan, over medium heat, melt the butter. Stir in the flour, blending into a smooth golden paste. Gradually blend in the pureed celery soup mixture. Bring to the boil, then reduce to a simmer and cook, stirring, for 10 minutes. Stir in the egg-cream mixture and, stirring, bring just to a simmer. Remove from the heat. Season with salt and pepper. Serve garnished with a sprinkle of chives.

CREAMY CHEESE SOUP

Serves 6:

2 tablespoons of butter
1 medium-sized white onion, minced
1 tablespoon of flour
2 cups of warm milk
2½ cups of chicken broth
2 cups of grated Gruyère or Cheddar cheese

¼ teaspoon of paprika
3 egg yolks, beaten with 1 cup of light cream
Salt to taste
½ cup of crumbled bacon, first cooked until crisp, then drained

In a large saucepan, over medium heat, melt the butter and cook the onion until soft. Stir in the flour. Cook, stirring, into a smooth paste. Add the milk gradually, stirring until smooth. Stir in the broth. Heat to a simmer. Lower heat, stir in the cheese and paprika, simmering until cheese is melted. Stir 3 or 4 tablespoons of the soup into the egg yolk-cream mixture, then stir back into the soup. Heat to a simmer (do not boil). Taste for seasoning and serve with bacon sprinkled over each serving.

EGG, CORN AND CRABMEAT SOUP

Serves 6 to 8:

7 cups of rich chicken broth
1 cup of corn kernels cut from fresh-cooked corn (or use frozen or canned kernels)
2 tablespoons of cornstarch, mixed with 2 tablespoons of water and 1 tablespoon of soy sauce

1 (6½-ounce) can of crab (or an equal amount of fresh or frozen crab), picked over and shredded
3 eggs, beaten
Salt to taste

In a large saucepan, heat the broth to a simmer. Stir in the corn and simmer for 1 minute. Stir in the cornstarch-soy sauce mixture, stirring until the soup has thickened slightly. Stir in half of the crabmeat. With broth at a simmer, slowly stir in the eggs. Remove from heat as soon as all of the egg has been added. Taste for seasoning. Serve with the remaining crabmeat sprinkled atop.

CREAM OF CRABMEAT SOUP
(OR SHRIMP OR LOBSTER)

Serves 6 to 8:

½ cup of dry white wine
1 (8-ounce) bottle of clam broth
1 bay leaf
⅛ teaspoon of dried thyme
1 pound of crabmeat, picked over to remove bits of shell and cartilage
5 tablespoons of butter
3 shallots, chopped, or 1 small white onion
1 small rib of celery, scraped and chopped

1½ quarts of chicken broth
1 teaspoon of Hungarian paprika
Salt and pepper to taste

beaten together
   3 egg yolks
   1 cup of heavy cream

¼ cup of dry sherry
2 tablespoons of chopped fresh parsley

In a saucepan, combine the wine, clam broth, bay leaf and thyme. Bring to a boil. Stir in the crabmeat. Heat to a simmer. Remove from heat. Remove crab and set aside. Remove bay leaf and reserve the liquid. In a large saucepan, over medium heat, melt 3 tablespoons of the butter. Stir in the shallots and celery and cook, stirring, for 1 minute, or until well coated with the butter. Stir in the chicken broth and reserved wine-clam broth mixture, and simmer until celery can be mashed against the side of the pan. Stir in the crabmeat. Cool slightly and puree in a blender, small amounts at a time. Return to the pot, add the paprika, salt and pepper. Heat just to a simmer. Stir in the egg yolk-cream mixture and heat, stirring, for about 2 minutes (do not boil). Stir in the sherry and the remaining 2 tablespoons of butter. Serve in hot soup bowls sprinkled with the parsley.

EGG DROP SOUP

Serves 6:

7 cups of rich chicken broth
2 tablespoons of dry sherry
⅛ teaspoon of ground
  ginger
1 tablespoon of soy sauce

3 eggs, beaten
Salt to taste
4 green onions, chopped
  (using part of the dark
  green tails)

In a large saucepan, bring the broth to a simmer. Stir in the sherry, ginger and soy sauce. Slowly stir in the eggs. Remove from heat when all of the egg has been added. Taste for seasoning. Serve immediately with the green onions sprinkled on top.

GARLIC SOUP WITH POACHED EGGS

Serves 6:

6 tablespoons of olive oil
6 cloves of garlic, peeled
  and mashed
6 (½-inch thick) slices of
  French bread
8 cups of rich chicken broth

Salt and pepper to taste
6 poached eggs, trimmed
  and kept warm
1 tablespoon of chopped
  fresh coriander

In a deep saucepan, heat the oil over medium heat and cook the garlic until lightly browned. Remove and discard the garlic. Sauté the bread in the oil until golden on both sides. Remove and cut each slice in half. Add the broth to the saucepan and heat to a boil. Taste for seasoning. Ladle into 6 soup bowls, placing an egg in each, with a half slice of bread on either side. Lightly sprinkle with the coriander.

MEATBALL SOUP

Serves 6:

3 tablespoons of butter
2 medium-sized onions, chopped
4 fresh mint leaves, chopped
1½ quarts of chicken broth
Salt and pepper to taste

well blended and formed into balls the size of acorns
  1 pound of finely ground beef
  1 egg

¼ cup of bread crumbs
Pinch of cinnamon
1 teaspoon of salt
¼ teaspoon of pepper

Flour

beaten together
  2 egg yolks
  ¾ cup of sour cream

2 tablespoons of chopped fresh parsley

In a large pot, over medium heat, melt the butter and cook the onion until soft. Stir in the mint leaves and broth and simmer for 15 minutes. Season with salt and pepper. Dust each meatball with flour. Add to the broth and simmer (do not boil), covered, for 30 minutes. Remove from the heat. Mix the egg yolk-sour cream mixture with 1 cup of soup. Stir it into the soup pot and cook, stirring, for about 2 minutes (do not boil). Serve sprinkled with parsley.

CREAM OF MUSHROOM SOUP

Serves 6:

6 tablespoons of butter
1½ pounds of mushrooms finely chopped
2 white onions, finely chopped
3 tablespoons of flour
1½ quarts of chicken broth

beaten together
  3 egg yolks
  ¾ cup of heavy cream

Salt and pepper to taste
2 tablespoons of Madeira
¼ cup of sour cream

In a large frypan, over medium heat, melt 3 tablespoons of the butter. Add the mushrooms and sauté until most of the mushroom liquid has cooked off, being careful not to burn them. Remove from heat and reserve.

In a large pot, over medium heat, melt the remaining 3 tablespoons of butter. Sauté the onion until soft. Stir in the flour and blend well. Gradually add the broth, stirring into a smooth thin sauce. Stir in the mushrooms. Cool slightly and puree in a blender, a small amount at a time. Return to the large pot and heat to a simmer. Remove from heat. Stir in the egg yolk-cream mixture and heat, stirring, for about 2 minutes (do not boil). Season with salt and pepper and stir in the wine. Serve wtih a dollop of sour cream floating on each serving.

COLD MUSTARD SOUP

Serves 4:

2 tablespoons of butter
2 tablespoons of flour
2½ cups of warm chicken broth
2½ cups of warm light cream
½ teaspoon of salt
¼ teaspoon of pepper
½ teaspoon of onion juice

beaten together
3 egg yolks
3 tablespoons of heavy cream

4 tablespoons of Dijon mustard
2 tablespoons of chopped parsley

In a saucepan, over medium heat, melt the butter. Add the flour, blending well. Gradually add the broth and light cream, stirring constantly until smooth. Add the salt, pepper and onion juice and simmer for 10 minutes. Cool slightly and stir in the egg yolk-cream mixture. Add the mustard, blending until smooth. Taste for seasoning. Refrigerate and serve cold in consommé cups. Sprinkle with parsley.

ONION AND EGG SOUP ALLA ROMANO

Serves 8:

6 tablespoons of butter
7 medium-sized onions,
  peeled and thinly sliced
2 cloves of garlic, minced
3 tablespoons of flour
8 cups of chicken broth
1 teaspoon of salt
½ teaspoon of pepper

beaten together
  4 egg yolks
  ¾ cup grated Parmesan
    cheese

6 thick slices of toasted Italian bread
3 tablespoons of minced
  broadleaf parsley

In a large saucepan, over medium heat, melt the butter. Add the onion and garlic and cook for 5 minutes. Stir in the flour and cook, stirring, for 2 minutes. Gradually stir in 2 cups of the broth, stirring constantly until broth and flour are well blended. Add remaining broth, salt and pepper. Cover and simmer for 20 minutes. Remove from heat and blend in the egg yolk-cheese mixture. Taste for seasoning. Place a slice of the bread in each soup bowl, ladle in the soup and sprinkle with parsley.

ZUPPA PAVESE

Serves 6:

4 tablespoons of butter
6 slices of Italian or French
  bread (no larger than 2½
  inches in diameter), cut
  ½-inch thick

6 tablespoons of grated Asiago or Parmesan cheese
8 cups of rich chicken broth
Salt and pepper to taste
6 eggs, poached, trimmed
  and kept warm

Melt butter in a frypan. Add the bread and fry until golden on both sides. Sprinkle 1 tablespoon of cheese on top of each slice of bread and run them under the broiler until the cheese melts. Heat the broth to a boil. Taste for seasoning. Divide the broth among 6 bowls. Float a slice of bread on the broth and place a poached egg on each slice.

STRACCIATELLA

Serves 6:

7 cups of rich, clear chicken
   broth
3 large eggs
3 tablespoons of tender
   chopped fresh spinach

4 tablespoons of grated Asi-
   ago or Parmesan cheese
Salt to taste
Pinch of nutmeg

While the broth is being heated, combine the eggs, spinach, cheese, salt and nutmeg in a bowl and beat thoroughly. When the broth comes to a slow boil, pour in the egg mixture, reduce the heat and simmer, stirring slowly until the eggs are set, floating in strands. Serve immediately.

TAPIOCA SOUP

Serves 6 to 8:

8 cups of chicken broth
3 tablespoons of tapioca
1 cup of diced cooked
   chicken

1 cup of diced cooked ham
Salt and pepper to taste
3 hard-cooked eggs,
   chopped

In a large saucepan, heat the broth over medium heat. Add the tapioca and simmer for 10 minutes. Stir in the chicken and ham and heat through. Season with salt and pepper. Serve hot with the eggs sprinkled on top.

TOMATO EGG DROP SOUP

Serves 6:

2 quarts of chicken broth
1 (1-pound) can of stewed
   tomatoes, mashed into
   small pieces

2 tablespoons of cornstarch,
   blended with ¼ cup cold
   water
3 eggs, beaten
2 whole young scallions,
   chopped

In a large saucepan, bring the broth to a boil, then stir in the tomatoes. When the mixture comes to a boil again, stir in the cornstarch. Reduce heat to a simmer, stirring until the soup thickens. Then slowly stir the beaten eggs into the simmering soup. Remove from the heat. Serve piping hot garnished with the scallions.

TOMATO MUSHROOM SOUP

Serves 4 to 6:

3 tablespoons of butter
2 cloves of garlic, minced
1 pound of small mushrooms, unpeeled (but stems removed), thinly sliced
2 small ripe tomatoes, peeled, seeded, chopped and cooked for 10 minutes to a mushlike consistency

2 tablespoons of finely chopped fresh chives
1½ quarts of chicken broth
Salt and pepper to taste

beaten together
   2 eggs
   2 egg yolks
   ⅛ teaspoon of nutmeg
   ½ cup of grated Romano cheese

In a large saucepan, over medium heat, melt the butter and sauté the garlic for 1 minute. Add the mushrooms, tomato and chives. Pour in the broth. Bring to a boil, then simmer, uncovered, stirring occasionally, for 30 minutes. Add salt and pepper. Add ½ cup of the soup to the egg-cheese mixture and mix well. Remove saucepan from the heat and stir in the egg mixture. Return to the heat and cook about 2 minutes, or until just hot (do not boil), stirring constantly.

ZUPPA TRASTEVERE

Serves 4:

1 quart of chicken broth
4 slices of Italian bread,
    toasted and crushed into
    bread crumbs (blender
    will do this nicely)

beaten together
    3 eggs
    ¼ cup of grated Asiago or
    Parmesan cheese

Salt and pepper to taste
Stracciata: 1½ cups of finely
    shredded escarole or ro-
    maine lettuce sautéed in
    butter until limp (do not
    overcook)
½ cup of grated Asiago or
    Parmesan cheese

In a large saucepan, bring the chicken broth to a boil, then
stir in the bread crumbs. Cook, stirring, for 3 minutes, or until thickened. Place the egg-cheese mixture in a large hot soup
bowl. Slowly pour the boiling soup in, beating it constantly,
until well blended. Taste and season with salt and pepper.
Serve garnished with the *stracciata* and pass the cheese.

PUREE OF VEGETABLE SOUP

Serves 6 to 8:

4 tablespoons of butter
¼ pound of cooked ham,
    diced
2 medium-sized potatoes,
    cubed
4 carrots, peeled and sliced
2 medium-sized onions,
    chopped
2 ribs of celery, scraped
    and chopped
¼ pound of green string
    beans, quartered

1 cup shelled of green peas
2 quarts of chicken broth
Salt and pepper to taste
3 egg yolks, beaten
Garlic croutons: make your
    own by frying slices of
    French or Italian bread in
    butter and garlic until
    golden on both sides, then
    cube the slices

In a large pot, over medium heat, melt 2 tablespoons of the
butter and sauté the ham, stirring, until light brown. Remove
with a slotted spoon and reserve. Melt the remaining 2 table-

spoons of butter in the pot and add the potatoes, carrots, onion, celery, beans and peas. Cook for 2 minutes, stirring, until well coated with butter. Pour in the broth and simmer, uncovered, for 30 minutes, or until the vegetables can be mashed against the side of the pot. Season with salt and pepper. Cool slightly and puree in a blender, a small amount at a time. Return to the pot. Heat just to a simmer. Blend 1 cup of soup with the egg yolks. Stir the egg yolk mixture into the pot and heat, stirring for about 2 minutes (do not boil). Serve with ham sprinkled over and pass the croutons.

EGG AND WATERCRESS SOUP WITH CHEESE DUMPLINGS

Serves 4:

2 tablespoons of butter
2 leeks (white part only), chopped
1 bunch of watercress (reserve ½ cup of uncooked, chopped leaves)

4 cups of chicken broth
Salt and pepper to taste
3 egg yolks, beaten with 1 cup of cream
Cheddar cheese dumplings (see below)

In a large saucepan, melt butter, over medium heat. Add leeks and cook for 5 minutes or until soft. Add watercress and broth, bring to a simmer and cook 10 minutes. Season with salt and pepper. Put into a blender and puree. Return to the saucepan and heat to a simmer. Stir in the egg yolk-cream mixture and heat, stirring, until well blended (do not boil). Taste for seasoning. Serve with the Cheddar cheese dumplings floating on top and the chopped watercress sprinkled over the dumplings.

CHEDDAR CHEESE DUMPLINGS

Make ¼ recipe for Cocktail Cheddar Cheese Shells (page 363) and instead of baking them, make tiny dumplings and cook them in simmering water until they rise to the top. They can be prepared in advance and kept warm in foil.

YOKOHAMA EGG SOUP

Serves 4 to 6:

2 quarts of chicken broth
1 tablespoon of fresh lemon juice
¼ teaspoon of minced ginger root
1 tablespoon of soy sauce
8 to 12 tender young snow peas

½ cup of bean sprouts
4 tender young scallions, chopped
6 small mushrooms, thinly sliced
4 to 6 jumbo eggs (depends on number being served)

In a large deep frypan, combine the broth, lemon juice, ginger and soy sauce. On medium heat, bring to the boil, then reduce heat and simmer for 8 minutes. Stir in the snow peas, bean sprouts, scallions and mushrooms, and simmer, stirring, for 5 minutes. Break eggs, one by one, in a saucer and slide them carefully into the soup. Poach to the desired degree of doneness. Remove eggs with a slotted spoon and place in individual hot soup bowls. Taste, then add salt. Spoon the soup and vegetables over them.

Chapter Three
Sauces

Once, a group of French three-star chefs were asked to name the most valuable ingredient in cooking, an ingredient that added finesse to their creations. To a man, the chefs agreed: The egg!

They went into detail (some of that is included in the foreward to this section) but mainly, they stressed sauces.

If it weren't for the egg, there wouldn't be such superb sauces as mayonnaise or hollandaise. Are these sauces not dressings? Both the words in cookery are almost interchangeable.

The world authority, Larousse Gastronomique, states "Sauce: By this word is understood every kind of liquid seasoning in food . . ."

Egg gives that "liquid" richness and authority, color and flavor. Examples: béarnaise and mousseline. Start turning the pages to add finesse to your own creations.

FRENCH AIOLI SAUCE

Makes about 1¾ cups: Good for just about anything—potatoes, eggs, fish, boiled beef—if you like garlic.

1 medium-sized potato, boiled and riced
2 hard-cooked egg yolks, riced
4 cloves of garlic, put through a garlic press
3 raw egg yolks
1½ cups of olive oil
2 tablespoons of fresh lemon juice
½ teaspoon of salt

In a bowl, combine the potato, egg yolks and garlic, blending well. Beat in the raw egg yolks, then gradually beat in the oil, beating constantly until the sauce becomes smooth. Then beat in the lemon juice and salt. Taste for seasoning.

GREEK VARIATION: SKORDALIA SAUCE

After the Aioli Sauce has been beaten and is smooth and thick, beat in:

1 tablespoon of fresh lemon juice

⅓ cup of ground toasted walnuts

1 teaspoon of Hungarian paprika

2 tablespoons of minced broadleaf parsley

SAUCE ANDALOUSE

Makes about 2½ cups: For cold fish and cold vegetables.

2 cups of mayonnaise

2 ripe tomatoes, peeled, seeded, minced and drained

1 small red pimiento, minced

1 teaspoon of fresh lemon juice

Salt and pepper to taste

In a bowl, place the mayonnaise. Beat in the tomato, pimiento and lemon juice. Season with salt and pepper.

EGG SAUCE ANTIBOISE

Makes about 1½ cups: Especially good with shellfish.

1½ cups of mayonnaise

2 teaspoons of anchovy paste

2 tablespoons of thick tomato sauce

¼ teaspoon of dried tarragon

In a bowl, combine all ingredients and blend well.

VARIATION OF EGG SAUCE ANTIBOISE: CYPRIOTE SAUCE

For vegetable salads.

Add 4 hard-cooked egg yolks, riced, and ¼ teaspoon of toasted, crushed fennel seeds.

AVGOLEMONO SAUCE

Makes about 1½ cups: This sauce is served over meat, fish or vegetables, or added to soups (chicken or lamb especially good) or stews to thicken them.

3 eggs
3 tablespoons of lemon juice
1 cup of hot broth (it can be chicken, fish or vegetable, depending on what it is served with)

In a bowl, beat the eggs until light and lemony with an electric beater, or blender. Gradually add the lemon juice, then the hot broth, beating constantly. Serve immediately.

If added to soups or stews, do not boil but heat over low heat, stirring until thickened.

BÉARNAISE SAUCE #1

Makes about 1 cup:

2 tablespoons of tarragon vinegar
2 shallots, minced
1 tablespoon of minced fresh tarragon or 1 teaspoon of dried
Pinch of salt
Pinch of cayenne
3 egg yolks (at room temperature)
¾ cup of warm melted butter
1 teaspoon of minced fresh tarragon

In a saucepan, simmer the vinegar, shallots, the 1 tablespoon of tarragon, salt and cayenne until most of the vinegar has evaporated. Strain and cool to lukewarm. Place in a heatproof bowl *over* hot water (or in the top of a double boiler) on low heat. Add the egg yolks, beating with a whisk until thickened, then gradually beat in the butter. Beat until the sauce has the consistency of hollandaise then blend in the 1 teaspoon of tarragon.

BÉARNAISE SAUCE #2

To Hollandaise Sauce (pages 407, 408), add 1 teaspoon of finely chopped parsley and 1 teaspoon of finely chopped tarragon (or 1 teaspoon tarragon vinegar).

EGG-CREAM SAUCE

Makes about 2¼ cups: Here is a fast and easy cream sauce, given new identity with its enrichment of eggs.

3 tablespoons of butter	3 egg yolks, lightly beaten
2 tablespoons of flour	1 teaspoon of salt
2 cups of light cream	¼ teaspoon of pepper

In a saucepan, over medium heat, melt the butter. Stir in the flour, blending into a smooth, golden paste. Reduce heat to low and gradually stir in the cream, stirring until smooth and thickened. Without boiling, blend in the egg yolks, salt and pepper, stirring, for 1 minute, or until hot. Taste for seasoning.

VARIATIONS OF EGG-CREAM SAUCE

Adding 2 tablespoons of Madeira, Marsala or sherry will give the sauce new personality. Substituting chicken broth for light cream converts this into an interesting *Allemande Sauce*. Stirring in 1½ tablespoons of minced broadleaf parsley makes it a *Poulette Sauce*. Add ½ cup of grated sharp Cheddar cheese to this egg-velouté and you create a *Fine Cheese Sauce*.

EGG SAUCE FERMIÈRE

Makes about 1½ cups: For fish and vegetables.

7 hard-cooked egg yolks, riced	⅛ teaspoon of cayenne
2 sticks (½ pound) of soft butter	¼ cup of dry white vermouth
1 teaspoon of salt	1 tablespoon of fresh lemon juice
½ teaspoon of pepper	1 teaspoon of Dijon mustard

406 THE CHICKEN AND THE EGG COOKBOOK

In a bowl, combine all ingredients, beat, blending well. Taste
for seasoning.

ISTANBUL EGG FISH SAUCE

Makes about 2½ cups:

4 egg yolks	1½ cups of olive oil
2 cups of fine bread crumbs	¼ cup of fresh lemon juice
2 cloves of garlic, put	½ teaspoon of salt
through a garlic press	¼ teaspoon of pepper

In a bowl, combine the egg yolks, bread crumbs and garlic,
beating together. Gradually beat in the olive oil, then the
lemon juice, salt and pepper. Taste for seasoning.

VOLGA COLD FISH SAUCE

Makes about 2½ cups:

½ cup of canned crabmeat, picked over to remove bits of shell and cartilage	2 cups of mayonnaise
	1 tablespoon of fresh lemon juice
2 tablespoons of red caviar	⅛ teaspoon of cayenne

In a bowl, combine crabmeat and caviar and mash into a
paste. Blend in the mayonnaise, lemon juice and cayenne.

CAMBRIDGE GAME SAUCE

Makes about 1¾ cups:

5 hard-cooked egg yolks, riced	¼ teaspoon of dried tarragon
	¼ teaspoon of dried thyme
½ teaspoon of salt	1½ cups of olive oil
3 anchovy fillets	¼ cup of wine vinegar
1 tablespoon of fresh chopped chives	2 tablespoons of chopped broadleaf parsley

In a large bowl, place the egg yolks. In a smaller bowl, combine the salt, anchovies, chives, tarragon and thyme and mash into a paste. Blend with the yolks in the large bowl. Slowly, small amounts at a time, beat in the olive oil, the vinegar, then the parsley. Taste for seasoning.

HARD-COOKED EGG SAUCE

Makes about 2½ cups: This is excellent for a poached chicken.

3 hard-cooked eggs	2 cups of hot chicken broth
2 tablespoons of butter	Good pinch of cayenne
1 tablespoon of flour	Salt to taste

Separate the yolks and whites of the eggs. Push them through a sieve, keeping them separate. In a saucepan, combine the egg yolks, butter and flour, blending well. Over low heat, gradually stir in the broth, stirring constantly. Cook at a bare simmer for 5 minutes. Stir in the cayenne and egg whites and season with salt.

CLASSIC HOLLANDAISE SAUCE

Makes about 2 cups:

4 egg yolks	Salt to taste
2 tablespoons of water	Pinch of cayenne
2 sticks (½ pound) of soft butter	Lemon juice to taste (start with 2 teaspoons)

Combine the egg yolks and water in the top of a double boiler, beating until well blended. Place over hot (not boiling) water in the double boiler and beat until mixture is creamy. Add a small amount of the butter, beating constantly, until butter has melted and sauce thickens. Continue adding small amounts of the butter, beating and blending well after each addition. Continue beating until sauce thickens. At no time allow the water in the double boiler to boil. Season with salt, cayenne and lemon juice. Keep warm over warm, not hot, water.

QUICK HOLLANDAISE SAUCE

Makes about ¾ cup:

2 egg yolks
1 tablespoon of lemon juice
½ teaspoon of salt

Dash of cayenne
1 stick (¼ pound) of melted butter

Combine the egg yolks, lemon juice, salt and cayenne pepper in a blender jar. Turn the blender on high, then turn right off. Turn it on high again and slowly pour in the melted butter. Check the seasoning, then turn blender on again for another second or two. Keep sauce warm over barely hot water. If there is sauce leftover, it can be frozen; then, when needed, warmed slowly over hot water.

QUICK MOUSSELINE SAUCE

Stir ½ cup of whipped cream into the above Quick Hollandaise Sauce.

HORSERADISH HOLLANDAISE

Blend ¼ cup peeled, freshly grated horseradish with ½ cup of whipped cream, then blend into the Quick Hollandaise sauce. Good with seafood.

HOLLANDAISE RAVIGOTE

Excellent with poached chicken.

4 tablespoons of butter, at room temperature
2 teaspoons of lemon juice
2 teaspoons of minced shallots
2 teaspoons of minced chives

2 teaspoons of minced parsley
1 teaspoon of minced fresh tarragon, or ⅓ teaspoon dried
1 recipe of Quick Hollandaise Sauce (page 408)

Combine all ingredients, except the hollandaise sauce, and using a blender or food processor, blend until smooth. Over warm water blend into the hollandaise sauce.

OTHER HOLLANDAISE VARIATIONS

ANCHOVY
To 1 cup of hollandaise, blend in 1 teaspoon of anchovy paste. For fish or vegetables.

CUCUMBER
To 1 cup of hollandaise, blend in 1 cup of well-drained minced cucumber. For fish.

CURRY
To 1 cup of hollandaise, blend in 1½ teaspoons of curry powder. For eggs and fish.

LEMONY
To 1 cup of hollandaise, blend in 2 teaspoons of grated lemon rind. For fish.

ORANGE
To 1 cup of hollandaise, blend in 1 tablespoon of fresh orange juice and 1 teaspoon of grated orange rind. For vegetables.

RED CAVIAR
To 1 cup of hollandaise blend in a 1-ounce jar of red caviar. For fish, eggs, vegetables.

EGG AND LEMON SAUCE
(Italian *Salsa di Limone*)

Makes about 1½ cups: To serve with roasted meats, hot or cold.

2 tablespoons of butter	Salt to taste
1 tablespoon of flour	1 tablespoon of minced
1 cup of milk	parsley
2 egg yolks, beaten with 2 tablespoons of lemon juice	1 tablespoon of small capers, or chopped large ones

In a saucepan, over medium heat, melt the butter. Add the flour, stirring into a smooth paste. Gradually add the milk, stirring, until sauce starts to thicken. Remove from heat. Stir in 3 or 4 tablespoons of the sauce into the egg yolk-lemon juice mixture. Blend this with the sauce in the saucepan. Season to taste. Over low heat, cook stirring, until sauce is hot and of the consistency desired (do not boil). Stir in the parsley and capers. Cool before serving.

MAYONNAISE
WITH 9 VARIATIONS

Makes about 2 cups:

2 egg yolks, at room temperature	2 tablespoons of tarragon vinegar
½ teaspoon dry mustard	2 tablespoons of lemon juice
½ teaspoon of salt	1 cup olive oil
Pinch of cayenne	1 cup of vegetable oil

In a bowl, with an electric hand beater (or use a blender), beat the yolks until thick and lemon-colored. Add the mustard, salt, cayenne, vinegar and lemon juice and beat well. Slowly, drop by drop, at first, beat in the oils. As mixture thickens, beat in larger amounts of the oils, being sure each addition is thoroughly absorbed before adding more.

If a less thick mayonnaise is desired, add small amount of cream.

BLUE CHEESE OR ROQUEFORT CHEESE MAYONNAISE

To 1 cup of mayonnaise, add ½ cup of heavy cream, whipped, and ¼ cup of crumbled blue or Roquefort cheese and 1 teaspoon of Worcestershire sauce, blending thoroughly.

BOMBAY MAYONNAISE

Add 1 teaspoon of curry powder, ¼ teaspoon of ground ginger, 1 tablespoon of lemon juice and 1 teaspoon of grated onion to 1 cup of mayonnaise, blending thoroughly.

BRANDY MAYONNAISE

Add 1 tablespoon of brandy and 1 tablespoon of dill weed to 1 cup of mayonnaise. Serve with fish.

CHANTILLY MAYONNAISE

Just before serving, add 1 cup of whipped cream to 1 cup mayonnaise.

For smoked or cold poached fish, add to the above Chantilly Mayonnaise 1 tablespoon of fresh grated horseradish and 1 tablespoon of sour cream, blending.

GARLIC MAYONNAISE

Add 1 clove of garlic put through the garlic press and 1 tablespoon of lemon juice to 1 cup of mayonnaise, blending.

GREEN MAYONNAISE

Add 1 tablespoon *each* of minced parsley, fresh tarragon, chives, watercress (or spinach) to 1 cup mayonnaise, blending.

RÉMOULADE SAUCE

To 1 cup mayonnaise, add ½ clove garlic, minced, 1 tablespoon chopped fresh tarragon, 1 tablespoon rinsed and dried capers, chopped, 1 teaspoon chopped parsley, 1 teaspoon prepared mustard, and, optional, ½ teaspoon anchovy paste, blending.

TARTAR SAUCE

To 1 cup mayonnaise, add finely chopped, 2 tablespoons shallots, 2 tablespoons of dill or sweet pickle, 1 hard-cooked egg, parsley and lemon juice to taste, blending.

THOUSAND ISLAND DRESSING

To 1 cup mayonnaise, add ¼ cup of chili sauce, 1 hard-cooked egg, chopped, 1 tablespoon minced onion, 1 tablespoon chopped parsley, blending.

MASKING MAYONNAISE

Makes slightly more than 1 cup: This sauce is used to cover cold dishes, such as breast of chicken or to cover canapés when ordinary mayonnaise wouldn't hold.

1½ teaspoons of unflavored
    gelatin
1 tablespoon of lemon juice

3 tablespoons of water
1 cup of mayonnaise

Soften gelatin in the cold lemon juice and water, then melt over hot, but not boiling, water, stirring until it becomes clear. Cool slightly (but not long enough for it to set) and blend with the mayonnaise.

RICH MORNAY SAUCE

Makes about 2½ cups:

4 tablespoons of butter
3 tablespoons of flour
Pinch of cayenne
Pinch of nutmeg
2 cups of milk
3 egg yolks, beaten with ½
    cup of heavy cream

¼ cup of grated Gruyère
    cheese
¼ cup of grated Parmesan
    cheese
Salt and pepper to taste

In a saucepan, over low heat, melt 3 tablespoons of the butter. Add the flour, stirring constantly into a smooth paste. Stir in the cayenne and nutmeg. Gradually add the milk, stirring into a smooth, medium-thick sauce. Stir 3 or 4 tablespoons of the sauce into the egg yolk-cream mixture, then stir back into the saucepan. Add the cheeses, stirring until melted (do not boil). Season with salt and pepper. Before serving, add the remaining tablespoon of butter, stirring until melted.

If sauce becomes too thick, thin with hot milk.

SAUCE PROVENÇALE

*Makes about 3 cups: For fish, especially good with frogs'
legs.*

7 hard-cooked eggs, chopped
4 ripe tomatoes, peeled,
   seeded, chopped and well
   drained
1 tablespoon of chopped
   broadleaf parsley

1 tablespoon of fresh lemon
   juice
3 cloves of garlic, put
   through a garlic press
½ teaspoon of salt
¼ teaspoon of pepper
2 cups of mayonnaise

In a saucepan, over low heat, combine the eggs, tomatoes,
parsley, lemon juice, garlic, salt and pepper. Stir, cooking,
until it bubbles. Remove from the heat and stir in the mayonnaise, blending well. Taste for seasoning.

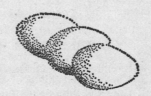

Chapter Four
Meals

Contained in the shell of the egg is not only an amazing storehouse of nutrients, but nestled there in that golden yolk encircled by the glistening white are enough meals to satisfy a regiment of epicures. Crack an egg, couple it with imagination, and out come almost endless varieties of breakfasts, lunches, suppers and dinners.

The key word of this chapter is "imagination," a creative cooking ability. Consider the eggs poached in red wine served by our mentor, the noted French chef Antoine Gilly, cooked for luncheon one rainy day. A neighbor created a "double," egg ring filled with chicken livers. Another friend made "Mexican" eggs, scrambled with tomatoes and chili powder.

Rather than divide all these ideas into separate chapters, omelets, poached, scrambled, etc., we decided to accentuate its versatility by imitating the egg itself. Make its mealtime magic compact. Here it is all in one place.

COOKING EGGS

A noted chef, Charles Virion, said of eggs, "You have to understand eggs. They have a sensibility of their own. Do not push them too far. Eggs will take only so much cooking then no more."

Another, an Escoffier-trained chef, Louis P. De Gouy, said, "Do not rush egg cooking. Eggs are like some people—rush them and they get tough. Cook eggs slowly."

All of which adds up to the fact that there are specific techniques for different kinds of egg cookery. But all agree: Do not overcook. Do not rush the cooking.

BAKING

Baked eggs are a unique and satisfying dish that are not difficult to cook. There are a few main points to remember:
Since eggs don't have any natural fat, make certain that the
dish is well buttered. They are easier to handle and more attractive to serve if baked in individual ramekins or dishes.
Preheat the oven for even baking. Like soufflés and pasta,
baked eggs should not wait for the guests, the guests should
wait for the baked eggs, which are ready to eat as soon as
they leave the oven.

Butter the ramekin, break in an egg or two, add a touch of
cream, tomato sauce, cheese, or whatever appeals, then salt
and pepper. Place in a *bain marie* (a pan of hot water). The
water should come about midway up on the dish containing
the eggs, then bake in a preheated 375°F. oven for 8 to 10
minutes, or slightly longer, depending upon on how well one
likes the eggs set.

Shirred eggs are baked eggs that have been started on top
of the stove. Butter a heatproof dish, break the eggs into it,
add seasonings and cook on medium heat on top of the stove
until the bottom is set. The advantage to this method is that
you can observe the "setting" more easily than that of the eggs
baking in the oven. When the shirred eggs are set properly,
place under a broiler or in a preheated 450°F. oven for 45
seconds or so until the yolks are filmed. Whites should be set
softly, yolks still somewhat liquid.

BOILING

Soft-boiled eggs are cooked basically the same way as hard-
cooked eggs (page 361, Appetizers). Place in a pan and
cover with 1 inch of cold water. Bring the water to the boil,
reduce to a simmer, then time: precisely. For soft-boiled
eggs with a firm white and slightly set yolk, cook 3 minutes.
To set the yolk a little more, cook 4 minutes. Immediately remove from water to stop further cooking.

Alternate method: After the water is brought to the boil,
remove from the heat, cover the pan and let set: 3½ minutes
for soft-boiled, 4 minutes for medium, 5 minutes for beyond
medium, for those who prefer a soft-boiled egg with a little
more substance, and 6 minutes, for so-called *mollet,* midway
between soft-boiled and hard-cooked.

Most people are particular about their soft-boiled eggs, so the important factor is timing.

CODDLING

Coddled eggs are recommended invalid food. True egg lovers also dote on them. Nutritious, easy to eat and digest, they are simple to prepare. Drop the eggs into rapidly boiling water, cover the pot, remove from the heat and let set for 10 minutes. Turn from the shell into a serving dish. They will be jellied, with little noticeable difference between the firmness of the white and the yolk.

FRYING

Next to boiling this is the simplest method of cooking an egg; yet there are many failures. Why are many fried egg yolks broken before leaving the pan? Because the eggs are carelessly broken onto the cooking surface, the eggs are not at room temperature (all eggs to be cooked should be at room temperature) or the eggs are turned or pushed around in the pan too soon. Often other foods, ham or potatoes, cooked in the pan first can be the culprits. The particles that remain make the egg stick, or make it difficult to turn. The most common error is cooking them too fast over too high heat, hardening the whole egg, toughening the white and overcooking the yolk.

Fried eggs are fussy eggs: Nearly everyone has a favorite, rarely do two people agree on a fried egg. Sunny-side down, sunny-side up. Basted. Covered, lightly steamed sunny-side up. Over easy, over medium, over well.

A properly fried egg should not be hard, should be unbrowned on the bottom, the white tender, the yolk soft, dunkable with a piece of toast, or soft enough to spread its golden personality on the top of a pancake or waffle.

The cooking surface of the frypan should be clean, the heat medium-high, then lowered, the pan should be covered with plenty of butter, margarine, cooking oil or bacon fat, so the egg won't stick. Reduce the amount of fat if the egg is to be cooked sunny-side up.

Break the egg to be fried in a small dish or saucer (some experts disagree and break it directly into the frypan), then carefully slide it onto the hot butter or fat in the frypan.

Breaking the egg first in a dish insures that there will be no broken yolk in the frypan. Breaking the egg into the pan, unless one is deft, is responsible for many a broken yolk and sloppily fried egg.

For a flavorful fried egg, fry several strips of bacon in the frypan first until almost crisp. Remove them, then fry the egg, basting with the bacon fat as it cooks. Or add several drops of water to the melted butter, cook the egg briefly, then cover the pan and allow the egg to self-baste.

Use the proper utensil, a pancake turner or spatula. Shake the pan a little first to loosen the egg, carefully slide the spatula under it, then turn it over, gently. Don't slap it down into the fat. The timing is a matter of choice. Technically, when the white begins to solidify, it is ready to turn.

As with all food, the French have a unique method for frying eggs—"black" butter eggs. Butter is heated in a frypan until it is almost black, but not burned. The egg is fried in it, removed, then more butter is added to the frypan along with ⅛ teaspoon of vinegar. This is stirred and simmered briefly, then spooned over the fried egg.

OMELETS

The word omelet is a formidable one to many of us, conjuring visions of much clever turning, flipping, rolling. In short, egg legerdemain that requires skill.

The word itself is used to cover a number of beaten egg dishes. Technically, it usually refers to the French-type omelet, tender and firm on the outside, soft and creamy inside, rolled or folded and often filled with anything from chicken livers to little cubes of tender young zucchini—or almost anything the imagination creates.

But omelet also refers to the dishes of other nations, the flat egg cake of Italy, the *frittata*; the flat cake filled with cooked potatoes, a favorite of Spain, *tortilla de patata*; the flat Chinese egg *foo yung*.

There is also the classic fluffy or soufflé omelet, with yolks and whites beaten separately.

The Danes cook a large flat omelet, place it on a plate, stuff it with hot pieces of chicken breast, roll it, surround it with cooked peas and fresh tomatoes, and top it with tiny cooked mushrooms.

Most nations have their own versions and adaptations of the omelet.

But to most of us the word refers to the French folded omelet, thus we offer information on that classic omelet, and also describe an easy short-cut that we use successfully.

Use 2 large eggs per person, and cook the omelets separately. It's the most effective way. Don't beat the eggs too long; don't use an eggbeater. Long beating and using anything but a fork, makes the omelet thin and tough.

The pan is important. It should have rounded or sloping shoulders to permit the eggs to quickly spread when the pan is tilted, and to make it easier for the omelet to slide out of the pan when cooked. The pan shouldn't be too small (it makes the omelet too thick), or too large (makes the omelet too thin and dry); 9 inches in diameter at the top is perfect for the 2- to 4-egg omelet.

The pan should be iron or aluminum, free of scratches that can cause sticking, and it should be "cured" to prevent sticking, by filling it with oil almost to the brim, then heating it until very hot, but not bubbling. Let it stand overnight, then pour the oil out. Wipe the pan out thoroughly, but do not wash. In fact, say the omelet experts, never wash an omelet pan, just wipe it out after use. If the pan does stand for a very long time unused, it will have to be washed and cured again, or else it might make the omelets taste somewhat rancid.

If you are going to fill an omelet, have all ingredients ready. Beat 2 large eggs for each omelet in a small bowl with salt and pepper and 2 teaspoons of heavy cream.

Place the pan on medium high heat. It should not be too hot, but should have an even, consistent heat. Test it by placing hard butter on a fork; if the heat is right, the butter will sizzle but won't brown. A heaping tablespoon of butter goes into the pan, tilt and turn the pan in all directions to completely coat it. When the butter stops foaming, pour in the beaten eggs. Stir for a couple of seconds with the flat back of a fork. Tilt the pan, so the fluid egg runs around the sides, and keep the pan moving, in a back-and-forth motion, so the omelet slides in the pan. With a fork or spatula, lift the edges of the setting omelet to allow the remaining liquid to run under and set. With a fork, fold the omelet, left side to the center, while the eggs are still soft. Give the handle of the pan a sharp blow with the edge of the hand to make it jump forward. Hold a plate close under the pan, then turn it completely over, depositing the omelet on the warm serving dish.

EASY BUT SUCCESSFUL METHOD

The trick: Use a pan with Teflon coating. Melt the butter as described. Add the eggs. Remember, the longer the egg is cooked, the tougher it gets. So, as soon as the omelet starts cooking, which is just about immediately, using a spatula, move the mixture, letting the liquid egg on top roll to the edges, replacing that portion that is already set. Continue until the entire omelet is cooked, but still soft and creamy in the center. Immediately, then fold half of the omelet over the other half, giving it about 3 seconds for the bottom to brown, then slide it out, upside down onto a warm plate.

POACHING

Of the numerous ways to poach eggs, we prefer the following: First, however, remember that to be perfectly poached an egg must be fresh, not more than several days old. The white of a really fresh egg is firm, compact, not runny, the not-so-fresh egg white is loose, does not cling to the yolk and produces a ragged, wide, thin white when poached in liquid. As very fresh eggs are often not available, there are a couple of ways around this:

1. If uncertain of the freshness of the egg to be poached, give it a quick heat treatment by lowering an unbroken egg into boiling water for exactly 9 seconds. Then break and poach.
2. Or use the French "egg ball" method of poaching: A pot is used rather than a shallow saucepan or frypan. To a nearly full small pot of boiling water, add 2 teaspoons of salt and 1 teaspoon of white vinegar. The water is then stirred (but not too fast) in a circular motion, until a little whirlpool or a hollow forms in the middle of the pot. The heat is lowered so the water simmers, the egg (broken into a dish or saucer) slipped into that hollow, the water constantly stirred (close to the side of the pot) in a circular motion, to keep the water circling the egg. The white will

wrap itself around the yolk producing a neat white ball. With this method only one egg can be done at a time.

Our method: In a saucepan, have water at least 2 inches deep. For 1 quart of water add 2 teaspoons of salt and 1 tablespoon of white vinegar, reducing these amounts accordingly. (The salt adds flavor and the vinegar helps in quickly setting the white so it doesn't shred or break up.) Eggs always should be first broken separately in a small dish or saucer, then slipped into the pan of boiling water. Do not crowd eggs in a pan. The water should completely cover the egg but should not boil after you add the eggs. Even a slight boil will bounce the eggs and may tear them apart. Lower the heat, and cook for about 5 minutes at a bare simmer, or until the white becomes opaque. Ideally, a poached egg should have firm whites and a soft yolk, at least in the center. The egg can be gently pressed with a fork or spoon to determine firmness. Remove with a slotted spoon and drain. Poached eggs also can be stored in cold water in the refrigerator for 2 days. Then drain them and use for cold eggs in aspic, or reheat by placing in hot, but not boiling, water long enough to just heat through but not cook. These stored poached eggs can also be used without heating for oven baked and sauced dishes.

Another method: In a saucepan, place enough water to completely cover the eggs to be poached, then add 2 teaspoons of salt and 1 tablespoon of white vinegar (if there is a quart of water; if less, reduce accordingly) and bring to the boil. Reduce the heat. When the water stops boiling slide 1 egg at a time from the saucer into the water. After all eggs are in the water, bring to a simmer again. Cover, take from the heat and let stand for 5 minutes.

There are also commercial "egg poachers" that do a decent job of poaching if directions are followed.

Flavor can be added to poached eggs by copying the French method of using liquids other than water. Soups, clear or creamed, cream, beef or chicken broth, milk, beer, wine, tomato juice or sauce. We have friends, Barbara and Bruno Valbona, who often serve an impressive dish at their popular Sunday brunches, "Eggs in Hell," poached in a very spicy, Sicilian tomato sauce.

SCRAMBLING

Someone has said, it is as easy to scramble eggs as it is hard to unscramble them.

The common mistake as with most egg dishes: overcooking. Scrambled eggs should be on the soft side, not stiff and hard with particles of white showing here and there. Do not add much liquid, or the eggs will be watery. One teaspoon per egg is about right. Milk, heavy cream, sour cream, wine, tomato sauce or tomato paste, all can be added. Many believe that eggs scrambled with cottage cheese are the ultimate.

Beat eggs with a fork until the whites and yolks are well mixed, add the desired liquid, salt and pepper and any other herb or spice preferred. Fresh chopped chives, for example, are excellent with scrambled eggs. The frypan should be well-buttered, at least ⅛ inch when melted.

On medium heat, cook the eggs (5 eggs for two), stirring until the eggs are the consistency of soft custard. Scrambled eggs should always be on the soft side; stored heat in them will continue cooking after they are removed from the heat.

If scrambled eggs aren't to be served immediately (and they should be), they will keep quite well for short periods, moist, soft, hot, in a double boiler over low heat.

Also excellent in scrambled eggs are parsley, tarragon, various grated cheeses, cream cheese, soy sauce, mushrooms. The eggs shouldn't be overwhelmed with outside influences, but some delicate touches do add flavor and sight appeal.

AMALFI EGGS

*Serves 6: This is a tasty meal-in-one, a Campania-style ome-
let, or sort of an omelet, as the eggs aren't broken or beaten,
prized by Italian priests.*

blended
   3 tablespoons of melted
      butter
   ¾ cup of fine bread
      crumbs

1 pound of mozzarella
   cheese, thinly sliced

6 eggs

blended
   ½ cup of grated Asiago or
      Romano cheese
   1 teaspoon of freshly
      grated black pepper

Line the bottom of a 2-inch-deep baking dish with the buttered bread crumbs. Cover the crumbs with a half of the
mozzarella slices, overlapping them, if necessary. Break the
eggs, one at a time, into a small dish, then slip them out,
spacing evenly, onto the cheese. Cover the eggs with the remaining slices of mozzarella. Sprinkle on the cheese-pepper
mixture. Bake, uncovered, in a preheated 400°F. oven for 15
minutes, or until the whites have firmly set and the yolks are
not yet completely set (but not runny).

BAKER'S WIFE'S EGGS AND POTATOES

Serves 4:

5 tablespoons of butter
4 medium-sized potatoes,
   peeled and cut into long
   thin slices

blended
   1½ teaspoons of salt

½ teaspoon of pepper
⅛ teaspoon of nutmeg

½ cup of grated Swiss cheese
8 eggs
½ cup of heavy cream

In a large frypan, melt the butter over medium heat and cook
the potatoes, turning often, until evenly browned and tender.
Sprinkle on half of the salt-nutmeg blend. Spread them
evenly on the bottom of a shallow baking dish and sprinkle
with the cheese. Break the eggs in a saucer or shallow dish
and slide them onto the cheese, dusting them with the re-

maining salt-nutmeg blend. Spoon the heavy cream over each
egg. Bake, uncovered, in a preheated 375°F. oven for 10
minutes, or until the eggs are set as preferred. Serve from the
baking dish.

EGGS BAKED IN BROCCOLI NESTS

Serves 4:

1 (10-ounce) package of
   frozen chopped broccoli,
   cooked according to package directions, well
   drained and chopped again
⅛ teaspoon of nutmeg
2 tablespoons of butter

1 tablespoon grated onion
5 tablespoons of heavy
   cream
4 jumbo eggs
Salt and pepper to taste
4 tablespoons of grated
   Swiss cheese

Sprinkle the broccoli with the nutmeg. In a saucepan, over
medium heat, melt the butter and cook the onion for 1
minute. Stir in the broccoli and 1 tablespoon of the cream,
blending well. Sauté for 2 minutes. Butter individual baking,
soufflé or custard dishes, coating bottoms and sides well with
the broccoli mixture. Break an egg into each little broccoli
nest and sprinkle lightly with salt and pepper. Spoon 1 tablespoon of the cream over each egg, and sprinkle each with 1
tablespoon of the cheese. Place in a pan with hot water coming halfway up on the baking dishes and cook for 12 minutes
in a preheated 325°F. oven, or until the eggs are set as preferred.

CHICKEN-BAKED EGGS

Serves 4:

blended
- ⅛ teaspoon of dried tarragon
- 1 tablespoon of minced fresh chives
- 2 tablespoons of soft butter

- ½ teaspoon of salt
- 1 tablespoon of heavy cream
- 1½ cups of minced cooked chicken
- 4 jumbo eggs

Butter 4 individual custard cups or small soufflé dishes. Reserve 2 teaspoons of the herb mixture, then add the chicken to the remainder, blending well. (It should be of spreadable consistency; if not, blend in a little more heavy cream.) Spread the chicken mixture evenly over the bottom and sides of the buttered cups. Break an egg into each. Top with a dab of the reserved herb mixture, then place the eggs in their cups in a pan of hot water (the water coming about halfway up the sides of the cups) and bake in a preheated 325°F. oven for 12 minutes, or until set. Whites should be just firm and the yolks about as soft as poached eggs.

EGG RING*

Serves 4:

- 2¼ cups of warm milk
- 6 eggs, plus 1 egg yolk
- ¾ teaspoon of salt
- ½ teaspoon of paprika

- ½ small white onion, minced and sautéed in 1 tablespoon of butter
- 1 tablespoon of chopped parsley

In a bowl, combine milk, eggs, egg yolk, salt, paprika and onion and beat with a wire whisk. Grease a 9-inch ring mold and sprinkle it with the parsley. Pour in the egg mixture. Set the mold in a pan of hot water. Bake in a preheated 325°F. oven for 20 to 25 minutes, or until the custard is set. Invert

* Especially Inexpensive

onto a heated serving dish. Sprinkle with more parsley, if
desired. Fill the ring with creamed mushrooms, chicken livers
or kidneys.

CREPES STUFFED WITH HERBED EGGS

Serves 4:

8 large eggs
Salt and pepper to taste
4 tablespoons of minced
  parsley
1 teaspoon of fresh chopped
  tarragon, or ½ teaspoon
  dried
3 tablespoons of heavy
  cream

6 tablespoons of butter
4 scallions, finely chopped
  (using some of the green
  tail)
8 (6-inch) crepes (see
  Basic Batter for Crepes
  page 475)
4 tablespoons of grated Parmesan cheese

In a large bowl, lightly beat together the eggs, salt, pepper, 2
tablespoons of the parsley, tarragon and heavy cream.

In a large frypan, over medium heat, heat 2 tablespoons of
the butter. Add the scallions and cook for 2 minutes, or until
they are crisp-tender. Add 3 tablespoons of butter to the frypan. When hot, turn the heat to low and stir in the beaten
egg mixture. Scramble the eggs, stirring constantly, until they
begin to set and are still quite soft. Divide the eggs among
the 8 crêpes. Roll the crepes and arrange them, seam side
down, in a buttered, shallow baking dish. Sprinkle with the
cheese, dot with remaining tablespoon of butter and bake in a
450°F. oven just long enough to heat them through and
slightly brown. Sprinkle with remaining parsley. Serve with
chicken livers, kidneys, mushrooms or bacon.

TUNA, EGG AND MUSHROOM CREPES

Serves 6:

7 tablespoons of butter
4 scallions (use ⅓ of the dark green ends)
4 medium-sized mushrooms, coarsely chopped
2 (7-ounce) cans of tuna, drained and broken into small chunks
3 jumbo hard-cooked eggs, coarsely chopped
Salt and pepper to taste

3 tablespoons of flour
2 cups of warm milk
1 teaspoon of Worcestershire sauce
½ teaspoon of celery salt
1 cup of warm heavy cream
1½ cups of grated Gruyère cheese
12 6-inch crepes (see Basic Batter page 475)

In a saucepan, over medium heat, melt 2 tablespoons of butter. Add the scallions and cook until they start to lose their crispness. Add 2 more tablespoons of butter; when melted add the mushrooms; cook 2 minutes. Remove the pan from the heat, stir in the tuna and eggs; season with salt and pepper. Set aside. In another saucepan, over medium low heat, melt the remaining butter; stir in the flour and cook, stirring constantly, into a smooth paste. Gradually add the milk and simmer, stirring, until the sauce is smooth and medium-thick. Stir in the Worcestershire sauce, celery salt, cream and half of the cheese. Continue stirring and cooking until the cheese has melted and the sauce is again medium-thick. Add enough sauce to the egg-tuna mixture to moisten it. Taste for seasoning.

Divide the mixture into 12 equal portions. Fill the crepes by spooning a portion of the mixture on the lower third of each crepe. Roll and lay seam side (but not touching) in a shallow, buttered baking dish. Spoon sauce on top. Sprinkle with the remaining cheese; bake in a preheated 375-degree oven for 15 minutes, or until heated through and golden on top. A long, narrow spatula is helpful in serving.

HARD-COOKED EGG AND CHEESE CASSEROLE

Serves 4:

6 hard-cooked eggs, sliced
(use an egg slicer)
2 ribs of celery, scraped
and finely chopped
4 medium-sized mushrooms,
sliced
2 scallions, (use ⅓ of the
green tails) finely chopped

¼ cup of chopped green pepper
⅔ cup of mayonnaise
Salt and pepper to taste
1 cup of grated sharp
Cheddar cheese
½ cup of cracker crumbs

Line a buttered 1-quart casserole with overlapping egg slices. Combine the celery, mushrooms, scallions, green pepper, mayonnaise, salt, pepper and one-half of the cheese, blending well. Spoon this mixture over the egg slices in the casserole. Sprinkle with remaining cheese, then the cracker crumbs. Bake, uncovered, in a preheated 350°F. oven for 25 to 30 minutes, or until bubbling and golden.

CURRIED HARD-COOKED EGGS

Serves 4:

6 tablespoons of butter
2 medium-sized onions,
chopped
1 clove of garlic, minced
1 small tart apple, peeled,
cored and chopped, or 3
tablespoons of applesauce
2 tablespoons of curry powder
2 tablespoons of flour

1 medium-sized ripe tomato,
peeled, seeded and
chopped
1 cup of chicken broth
1 teaspoon of salt
Pinch of cayenne
1 cup of heavy cream
6 hard-cooked eggs, cut into
thick slices
2 tablespoons of chopped
parsley

In a saucepan, over medium heat, melt the butter. Add the onion, garlic and apple. Cook for 5 minutes, or until the onion is soft (do not brown). Sprinkle in the curry powder and flour. Simmer for 3 minutes, stirring to blend well. Gradually add the tomato, broth, salt, cayenne and cream, stirring constantly. Cook for 5 minutes, or until the sauce thickens. Force through a strainer. Taste for seasoning. Place the egg slices in a saucepan and cover with the strained sauce. Heat through. Serve on hot buttered toast with parsley sprinkled over the top, or with rice and accompaniments such as raisins, chopped peanuts, chutney, coconut or chopped scallions.

FINNISH EGGS

Serves 4:

3 tablespoons of butter
3 tablespoons of flour
1½ cups of light cream
1 (10½-ounce) can of condensed tomato soup
1 cup grated Fontina or Gruyère cheese

1 teaspoon of Worcestershire sauce
1 teaspoon of grated onion
8 hard-cooked eggs, sliced
Salt and pepper to taste
6 slices of toast, cut into halves

In a saucepan, over medium heat, melt the butter. Stir in the flour and cook, stirring into a smooth paste. Gradually add the cream and soup, stirring constantly, until you have a smooth, thickened sauce. Add the cheese, Worcestershire and onion and stir until the cheese is melted. Carefully stir in the eggs. Season with salt and pepper. Heat through and serve on the toast halves (3 for each serving).

CREAMED HAM AND EGGS

Serves 4 to 6:

3 tablespoons of butter
1 small onion, minced
3 tablespoons of flour
1 cup of milk
1 cup of medium cream
Pinch of cayenne
½ teaspoon of dry mustard
2 cups of cubed cooked ham

2 tablespoons of minced parsley
6 hard-cooked eggs, sliced (use an egg slicer)
Salt (if needed)
4 to 6 frozen patty shells, baked according to package directions

In a saucepan, over medium heat, melt the butter. Add the onion and cook for 2 minutes, or until soft. Stir in the flour and cook, stirring, until well-blended. Gradually add the milk and cream, stirring constantly until the sauce is smooth and medium-thick. Stir in the cayenne, mustard, ham and parsley, blending well. Carefully stir in the eggs and cook until eggs are heated through. Taste; if ham hasn't provided enough salt, add more. Serve in the patty shells.

EGG AND ELBOW MACARONI BAKE*

Serves 4:

4 tablespoons of butter
2 tablespoons of flour
2 cups of light cream or half-and-half
1 cup of grated Monterey Jack cheese
Salt and pepper to taste
1 small onion, minced

1 tablespoon of freshly grated horseradish (or prepared)
½ pound of elbow macaroni, cooked *al dente* in salted water and drained
6 hard-cooked eggs, cut into ½-inch slices
½ cup of bread crumbs

In a frypan, over medium heat, melt 2 tablespoons of the butter. Add the flour and cook, stirring into a smooth paste. Gradually add the cream and cook, stirring until the sauce is smooth and medium-thick. Add cheese and stir until melted. Stir in salt, pepper, onion and horseradish.

In a deep buttered 1½-quart casserole, arrange one-third of the macaroni. Arrange one-half of the egg slices over it. Spoon on one-third of the sauce. Repeat another layer of macaroni, egg slices and sauce, saving one-third macaroni and one-third sauce for the top. Sprinkle with the bread crumbs and dot with the remaining 2 tablespoons of butter. Bake in a preheated 350°F. oven for 30 minutes, or until heated through, bubbly and golden.

* Especially Inexpensive

SCOTCH EGGS

Serves 4: (Famous in Scotland and the British Isles, this is an all-out imaginative push from the Scots who are not noted for creative touches with food.)

8 hard-cooked eggs, shelled
Flour for dredging

blended
  1 pound of sausage meat
  1 tablespoon of chopped
    fresh chives
  1 small clove of garlic,
    minced

½ teaspoon of salt
½ teaspoon of pepper

2 eggs beaten with 2 table-
  spoons of water
Bread crumbs for dredging
Oil for deep frying

Roll the eggs in flour. Completely encase each egg with sausage meat blend. Again roll the sausage-covered eggs in flour. Dip each egg in the egg-water mixture, then dredge with bread crumbs. Let the eggs stand for 20 minutes. Fry in hot deep fat just until crisp and golden. In Scotland, they are usually served hot and whole, sometimes just with a salad, sometimes with a tart tomato sauce.

SIMPLE EGGS BENEDICT

Serves 4:

8 (½-in-thick) round slices
  of bread, toasted and buttered*
8 slices of Canadian bacon,
  lightly sautéed in butter

8 eggs, poached
1 cup of Hollandaise Sauce
  (pages 407, 408)

Have all ingredients hot. Place a slice of Canadian bacon on each slice toasted bread and top with a poached egg. Spoon over the hollandaise sauce and serve immediately.

* We find English muffins tough, difficult to cut.

BILL CARR'S EGGS BENEDICT NIÇOISE

Serves 4:

8 frozen patty shells, baked
  according to package
  directions
1½ cups of minced cooked
  ham, sautéed in 2 tablespoons of butter and 2
  ounces of sherry

8 eggs, poached and
  trimmed
1 cup of Hollandaise Sauce
  (pages 407, 408)

Have all ingredients hot. Spoon a tablespoon of the ham onto
the bottom of each patty shell. Top with a poached egg and
cover with hollandaise sauce. Sprinkle the remaining ham
over the top and serve immediately.

POACHED EGGS WITH CREAMY CHICKEN HASH

Serves 4:

4 (3-inch-thick) slices of
  sandwich bread

¼ to ½ pound of unsalted
  butter, melted

Trim the crusts from the bread so the sides are even and they
measure about 4 inches square. Hollow out the centers of the
thick bread slices with a sharp serrated paring knife, making
a bowl about 3 inches wide and 1½ inches deep. Brush the
entire surface of each (inside and out) with the melted butter. Place under a broiler turning to brown all sides. Keep
warm. (Frozen, commercial patty shells, baked according to
the package directions, may also be used, but they won't taste
so good as your own "croustades.")

4 tablespoons of butter
4 medium-large mushrooms,
  coarsely chopped
1 tablespoon of flour
½ cup of heavy cream
2 cups of Creamy Chicken
  Hash (page 215)

2 (¼-inch-thick) slices of
  boiled ham, chopped
Salt and pepper to taste
4 eggs, poached
1 cup of Hollandaise Sauce
  (pages 407, 408)

In a saucepan, over medium heat, melt the butter. Add the mushrooms and cook for 2 minutes. Add the flour and stir until well-blended. Add the cream and cook, stirring, until the sauce is smooth and medium-thick. Stir in the chicken hash, ham, salt (the ham may provide enough salt) and pepper and simmer 3 minutes, or until heated through. Taste for seasoning. Arrange the croustades on a shallow baking dish and spoon equal amounts of the hash-ham mixture into the bowl of each. Top each with an egg. Spoon the hollandaise over the eggs. Before serving, bake in a preheated 400°F. oven for 8 minutes, or until the top is golden.

POACHED EGGS WITH MUSHROOM SAUCE

Serves 2 or 4:

2 tablespoons of butter
½ pound of medium-sized fresh mushrooms, cut into ¼-inch-thick slices
1 clove of garlic, minced
1 (1-pound) can of tomatoes, drained and chopped
1 cup of chicken broth
Salt and pepper to taste
½ teaspoon of cumin

4 (½-inch-thick) slices of bread, cut into large rounds, sautéed in butter until golden on both sides and kept warm
4 slices of warm cooked ham, same size and shape as the sautéed bread
4 eggs, poached, drained, trimmed and kept warm

In a saucepan, over medium heat, melt the butter. Add the mushrooms and cook for 3 minutes, stirring several times. Remove with a slotted spoon and reserve. Add the garlic to the pan and cook for 1 minute (do not brown). Stir in tomatoes, broth, salt and pepper and simmer, uncovered, for 15 minutes, stirring until the sauce thickens. Stir in the cumin. Return the mushrooms to the pan and cook 2 or 3 minutes until heated through.

Place a slice of ham on each slice of bread and top with a poached egg. Spoon a tablespoon of sauce over each egg, the remaining sauce around the sautéed bread.

EGGS POACHED IN TOMATO SAUCE

Serves 4:

3 tablespoons of vegetable oil

1 medium-sized onion, chopped

1 clove of garlic, minced

1 (1-pound, 12-ounce) can of tomatoes, broken up

1 teaspoon of salt

¼ teaspoon of pepper

⅛ teaspoon of dried oregano

8 eggs

2 tablespoons of chopped parsley

In a large frypan, over medium heat, heat the oil. Add the onion and garlic and cook for 4 minutes, or until the onion is soft. Add the tomatoes, salt, pepper and oregano and simmer, uncovered, stirring from time to time, for 20 minutes, or until most of the watery content of the tomatoes has cooked off. Break the eggs, one at a time, into a small bowl, then slip them into the sauce. Simmer, uncovered, until the egg whites are firmly set (the yolks should be less firmly set), spooning the sauce over them. Taste for seasoning. Sprinkle with the parsley.

POACHED EGGS WITH RED FLANNEL HASH

Serves 4: This famous conbination perhaps gets its name from the beet coloring. It's delicious.

2 small onions, minced

3 cups of finely chopped boiled or baked potatoes

2 tablespoons of minced broadleaf parsley

2 tablespoons of heavy cream

½ cup of diced cooked beets

2 cups of finely chopped corned beef

1 teaspoon of salt

½ teaspoon of pepper

5 tablespoons of butter

4 jumbo eggs, poached

In a bowl, combine onion, potatoes, parsley, cream, beets, corned beef, salt and pepper, blending thoroughly. In a large frypan, over medium heat, melt half of the butter. Add the hash mixture, pressing it down like a large pancake. Cook for 15 minutes, or until hot and brown and crisp on the bottom. Loosen with a spatula. Invert a large plate over the top of the frypan. Turn frypan over so hash falls out onto the plate, brown side up. Melt remaining butter in the frypan. Slide the hash back into the pan, brown side up, and cook until bottom is brown. Cut into 4 wedges of equal size, place on 4 hot plates, top each wedge with a poached egg.

EGGS POACHED IN RED WINE

Serves 4: This is French, taught us by our mentor, great chef Antoine Gilly. A unique luncheon dish, it always receives bravos from guests who have never experienced this mating of eggs and wine.

4 slices of bread, cut ½ inch thick and 3½ inches square, crusts removed, rubbed with a cut clove of garlic and fried in butter on both sides until golden and crisp
5 tablespoons of butter
8 medium-sized mushrooms, stems removed but reserved
3 cups of dry red wine
1 cup of chicken broth
1 rib of celery, chopped

4 shallots, or 2 small white onions, chopped
1 bay leaf
½ teaspoon of sugar
⅛ teaspoon of dried thyme
½ teaspoon of salt
¼ teaspoon of pepper
8 eggs
3 tablespoons of butter, kneaded with 2 tablespoons of flour
2 tablespoons of chopped parsley

Keep the fried bread warm. In a large saucepan, heat 2 tablespoons of the butter and sauté the mushrooms (not the stems) for 3 minutes, or until evenly browned (do not overcook, they should be firm). Remove the mushrooms. In the same saucepan combine the wine, broth, celery, mushroom stems, shallots, bay leaf, sugar, thyme, salt and pepper. Simmer for 25 minutes, uncovered. Strain this liquid and return it to the saucepan. Bring to a boil, then reduce to a steady simmer. Break the eggs, one at a time, into a small bowl and slip them into the simmering liquid. Poach 2 or 3 eggs (or whatever number can be poached at one time without crowding) until the whites are firm. Remove the cooked eggs with a slotted spoon and keep warm. When the eggs are all cooked, stir the butter kneaded with flour into the simmering

wine sauce and cook, stirring, until the sauce thickens. Taste
for seasoning. Arrange the warm fried bread on four individual heated dishes. Place two eggs on each slice of bread and
top with a mushroom cap. Stir the remaining 3 tablespoons
of butter into the thickened sauce and spoon it over the eggs.
Sprinkle with the parsley.

EGGS SARDOU

Serves 4:

2 (10-ounce) packages of fresh spinach, or 2 (10-ounce) packages of frozen spinach, defrosted but not cooked	Pinch of nutmeg
	8 artichoke bottoms (canned)
	8 eggs, poached and kept warm
5 tablespoons of butter	1 cup of Hollandaise sauce
Salt and pepper to taste	(pages 407, 408), kept warm

If fresh spinach is used, bring 3 quarts of water to the boil.
Add one package of the spinach, pushing it down with a
fork. After the water comes to the boil a second time, cook
the spinach for 2 minutes, then remove it with a fork and
drain. Cook the second package of spinach in the same
water. Drain well and when cool enough squeeze as much
liquid from it as possible. Using a blender or food processor,
finely chop the spinach. This can be done well in advance.

Heat 3 tablespoons of the butter in a saucepan over
medium heat. Add the spinach (fresh cooked or frozen defrosted), season with salt, pepper and nutmeg. Cook for 3
minutes, uncovered, stirring. Keep warm.

In a frypan, heat the remaining 2 tablespoons of butter,
add the artichoke bottoms and cook for 1 minute on each
side to heat through. Season with salt and pepper.

Have all ingredients hot. Place 2 artichoke bottoms on individual heated plates. Spoon the spinach onto the artichoke
bottoms. Place a poached egg on each spinach-filled artichoke
bottom and spoon the hollandaise sauce over the eggs.

COUNTRY CHEESE OMELET WITH POTATO AND ONION

Serves 2:

3 tablespoons of butter
1 medium-sized potato, cut into ½-inch cubes
2 small onions, sliced, dredged with flour, crisply fried in oil and drained on paper towels

blended
   3 eggs, lightly beaten
   2 tablespoons of heavy cream
   ½ cup of grated provolone cheese

Salt and pepper to taste

In a frypan, over medium heat, melt the butter. Add the potatoes and cook until golden and tender. Stir in the onion. Pour in the egg-cheese mixture, season with salt and pepper. As the egg cooks, lift the edges of the omelet permitting the uncooked egg to flow under. When the egg has set, but is still creamy in the center, fold the omelet and turn out onto a hot serving dish.

EGG FOO YUNG

Serves 4:

8 eggs, beaten
1½ cups of diced fresh shrimp, sautéed in butter for 1 minute, or until they just turn pink
½ cup of frozen tiny peas, thawed
1 cup of bean sprouts, drained

12 very small mushrooms, thinly sliced
4 whole young scallions, chopped
1 teaspoon of sugar
¼ teaspoon of salt
3 tablespoons of soy sauce
½ cup of chicken broth
Peanut oil

In a large bowl, blend all ingredients except the oil. In a large frypan, heat ½ inch oil to a light sizzle. Using a small ladle, pour egg mixture into frypan. When it begins to set and stops spreading, add another ladle next to it, but allow for spreading (as you would for pancakes). Do not crowd. Cook until golden brown on each side, a little less than 1 minute on each side. Drain on paper towels. Place the omelets in a 200°F. oven to keep warm until all are cooked. Serve with a spoonful of the following sauce on each omelet.

SAUCE FOR EGG FOO YUNG

2 cups of chicken broth
¼ teaspoon of salt
⅛ teaspoon of pepper

2½ tablespoons of soy sauce
1½ tablespoons of cornstarch

In a saucepan, blend all ingredients well. Cook over medium heat, stirring, until thickened.

SIMPLE FRENCH OMELET**

Serves 2:

lightly beaten together
  5 eggs
  2 tablespoons of heavy cream

Salt and pepper to taste

2 tablespoons of butter

In an omelet pan or frypan over medium-high heat, melt the butter. Pour in the egg mixture, shake the pan and simultaneously stir the egg mixture with the back of a fork until it starts to set. When the omelet is set, but still creamy in the center, fold. Turn it out onto a hot plate and serve immediately.

** Fast and Easy

INDIVIDUAL FRENCH OMELETS FILLED WITH BRANDIED CRABMEAT

Serves 4:

BRANDIED CRABMEAT

2 cups of fresh crabmeat, picked over to remove any shell or cartilage, coarsely chopped and sautéed in 2 tablespoons of butter for 2 minutes

2 tablespoons of butter
2 tablespoons of flour
½ cup of chicken broth
1 cup of heavy cream
3 tablespoons of cognac
Salt and pepper to taste

In a saucepan, over medium heat, melt the butter. Add the flour, stirring into a smooth golden paste. Gradually stir in the broth, cream and cognac, cook, stirring, until the sauce is smooth and thickened. Season with salt and pepper. Add the crabmeat, lower heat and cook, gently stirring, for 2 minutes. Set aside to fill the omelets. Keep warm.

OMELETS

4 teaspoons of butter
12 eggs

Salt and pepper to taste
4 teaspoons of heavy cream

In a Teflon frypan, over medium heat, melt 1 teaspoon of the butter, and pour in 3 eggs that have been beaten with salt and pepper added and 1 teaspoon of cream. Lift the omelet, letting the uncooked part of the eggs flow to the edge replacing the portion that is set. Continue until omelet is set but soft and creamy in the center. Spoon one-fourth of the crabmeat mixture in the center and fold the omelet over. Transfer to a hot plate. Repeat with the remaining omelets.

FRITTATA WITH FIVE VARIATIONS*

Serves 6: We all know the omelet was originated by the French. But not everybody is familiar with the frittata, *an unusual Italian omelet. Resembling a puffy, golden cake, it is a delicious variation that requires no particular expertise.*

3 tablespoons of olive oil
3 tablespoons of butter
3 small white onions, sliced wafer thin

lightly beaten together
8 eggs
½ cup of grated Parmesan cheese
Salt and pepper to taste

In a large frypan, heat 2 tablespoons of the oil and 1 tablespoon of the butter and sauté the onion until soft. Spoon the onion into a strainer to drain off the oil. Combine the drained onion with the egg-cheese mixture, blending well. Heat the remaining oil and butter and pour in the egg-cheese-onion mixture. With the heat at medium, cook for 5 minutes, or until the bottom and sides are set and golden and the top not too runny. Loosen with a spatula, and with a plate on top of the pan, flip the *frittata* onto the plate, the uncooked side down. Slide the frittata back into the frypan (uncooked side down) and cook for 4 minutes, or until the bottom is set and golden. Serve immediately with small boiled potatoes and a nippy mustard on the side.

This is a basic *frittata*. It can be varied in interesting ways by adding, with the onion, chopped fresh tomatoes that have been sautéed in butter for 10 minutes, then drained, or diced leftover cooked meat or vegetables. Three classics: sliced, lightly cooked young zucchini, or fresh, uncooked spinach, washed, dried and coarsely chopped, or the lightly cooked, chopped flowerets of tender, young broccoli. All should be mixed with the beaten eggs.

* Especially Inexpensive

JAPANESE CHICKEN OMELET

Serves 4: The Japanese call this dish Oyako Domburi, *and serve it on individual bowls of rice.*

8 dried mushrooms, soaked in water for 20 minutes, drained, then coarsely chopped

4 whole scallions, chopped

1 whole uncooked chicken breast, skinned, boned and cut into small cubes

½ cup of chicken broth

¼ cup of *mirin* (sweet sake) or sherry

3 tablespoons of soy sauce

2 teaspoons of minced fresh ginger

3 tablespoons of peanut oil

6 eggs, beaten

4 bowls of hot, cooked short-grain rice (keep warm in a 200°F. oven or warmer)

In a bowl, combine the mushrooms, scallions and chicken. Pour in the broth, wine and soy sauce. Add ginger and blend well. In a 10-inch frypan or omelet pan, over medium heat, heat the oil and stir in the chicken mixture. Bring to a boil; reduce heat and simmer, covered, for 5 minutes, or until the chicken is almost cooked. Pour in the eggs, cover and cook for 4 minutes, or until eggs are set. Divide the omelet into 4 portions, serving each portion on top of a bowl of hot rice.

BASQUE PIPÉRADE

Serves 4 to 6:

3 tablespoons of butter

3 tablespoons of olive oil

½ cup *each* of green and red peppers, cored, seeded and cut into thin strips

1 clove of garlic, chopped

½ cup of thinly sliced white onion

1 cup of diced cooked ham

2 ripe tomatoes, peeled, seeded, coarsely chopped and drained

Salt and pepper to taste

9 eggs, beaten

3 anchovy fillets, drained and cut into thin strips

In a large frypan, over medium heat, heat the butter and oil. Add the peppers, garlic, onion and sauté for 5 minutes, or until soft. Stir in the ham and tomatoes, seasoning with salt and pepper. Simmer, uncovered, for 15 minutes, or until most of the liquid from the tomatoes has cooked off. Blend the anchovies with the eggs and stir them into the vegetable mixture. Raise the heat, stirring, scrambling the eggs for 1 minute, or until almost firm. Lower heat and cook for 3 minutes, or until the bottom of the omelet is set. Give the pan several hearty shakes, or use a spatula to loosen the *pipérade*. Slide it out onto a warm platter like a cake. Cut into wedges to serve.

POLISH EGG CAKE

Serves 6:

1 stick (¼ pound) of butter
4 tablespoons of olive oil
3 medium-sized potatoes, peeled and cut into ⅛-inch-thick slices
2 teaspoons of salt
3 medium-sized onions, chopped

1 clove of garlic, minced
½ pound of kielbasa, pricked, parboiled 3 minutes, drained, broiled 5 minutes (or until browned), then sliced into ⅛-inch-thick rounds
7 eggs

In a large frypan, over medium heat, heat half of the butter and half of the oil. Place the potatoes into the hot fat, turning until well coated, then sprinkle with 1 teaspoon of the salt. Cook, turning, for 10 minutes, or until lightly browned. Push potatoes to one side in the pan, add the garlic and onion and cook for 3 minutes. Blend the potatoes, onion, garlic and sausage in the pan and cook 5 minutes. Transfer with a slotted spoon to a strainer to drain off any fat.

In a large bowl, break the eggs, add the remaining 1 teaspoon of salt and beat until frothy. Stir the drained potatoe mixture into the eggs, blending. In a 9-inch deep frypan, heat the remaining butter and oil, over medium heat. When hot, pour in the egg mixture, spreading so it will cook evenly. Occasionally take the pan off the heat and shake vigorously or loosen with a spatula to prevent sticking. When the bottom is set (about 4 minutes), remove from the heat and place a large plate over the pan to cover. Holding the pan handle with one hand and the plate tight against the pan with the other, turn the egg cake onto the plate, (cooked side will be up). Slide the cake off the plate back into the frypan. Cook for 3 minutes longer, or until bottom is cooked.

SHELLFISH OMELET

Serves 3:

5 tablespoons of butter
2 scallions (including ⅓ of the green ends), finely chopped
1 tablespoon of flour
Dash of Tabasco
Dash of soy sauce
2 tablespoons of cream

1 cup of cooked shrimp, crabmeat, lobster, or a combination, cut into small pieces
6 eggs, lightly beaten with 2 tablespoons of cream and salt to taste

In a frypan, over medium heat, melt 2 tablespoons of the butter. Add the scallions and cook for 1 minute. Sprinkle on the flour, stirring until well-blended. Stir in the Tabasco, soy sauce and cream and simmer for 1 minute, or until smooth and very thick. Add the shellfish to heat through.

In an omelet pan or frypan, melt the remaining 3 tablespoons of butter. Pour in the egg mixture and cook, stirring with the bottom of a fork. As the egg cooks, lift the cooked portion permitting the uncooked egg to flow under. When the egg is set to your taste, spoon the shellfish mixture onto the center. Fold and turn out onto a hot serving dish.

VENEZUELAN MINI OMELETS

Serves 4: *In South America these might be served with strips of rare broiled beef. But they are excellent as a luncheon dish with hot broiled tomatoes and a green salad, or an avocado salad.*

8 eggs
1½ cups of grated Gouda or Cheddar cheese
1 teaspoon of salt
⅛ teaspoon of cayenne

4 cups of cooked narrow noodles, chopped into very small pieces
6 tablespoons of butter

In a bowl, beat the eggs, then blend in the cheese, salt, cayenne and noodles. In a frypan, over medium heat, melt 2 tablespoons of the butter. When the butter is hot, spoon in 2 tablespoonfuls of the egg-noodle mixture for each omelet. Cook 1 minute on each side, or until golden brown (do not crowd in pan). Add more butter as needed. Keep cooked omelets warm in a 200°F. oven until all are cooked.

SPICY CHEESE PIE

Serves 4:

4 eggs, lightly beaten in a large bowl
½ teaspoon of salt
½ teaspoon of Tabasco
1 cup of medium cream
½ cup of milk

2 cups of grated sharp Cheddar cheese
2 tablespoons of Dijon mustard, or other sharp mustard
1 partially baked 9-inch pastry shell

Add all other ingredients, except the pastry shell, to the egg bowl and beat to blend well. Pour into the pastry shell, place on a baking sheet and bake in a preheated 350°F. oven for 45 minutes, or until set, puffed and golden.

RICOTTA AND SPINACH CROSTATA

Serves 4:

3 tablespoons of butter
4 tablespoons of minced onion
1½ cups of chopped cooked spinach, squeezed dry
Salt and pepper to taste
¼ teaspoon of nutmeg
2 whole eggs, plus 2 egg yolks

1½ cups of medium cream
½ teaspoon of sugar
¾ cup (½ pound) of ricotta (thoroughly drained in a strainer)
¾ cup of grated Asiago or Parmesan cheese
9-inch partially baked pastry shell

In a frypan, over medium heat, melt the butter and cook the onion for 2 minutes, or until soft. Off heat, stir in the spinach, salt, pepper and nutmeg, blending well. In a bowl, beat the eggs and yolks, cream and sugar. Blend in the ricotta, the spinach mixture and half of the grated cheese. Pour into the pastry shell and sprinkle the remaining cheese on top. Place on a baking sheet and bake in a preheated 375°F. oven for 30 minutes, or until set, puffed and golden (do not overcook).

SALMON QUICHE WITH MUSHROOM SAUCE

Serves 4:

1 (1-pound) can of red salmon
2 tablespoons of butter
3 tablespoons of minced shallots
3 whole eggs, plus 1 egg yolk
1½ cups of light cream
4 tablespoons (2 ounces) of sherry

1 teaspoon of salt
¼ teaspoon of pepper
1 tablespoon of fresh minced dill, or 1 teaspoon of dried dill weed
9-inch partially baked pastry shell
Mushroom Sauce (see below)

Drain the salmon, reserving ⅓ cup of liquid. Remove and discard the skin and bones, then mash the salmon. Set aside. In a frypan, over medium heat, melt the butter and cook the shallots for 4 minutes, or until soft. In a bowl, beat the eggs and yolk, cream and sherry. Blend in the salmon, the reserved liquid, shallots, salt, pepper and dill. Pour into the pastry shell. Place on a baking sheet and bake in a preheated 375° oven for 30 minutes, or until set, puffed and golden. An inserted knife blade will emerge clean when the quiche is done (do not overcook). Serve with the Mushroom Sauce.

MUSHROOM SAUCE

About 2½ cups:

7 tablespoons of butter
4 tablespoons of minced
  white onion
½ pound of small
  mushrooms, thinly sliced

Salt and pepper to taste
3 tablespoons of flour
2 cups of chicken broth
½ cup of heavy cream

In a frypan, over medium heat, melt 2 tablespoons of the butter and cook the onion for 2 minutes, or until soft. Stir in 2 more tablespoons of butter and the mushrooms. Cook for 2 minutes, or until mushrooms are brown but still firm. Season with salt and pepper. Reserve.

In a saucepan, melt the remaining 3 tablespoons of butter. Stir in the flour and cook, stirring into a smooth golden paste. Gradually stir in the broth. Cook, stirring, until the sauce is smooth and medium-thick. Blend in the cream, the mushroom-onion mixture and simmer, stirring, until the mushroom sauce is medium-thick.

SAUSAGE CROSTATA

Serves 4: A crostata is an Italian quiche; or a quiche is a French crostata, as the Italians came up with this unique egg custard meal pie before the French even learned to eat with a knife and fork.

½ pound of sweet Italian
  sausages
Butter 9-inch partially baked
  pastry shell
2 whole eggs, plus 2 egg
  yolks
¾ cup of medium cream
¾ cup of tomato sauce

½ teaspoon of salt
¼ teaspoon of pepper
⅛ teaspoon of oregano
½ cup of grated Asiago **or**
  Parmesan cheese
½ cup of grated Fontina
  cheese

Prick the sausages with the point of a knife in several places and poach in simmering water for 15 minutes. Drain, then sauté them in butter until evenly browned, cooking off most of the fat. Cut the sausages into halves lengthwise, then cut the halves into ¼ inch slices. Arrange them on the bottom of the pastry shell. In a bowl, beat together the eggs and yolks, cream, tomato sauce, salt, pepper and oregano. Stir in the cheeses. Spoon the mixture over the sausage slices in the pastry shell. Place on a baking sheet and bake in a preheated 375°F. oven for 40 minutes, or until set, puffed and golden (do not overcook).

SCALLOP QUICHE

Serves 6:

3 tablespoons of butter
2 tablespoons of minced celery
3 tablespoons of minced scallions (white part only)
1 pound of whole bay scallops (or sliced sea scallops, but bay are best)
9-inch partially baked pastry shell

¼ cup of grated Emmentaler cheese
2 whole eggs, plus 2 egg yolks
1½ cups of light cream
⅛ teaspoon of mace
1 tablespoon of flour
4 tablespoons (2 ounces) of white vermouth
1 teaspoon of salt
¼ teaspoon of pepper

In a frypan, over medium heat, melt 2 tablespoons of the butter. Add the celery and scallions and cook for 2 minutes, or until crisp-tender. Blend with the scallops and evenly spread over the bottom of the pastry shell. Sprinkle with the cheese. In a bowl, beat the eggs and yolk, cream, mace, flour, vermouth, salt and pepper, blending well. Pour into the pastry shell. Dot with remaining 1 tablespoon of butter. Place on a baking sheet in a preheated 375°F. oven and bake for 30 minutes, or until set, puffed and golden (do not overcook).

SCRAMBLED EGGS WITH CREAM CHEESE AND MUSHROOMS

Serves 3:

blended
- ½ stick (4 tablespoons) of butter
- 6 eggs, lightly beaten
- ¼ cup of light cream
- ½ teaspoon of salt
- ¼ teaspoon of pepper
- 1 tablespoon of chopped fresh tarragon, or 1 teaspoon of dried

- 1 (3-ounce) package cream cheese, cut into small pieces
- 4 medium-sized mushrooms, sliced, sautéed for 1 minute in 2 tablespoons of butter and drained
- 2 tablespoons of chopped pimiento

In a frypan over medium heat, melt the butter. Add the egg-cream mixture and cook, stirring frequently, until the eggs begin to set. Stir in the cheese, mushrooms and pimiento and cook, stirring, until the eggs are set to your taste.

BETTY PETER'S MEXICAN EGGS

Serves 6: This simple dish, prepared in mere minutes, is perfect to serve guests who have spent the night and need to be revived next morning with an exhilarating drink and stimulating meal. The consistency should be that of scrambled eggs.

- 4 tablespoons of butter
- 1 medium-sized yellow onion, finely chopped
- 2 medium-sized ripe tomatoes, peeled, seeded and chopped
- 1½ teaspoons of chili powder

- 2 tablespoons of chopped broadleaf parsley
- 12 eggs, beaten with 4 tablespoons of heavy cream and salt and pepper to taste

In a large frypan, melt the butter over medium heat. Sauté the onion until soft. Stir in the tomatoes and chili powder and simmer until all of the liquid from the tomato has cooked off. Stir in the parsley, then the egg-cream mixture.

Stir gently, letting the uncooked part of the egg work its way to the bottom of the pan until the eggs are cooked but not dry (10 minutes over medium heat should do it).

SALAMI-SCRAMBLED EGGS

Serves 4: An excellent breakfast for those guests who stayed after a hard night of elbow-bending. Serve with Bloody Marys.

6 tablespoons of butter
4 medium-sized onions, coarsely chopped
1 cup of diced salami
½ cup of diced provolone (or other very sharp) cheese

beaten together in a large bowl
8 eggs
⅔ cup of light cream

4 medium-sized ripe tomatoes, skinned, seeded and thickly sliced
2 tablespoons of chopped fresh basil

In a deep frypan, over medium heat, melt 3 tablespoons of the butter and cook the onion, stirring, for 5 minutes, or until soft. Add the onion, salami and cheese to the egg-cream bowl and blend well. In the frypan in which the onion cooked, over medium heat, melt the remaining 3 tablespoons of butter. Pour in the egg mixture and cook, stirring, until just set. Taste for seasoning. Serve garnished with tomato slices sprinkled with the basil.

EGGS SCRAMBLED WITH SHRIMP**

Serves 6:

10 eggs, lightly beaten
8 whole scallions, chopped
2 teaspoons of salt
6 tablespoons of peanut oil

1 pound of medium shrimp, shelled, deveined and each cut into 3 pieces

** Fast and Easy

In a bowl, combine the eggs, scallons, salt and 2 tablespoons of the oil, blending well. In a large frypan, over medium heat, heat remaining 4 tablespoons oil and stir-fry the shrimp for 10 seconds, or just until they begin to turn pink. Lower heat, and pour the egg mixture over the shrimp. Stirring gently, let the uncooked part of the eggs work to the bottom of the pan. Continue until the eggs are just set but still creamy and soft.

EGG SCRAPPLE*

Serves 6:

4 tablespoons of butter	1 teaspoon of salt
1 tablespoon of olive oil	½ teaspoon of pepper
2 small green peppers, cored, seeded and diced	2 medium-sized ripe tomatoes, peeled, seeded and diced
2 small white onions, chopped	8 eggs, separated
4 small potatoes, peeled and diced	

In a large, shallow top-of-the-stove-to-oven pan, heat the butter and oil over medium heat. Sauté the peppers and onion for 4 minutes, or until tender-crisp. Stir in the potatoes and season with salt and pepper. Cover the pan, lower heat and simmer for 15 minutes, or until potatoes are tender. Stir in the tomatoes. Remove from heat. In a bowl, beat the egg yolks until light and fluffy. In another bowl, beat the egg whites until stiff. Fold the whites into the yolks, then blend with the tomato mixture. Bake covered, in a preheated 350°F. oven for 15 minutes. Remove cover and cook 10 minutes longer, or until set and golden brown.

* Especially Inexpensive

FRENCH TOAST

Serves 4: This is an excellent luncheon dish served with bacon, ham or sausage. Called Pain Perdu, *"lost bread," in French, it actually means stale bread.*

5 jumbo eggs	½ teaspoon of vanilla
1 tablespoon of sugar	8 large slices of French or
2 cups of heavy cream	Italian bread
⅛ teaspoon of mace	7 tablespoons of butter

Beat together the eggs, sugar, cream, mace and vanilla (use an electric beater on low speed). In a shallow casserole or baking dish, place the bread, not overlapping, and cover each slice with the egg mixture. Refrigerate overnight to allow bread to absorb the egg mixture.

In a large frypan, melt the butter over medium heat and brown the bread evenly. Serve warm, as you serve pancakes with the same accompaniments.

ITALIAN FRIED EGGS**

Serves 2:

3 tablespoons of olive oil	⅛ teaspoon of finely
4 eggs	crushed red pepper flakes
1 teaspoon of salt	4 teaspoons of grated Romano cheese

In a frypan, over medium heat, heat oil. Break eggs, one at a time, in a saucer and slide them into the hot oil. Fry gently, sprinkle with salt and red pepper, and remove from heat when eggs are set to taste. Sprinkle 1 teaspoon of cheese over each egg. Run the eggs under a broiler until the cheese is melted.

** Fast and Easy

SPAGHETTI CARBONARA

Serves 6:

2 tablespoons of butter
2 tablespons of olive oil
2 small white onions,
  chopped
½ cup of dry white wine
5 slices of bacon, diced

beat together
  3 eggs

⅔ cup of grated Asiago or
  Parmesan cheese
2 tablespoons of chopped
  parsley

1 pound of spaghetti, cooked
  al dente in salted water,
  drained and kept hot
Black pepper

In a saucepan, over medium heat, heat the butter and oil. Add onion and cook until soft. Stir in the wine and bacon. Raise heat to quickly cook off the wine. Continue cooking until the bacon just begins to brown. Remove pan from heat and quickly mix in the egg-cheese mixture. Toss carefully with the hot spaghetti, generously milling on black pepper. Serve immediately before the hot bacon and hot pasta can completely set the eggs.

SPINACH EGG CUSTARD

Serves 6 to 8:

2 tablespoons of oil
1 tablespoon of butter
2 medium-sized onions,
  chopped
1 clove of garlic, minced
2 (10-ounce) packages
  frozen chopped spinach,
  defrosted and liquid
  squeezed out

1 teaspoon of salt
¼ teaspoon of pepper
1½ cups of shredded Muen-
  ster cheese
1 cup of shredded sharp
  Cheddar cheese
½ cup of cottage cheese
6 eggs, beaten with ½ cup of
  light cream in a large bowl

In a saucepan, over medium heat, heat the oil and butter and sauté the onion and garlic for 3 minutes, or until soft. Lower heat, add the spinach and cook 2 minutes longer, stirring. Stir the salt, pepper and cheeses into the egg-cream bowl, blending thoroughly. Combine the spinach mixture with the egg-cream-cheese mixture and blend well. Pour into a buttered 2-quart baking dish and bake, uncovered, in a preheated 375°F. oven for 40 minutes, (stirring twice during the first 20 minutes of cooking time), or until just set. Do not overcook.

WELSH RABBIT

Serves 4: Sometimes it is called "rarebit," but always pronounced "rabbit."

2 tablespoons of butter

beaten together
  2 egg yolks
  ½ teaspoon of paprika
  ½ teaspoon of salt
  1 teaspoon of Worcestershire sauce

½ teaspoon of dry mustard
⅛ teaspoon of Tabasco
½ cup of beer

½ pound of grated sharp Cheddar cheese
4 large slices of toast (Italian bread is excellent)

In a double boiler, over barely simmering water, melt the butter. Stir in the beaten egg yolk mixture. When it is hot (do not boil) and starts to thicken, add the cheese, large tablespoonfuls at a time, stirring constantly until the cheese has melted and the sauce is creamy smooth. Taste for seasoning. Spoon over the toast.

VARIATION: GOLDEN BUCK
Place a poached egg atop each piece of toast, then spoon the cheese mixture over it.

Chapter Five

Croquettes, Fritters, Non-Dessert Puddings, Non-Dessert Souffles, etc.

The marriage ties that bind in cookery are eggs. Without their cohesive influence such tasty and unique foods as croquettes and fritters would be impossible; puddings would be poorer, many dumplings would have to be dumped, soufflés would end up as sauces. Actually, soufflés are simply sauces that have been enriched by egg yolks, lightened by beaten egg whites and baked in the oven. They emerge puffed high, golden brown, fragile castles in the air that collapse quickly. So they must be served even more quickly.

Constructed of many fine ingredients, cheese, chicken, fish, seafoods, herbs and vegetables, these soufflés that make a meal, might be called gossamer or cloud omelets. But they aren't, for soufflés rise above comparison. With a distinct personality of their own, soufflés are among the most special of all egg creations, impressive to behold, a light and delectable food without equal.

EGG CROQUETTES

Serves 4:

1 tablespoon of butter	Salt to taste
1 tablespoon of flour	Cracker crumbs for dredging
⅔ cup of light cream	(about 2 cups)
⅛ teaspoon of cayenne	1 egg, beaten
6 hard-cooked eggs, finely chopped	Vegetable oil for deep frying

In a frypan, over medium heat, melt the butter. Add the flour and stir into a smooth paste. Gradually pour in the cream and stir into a smooth thick sauce. Add cayenne and cool. Add the eggs to the sauce, mixing well. Season to taste. Form into 12 or more croquettes. Dredge with crumbs, dip in egg then back into the crumbs. Deep fry in hot vegetable oil until golden and crisp. Drain on paper towels.

EGG-RICE CROQUETTES

Serves 6:

8 hard-cooked eggs, minced	⅛ teaspoon of Tabasco
2 eggs, beaten	1 teaspoon of salt
1 cup of cooked rice	Bread crumbs for dredging
2 tablespoons of catsup	5 tablespoons of butter
1 small onion, minced	1 tablespoon of olive oil
¼ teaspoon of paprika	

In a bowl, combine all ingredients except the bread crumbs, butter and oil, and blend well. Shape into small croquettes and dredge with bread crumbs. In a frypan, over medium heat, heat the butter and oil and fry the croquettes, turning, about 5 minutes, or until crisp and golden brown. Add more butter, if needed.

CROQUETTES, LAKE FUSCHL STYLE

Serves 4:

4 medium-sized unpeeled potatoes (about 1½ pounds),
cooked, drained, dried,
peeled and riced
3 eggs, beaten
¾ cup of flour
½ cup of white cornmeal

3 tablespoons of soft butter
1 tablespoon of minced onion
1½ teaspoons of salt
½ teaspoon of pepper
Oil for deep frying

In a large bowl, combine all the ingredients except the oil, blending well. If potatoes were hot when mixed, cool mixture. Heat the oil in a deep frypan, over medium heat, to about 375°F. Carefully lower the croquettes by the tablespoonful into the hot oil (do not crowd). Cook until crisp and evenly browned, about 5 minutes. Remove with a slotted spoon and drain on paper towels.

HAM AND EGG CROQUETTES

Serves 6:

5 tablespoons of butter
4 medium-sized mushrooms,
minced
4 tablespoons (2 ounces) of
sherry
2 cups of minced cooked
ham
3 hard-cooked eggs, minced

3 tablespoons of flour
1 cup of light cream
2 egg yolks, beaten
Salt and pepper to taste
Flour for dredging
2 eggs, beaten
Bread crumbs for dredging
Oil for deep frying

In a saucepan, over medium heat, melt 2 tablespoons of the butter and sauté the mushrooms for 1 minute. Stir in the wine and ham and cook until most of the wine and mushroom liquid has evaporated. Stir in the minced eggs and set aside. In another saucepan, over low heat, melt the remaining 3 tablespoons of butter, add flour and cook, stirring, into a smooth golden paste. Gradually add the cream, stirring constantly, until the sauce is smooth and thick. Cool for 10 minutes, then stir in the egg yolks. Spoon enough of the sauce into the ham mixture to bind well. Season with salt and pepper. Chill. Roll into cylinders 1 inch in diameter and 2 inches long. Dredge cylinders in flour, dip in the beaten egg, then dredge in bread crumbs. Fry in hot deep fat (390°F.) until crisp and golden, about 3 to 4 minutes. Drain on paper towels and keep warm in a 200°F. oven until all are cooked. Served with a sauce of your choice.

AUSTRIAN DUMPLINGS

Serves 4:

7 slices of bacon
2 onions, minced
2 tablespoons of minced broadleaf parsley
¼ teaspoon of savory
4 cups of bread crumbs

3 eggs, beaten with ¼ cup of light cream
½ cup of flour
½ teaspoon of salt
½ teaspoon of pepper
Flour

In a frypan, fry the bacon until almost crisp. Cool and mince. Add the onion to the bacon fat and cook over medium heat for 3 minutes, or until soft. Remove with a slotted spoon, leaving the bacon fat in the frypan. In a bowl, combine the bacon, onion, parsley and savory, blending well. Set aside.

Over low heat, sauté the bread crumbs in the bacon fat, stirring, for 4 minutes. In a large bowl, mix the bread crumbs with the beaten eggs and cream, blending well. Beat in the flour, salt and pepper. Cover and let set for 20 minutes. Sprinkle flour lightly on waxed paper. Spoon the bread crumb dough out of the bowl in tablespoonfuls onto the flour, pressing each spoonful of dough down into flat 3-inch circles. Place a teaspoon of the bacon mixture in the center of each circle. With your hands, carefully roll into balls, encasing the bacon filling. In a pot, bring water to a boil, reduce heat so water barely simmers. Carefully spoon the dumplings in, cooking them about 4 minutes, or until they float to the top. Remove from the pot with a slotted spoon and drain on paper towels.

CLAM FRITTERS

Serves 4:

4 egg yolks
3 whole tender young scallions, minced
⅛ teaspoon of dill weed
½ teaspoon of salt
⅛ teaspoon of cayenne

¼ cup of flour, sifted
2 cups of minced canned
clams, drained
4 egg whites, stiffly beaten
Oil for deep frying

In a bowl, beat the egg yolks with the scallions, dill weed, salt, cayenne and flour. Blend in the clams. Fold the egg whites into the clam mixture. In a deep frypan, or deep fryer, using medium-high heat, heat the oil (at least 2 inches) and drop the clam mixture in by the tablespoonful (do not crowd). Fry until crisp and evenly browned. Drain on paper towels. Serve hot with mustards or sauces of your choice. An extra spicy tartare sauce is excellent.

VARIATIONS
Substitute conch, crab, oysters, mussels or shrimp for the clams.

VEGETABLE VARIATIONS FOR CLAM FRITTERS
Substitute grated, well-drained zucchini, carrot or other vegetables for the seafood, in the same amount, adding other herbs and spices as preferred.

SOUTHERN CORN FRITTERS

Serves 4:

2 eggs, beaten
2 cups of cooked corn kernels (fresh is best, but
canned or frozen, drained,
may be used
2½ tablespoons of flour

½ teaspoon of salt
¼ teaspoon of pepper
½ teaspoon of sugar
⅛ teaspoon of nutmeg
4 tablespoons of butter
1 tablespoon of cooking oil

In a bowl, combine the eggs, corn, flour, salt, pepper, sugar and nutmeg, blending well. In a frypan, over medium-high heat, heat the butter and oil (do not let the butter brown). Ladle the corn mixture in, 1 heaping tablespoonful at a time, with space between each spoonful. Each panful will take about 3 minutes, 1½ minutes on each side. Add more butter, if needed. Fritters should be crisp and golden-brown. Drain on paper towels, and keep warm in a low oven until the Southern Fried Chicken (page 142) is ready.

VARIATION

Some Southern cooks separate the eggs, adding the beaten yolks first with the corn mixture, then beating the whites until stiff and folding them in just before cooking. This produces lighter fritters.

ZUCCHINI FRITTERS

Serves 4:

5 medium-sized zucchini, unpeeled and cut into ½-inch slices
Salt and pepper
Flour for dredging

3 eggs, beaten with 1 tablespoon of milk
Bread crumbs for dredging
Oil for frying

Sprinkle zucchini slices with salt and pepper, dredge in flour, dip in beaten egg, then dredge in bread crumbs. In a deep frypan, over medium high heat, heat oil just to sizzling and fry the zucchini slices, completely submerged in the hot oil, until crisp and evenly browned. Drain on paper towels and serve hot as an unusually tasty vegetable.

COD PUDDING*

Serves 6:

2½ pounds of fresh codfish (or any inexpensive sea fish)
1 small bay leaf
2 carrots, sliced
2 onions, sliced
1½ teaspoons of salt
½ teaspoon of pepper
3 tablespoons of butter
3 tablespoons of flour

1 cup of fish stock (see below)

beaten together
1 cup of milk
2 eggs

Salt and pepper to taste
½ cup of buttered bread crumbs

In a large saucepan, place the cod, bay leaf, carrots, onions, salt and pepper. Cover with water, bring to a boil, reduce heat and simmer for 12 minutes, or until the fish can be flaked with a fork. Remove the cod, drain and flake it. Over high heat, reduce the liquid the fish cooked in to 1 cup. Strain and set aside. In a saucepan, over medium heat, melt the butter, add the flour, stirring into a smooth golden paste. Gradually stir in the reduced fish stock and cook, stirring, until smooth and thickened. Reduce heat and stir in the milk-egg mixture. Cook, stirring, into a smooth thick sauce (do not boil). Season with salt and pepper. Stir in the flaked fish and heat through. Butter a casserole, pour in the fish-sauce mixture. Sprinkle with the bread crumbs and bake, uncovered, in a preheated 375°F. oven for 25 minutes, or until crusty-brown on top.

* Especially Inexpensive

MARIAN LOVING'S VIRGINIA CORN PUDDING**

Serves 4: This can be prepared 2 hours before baking.

2 cups of fresh corn kernels
3 egg yolks, beaten
2 tablespoons of sugar
¼ teaspoon of salt

2 tablespoons of melted butter
1½ cups of milk
1 tablespoon of tapioca
3 egg whites, stiffly beaten

In a large bowl, blend the corn, egg yolks, sugar, salt, butter, milk and tapioca. Fold in the egg whites. Pour into a buttered baking dish and bake, uncovered, in a preheated 350°F. oven for 45 minutes, or until the center of the pudding is set.

** Fast and Easy

POLENTA

Serves 6: Polenta, or Italian corn pudding, is excellent served with meats or poultry cooked in tomato sauce.

2 teaspoons of salt	5 tablespoons of butter, in small pieces
5 cups of boiling water in a large saucepan	1 cup of grated Asiago or Parmesan cheese
2½ cups of yellow cornmeal	1 large egg, beaten

Add the salt to the boiling water. Stir in the cornmeal, small amounts at a time, stirring constantly, and keeping the water boiling. When all of the cornmeal has been added, reduce the heat to low, and simmer for 30 minutes, uncovered, stirring almost constantly so that it won't become lumpy or stick to the pan. When it is finished cooking, a spoon will stand upright in the thick smooth mush. Off the heat, stir in the butter and cheese, blending well until the cheese has melted. Stir in the egg. Cover the pot and let stand for 10 minutes.

CZECHOSLOVAKIAN EGG-POTATO PUDDING

Serves 6:

4 large baking potatoes, peeled and finely grated	1½ teaspoons of salt
2 medium-sized onions, finely grated	2 teaspoons of paprika
5 eggs, beaten	½ teaspoon of pepper
2 tablespoons of minced broadleaf parsley	2 tablespoons of melted butter, blended with 1 tablespoon of olive oil

Butter a ring mold large enough to hold all ingredients. Place the potatoes in a strainer for 5 minutes to drain excess water. In a bowl, combine potatoes, onion, eggs, parsley, salt, paprika and pepper. Blend well. Spoon the mixture into the mold. Dribble the butter-oil mixture over the top. Place on a baking sheet and bake in a preheated 400°F. oven for 50 minutes, or until the top forms a golden crust. Loosen sides with a spatula and invert onto a hot serving dish. The center of the ring can be filled with a variety of creamed vegetables, or sour-creamed dried beef or chicken, etc. Or the pudding can be served in thick slices just as it is.

TURNIP PUDDING

Serves 6:

4 tablespoons of butter	1 teaspoon of salt
¼ cup of minced celery	½ teaspoon of pepper
1 small onion, minced	¼ teaspoon of mace
1½ tablespoons of flour	2 eggs, beaten
1 tablespoon of sugar	½ cup of buttered bread crumbs
1½ cups of hot light cream	
1 medium-sized turnip, cooked, drained and mashed	

In a saucepan, over medium heat, melt 2 tablespoons of the butter and cook the celery and onion for 3 minutes, or until soft. Stir in the remaining 2 tablespoons of butter and flour, stirring, blending well and cooking 1 minute. Stir in the sugar. Gradually add the cream and cook, stirring, until thickened. Place in a bowl and blend in the turnip, salt, pepper, mace and eggs. When well mixed, pour into a buttered casserole of sufficient size. Sprinkle with the bread crumbs and bake, uncovered, in a preheated 350°F. oven for 35 minutes, or until an inserted knife blade emerges clean.

VARIATION
Make a variety of these vegetable puddings, substituting for the turnip, carrots, parsnips, Brussels sprouts, broccoli, etc.

SIMPLE BROCCOLI SOUFFLÉ**

Serves 6:

¼ cup of flour
½ cup of mayonnaise
1½ cups of milk
1 teaspoon of salt
½ cup of grated Asiago or
Parmesan cheese

1 (10-ounce) package of
frozen chopped broccoli,
defrosted and drained
4 egg yolks, lightly beaten
5 egg whites, stiffly beaten

In a saucepan, combine the flour and mayonnaise and blend well. Place on low heat, slowly add the milk. Cook, stirring, until thickened. Stir in the salt and cheese and cook, stirring, until the cheese has melted. Remove from heat and cool briefly. Blend in the broccoli and egg yolks. Fold in the egg whites. Pour into a buttered 1½-quart soufflé dish or a round casserole. Bake, uncovered, in a preheated 300°F. oven for 1 hour, or until brown and puffed.

** Fast and Easy

ITALIAN CHEESE SOUFFLÉ

Serves 6:

3 tablespoons of butter
3 tablespoons of flour
1½ cups of light cream
5 egg yolks, beaten
1 cup of finely crumbled
Gorgonzola cheese
1 teaspoon of Dijon mustard

⅛ teaspoon of cayenne
⅛ teaspoon of nutmeg
7 egg whites, stiffly beaten
with ⅛ teaspoon of salt
and ⅛ teaspoon of cream
of tartar

In a saucepan, over medium heat, melt the butter. Add the flour, stirring into a smooth golden paste. Gradually stir in the cream, stirring until the sauce is smooth and thick. Remove from the heat. Blend in the egg yolks, cheese, mustard, cayenne and nutmeg. Fold in (but do not overfold) the egg whites. Pour into a buttered 8-cup soufflé dish. Place on a baking sheet and bake in a preheated 375°F. oven for 35 minutes, or until set, puffed and golden. The top should be firm to the touch.

BREAST OF CHICKEN SOUFFLÉ

Serves 4:

3 tablespoons of butter
2 tablespoons of flour
1 cup of hot milk
½ cup of chicken broth
1 teaspoon of salt
½ teaspoon of pepper
¼ teaspoon of dried thyme
⅛ teaspoon of nutmeg

2 tablespoons of Madeira
½ cup of bread crumbs
½ teaspoon of grated lemon rind
1 cup of minced cooked breast of chicken
3 egg yolks
4 egg whites, stiffly beaten

In a saucepan, over medium heat, melt the butter and stir in the flour, blending into a smooth golden paste. Gradually stir in the milk and broth, stirring until it is smooth and thickish. Stir in the salt, pepper, thyme, nutmeg and wine, blending well. Blend in the bread crumbs, lemon rind and chicken. Then beat in the egg yolks, one at a time. Fold in the egg whites. Pour into a buttered soufflé dish. Bake, uncovered, in a preheated 400°F. oven for 35 minutes, or until the soufflé is puffed, set in the center and golden.

GRITS SOUFFLÉ

Serves 6: Good with stew type dishes or simply cooked red meat.

2 cups of milk
2 cups of water
1 cup of grits
1 teaspoon of salt
1 stick (¼ pound) of butter

2 cups of grated Cheddar cheese
2 egg yolks, beaten with ¾ cup milk
3 egg whites, stiffly beaten

In a saucepan, bring the milk and water to a boil, add grits and salt. Lower heat and simmer, stirring constantly, until mixture is very thick. Add the butter and cheese and stir until melted. Remove from heat, cool about 10 minutes, then quickly stir in the egg yolk-milk mixture. Fold in the egg whites and pour into a buttered, shallow baking dish. Bake in a preheated 325°F. oven for 45 to 60 minutes until set and golden on top.

CURRIED LAMB SOUFFLÉ

Serves 4:

2 tablespoons of butter
6 scallions (white part only), chopped
2 teaspoons of curry powder
¼ teaspoon of cumin
1½ tablespoons of flour
¾ cup of beef broth

4 egg yolks, beaten
¾ cup of cooked chopped lean lamb
5 egg whites, stiffly beaten with ⅛ teaspoon of salt and ⅛ teaspoon of cream of tartar

In a saucepan, over medium heat, melt the butter and sauté the scallions for 3 minutes, or until soft. Stir in the curry powder and cumin and cook for 1 minute, stirring. Add the flour, blending well. Gradually add the broth, stirring, until the sauce is thick and smooth. Remove from the heat and add the egg yolks, blending well. Blend in the lamb. Fold in (but do not overfold) the egg whites. Butter 4 individual soufflé dishes. Spoon the mixture in, place on a baking sheet and bake in a preheated 400°F. oven for 15 minutes, or until set, puffed and golden. Tops should be firm to the touch.

POTATO-CHEESE SOUFFLÉ

Serves 4 to 6:

3 cups of mashed potatoes (3 large potatoes, about 1½ pounds)
¼ cup of milk
3 eggs, beaten

4 scallions, (⅓ of the green tail), minced
½ teaspoon of salt
½ teaspoon of pepper
2 cups of shredded sharp Cheddar cheese

In a large bowl, combine the potatoes with the milk. Stir in the remaining ingredients. Pour into a buttered soufflé dish and bake in a preheated 375°F. oven for 50 minutes, or until set in the center and golden on top. Serve immediately.

SOUFFLÉED BAKED POTATOES

Serves 6:

6 large, long baking potatoes
Oil
6 tablespoons of butter
¼ cup of cream
Salt and pepper to taste
1 tablespoon of chopped
  fresh chives

3 slices of bacon, cooked until crisp, drained and
  crumbled
2 egg yolks, slightly beaten
2 egg whites, stiffly beaten

Wash, dry and rub the potatoes with oil. Prick in several places with the point of a knife and bake in a preheated 425°F. oven for 40 to 60 minutes, or until tender. Cut a slice off each potato lengthwise, about one-third (or less) the size of the potato. Scoop out all of the pulp and put through a ricer. Discard the skin from the smaller part. In a bowl, combine the riced potato, butter, cream, salt, pepper, chives and bacon and blend well. Beat in the egg yolks. Fold in the egg whites. Heap the mixture back into the potato shells and bake in a preheated 375°F. oven for 15 minutes, or until the potatoes are puffed and golden. Serve immediately.

SPINACH SOUFFLÉ

Serves 4 to 6:

1 (10-ounce) package of
   fresh spinach, or 1 (10-
   ounce) package of frozen
   chopped spinach, defrosted
   and drained
4 tablespoons of butter
6 shallots
¼ cup of flour

1 cup of milk
1 teaspoon of salt
½ teaspoon of pepper
¼ teaspoon of mace
1 cup of grated Gruyère
   cheese
4 egg yolks, lightly beaten
5 egg whites, stiffly beaten

If fresh spinach is used, remove tough stems and wash. In a
large pot bring 3 quarts of water to a boil. Add the spinach,
pushing it down into the water with a large fork. Bring the
water to a boil again, cook the spinach for 1 minute, pushing
it down into the water as it floats to the top, then lift it out
with the fork. Drain well and chop.

In a large saucepan, over medium heat, melt the butter and
sauté the shallots just until soft, about 1 minute. Stir in the
flour. When well blended and smooth, gradually stir in the
milk, salt, pepper and mace. Simmer, stirring constantly, until
the sauce is smooth and thickened. Add the cheese and stir
until melted. Remove pan from the heat, stir in the spinach,
cool slightly, then stir in the beaten egg yolks. Fold in the
whites (do not overmix). Pour into a buttered soufflé dish
with a collar and bake in a preheated 375°F. oven for 30
minutes, or until set, puffed and top is golden (do not overcook). Serve immediately.

FRENCH FRIED EGGS

*Serves 4: Here's a unique dish none of your guests will have
had.*

1 cup of cooking oil
8 eggs
Salt and pepper

8 slices of Canadian bacon,
   sautéed in butter until
   slightly browned

In a deep frypan, over medium high heat, heat the oil until
very hot. Break an egg into a small saucer. Salt the white

lightly. Hold the pan at a slight angle and slide the egg into the sizzling oil. Immediately turn the egg over, as the white should not bubble. Gently push the white down, just until the underside of the egg is brown. Turn it over and brown the other side. Quickly and gently does it. Drain the egg and keep warm in a 200°F. oven until the other eggs are cooked. Cook only 1 egg at a time. Serve the eggs on top of the sautéed Canadian bacon, sprinkled lightly with salt and pepper. Also serve hot French bread toasted and buttered.

CHICKEN QUENELLES WITH MADEIRA SAUCE

Serves 6: Make the sauce first as the quenelles are best served as soon as possible after being poached.

MADEIRA SAUCE

¼ pound of medium-sized mushrooms, sliced	*blended*
3 tablespoons of butter	1 egg yolk
1½ tablespoons of flour	1 cup of heavy cream
1 cup of chicken broth	4 tablespoons (2 ounces) Madeira wine
	Salt and pepper to taste

In a saucepan, over medium heat, cook the mushrooms in the butter until just brown, but still very firm. Sprinkle with the flour and mix well. Gradually stir in the broth, stirring until the sauce is smooth, seasoning with salt and pepper. Lower heat and stir in the egg yolk mixture. Cook (do not boil), stirring, until the sauce thickens.

QUENELLES

2 egg whites	Pinch of cayenne
1½ pounds of raw chicken breast put through fine blade of food chopper three times or pureed in a food processor	1 teaspoon of salt
	2½ cups of very cold heavy cream
¼ teaspoon of nutmeg	Chicken broth for poaching *quenelles*

In a large bowl, over a bowl of ice, very gradually beat the egg whites into the chicken meat with a wooden spoon. Add the nutmeg, cayenne and salt. Thoroughly chill in refrigerator. Add the cream, again very gradually, mixing well each time part of the cream is added. Refrigerate again to chill thoroughly.

Have a well-buttered pan ready (a frypan or any shallow pan that can be set on heat). Shape the *quenelles* by using two soupspoons or teaspoons (depending on the size you want, remembering that they will double in size as they cook). Dip both spoons into hot water, scoop out a spoonful with one and cup it with the other spoon to give it an egg shape. Dip the spoons in the hot water before making each *quenelle*. Arrange them in the buttered pan, side by side, slightly spaced (for allowing expansion). Pour enough simmering chicken broth around the *quenelles* (not on top of them as they can disintegrate easily) to cover them and simmer 5 minutes over low heat, or until they rise to the surface. Remove the *quenelles* with a slotted spoon and keep warm. Serve with the Madeira Sauce spooned over them.

SQUASH PIE

Serves 6: Here, the eggs in this unique dish solve the problem of serving the same old vegetables.

unpeeled and coarsely grated
  ½ pound of zucchini
  ½ pound of summer
     squash

1 teaspoon of salt
4 eggs, beaten

2 cups of grated Gruyère
  cheese
½ teaspoon of dill weed
¼ teaspoon of dried oregano
½ cup of grated Asiago or
  Parmesan cheese
Tomatoes and cucumbers,
  peeled and sliced

In a bowl, place the squash, sprinkle with salt and set aside for 20 minutes. Place in a cloth and squeeze out all liquid. In a bowl, combine the squash, eggs, Gruyère cheese, dill weed and oregano and blend well. Pour into a buttered 8-inch-square baking pan or dish, or a quiche pan of sufficient size, sprinkling the top with the Asiago or Parmesan cheese. Bake, uncovered, in a preheated 350°F. oven for 35 minutes, or until the pie is set in the center and all edges golden brown. Serve with the tomatoes and cucumbers.

SPOON BREAD

Serves 6:

2 eggs
1 cup of milk
1 cup of buttermilk
⅓ cup of white cornmeal
2 teaspoons of baking powder

½ teaspoon of baking soda
½ teaspoon of salt
2 tablespoons of melted butter

In a bowl, beat the eggs until light and fluffy. Stir in the remaining ingredients, blending well. Butter a casserole and pour the mixture into it. Bake, uncovered, in a preheated 450°F. oven for 30 minutes, or until the center is set. When cooked properly, it is custardlike and light.

SAVANNAH SPOON BREAD

Serves 6 to 8:

1 cup of white cornmeal
1½ cups of water
2½ cups of light cream, scalded
1 teaspoon of salt
8 small mushrooms, minced and sautéed in 4 table-

spoons of butter for 4 minutes
1 cup of minced good ham, preferably Smithfield
¼ teaspoon of nutmeg
4 egg yolks, beaten
4 egg whites, stiffly beaten

In a saucepan, stir the cornmeal into the water, then stir in the cream and cook over low heat, stirring constantly, until thick. Stir in the salt, mushrooms, ham and nutmeg, blending well. Remove from heat, cooling slightly. Blend in the egg yolks, then fold in the egg whites. Pour into a buttered baking dish or soufflé dish, and bake, uncovered, in a preheated 400°F. oven for 40 minutes, or until puffed, set in the center and golden.

Chapter Six

Specialties, Pasta, Breads, Pancakes, etc.

Here are those foods that wouldn't be possible, or at the very least, wouldn't be nearly as palatable if it weren't for the egg. Lacy, delectable crêpes stuffed with so many delicious fillings, popovers, waffles, certain breads and pancakes.

The egg is many things to many people, but, above all, it is a specialist, too.

A specialist in making those batters and doughs without which our cuisine would be much poorer.

OLD-FASHIONED CORN BREAD

Serves 8 to 10:

2 cups of white or yellow cornmeal
¾ cup of sifted flour
4 teaspoons of baking powder
1½ teaspoons of salt
2 teaspoons of sugar

blended
4 eggs, beaten
1½ cups of milk

⅓ cup of medium cream
½ cup of melted butter
Lard

In a bowl, combine the cornmeal, flour, baking powder, salt and sugar, blending well. Mix in the eggs-milk. Beat into a smooth batter. Beat in cream and butter. Rub an oven-proof frypan with lard and place on high heat just until it begins to smoke. Remove. Pour the batter evenly into the hot skillet. Bake in a preheated 400°F. oven for 25 minutes, or until the corn bread is golden brown and an inserted knife blade emerges clean.

EGG BREAD

Makes 2 loaves:

2 cups of scalded milk
1 stick (¼ pound) of butter, in small pieces
2 tablespoons of honey

combined in a measuring cup, stirred well and covered

2 packages of active dry yeast
⅓ cup warm water
2 teaspoons of sugar

4 egg yolks, beaten
2 teaspoons of salt
6 cups of unbleached flour

In a bowl large enough to hold all the ingredients, combine the milk, butter and honey, stirring until the butter has melted. When the yeast has doubled in volume and is foaming, add it to the milk, blending well. Stir in the egg yolks, salt and 2 cups of the flour, beating well until blended and bubbling. Work in the remaining flour, ½ cup at a time, making a soft to slightly firm dough. Knead on a lightly floured pastry board for 15 minutes. Butter a warm bowl, add the dough, turning to completely coat it with the butter. Cover and set in a warm place until dough doubles in volume. Punch down and let rise again. Shape into two loaves of equal size on a lightly floured board. Put into buttered lightly floured bread pans of sufficient size. Cover, set in warm place until dough doubles in volume, or reaches the top of the bread pans. Bake in a preheated 400°F. oven for 10 minutes, reduce heat to 350°F. oven and bake for 30 minutes, or until golden brown.

BAVARIAN WHITE POTATO BREAD

Makes 1 loaf:

3 eggs, beaten
½ cup of unseasoned mashed potatoes
1 teaspoon of salt
3 tablespoons of melted butter

combined in a measuring cup, stirred well and covered

1 package of active dry yeast
½ cup of milk, scalded then cooled to lukewarm
1 teaspoon of sugar

½ teaspoon of baking powder
3 cups of unbleached flour

In a bowl large enough to hold all ingredients, combine the eggs, potatoes, salt and butter, blending well. When the yeast has doubled in volume and is foaming, add it to the bowl with the baking powder and 1 cup of flour. Blend well. Add remaining flour ½ cup at a time, mixing thoroughly. Knead well on a lightly floured pastry board for about 15 minutes, or until the dough is smooth, firm and elastic. Butter a warm bowl, add the dough, turning to completely coat it with butter. Cover, set in a warm place until dough doubles in volume. Punch down and let rise again until doubled. Knead well again and shape into a loaf. Place in a buttered, lightly floured bread pan. Cover and let rise in a warm place until doubled in volume, or until dough reaches top of pan. Bake in a preheated 400°F. oven for 10 minutes. Reduce heat to 375°F. and bake for 30 minutes longer, or until loaf is golden brown. Cool on a wire rack.

WHOLE-WHEAT BREAD

Makes 2 loaves:

4 eggs, beaten
1 tablespoon of salt
¼ cup of vegetable oil
1 cup milk

combined in a 4-cup measuring cup, mixed well and covered

1½ cups of warm water
2 packages of active dry yeast
⅓ cup of molasses

8 cups of whole-wheat flour

In a bowl large enough to hold all ingredients, combine the eggs, salt, vegetable oil and milk, blending well. When the yeast mixture doubles in volume and is foaming add it to the bowl and blend. Stir in 2 cups of the flour, stirring vigorously until well blended. Gradually, stir in the remaining flour ½ cup at a time, blending well. Knead the dough on a lightly floured pastry board for 15 minutes. If dough becomes sticky, sprinkle in additional flour. Butter a bowl and place the dough in it, turning so it is evenly coated with butter. Cover, let rise in a warm place until doubled in volume. Punch down, knead briefly and let rise again until doubled in volume. Punch down again, knead briefly again, divide dough and shape into two equal-sized loaves. Place in 2 buttered bread pans. Cover and place in warm place until doubled in volume or dough reaches top of pans. Bake in a preheated 350°F. oven for 45 minutes, or until golden brown. Test for doneness by tapping the bread. If it has a hollow sound, it is ready.

ORANGE BISCUITS

Makes about 2 dozen, depending upon size:

1¼ cups of milk, scalded
1 stick (¼ pound) of butter, in small pieces
⅓ cup of sugar
1 teaspoon of salt
one ¼-ounce package of active dry yeast

2 eggs, beaten
¼ cup of orange juice
2 tablespoons of grated orange rind
5 cups of flour

In a large bowl, combine the milk, butter, sugar and salt, blending well. When it has cooled to lukewarm, stir in the yeast. Cover, and when it increases in volume and is foaming, add the eggs, orange juice and rind, blending well. Gradually add the flour, mixing into a soft dough. Cover and let rest for 10 minutes. Knead well on a lightly floured pastry board. Place in a buttered bowl, turning dough to evenly cover with butter. Cover and let rise in a warm place until dough doubles in volume (this may take 2 hours). Punch down. Roll dough out ½-inch thick. Cut into biscuits of preferred size with a cutter. Arrange on a buttered baking pan. Cover and let rise. Bake in a preheated 400°F. oven for 15 minutes.

MINA'S SOUR CREAM COFFEE CAKE

Serves 6 to 8:

1 stick (¼ pound) of butter, softened
1 cup of sugar
2 eggs, beaten
1 cup of sour cream
1 teaspoon of vanilla

2 cups of flour
1 teaspoon of baking soda
1 teaspoon of baking powder
½ teaspoon of salt
Topping (see below)

In a bowl, cream the butter and sugar. Add the eggs, sour cream and vanilla, blending well. Stir in the flour, baking soda, baking powder and salt, blending well. Pour one-half of the mixture into a lightly buttered square 9-inch baking pan. Sprinkle one-half of the topping mixture over it. Pour on the rest of the batter and sprinkle with the remaining topping. Bake in a preheated 350°F. oven for 50 minutes.

TOPPING

¼ cup of granulated sugar
⅓ cup of brown sugar
1 teaspoon of cinnamon

½ cup *each* of chopped pecans and walnuts

In a bowl, place all ingredients and blend thoroughly.

BASIC BATTER FOR CREPES

To make about 24 (6-inch) crepes or 30 (5-inch) crepes:

1 cup of milk
1 cup water (this can be varied with other liquids to give the crepe flavor— clam juice, club soda, broth, tomato juice, etc. depending on the crepe filling)

4 eggs
1 teaspoon of salt
2 cups of sifted all-purpose white flour (measured after sifting)
4 tablespoons of melted butter

Place all ingredients except the melted butter into an electric blender jar. Blend at highest speed for 1½ minutes (scrape flour sticking to the sides down into the batter). Add the melted butter, cover and blend for another 30 seconds. Refrigerate in the blender jar for 3 hours. This gives the flour time to expand, producing light and tender crepes. The batter must be the consistency of medium cream and should coat a spoon. If too heavy, it not only makes thick crepes, but spreads too slowly in the pan and lumps can form in the center. If necessary, the batter can be thinned by stirring in small amounts of milk. Remove from the refrigerator and blend again.

A true crepe must be parchment-thin, no thicker than 1/16 of an inch, so be careful about the amount of batter you pour into the pan. We use a spouted glass jigger marked in ounces and pour in just under 1 ounce for a 5-inch crepe; just barely over 1 ounce for a 6-inch crepe. In tablespoons this would be 1½ tablespoons for a 5-inch crepe and just barely 2 tablespoons for the 6-inch. A small ladle is handy, but with the cooking of a few crepes, you'll work out the precise amount of batter without any problem.

Brush a treated crepe pan lightly with oil. Place it over high heat, testing it with a drop of cold water. When the water instantly evaporates, you are ready. Reduce heat to medium. Place the blender jar with batter in a convenient place, a long spoon beside it to stir the batter frequently. Pour the measured batter into the pan, then quickly tip the pan in several directions to completely cover the bottom with a thin coating of batter. Pour any excess batter back into the blender jar. Place the pan on medium heat (if holes appear in the crepe, spoon small amounts of batter just to cover).

When the crepe begins to look dry and is browning slightly around the edges, loosen those edges with a spatula and flip it over. The entire cooking operation takes about 1 minute for both sides, more for the first side than the second. With practice you'll get the timing.

The first is a test, so discard it. You'll note that the side cooked first will be golden brown and the second side spotty. That's as it should be. The second side is the inside, the portion that the filling is put on, and doesn't show after the crepe is rolled. Pile the cooked crepes on top of one another to keep them moist and in shape.

They can be made and frozen in well-wrapped packages of 2, 4, 6 or 8, etc., depending on the number you'll use at one time.

OLD-FASHIONED PANCAKES

About 12 medium-sized pancakes:

1 cup of milk, room temperature	*sifted together*
	1½ cups of pastry flour
3 tablespoons of melted butter	1 teaspoon of salt
	2 tablespoons of sugar
2 eggs, beaten	1½ teaspoons of baking powder

In a bowl, combine milk, butter and eggs. Add the dry ingredients and beat into a smooth batter. Drop onto a greased hot griddle by tablespoonfuls, or more, depending upon how large or how thick pancakes are preferred.

VARIATIONS

Buckwheat pancakes: Use one-half buckwheat and one-half white flour.

Whole-wheat: ½ cup of whole-wheat flour, 1 cup of white flour.

Buttermilk pancakes: Substitute buttermilk for sweet milk.

Blueberries or chopped apple can be added and beaten into the batter.

HAM AND EGG PANCAKES

To make about 24 (6-inch) pancakes:

1 recipe for Basic Batter for
  Crepes (page 475)
1 teaspoon of sugar

1 teaspoon of baking powder
¾ cup of minced cooked
  ham

To the crepe batter, add the remaining ingredients, blending
thoroughly. Cook the pancakes in a 6-inch crepe pan or on a
regular pancake griddle until golden brown on the bottom.
Flip and cook the other side until golden brown.

For breakfast, serve with syrup.

For lunch or supper, these may be filled with equal parts
of chopped cooked chicken and Gruyère cheese, rolled and
placed seam side down, in a shallow baking dish and topped
with a tablespoon of Rich Mornay Sauce (page 412). Bake
in a preheated 375°F. oven until heated through and top is
golden.

RICOTTA GNOCCHI

Serves 4:

1 cup of ricotta cheese,
  drained
2 cups of flour

1 tablespoon of salt
1 egg, beaten

In a bowl, combine the ingredients, blending thoroughly.
Knead well on a lightly floured board. Roll into long finger-
like rolls and cut into ¼-inch pieces. Roll these small pieces
into uniform shapes. Bring a large pot of water to a boil.
Reduce to a simmer and drop in *gnocchi* without crowding.
Cook for about 6 minutes. Serve with butter and cheese or
any sauce desired. Recipe may be doubled.

HUSH PUPPIES

To make about 12 (2-inch) puppies:

1½ cups of yellow cornmeal
3 tablespoons of minced
   whole scallions
1 teaspoon of salt

½ teaspoon of baking
   powder
2 eggs, beaten with ½ cup of
   milk
Oil for deep frying

In a bowl, combine the cornmeal, scallions, salt and baking powder, blending well. Stir in the eggs and milk, again blending. Form into fingers. Using a deep frypan or a deep fryer, heat about 1 inch of oil until it sizzles when a tiny ball of the dough is dropped in. Fry the hush puppies until evenly golden and crisp. Drain on paper towels.

KLUSKI NOODLES WITH BACON AND CHEESE

Serves 4 to 6:

2½ cups of sifted flour
2 eggs, beaten

½ teaspoon of salt
3 tablespoons of warm water

Mound the flour on a pastry board, forming a well in the center. Put the eggs and salt in the well and work into the flour, adding the water gradually as the flour is worked, kneading it into an elastic dough. When tiny bubbles begin to form, divide the dough into 2 balls. Clean off the pastry board and lightly flour it. With a pastry roller, roll the dough into ⅛-inch sheets. Let the dough stand for 15 minutes, then roll each sheet up as for a jelly roll. Cut the roll straight across into desired width (anywhere from ¼ inch to 1 inch). Shake them out into noodle lengths. Cook in boiling salted water until *al dente* and drain.

CHEESE AND BACON

1 pound of pot cheese, at
   room temperature
6 slices of bacon, cooked un-

til crisp, drained and
crumbled (reserve the
bacon fat)

Combine cheese and noodles in a bowl and toss. Top with the crumbled bacon and the bacon fat.

PASTA DOUGH

About 2 pounds:

4 cups of flour	2 teaspoons of olive oil
2 teaspoons of salt	2 teaspoons of warm water
4 eggs, lightly beaten	

Sift the flour and salt onto a pastry board. Make a well halfway down into the mound of flour. Pour in the eggs, olive oil and water, adding the liquid gradually to make the dough soft enough to handle. Blend everything well with your hands and form the dough into a ball. Lightly flour a pastry board and knead the ball of dough well, slapping it and pressing down with the heels of your hands until the dough is smooth and pliant (this should take about 15 minutes). Invert a bowl over the dough and let it rest for 15 minutes.

Divide the ball of dough into 4 pieces. Clean the pastry board and lightly flour it. With a rolling pin, roll each piece of dough into as thin a sheet as possible. (Meanwhile, keep the other dough covered.) Cut the flat sheets of pasta into the widths or shapes desired. Place on clean white cloth and allow to dry for 30 minutes to 1 hour before cooking.

FOOD PROCESSOR PASTA DOUGH

About 1 pound:

2 eggs	¼ cup of water
1 teaspoon of salt	2 cups of flour
1 teaspoon of olive oil	

With cutting blade in, pour into the work bowl, the eggs, salt, olive oil and water. Process 15 seconds. Through the tube, pour in 1 cup of flour, slowly with processor running, for 15 seconds. Then, very slowly, pour in remaining cup of flour, processing until the dough has proper consistency (firm, pulling away from the sides of the bowl). Divide in half. Roll out one half at a time on a lightly floured pastry board as thin as possible. Cut to desired width, then dry 30 minutes to 1 hour before cooking.

CHEESE POPOVERS

10 to 12 popovers:

1⅓ cups milk

sifted together into a bowl
  1½ cups flour
  ½ teaspoon of dry
    mustard

1 teaspoon salt

8 eggs, well beaten
2 cups of grated Gruyère
  cheese

Add the milk to the bowl with the flour and beat with a rotary beater until smooth. Add eggs and cheese and beat until well blended. Grease popover pans or muffin tins and fill one-third full with batter. Bake in a preheated 450°F. oven for 10 minutes. Reduce heat to 350°F. and bake 20 minutes longer, or until golden and puffed.

RICE WITH EGGS AND LEMON

Serves 6:

3 tablespoons of butter
3 cups of cooked rice

beaten together
  Juice of 1 lemon (at least
    3 tablespoons)

3 eggs
½ cup of grated Parmesan
  cheese
2 tablespoons of chopped
  parsley

In a saucepan, over medium heat, melt the butter. Add the rice and fluff with a fork mixing with the butter and heating it through. Lower heat and blend the lemon juice-egg mixture thoroughly with the hot rice. Cook until the eggs begin to set.

SCONES

This famous Scottish and English bread-cake is served at tea—warm, spread with jam and whipped cream. However, we enjoyed them most one balmy morning in South Africa, when we stopped at a small restaurant on the veldt while riding from Johannesburg to Kruger Park. Number of scones depends upon their size:

blended
  1 cup of milk
  3 eggs, beaten

sifted together in a bowl
  3 cups of flour
  ½ teaspoon of salt

5 teaspoons of baking powder

3 tablespoons of sugar
3 tablespoons of melted butter

Pour the milk-egg blend into the bowl with the flour and beat, blending well. Beat in the sugar and butter. Cook on a hot griddle, dropping by the tablespoonful amounts of preferred size for the scone. Turn gently several times, until evenly golden brown.

SPAETZLE

Serves 4 to 6:

2½ cups of flour
1 teaspoon of salt
¼ teaspoon of pepper
¼ teaspoon of nutmeg

3 eggs, beaten
¼ to ½ cup of milk
2 tablespoons of butter

In a bowl, combine the flour, salt, pepper and nutmeg. Make a well in the center, pour in the eggs and one-half of the milk. Blend into a thick, firm dough that comes away from the sides of the bowl, adding more milk if too stiff. Knead the dough on a lightly floured board until smooth. Divide the dough into 3 balls. Over a pot of boiling salted water, push the dough, wormlike, through a large-holed colander into the water. When cooked, in about 5 minutes, the *spaetzle* will float. Drain and toss with the butter. Serve instead of potatoes, or with a sauce and cheese.

TARHONYA

Serves 6:

3 cups of flour
1 teaspoon of salt
3 eggs, beaten
1 egg yolk, beaten

⅓ cup of butter
2 teaspoons of sweet Hungarian paprika

In a bowl, sift the flour and salt, blending in the eggs and egg yolk. Knead the mixture, working into a stiff dough. (If dough seems too soft, add a little flour.) Knead the dough on a lightly floured pastry board for 5 minutes. Cover with a bowl and let rest for 15 minutes. On the large opening of a grater, grate the dough, then spread it out on a cloth or baking sheet and let it dry for 24 hours, turning occasionally. In a frypan, melt the butter, stir in the paprika and over medium heat cook the dried pasta, stirring and turning until it is well coated with butter and evenly colored. Cool well and store in airtight jars, or freeze until ready to use. Cook as you do other pasta in boiling, salted water.

WAFFLES

To make about 10:

blended
3 egg yolks, beaten
1 cup of milk
5 tablespoons of melted butter

2 teaspoons of baking powder
⅓ teaspoon of salt
1 tablespoon of sugar (omit if very crisp waffles are desired)

sifted together into a bowl
1½ cups of flour

3 egg whites, stiffly beaten

Pour the egg-milk-butter blend into the bowl with the flour and beat into a batter. Fold in the egg whites. Batter should be thin enough to pour. If it isn't, blend in more milk. Oil or grease the waffle iron well. Heat until very hot. Brush lightly with butter (or follow manufacturer's directions) and cook the waffles, slowly pouring in the batter to allow spreading. Cook about 30 seconds, or until it stops steaming.

For cheese waffles: Beat in ½ cup of grated sharp Cheddar cheese with the egg yolks and milk.

SIMPLE YORKSHIRE PUDDING

Serves 6: The English made this famous, serving it with roast beef.

1 cup of flour, sifted	2 eggs, well beaten
½ teaspoon of salt	½ cup of water
½ cup of milk	½ cup of butter, melted, hot

All ingredients must be at room temperature. In a bowl, combine flour and salt. Spoon a well in the center, pour in the milk and mix it well with the flour. Stir the eggs into the flour mixture and beat into a smooth batter. Add the water, beating constantly until large bubbles form. Cover the bowl and refrigerate for 1 hour. Beat well again. Muffin tins are excellent for cooking the pudding. Heat the tins. Spoon one-quarter inch of hot melted butter into each muffin circle. Pour in the batter to a depth of ⅝ inch. Bake in a preheated 425°F. oven for 15 minutes. Reduce heat to 350°F. and bake for another 20 minutes, or until pudding peaks, is dark golden brown and very light.

Chapter Seven
Desserts

That question of which came first, the chicken or the egg may never be solved. We believe, however, that we offered a reasonable theory about which of the two was the first food.

We will state flatly here that when it comes to desserts, the egg is definitely first. Are there any chicken desserts? We've never heard of one.

But the egg. Astounding. It is responsible for those desserts of which dreams are made.

Crème brulée. You don't know this one? Then this chapter will be a revelation. Pots-de-Crème, flans and a variety of other custards. Pies, cakes, cookies, puddings.

With the egg as base and enhancer, these truly are just desserts.

ANGEL FOOD CAKE WITH FRESH ORANGE ICING

Serves 6:

1¼ cups of egg whites (8 to 10 whites)
1 teaspoon of cream of tartar
1 cup of cake flour, sifted before measuring

1¼ cups of fine granulated sugar, sifted
¼ teaspoon of salt
¼ teaspoon of almond extract
1 teaspoon of vanilla extract

In a large bowl, beat the egg whites until foamy. Add cream of tartar and beat until stiff, but not dry. Sift flour and sugar together 4 times. Fold gently into the beaten whites, a couple of tablespoons at a time, also adding the salt, almond extract and vanilla, carefully folding over and over until the mixture is evenly blended. Spoon evenly into a 9-inch ungreased tube angel food cake pan. Bake in a preheated 350°F. oven for 50 minutes. Turn off the oven and bake 10 minutes longer.

FRESH ORANGE ICING

⅓ cup of butter, softened
1 egg yolk
Grated rind of 1 orange

2 tablespoons of orange juice
1 cup of confectioners' sugar

Combine all ingredients in a bowl and blend into a smooth mixture.

UNIQUE APPLE-PIE-CAKE

Serves 6:

6 eggs, beaten lightly
1¼ cups of milk
¼ cup of brandy
1 cup of flour
¼ cup of sugar

½ teaspoon of salt
½ teaspoon of cinnamon
¼ cup of butter
2 tart apples, peeled, cored and thinly sliced

In a bowl, combine the eggs, milk, brandy, flour, sugar, salt and cinnamon, blending well. In a preheated 425°F. oven, melt the butter in a 9- by 13-inch baking dish. As soon as melted, immediately add the apples, covering the bottom of the dish, cooking just until the butter bubbles. Spoon the batter over the apples and cook for 20 minutes, or until puffed and golden. Serve with rather soft vanilla ice cream or whipped cream.

BAKED ALASKA

Serves 8:

½-inch layer of Sponge Cake (page 505) slightly larger than the brick of ice cream (see below)

6 egg whites

6 tablespoons of superfine sugar

1 (2-quart) brick of strawberry ice cream, solidly frozen

Fresh strawberries for garnish, marinated in sugar and kirsch

Place the sponge cake on an ovenproof oval serving platter and refrigerate. In a large bowl, beat the egg whites until they peak and gradually add the sugar, beating well after each addition (the whites should be stiff but still moist). Place the ice cream on the layer of sponge cake and completely mask with the meringue right down to the bottom edge. Immediately, place the ice cream in a preheated 500°F. oven for 2½ minutes, or until golden brown. Remove the baked Alaska and serve at once, garnished with the drained kirsch-soaked strawberries. Use a warm, sharp knife, slicing thick slices. Work quickly so the ice cream does not melt before it is served.

BUTTER AND EGG CAKE

Serves 8:

6 jumbo eggs, at room temperature

1 cup of sugar

2 teaspoons of Grand Marnier

2 teaspoons of finely grated orange rind

1 cup of sifted cake flour

½ cup of butter, at room temperature (Melt butter, pour off and reserve yellow liquid that comes to the top and keep warm. Discard the milky liquid that settles to the bottom.)

First, butter 3 9-inch layer-cake pans, then line with waxed paper. Butter the waxed paper.

In a warm mixing bowl, beat the eggs until foamy. With an electric beater at high speed, gradually beat in the sugar until the mixture is light and almost doubled in volume. Beat in the liqueur and orange rind. Stir in the flour, 1 tablespoon at a time, then the butter, also 1 tablespoon at a time. Blend all well. Pour the batter into the pans. Bake in a preheated 350°F. oven for 35 minutes, or until a toothpick comes out clean. Cool. Construct the layer cake, frosting with a favorite icing. The Fresh Orange Icing (page 485) is excellent.

RUM CHEESE CAKE

Serves 10 to 12:

CRUST

2 cups of graham cracker crumbs	1 stick (¼ pound) of butter, melted
⅓ cup of sugar	⅛ teaspoon of cinnamon

Combine all the ingredients, blending well. Reserving ½ cup of the crumb mixture, press the remaining onto the bottom of a 9-inch springform pan. Chill before adding the filling.

FILLING

1 envelope of unflavored gel- atin, dissolved in ¼ cup of lemon juice over hot water	2 (8-ounce) packages of cream cheese, at room temperature
¾ cup of sugar	4 egg whites, beat until peaks form then gradually beat in 3 tablespoons of sugar
¼ cup of light rum	
1 tablespoon of grated lemon rind	
4 egg yolks, beaten	1 cup of heavy cream, whipped

In a saucepan combine the gelatin in the lemon juice and sugar, blending well. Stir in the rum, lemon rind and egg yolks. Cook over low heat, stirring constantly, until the mixture begins to thicken (do not allow to boil). Remove from heat and cool slightly. Beat in the cream cheese until smooth. Fold in the egg whites and whipped cream. Spoon into the crumb crust. Sprinkle with the reserved ½ cup of crumbs and chill until firm. Run a spatula around the edge of the cake before removing the mold.

CHOCOLATE MOUSSE CAKE

Serves 8:

30 ladyfingers, split, but not separated

⅓ cup of white rum (more or less, depending upon taste), plus 2 tablespoons

16 ounces of semisweet chocolate

6 eggs, separated

½ cup of superfine sugar

1 teaspoon of vanilla extract

3 tablespoons of strong coffee

1½ cups of heavy cream, whipped

½ cup of coarsely chopped hazelnuts (optional)

Brush the flat sides of the ladyfingers with the ⅓ cup of rum and line the sides and bottom of a springform pan, round sides against the mold. Melt the chocolate in the top of a double boiler over hot water, stirring until smooth. Set aside. In a large bowl beat the egg whites until stiff. Gradually beat in 2 tablespoons of the sugar and beat until stiff peaks form. Set aside. In a separate large bowl, beat the egg yolks at high speed until foamy. Gradually beat in the remaining sugar, beating until light. Reduce speed and beat in the 2 tablespoons of rum, vanilla and coffee.

Fold 1 cup of the egg whites into the chocolate to lighten it. Fold the chocolate-egg whites mixture into the egg yolk bowl, then fold in the remaining egg whites and the whipped cream. Spoon into the lined mold. Sprinkle top with nuts if you like. Freeze until firm.

Remove from the freezer an hour or two before serving, or until somewhat softened, then refrigerate until ready to serve.

VELVET CHOCOLATE FOOD PROCESSOR PIE

Serves 6: This is a rich, delicious pie with a velvety texture—for the food processor fans.

1 cup of sugar
¾ cup of butter, in small pieces
3 (1-ounce) squares of unsweetened chocolate, melted and slightly cooled but still pourable

1½ teaspoons of vanilla extract
3 eggs
9-inch fully baked pastry shell, cooled
Whipped cream

With steel cutting blade in processor work bowl, blend sugar and butter until very smooth, scraping down the sides of the bowl when necessary. With processor running, pour melted chocolate and vanilla through feed tube. Through the tube, processor still running, add the eggs, one at a time. Process until mixture is smooth. Pour into the baked pastry shell and refrigerate overnight. Garnish lavishly with whipped cream.

CHOCOLATE ROLL

Serves 6 to 8:

5 large eggs, separated
sifted together
  ¾ cup of sugar
  2 tablespoons of flour

6 ounces of semisweet chocolate

3 tablespoons of cold water
¼ teaspoon of cream of tartar
Grated chocolate or cocoa
1 cup of heavy cream
½ teaspoon of vanilla extract
1 teaspoon of sugar

In a bowl, beat the egg yolks, add the sugar and flour and beat to a light, creamy consistency. Break up the chocolate and place in a pan with the cold water. Without letting it get too hot, melt over low heat, stirring until smooth. Cool slightly. Blend the chocolate into the egg yolk bowl. In another bowl, with a clean, dry beater, beat the egg whites with the cream of tartar until stiff. Fold into the egg yolk-chocolate bowl. Butter a jelly roll pan, cover with waxed paper and butter that. Pour the batter into the pan (onto the waxed paper) and gently spread evenly. Bake in a preheated 350°F. oven for 10 minutes. Reduce the heat to 325°F. and bake for another 5 minutes, or until a toothpick comes out clean. Cover with a cloth dipped into cold water and thoroughly wrung out. Refrigerate for 1 hour. Remove the cloth and carefully loosen the pastry from the pan (a thin spatula is useful for this). Dust the top generously with grated chocolate or cocoa. Lay a sheet of waxed paper, slightly longer than the pan, over it. Invert pan to turn the pastry out onto the waxed paper. Carefully peel off the paper. Beat the cream with the vanilla and sugar. Spread over the pastry and roll up like a jelly roll, using the waxed paper to help roll it.

CLASSIC COCONUT CUSTARD PIE

Serves 6:

3 egg yolks

sifted together
  ½ cup of sugar
  1 tablespoon of flour

2 whole eggs, beaten with a
  pinch of salt

1 teaspoon of vanilla extract
1½ cups of medium cream
½ cup of milk
¾ cup of shredded coconut
one partially baked 8-inch
  pastry shell

In a bowl, beat the yolks, add the sugar and flour, beating until well blended. Beat in the whole eggs, vanilla, cream and milk. Stir in the coconut, blending well. Pour into the pastry shell. Place on a baking sheet and bake in a preheated 350°F. oven 35 minutes, or until golden and set.

ST. JOSEPH'S CREAM PUFFS

Makes about 15 or more, depending on size:

1 stick (¼ pound) of butter,
  in small pieces
1 cup of water
¼ teaspoon of salt

1 cup of flour
4 eggs
Custard (see below)

In a saucepan, combine the butter, water and salt. Bring to a boil. Over medium heat, add the flour, stirring constantly. When the mixture leaves the sides of the pan, remove from heat. Cool. Beat in the eggs, one at a time. Drop by spoonfuls (amount depends on size desired) onto a greased cookie sheet. Leave a space between as they will spread a little. Bake in a preheated 450°F. oven for 20 minutes. Reduce heat to 350°F. and bake for 20 minutes longer, or until puffed and golden brown. Cut part way through the center (as you would a hamburger roll) and fill with custard.

CUSTARD

3 cups of milk	⅔ cup of sugar
blended	½ teaspoon of salt
2 tablespoons of flour	2 eggs, beaten
2 tablespoons of corn-starch	3 teaspoons of Marsala
	1 cup of whipped cream

In a sauce pan, over medium heat, scald the milk. Stir in the flour-mixture and cook, stirring, until thick. Quickly stir in the beaten eggs and cook, stirring constantly, for 1 minute. Remove from heat. Cool. Stir in the Marsala and fold in the whipped cream.

CRÈME BRULÉE

Serves 6 to 8:

1 quart of medium cream	2 tablespoons of Amaretto liqueur (or 2 teaspoons of vanilla extract)
2 tablespoons of sugar	
8 egg yolks	Soft light brown sugar, free of any lumps

Heat the cream in the top of a double boiler until barely hot (if cream is too hot, the egg yolks will curdle). Add the sugar and stir until dissolved. Beat the egg yolks until very light. Add to the cream with the Amaretto. Blend well. Strain into a shallow glass baking dish of a size that the custard will be 1½ inches thick. Place the dish in a pan of hot water (water coming halfway up the sides of the dish) and bake in a preheated 325°F. oven for 45 minutes, or until just set. Remove from the oven, cool, then place in the refrigerator until thoroughly chilled. Preheat broiler. Cover the surface of the custard evenly with a ¼-inch-thick layer of the brown sugar. Place the custard under the broiler and watch constantly. The sugar will melt and form a dark-brown glaze. When the entire surface is glazed, remove and cool. Refrigerate to cool. It should not be served too cold.

DATE DELIGHT

Serves 6:

3 eggs, beaten
1 cup of sugar
1 cup of sifted enriched
   flour
1 teaspoon of baking powder

¼ teaspoon of salt
1 cup of chopped dates
½ cup of chopped walnuts
1 cup of heavy cream,
   whipped

In a large bowl, beat the eggs and sugar until light. Stir in the flour, baking powder, salt, dates and nuts. Blend well. Pour mixture into a buttered 8-inch square, 2-inch deep baking dish. Place the dish in a pan with an inch of hot water. Bake in a preheated 350°F. oven for 50 minutes. Serve warm with whipped cream on top.

EGGNOG

To make about 30 (4-ounce) servings: This, of course, is a holiday drink, but real drinkers consider it dessert.

8 eggs, separated
1 cup of sugar
6 tablespoons (3 ounces) of
   rum

Fifth of whiskey or brandy
3 pints of heavy cream,
   beaten until stiff
Nutmeg

Beat the egg yolks and whites separately. Gradually add the sugar to the whites, beating until stiff. Combine the yolks with the whites and mix thoroughly. Place in a large bowl or punch bowl. Add the rum and whiskey. Beat. Fold in the whipped cream. Serve with a sprinkle of nutmeg over each serving.

For a lighter eggnog, substitute 1 pint of milk for 1 pint of cream and add it before you fold in the cream.

HUGUENOT TORTE

Serves 6:

- 2 eggs

sifted together
  1½ cups of sugar
  3 tablespoons of flour
  2½ teaspoons of baking powder
  ¼ teaspoon of salt

1 cup of chopped tart apples (no skin or seeds)
1 cup of chopped walnuts
1 teaspoon of vanilla extract
1 cup of heavy cream, whipped

In a large bowl, beat the eggs until light and lemony. Gradually add the sifted dry ingredients, beating well after each addition. Stir in the apples, nuts and vanilla, blending well. Pour into a generously buttered 9-inch springform mold. Place on a baking sheet and bake in a preheated 300°F. oven for 1 hour, or until the top is golden and crusty. Serve with a generous topping of whipped cream (or soft vanilla ice cream).

J.D.S.'S RICH FRENCH EGG-VANILLA ICE CREAM

About 1 quart:

1½ cups of half-and-half
6 jumbo egg yolks
11 tablespoons of sugar

1 cup of heavy cream
2 teaspoons of vanilla extract
4 tablespoons of butter

In a saucepan, over medium heat, gradually bring the half-and-half to a boil. Refrigerate for 5 hours. In a bowl, cream egg yolks with one-half of the sugar. Set aside. In another saucepan, over medium heat, combine the cream, vanilla and remaining sugar, blending well. Slowly, stirring constantly, bring to the boil. Remove from heat and cool briefly. In still another saucepan, pour the egg yolk-sugar mixture, and, stirring constantly, add one-third of the cream-vanilla-sugar mixture, then quickly stir it all in. On medium heat, slowly bring to just below the boiling point. Remove from the heat and stir in the butter, blending well. Place pan midway up in another pan of ice water, stirring constantly to stop further cooking and to cool the mixture. Strain this, then take the chilled half-and-half from the refrigerator and beat it in, blending well. Pour into ice cream maker and churn according to directions.

GEORGE HERZ'S LEMON FLUFF

Serves 4 to 6: This unique dessert creates its own sauce.

3 tablespoons of butter
1 cup of sugar
4 egg yolks, well beaten
3 tablespoons of flour
¼ cup of fresh lemon juice

2 teaspoons of grated lemon rind
½ teaspoon of vanilla extract
1 cup of milk
4 egg whites, stiffly beaten

In a bowl, cream the butter and sugar. Add the egg yolks, flour, lemon juice and rind and vanilla, blending well. Pour in the milk, blending all thoroughly. Fold in the egg whites. Pour into a buttered 6-inch soufflé dish and place in a pan of hot water, 1 inch deep. Bake in a preheated 350°F. oven for 40 minutes.

LEMON SPONGE PIE

Serves 6:

1 cup of sugar
3 tablespoons of soft butter
Pinch of salt
3 egg yolks
Juice (at least ¼ cup) and grated rind of 1 lemon

3 tablespoons of flour
1 cup of milk
3 egg whites, stiffly beaten
9-inch partially baked pastry shell
Whipped cream (optional)

In a bowl, combine the sugar, butter, salt and egg yolks and beat until well-blended. Add the lemon juice and rind. Beat in the flour and milk. Fold in the egg whites. Spoon into the pastry shell and bake in a preheated 325°F. oven for 45 minutes, or until set. It will be custardy on the bottom and cakelike on the top. Top with whipped cream, if desired.

LEMON SQUARES

Makes 16 (2-inch) squares:

blend as you would a pie crust	½ cup of butter extract
1 cup of flour	¼ cup of confectioners' sugar

Place the dough into an 8-inch-square baking dish. Bake in a preheated 350°F. oven for 10 minutes to partially cook.

2 eggs, beaten	Grated rind and juice (at least 3 tablespoons) of 1 lemon
1 cup of sugar	
½ teaspoon of salt	
2 tablespoons of flour	1 cup of coconut
½ teaspoon of baking powder	Confectioners' sugar

In a bowl, combine all the ingredients, except the confectioners' sugar, blending thoroughly. Pour over the partially baked crust and bake in a preheated 350°F. oven for 30 minutes. Sprinkle with confectioners' sugar and cut into squares.

MERINGUE SHELLS FILLED WITH LEMON CUSTARD

Makes 8 or more meringue shells, depending on size:

4 large egg whites	1 cup of superfine sugar
Pinch of salt	½ teaspoon of vanilla extract
¼ teaspoon of cream of tartar	

In a large bowl, beat the egg whites with the salt until stiff and dry. Beat in the cream of tartar. Add ½ cup of the sugar, 1 tablespoon at a time, beating well after each addition. Then beat in larger amounts of the remaining sugar. Beat until the meringue holds its shape. Add vanilla.

Put the egg white mixture into a pastry bag and, onto a buttered and floured cookie sheet, make individual shells 2½ to 3 inches in diameter. First circle a solid base, then build up the sides with 1 ring of the mixture (or spoon some of it onto the paper, making a depression in the center, shaping into shells). Allow space between each shell as they will spread. Bake in a preheated 275°F. oven for 1 hour. Turn oven off and leave in the oven 15 minutes longer. They will be rather soft when taken from the oven, but will crisp up when cooled.

If the meringues become sticky as they sometimes can on a humid day, if not in an airtight container, place them into a low oven for a few minutes, then cool.

FILLING

6 large egg yolks, beaten	1½ tablespoons of grated
¾ cup of sugar	lemon rind
Pinch of salt	¾ cup of heavy cream,
6 tablespoons of lemon juice	whipped

In the top of a double boiler, combine the egg yolks, sugar, salt and lemon juice, blending well. Cook over hot (not boiling) water, stirring constantly, until thickened (do not allow the egg mixture to boil or it will curdle). Remove from the heat and cool. Add the lemon rind and fold in the whipped cream. Spoon the lemon custard into the meringue shells and serve immediately.

CALVADOS MOUSSE

Serves 6:

6 egg yolks	4 cups of heavy cream
blended	½ cup of calvados
¼ cup of cornstarch	Crystallized violets
½ cup of sugar	Slivered almonds, toasted

In a bowl, beat the egg yolks until smooth and lemony. Stir in the sugar-cornstarch mixture. Gradually stir in 3 cups of the cream. Stir until well-mixed. In a saucepan, over low heat, cook, stirring constantly, until thick and creamy (do not allow to boil). Cool to lukewarm and stir in the calvados. Refrigerate until well-chilled. Whip the remaining heavy cream. Fold half of it into the chilled mousse. Spoon into a soufflé dish. Pipe with a pastry bag (or spoon) the remaining whipped cream around the edge of the mousse. Decorate with the crystallized violets and almonds.

ANTOINE GILLY'S POT DE CRÈME

To make 6 pots:

2 cups of milk	6 tablespoons of sugar
1-inch piece of vanilla bean	1 tablespoon of instant
6 egg yolks	coffee crystals dissolved in
2 whole eggs	1 tablespoon of hot water

Scald the milk with the vanilla bean. Beat the egg yolks and eggs until light and fluffy. Beat in the sugar and coffee. Remove and discard the vanilla bean and slightly cool the milk. Slowly pour it into the egg mixture, stirring constantly. Strain into ovenproof porcelain pots or custard cups. Set the pots in a pan of hot water and bake in a preheated 275°F. oven for about 20 minutes, or until no pocket is formed when the pot is slightly tipped (or if a knife inserted comes out clean). Cool before serving.

TWO LAYER PRUNE CAKES

Serves 8 to 10:

sifted together into a large bowl
2½ cups of sifted flour
1⅓ teaspoons of baking soda
2 cups of sugar
1⅓ teaspoons of cinnamon

1 teaspoon of nutmeg

4 eggs, beaten
1⅓ cups of vegetable oil
1⅓ cups of buttermilk
⅔ teaspoon of salt
2 cups of chopped cooked prunes
Confectioners' sugar

To the bowl with the flour, add the eggs, oil, buttermilk, salt and prunes, beating into a completely blended mixture. Lightly butter and flour two 9-inch baking pans and pour in the prune mixture. Place in a preheated 350°F. oven for 45 minutes, or until an inserted toothpick emerges clean. When cake has cooled, sprinkle the confectioners' sugar evenly over the top.

SPICY OLD-FASHIONED PUMPKIN PIE

Serves 6 to 8:

1 (10-ounce) package of frozen squash, cooked according to package directions
3 eggs, beaten
1½ cups of milk
¼ cup of molasses
1 tablespoon of honey

½ cup of sugar
½ teaspoon of ginger
½ teaspoon of nutmeg
1 tablespoon of melted butter
9-inch partially baked pastry shell
Cinnamon

In a bowl, combine the squash, eggs, milk, molasses, honey, sugar, ginger, nutmeg and butter, blending well. Pour into the pastry shell and sprinkle lightly with cinnamon. Bake in a preheated 450°F. oven for 10 minutes, then, reduce heat to 350°F. and cook for 40 minutes longer, or until set. Do not overcook.

RASPBERRY MERINGUE PIE

Serves 6:

MERINGUE SHELL

4 egg whites, room temperature

¼ teaspoon of salt

¼ teaspoon of cream of tartar

1 cup of sugar

1 teaspoon of vanilla extract

⅓ cup of finely ground walnuts

In a large bowl, beat the egg whites until frothy. Beat in the salt and cream of tartar, beating until stiff. Beat in the sugar, 1 tablespoon at a time. Beat in the vanilla and nuts. Cover a cookie sheet with waxed paper. Butter and lightly flour it. Using a pastry bag or a spoon make an 8-inch circle of the egg whites, building up the sides slightly to hold the filling. (If using a pastry bag, start in the center of the circle, press out the batter in one long finger width strip, circling until the circle is the desired diameter. Build up the sides by adding 1 or 2 more circles to the outside ring of meringue. Bake in a preheated 250°F. oven for 1 hour. Turn off heat and let set for 15 minutes. It should be firm and dry and still quite white. Carefully remove from pan and cool.

Note: For garnish, make a number of small rosettes with the meringue and bake along with the meringue shell.

RASPBERRY MOUSSE FILLING

3 pints of fresh raspberries, or 2 (10-ounce) packages of frozen

Sugar to taste

1 envelope of gelatin

¼ cup of cold water

1 cup of heavy cream, whipped

Reserve ½ cup of the best raspberries for garnish. If frozen berries are used, select the largest and freeze separated on a flat surface (such as a plate), until ready to serve the pie. Press berries through a fine sieve to eliminate seeds. If fresh, add sugar to taste, but they should be tart. Refrigerate. Stir the gelatin into the cold water, then dissolve over hot water. Stir the gelatin into the raspberry puree and chill again. When it begins to set, fold in the whipped cream. Spoon into the cooled meringue shell and refrigerate for several hours. Just before serving, garnish with the reserved raspberries and meringue rosettes.

LEMON CREAM ROULADE

Serves 6 to 8:

SPONGE ROULADE

4 eggs, separated
½ cup of sugar
¾ cup of sifted flour

¾ teaspoon of baking powder
1 teaspoon of vanilla extract
Grated rind of 1 lemon

In a bowl, beat the egg yolks until light and lemony. Gradually beat in the sugar, then the flour, baking powder, vanilla and lemon rind. With a clean dry beater, beat the egg whites until stiff. Fold the egg whites into the egg yolk mixture. Butter a jelly roll pan. Line it with waxed paper and butter the paper. Pour the batter into the pan (onto the waxed paper) and bake in a preheated 400°F. oven for 10 minutes. Reduce heat to 350°F. and bake 5 minutes longer, or until slightly golden. Place a moist kitchen towel over the *roulade* and cool.

LEMON CREAM FILLING

¾ cup of sugar
4 tablespoons of cornstarch
3 tablespoons of flour
1½ cups of boiling water
Grated rind and juice of 2 lemons (at least ¼ cup of juice)

4 tablespoons of butter, softened
4 egg yolks, slightly beaten
Confectioners' sugar

In the top of a double boiler, combine the sugar, cornstarch and flour and mix well. Gradually add the boiling water, stirring constantly. Bring to a simmer right on the heat. Then cook over hot water for 20 minutes, or until the mixture thickens, stirring several times. Remove the pan from the hot water. Stir in the lemon rind and juice. Quickly mix in the butter and egg yolks. Place the pan over the hot water and continue to cook, stirring, until thick and smooth. Cool thoroughly.

Remove the towel from the roulade. Sprinkle confectioners' sugar over it. Lay a piece of waxed paper, slightly longer than the pan, over it. Invert pan to turn the roulade out onto the waxed paper (you may have to use a narrow spatula first to loosen it). Carefully peel off the waxed paper. Spread the lemon cream evenly over the sponge and roll, using the waxed paper to help roll it. Just before serving, sprinkle with confectioners' sugar.

COLD LEMON SOUFFLÉ

Serves 6 to 8:

1 envelope of gelatin
¼ cup of cold water
3 egg yolks
1 cup sugar
⅓ cup plus 2 tablespoons of lemon juice
1½ tablespoons of grated lemon rind

1 teaspoon of vanilla extract
3 egg whites, stiffly beaten
2 cups of heavy cream, beaten until it mounds
Bitter chocolate (optional)
Raspberries soaked in kirsch (optional)

Stir the gelatin into the cold water. In a bowl, large enough to hold all ingredients, beat the yolks until light and lemony. Add the sugar, small amounts at a time, beating well after each addition. Beat in the lemon juice, rind and vanilla. Dissolve the gelatin over hot water until it is transparent and liquid. Stir well into the egg yolk mixture. Place in the refrigerator until just beginning to set. Fold the egg whites and cream into the egg yolk bowl. Spoon into a large soufflé dish or individual ones. Refrigerate. Before serving, coarsely grate bitter chocolate over the top. Or garnish with large raspberries that have been soaked in kirsch and well-drained.

MOCHA SOUFFLÉ

Serves 6:

2 (1-ounce) squares of unsweetened chocolate,
   melted over hot water
⅓ cup of sugar
2 teaspoons of instant es-
   presso coffee, stirred into
   ⅓ cup of boiling water
3 tablespoons of butter
2 tablespoons of flour

1 cup of milk, scalded
4 egg yolks, beaten
2 teaspoons of vanilla extract
6 egg whites, beaten stiff
   with ¼ teaspoon of cream
   of tartar, then with 3
   tablespoons of sugar
   gradually added

In a bowl, blend well the melted chocolate and sugar. Pour in the hot coffee, blending. In a saucepan, over medium heat, melt the butter, add the flour and cook, stirring, into a smooth paste. Add the milk gradually, stirring into a smooth thickish sauce. Add the chocolate-coffee mixture, blending it in well. Cool. Stir in the egg yolks and the vanilla. Fold in the egg whites. Butter a 2-quart soufflé dish, sprinkle with sugar and shake out the excess. Pour in the soufflé mixture. Bake in a preheated 375°F. oven for 5 minutes, then lower heat to 350°F. and bake for 20 minutes longer, or until puffed, crusty and brown. Serve immediately with whipped cream.

SOUFFLÉ VARIATIONS

LEMON
This is a substitute for other flavorings, chocolate, coffee, etc. Into the batter beat the finely grated rind of 2 lemons plus 2 teaspoons of lemon juice.

GRAND MARNIER
Beat into the batter the finely grated rind of ½ orange and 2 ounces of Grand Marnier.

STRAWBERRY
Beat into the batter ½ cup of chopped and drained fresh ripe strawberries and 2 ounces of wild strawberry liqueur

QUICK SAUCES FOR SOUFFLÉS

CRÈME DE CACAO

1 cup of chocolate ice
cream, at room tempera-
ture for 10 minutes

⅓ cup of heavy cream,
whipped
2 ounces of crème de cacao

Fold the whipped cream and the crème de cacao into the soft
ice cream and serve immediately with the hot soufflé.

GRAND MARNIER

⅓ cup of heavy cream,
whipped
2 ounces of Grand Marnier

1 cup of vanilla ice cream,
at room temperature for
10 minutes

Fold the whipped cream and Grand Marnier into the ice
cream and serve immediately with the hot soufflé.

MINA THOMPSON'S CHEWY VANILLA-PECAN SQUARES

Number of squares depends upon size desired:

4 eggs
1 pound of light brown
sugar
1¾ cups of flour

1 tablespoon of baking powder
¾ teaspoon of salt
2 teaspoons of vanilla extract
2 cups of chopped pecans

Beat eggs lightly in top of double boiler. Place over the hot
water. Stir in the sugar and cook, stirring for 10 minutes. Remove from heat and cool. Stir in the remaining ingredients,
blending well. Pour into a buttered 9- by 13-inch baking dish
and bake in a preheated 350°F. oven for 35 minutes.

DESSERT WAFFLES

Makes about 10 depending on size:

4 tablespoons of sugar (this
  is in addition to the sugar
  in the Waffles recipe)
2 squares of semisweet chocolate, melted

1½ teaspoons of vanilla
  extract
1 recipe for Waffles (page
  482)

Combine the sugar, chocolate and vanilla with the waffle batter and cook in waffle iron, buttering the iron well.

Serve with ice cream.

ZABAGLIONE

Serves 4:

6 egg yolks
5 tablespoons superfine sugar

Pinch of salt
6 tablespoons of Marsala

Combine all the ingredients in the top of a round-bottomed
double boiler, stirring well to blend. Place over simmering
water and beat with a rotary beater, constantly, until it thickens and is light and fluffy. (During this cooking period, occasionally scrape the sides of the pot so all will cook evenly.)
Take the pot holding the zabaglione away from the hot water
and continue to stir with a spoon to stop the cooking.

Serve hot in stemmed (not hollow stemmed) glasses, or
cool in the refrigerator before serving, sprinkling with a little
nutmeg.

VARIATIONS

Stir in 1 tablespoon of whipped cream per person. Or serve
over raspberries that have been soaked in a little kirsch or
strawberries soaked in brandy or any other fruit soaked in
some liqueur.

ZUPPA INGLESE
(Classic Italian Rum Cake)

Serves 8 to 10:

½ cup of sugar
¼ cup of flour
¼ teaspoon of salt
2 cups of scalded milk
4 egg yolks, beaten
½ teaspoon of vanilla
 extract
2 tablespoons of dark crème
 de cacao

3 layers of sponge cake (see
 below)
1 cup of light rum
1 cup of heavy cream,
 whipped
Angelica and candied cherries
Split toasted almonds

In the top of a double boiler, blend the sugar, flour and salt.
Place over the simmering water and gradually add milk, stirring, until thickened. Remove from heat. In a bowl, place egg
yolks and gradually add part of the milk mixture to them,
stirring constantly. Then pour the egg yolk mix into the hot
mixture in the double boiler. With water barely simmering,
cook, stirring until the mixture is very thick. Cool and chill.
Divide this custard into 2 parts. Blend vanilla into one part
and the crème de cacao into the other.

Split sponge cake to make 3 layers. Place one on a serving
plate. Sprinkle that layer with one-third of the rum and cover
with one of the custard mixtures. Repeat with the second
layer, using the other custard mixture. Cover with third layer,
sprinkling it with the remaining rum. At serving time, spread
whipped cream over top and sides of cake and decorate top
and sides with the candied fruits and split toasted almonds.
The Zuppa Inglese should be made the same day it is served,
as refrigeration detracts somewhat from its flavor.

SPONGE CAKE

4 eggs
1 cup of sugar

sifted together 4 times
   1 cup of sifted cake flour

1 teaspoon of baking pow-
   der
¼ teaspoon of salt

2 tablespoons of lemon juice
6 tablespoons of hot milk

In a large bowl, beat the eggs well. Gradually add sugar and beat until thick and lemon colored. Add dry ingredients, then lemon juice and milk, blending well. Pour into a 9-inch tube pan and bake in a preheated 350°F. oven for 35 minutes.

Index

ABOUT THE AUTHORS

MARIA LUISA SCOTT and JACK DENTON SCOTT are among the most experienced in microwave cooking in the country. They have been working with the medium for over eight years and were asked by *Reader's Digest* to present the story of the microwave oven to its millions of readers. The Scotts are magnificent cooks, and have worked closely with one of the world's greatest living French chefs, Antoine Gilly, winner of the world's outstanding awards of chefdom. In collaboration with Antoine Gilly, the Scotts wrote *Feast of France*. The *Wall Street Journal* called it one of the best cookbooks ever written. In addition to cooking as a hobby, Jack Denton Scott is a successful writer, with novels, travel books, natural history, adventure and children's books to his credit. Maria Luisa Scott, aside from being a superb cook, is a copy editor, typist, researcher and severe critic. Among the Scotts' other books are *The Complete Book of Pasta*, which was ten years in the making and is now considered a classic, *Informal Dinners for Easy Entertainment*, which includes easy, but elegant recipes where the food can be eaten informally without the use of a knife, and *Fork Dinners*, the first cookbook to concentrate on the new informality sweeping the country where the guest is served dinner with a plate for one hand, and a fork for the other hand. The Scotts' other recent book is *Cook Like a Peasant, Eat Like a King*, which has been hailed as a great collection of simple country recipes from around the world.

KITCHEN POWER!

☐ 11888 **CROCKERY COOKERY** Mable Hoffman $2.25

☐ 20076 **COOKING WITHOUT A GRAIN OF SALT** $2.95
Elma Bagg

☐ 20157 **GREAT POTATO COOKBOOK** Scotts $2.95

☐ 14926 **THE ROMAGNOLIS' TABLE** The Romagnolis $2.75

☐ 13329 **ALL NEW SOPHIE LEAVITT'S PENNY** $2.95
PINCHER'S COOKBOOK Sophie Leavitt

☐ 13168 **COMPLETE BOOK OF PASTA** Scott $2.25

☐ 20249 **UNABRIDGED VEGETABLE COOKBOOK** $3.95
Hazleton

☐ 13056 **THE FRENCH CHEF COOKBOOK** Julia Child $3.50

☐ 13437 **WHOLE EARTH COOKBOOK** Cadwallader & $2.25
Ohr

☐ 13454 **GREAT COOKING OUTDOORS** Holsmans $2.50

☐ 20334 **BLEND IT SPLENDID: THE NATURAL FOODS** $2.75
BLENDER BOOK The Dworkins

☐ 20656 **BETTY CROCKER'S DINNER FOR TWO** $2.95

☐ 12815 **BAKING BREAD THE WAY MOM** $2.25
TAUGHT ME Mary Anne Gross

☐ 12908 **CREPE COOKERY** Mable Hoffman $2.25

Buy them at your local bookstore or use this handy coupon for ordering: